GOOD CITY FORM

The MIT Press   Cambridge, Massachusetts, and London, England

Kevin Lynch   GOOD CITY FORM

Tenth printing, 1996
First paperback edition, 1984
© 1981 by
Massachusetts Institute of
Technology

Material in chapter 17 was
originally published in
slightly different form as
"Grounds for Utopia,"
in *Responding to Social
Change* (Stroudsberg,
Pennsylvania: Dowden,
Hutchinson & Ross,
1975). It appears here
with the permission of
Dowden, Hutchinson &
Ross.

This book was set in VIP
Palatino by Grafacon, Inc.
and printed and bound in
the United States of
America.

Library of Congress
Cataloging in Publication
Data

Lynch, Kevin.
  Good city form.

  Originally published: A
theory of good city form.
c1981.
  Bibliography: p.
  Includes index.
  1. City planning—
Philosophy. 2. Sociology,
Urban. 3. Cities and
towns—History. I.
Title.
[HT166.L96 1984] 307.7′6′01
83–24824
ISBN 0–262–62046–4 (p)
    0–262–12085–2 (h)

"All men in their native powers are craftsmen, whose destiny it is to create . . . a fit abiding place, a sane and beautiful world."
Louis Henry Sullivan,
January 27, 1924

Contents

GOOD CITY FORM

Prologue: A Naive Question

"What makes a good city?" might be a meaning-less question. Cities are too complicated, too far beyond our control, and affect too many people, who are subject to too many cultural variations, to permit any rational answer. Cities, like continents, are simply huge facts of nature, to which we must adapt. We study their origin and function, because that is interesting to know and handy for making predictions. Someone might say "I like Boston," but we all understand that this is merely a trivial preference, based on personal experience. Only a Sunday journalist rates Boston in comparison to Atlanta. Scholars analyze hard data, such as population, dollars, and traffic flow.

This essay addresses that naive question, with all the qualifications, stratagems, and doubts that will soon be apparent. Decisions about urban policy, or the allocation of resources, or where to move, or how to build something, *must* use norms about good and bad. Short-range or long-range, broad or selfish, implicit or explicit, values are an inevitable ingredient of decision. Without some sense of better, any action is perverse. When values lie unexamined, they are dangerous.

It is a common feeling that most urban places are less than satisfactory—uncomfortable, ugly, or dull—as if they were being measured on some absolute scale. Only fragments of the settled world are generally excepted from this dismal view: an affluent suburb, a fine park, a historic town, the vital center of some great city, an old farming re-gion. If we could be articulate about why we feel that way, we might be prepared to make effective changes.

The purpose of this essay is to make a general statement about the good settlement, one relevant and responsive to any human context, and which connects general values to specific actions. The statement will restrict itself to the connection be-tween human values and the spatial, physical city, although that last is meant in a broader sense than is commonly intended. It will only be a partial theory, not so much because it is confined to this physical aspect, but because a comprehensive theory should connect statements about how a city works with statements about its goodness. The normative theory to follow, which deals only with the latter, while making assumptions about the former, is as partial in its way, then, as the prevalent functional theories so unconsciously are in their own peculiar ways. The distinction between normative and functional theory, and the need for a connection between them, are discussed in chapter 2.

Normative theories of city form are not new. Three leading varieties will be described in chapter 4. They will be preceded in part I by a little history, a discussion of the nature of city form, and a scraping of form values from various sources—a springboard for our first jump. The three normative theories of chapter 4 are powerful theories, not just in the intellectual sense, but because of their long influence on actual city decisions. I demonstrate their inadequacies. A more general theory is laid out in part II, based on "performance dimensions." It has some problems of its own, as will be seen. Still, it is a beginning. Part III applies that theory to current city issues and models, and illustrates it with a utopian sketch.

The normative theory of city form is in woeful state. Academic attention has been drawn to the socioeconomic aspects of human settlements, or to an analysis of how the physical form works, or to tales of how it got to be the way it is. Many value assumptions are cleverly concealed within those immaculate scientific structures. Practitioners, meanwhile, cling to those obvious values that everyone agrees with. Anyone knows what a good city is. The only serious question is how to achieve it. Should such value questions continue to be taken for granted?

I VALUES AND CITIES

1

Form Values in Urban History

Impersonal forces do not transform human settlements. Or at least they do so only on rare occasions, and these are natural disasters: fire, flood, earthquake, and pestilence. Otherwise, the modification of settlement is a human act, however complex, accomplished for human motives, however obscure or ineffective. Uncovering those motives gives us some first clues to the connections between values and environmental form. A brief narration of several striking cases of urban transformation will give us something to chew on.

The primeval transformation is the emergence of the city itself. Why were these peculiar environments created in the first place? Since the first cities precede the first written records, we have only indirect evidence, but archeology and myth tell us something. The independent and relatively sudden jump to civilization has occurred some six or seven times in world history.* This jump has always been accompanied by the appearance of cities, that is, by large, relatively dense settlements of heterogeneous people, which organize a large rural territory around themselves. And with cities and civilization there appear a stratified society, unequal ownership, full-time specialists, and usually writing, science, war, realistic art, luxury crafts, long distance trade, and monumental ceremonial centers. Why these things should repeatedly be linked together is a fundamental problem. It is interesting to speculate about what cities had to do with it, and what this tells us about city values.

In every case, the first cities emerged only after a preceding agricultural revolution, during which plants and animals were domesticated and small permanent settlements of cultivators appeared. This was a necessary, but not a sufficient, condition. In many cases, permanent agriculture did not

Adams

See fig. 1

*In Sumer and perhaps independently in Egypt; in the Indus Valley; Shang China; Mesoamerica and perhaps independently in Peru; and just possibly in certain areas of Southeast Asia or Africa not yet thoroughly studied.

lead to an independent appearance of cities.* In those few favored (?) cases where urban civilization did appear, it came a millennium, more or less, after the fundamental agricultural revolution occurred in that region. Domesticated plants appeared in Sumer about 5000 B.C., while Eridu—the first city that we know of in that area—existed by 4000 B.C., housing several thousand persons. By 3500 B.C., there were 15 to 20 city states in Sumer, including Ur, Erech, Uruk, Lagash, Kish, and Nippur—all of them full-scale cities, and some with populations of 50,000. Ur was four square miles in extent.

Oates

See fig. 2

These are walled cities, and the contrasts of size between their several houses, and of the value of goods in their graves, indicates marked differences of rank and power. The cities boast large elaborate temples on high platforms, carefully oriented. The temples were built on successive ruins of older, smaller temples. There were specialist crafts in stone, metal, pottery, wood, and glass. Trade was organized, reaching as far as Syria or the Indus Valley. Food and other goods were gathered as tribute from peasants and outlanders and distributed among citizens by a priestly class, who were at the center of society.

Writing, an invention which was to have explosive consequences, developed from the pictographs and counters used to tally goods. It flowered into a complicated cuneiform system, taught in scribal schools and based on lexical lists common throughout the region. Regular astronomical observations were made; a number system was developed. Bronze and some iron appeared by 3000 B.C.; there was a precocious leap in art and technology. The wheel was invented.

Yet the wheeled cart was used in battle and religious ceremony for a thousand years before it was used to carry cargo. The imported goods were luxuries, the specialized crafts and the new technology served war and ritual, not daily use. Gradually, the relative equality of the village was converted to a stratified society, one which shifted its dominant

*Moreover, in at least one case—Jericho—urban development may have been a stillbirth. Jericho apparently had no direct successors and led to no permanent civilized states.

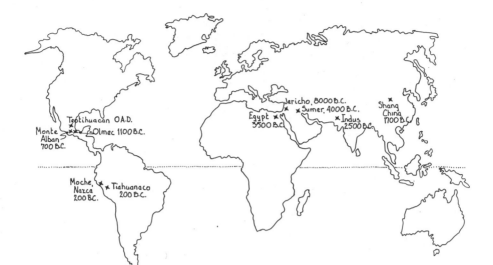

1 The known or possible
locations where cities
appeared independently.

2 Plan of a portion of the
ancient Sumerian city of
Ur, as it was about 1900
B.C. *A, B, C,* and *D* are
wayside chapels. Number
1 at the upper corner was
the house of a merchant
in the copper trade with
Dilmun (present Bahrein),
and number 14 on the
lower left was a res-
taurant.

social relations from kin to class. The social pyramid ran up from slave and peasant, through overseers and soldiers, to state officials and priests. The ownership of land was concentrated in the hands of the latter. The border wars between city states led to permanent war leaders, professional armies, and perpetual aggression. Priest and king became separate, and in time the latter dominated. Finally, with the rise of Sargon of Akkad in 2400 B.C., we enter the period of military empire.

As far as we can tell, this same tale seems to have been repeated in other regions: in Shang China, in Mesoamerica, perhaps also in the Indus Valley, Egypt, and Peru—not always with just the same features, of course, but essentially in parallel. What did the physical city have to do with it? There have been a number of explanations. Cities were said to have appeared as warehouses and breakpoints in trade, or as fortified centers for war, or as administrative centers for managing complex and centralized public works such as irrigation systems. But organized war, trade, and public works seem to have appeared *after* the emergence of the city. They seem to have been the products of city society, and not its causes.

Apparently, the first leap to civilization has occurred along a single path, one taken independently several times in human history. Once it is made, the ideas of civilization—such as cities and writing and war—can be transmitted to other human communities, who then move along different, shorter trajectories. But the classical, independent path seems to start from a settled peasant society, which is capable of producing a food surplus and which, in local shrines and rituals, has articulated its pervasive anxieties about fertility, death, disaster, and the continuity of the human community. A particularly attractive shrine begins to gain a reputation, drawing pilgrims and gifts from a larger area. It becomes a permanent ceremonial center, served by priest specialists, and they develop their ritual and physical setting to compound the attractiveness of the place. Place and ceremony offer pilgrims a release from anxiety and become in themselves fascinating and stimulating experiences. Goods, ceremonies, myths, and power accumulate.

New skills develop to serve the new elite, to manage their affairs, or to impose their will on surrounding populations. The voluntary gifts and adherence of the rural population are converted into tribute and submission. The central collection of food has secondary advantages, since it serves as a reserve in famine, and as a way of exchanging complementary products.

The physical environment plays a key role in this unfolding. It is the material basis of the religious idea, the emotional stimulus that binds the peasantry to the system. The city is a "great place," a release, a new world, and also a new oppression. Its layout is therefore carefully planned to reinforce the sense of awe, and to form a magnificent background for religious ceremony. Built with devotion and also with conscious intent, it is an essential piece of equipment for psychological

See fig. 3

domination. At the same time, it is a glorious expression of human pride, relief, and awe. As the civilization develops, of course, the city takes on many other roles in addition to this primary one. It becomes storehouse, fortress, workshop, market, and palace. First, however, it is a holy place.

Andrews
Hardoy

A number of urban centers in Mesoamerica followed similar paths, including the early Olmec center at La Venta, and later places such as Monte

See fig. 4

Albán, Tula, the Mayan cities, and Tenochtitlán (now Mexico City). One of the greatest of these centers was Teotihuacán, just to the northeast of Mexico City. Although the Olmec sites are earlier, Teotihuacán was the great metropolis of Mesoamerica in its day, unparalleled in its size and intensity of urbanization, and the first in a succession of power centers that culminated in Aztec Tenochtitlán. Teotihuacán has been carefully in-

Millon

vestigated as a whole urban system by René Millon and his associates.

At its zenith around 450 A.D., the city may have contained up to 200,000 people and was only par-

See fig. 5

tially walled. It was laid out along a great monumental avenue which ran straight across the valley, rising by gradual steps for some 5 kilometers. Toward the north, this main avenue was intersected by a major cross-avenue. At this crossing were two great compounds, one a market and

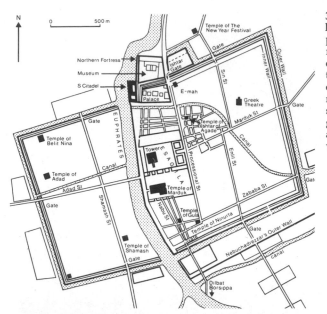

3 Plan of the city of Babylon at the height of its power, about 600 B.C. The religious features were dominant, especially the temple of Marduk, the city god, the temple of the new year festival (the spring equinox), and the great processional way, along which that festival was celebrated.

4 A reconstruction of the great ceremonial area at the center of Tenochtitlán, as it was just before the Spanish conquest. In the right foreground is the Temple of the Sun, and in the left corner the school for the children of noblemen. The twin temples on the main pyramid are those of the sun god Huitzilopochtli, and Tlaloc, the rain god. On the round pyramid in the center is the temple of Quetzalcóatl, the feathered serpent. The royal palaces and the offices of the central administration surrounded this walled, sacred precinct, now occupied by the cathedral and central square of Mexico City (see fig. 14).

5 Plan of the central portion of Teotihuacán, showing the great ceremonial way, which terminated at the Pyramid of the Moon on the north but ran southward across the valley for over five kilometers. The Citadel and the Great Compound were the administrative and commercial centers of the city, located at the major cross street (East Avenue–West Avenue). Temples and houses of the nobility lined the great way, which ascends by intermittent steps toward the monumental pyramids. Walled residential and industrial compounds make up the basic texture of the city. The plan shows the city at the height of its power in 450 A.D., when it covered eight square miles, and may have held up to 200,000 people.

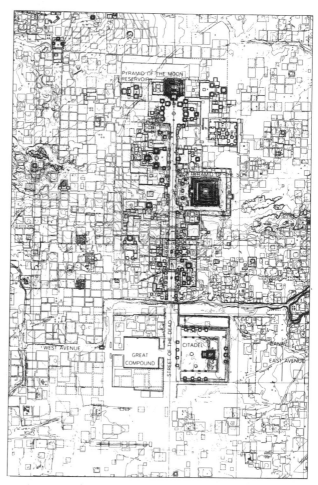

6 Looking south along the great way in Teotihuacán, from the Pyramid of the Moon, past the pyramid of the Sun (which contains over a million cubic yards of material), toward the Citadel in the background. The modern roads overlie and encircle the site, but the traditional field pattern still reflects the ancient orientation of the compounds.

the other an administrative center. Along the great avenue and at its head stood awe-inspiring, man-made mountains and a continuous string of temples and great houses. The entire settled area was laid out in a regular network of rectangular compounds. The orientation of avenues and compounds (15°30′ E of N) is close to exact.* The compounds were group residences for 30 to 100 persons, many of them craft specialists working where they lived. Five hundred craft workshops have been identified, mostly devoted to preparing obsidian for export. Teotihuacán was in communication with Oaxaca, and its armed traders are depicted in Mayan murals. Its influence reached Kaminaljuyú, 600 miles away. It was the great religious and market center of its time, drawing in pilgrims and traders from an immense region.

There had been a village of moderate size there as early as 500 B.C., but the sudden leap to city occurs in the first century A.D. At that time, the great avenue and cross-avenue were laid far out across the empty land, somewhat to the south and east of the original village site, and the pyramids were begun and then enlarged. These vast public works controlled the planning of the city's growth for the next six centuries, and there is evidence that locations were provided in this initial planning that never were fully utilized. The labor for these enormous works must have been drawn from the surrounding foodshed, and most likely it drew on the contributed efforts of pilgrims as well.

Early in its history, Teotihuacán controlled an important source of obsidian, and certainly much of its later influence is based on obsidian-working and the trade in obsidian. But it appears that religious exaltation powered the first leap to urban status. The physical form of the city, and the great ceremonies that it housed, were the basis of its attraction. Surely the motive for such an extraordinary physical effort was to honor the gods, but also to induce pride and awe and to secure the city's position as a center of pilgrimage and tribute. Once the

See fig. 6

*Surveying marks have been found for a line three kilometers long, laid off at right angles to the main avenue with no more than 10 minutes of error.

Wheatley

Boyd

See fig. 7

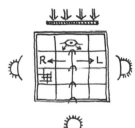

See fig. 9

Kates

urban machine was in motion, the additional economic and political advantages of concentration may have been self-generating.

When we look at an early city such as Teotihuacán, which has left no written records, we can only infer the motives of its builders. In civilizations possessed of writing, the trace of motive is more direct. In China, for example, the same succession of settled agriculture followed by cities and a stratified society occurs in the middle reaches of the Yellow River valley. In the earliest capital of Shang China, pillared buildings rose on earthen platforms, and there was a human sacrifice under each important building, or even under every pillar. Anxiety and guilt accompanied city building. The earth spirits must be propitiated and controlled. Chang'an, great capital of Han and T'ang, was run like a ritualized military camp. There were 160 wards within the city wall, like the compounds of Teotihuacán. Each ward had its own wall, and but a single gate. All gates closed at sunset to the sound of drums, and opened to drums again in the morning. Only military patrols moved through the streets at night.

This urban tradition is continuous in China from 1500 B.C. almost to the present, and the concept of the ideal Chinese city was gradually codified in writing. It should be square, regular, and oriented, with an emphasis on enclosure, gates, approaches, the meaning of the directions, and the duality of left and right. Creating and maintaining religious and political order was the explicit aim. Ritual and place were fitted together. They expressed, and indeed were believed actually to sustain, the harmony of heaven and men, which it was disastrous to disturb. The world, within this place of orderly location, orderly timing, and fitting behavior and dress, was safe and secure. Not incidentally, the hierarchical social structure was also unassailable there. A substantial literature describes this intertwining of thought and place. Its psychological power, even in relatively recent times and for a non-Chinese, is vividly conveyed in George Kates's memoirs of his life in Peking, in the twilight of the Chinese empire.

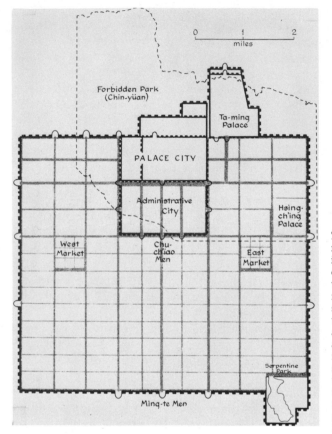

Forbidden Park
(Chin-yüan)

Ta-ming
Palace

PALACE CITY

Administrative
City

Hsing-
ch'ing
Palace

West
Market

Chu-
ch'iao
Men

East
Market

Serpentine
Park

Ming-te Men

0   1   2
miles

7 Plan of Chang'an (the
modern Sian) in China, as
it was under the T'ang
dynasty, about 700 A.D.,
when it contained one
million people and its
splendor was a byword. It
was divided into a palace,
an administrative city,
and an outer city, and its
markets and roads were
strictly supervised. Prices
were controlled, and
trades occupied separate
streets. The outer city, consisting of approximately
110 regular blocks, was
symmetrically divided by
Red Bird Street into west
and east administrative
areas, each with its own
market. Chang'an lay
close to the site of the earlier Han capital, estab-
lished about 200 B.C., and
in a region in which older
capitals had been built before 1000 B.C. By the T'ang
period, the classic model
of the Chinese city was
already well developed, in
the form that would in-
fluence later cities
throughout East Asia (see
fig. 37).

8 Air view of one of the
so-called citadels of Chan
Chan, capital of the Chi-
mu empire in Peru about
1000 A.D. The city con-
sisted of a mosaic of these
walled domains, unified
in orientation, but of unknown use and signifi-
cance. While there were
some built-up areas be-
tween the citadels there
were no important streets,
and the citadels often contained large open spaces.
The city was a set of boxes
within boxes.

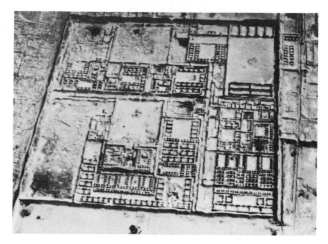

9 Diagram of the awe-
some formal approach to
the imperial audience hall
in Peking. The suppliant
passed through court after
court, gate after gate.

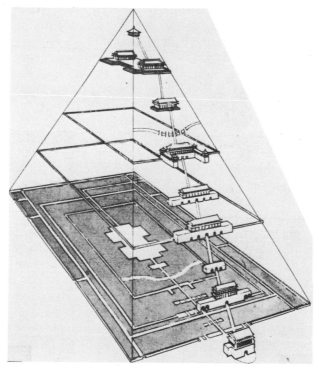

Once the idea of city was conceived, it acquired new functions and new values. Some of these appear when we study those deliberate plantations made by people already familiar with the city's usefulness. Company towns were built for clear motives of exploitation and profit, and their success or failure in achieving them has often been recorded. Another example, the colonial city, appears in two forms. First, there are the colonies in the wilderness, fixed in places where there are no other human beings, or where they are so scattered or so primitive that the colonizers see no use in them—that is, where the indigenes are either ignored or driven out. The new urban settlement is created to control some resource, or to relieve overpopulation at home. It is a small space of familiar order in an impersonal and alien region, and so the principal concerns are safety, efficient extraction of the sought resource, and a clear allocation of place and goods, so that a functioning society can be put in place as quickly as possible. Nostalgia for the homeland is a prominent feeling, and often there is a sense of temporariness, real or imagined. These places tend to be deliberately designed, quickly built, sharply defined from their surroundings, orderly in a rather simple way, and full of the conservative symbols of home.

The Greek colonies which spread along the shores of the Mediterranean and the Black Sea during the fourth and fifth centuries B.C. are classic examples of such cities in the wilderness. Most of them were laid out to a common pattern of long, slim blocks separated by narrow feeder streets. The feeder streets led into a few wider main streets at right angles. This is a repetitive pattern, applied heedless of topography. The city is enclosed by an irregular wall which responds to the defensibility of the terrain, having no apparent relation to the street pattern within. Defense, order, and a rapid and equitable allocation of house site and access seem to be the principal motives. Military camps and many nineteenth-century North American cities have similar features. We will see many of these characteristics once again, when we begin to build space stations.

See fig. 10

Wycherley

See figs. 11, 12

See fig. 13

10 View of the company
town of Sewell, built to
house workers of the El
Teniente copper mine, in
the arid highlands of
Chile. Mine buildings
occupy the only relatively
level ground. There is no
public open space, and
goods are carried by hand
and back, up the steep
streets. Mine workers are
housed in the long, five-
story *camorotes* ("ship's
bunks"). Employees paid
in U.S. dollars live in one-
family houses on the
north-facing (in the
Southern Hemisphere,
sunny) slope above.

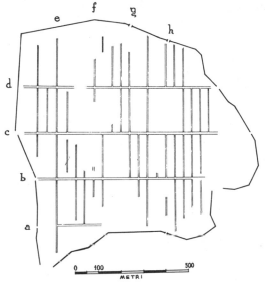

11 Air photo of the center
of Naples, together with a
plan of the corresponding
streets of the original
Greek colony of Neapolis
("new city"), whose
streets followed the typical pattern called *per strigas*
(by row, or furrow). The
defensive wall is related
to the form of the ground,
and not to the street pattern. This layout has persisted for 2600 years.

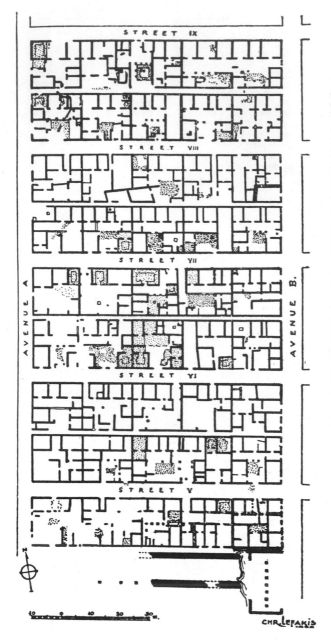

12 Five residential blocks of the new section of the Greek city of Olynthus, built about 430 B.C. and destroyed in 348 B.C. Although the older city is irregular, this new portion is regularly planned, with long, paved avenues running north and south, small cross streets at short intervals, and smaller alleys for drainage, making blocks about 120 by 300 feet. Note the modular plan of the houses and the consistent orientation of the open courts to the sun, regardless of the street entrance. The repetitive form is overlaid by subsequent remodelings. In the entire city, there was no great differentiation among the houses, except for a very few large structures, and some poorer houses in one quarter.

13 A bird's-eye view of
Fort Worth, Texas, in
1876, a typical North
American frontier city,
laid out in a regular grid
for rapid development
and the easy exchange of
land.

There is also a different type of colonial city, created within some well-populated region by an external power. Here, the local population is part of the resource to be exploited. Its usefulness and also its threat must be controlled. The resulting conflicts of culture must be faced. The Spanish ritual of town founding in the Americas began with the planting of a pike, the utterance of a challenge, and the cutting of weeds, as an act of possession. A gallows was erected, and only then was the cross raised and the founding mass celebrated. Indigenous systems of land tenure were abolished or absorbed into a system of rights imposed by the conquerors. A floating population of displaced Indians soon invaded the designated common lands and the town margins, distorting their orderly patterns, as may be seen in many early town surveys. Segregated Indian communities were created, to which the natives were removed by force and there subjected to religious teaching and social reorganization. Lima, for example, founded by Pizarro after the conquest of the native capital of Cuzco, had a walled *cercado* at its eastern end for Indians (from which they persisted in running away). Not that the indigenes were wholly excluded from the new center. The Laws of the Indies propose that they be kept out during construction, and only admitted when it was splendid and complete. The strange new city is to awe them into submission, just as the first cities awed their peasants. The house of the rulers should be distant but approachable. The double settlement (the familiar bipolar form) appears early in colonial history. Peking is one striking example.

The British built many examples of this type of dominating colony, in which the prime motive is the control of others, and the leading emotions of the conquerors are pride, fear, and a sense of exile. Delhi was the old locus of Moghul rule, in the center of India, on the main invasion route from the northwest. In 1911, the Queen's viceroy removed from Calcutta to Delhi, and a new capital was laid out, south of the old city. It was disposed along a set of great axial avenues of baroque inspiration, with ample space for the display of military force and civil grandeur. Society was minutely ranked, and the ranks were carefully located in precedence, pay,

20
Spanish colonies

Gakenheimer

See fig. 14

King

and place of residence in the new city. Height of ground and axial visibility were employed to express social dominance.

The English themselves lived in low-density compounds, in which English landscapes were recreated, as far as possible. Space was used to express social distance and to control the contacts between native and colonist. Indian servants lived and ate apart. The new city was sharply defined from the old, crowded native city. The entire landscape, from the form of chairs to the hierarchical naming of roads, was used to make the imposed social structure visible and concrete. Separation and control were maintained, while the nostalgia and anxiety of the intruders was made manageable.

These centers of colonial power use common physical devices: spatial separations, gates, and barriers; open views and fields of fire which extend the range of control; symmetrical axes of approach and parade; order, formality, cleanliness, level ground, standard parts, and things in lines; height and size as expressions of power; naming, marking, and fixing things in space and time; the regulation of spatial behavior and a luxuriance of ritual—all coupled, however, with special places of escape, in which the rulers can relax into informality. Commonly, these colonial settlements are bipolar cities, in which two zones lie side by side: old and new, crowded and extensive, disorderly and orderly, poor and rich, native and foreign.

Similar features, serving the same motives, can often be found when colonization is internal—when one clearly demarcated group exploits and controls another. Johannesburg in South Africa is an extreme example of the bipolar city of internal colonization. Border cities between nations of widely divergent power, such as the cities along the border between Mexico and the United States, have some of these same characteristics.

How does the colonized population deal with this inherited bipolar form, once the colonial hold is broken? Sometimes, as in Delhi today, the hierarchies and segregations are simply taken over and perpetuated by a new native elite. In other cases, as in Havana, the old colonial shell is uneasily inhabited by a completely different society, and it is not

See fig. 15

See fig. 16

14 A plan of Mexico City
in 1750, as rebuilt by the
Spanish conquerors on the
ruins of Aztec Tenochtit-
lán (see fig. 4). The city
core has a regular "bas-
tide" plan and a ring of
irregular "squatter" housing surrounds it.

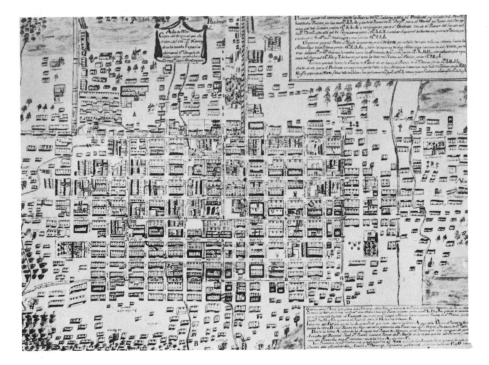

15 Aerial view of the boundary between Old and New Delhi, taken in 1942. The "greenbelt" is the clearance for gunfire which the British military government created just outside the old city walls after the Sepoy rebellion. The contrast in scale and texture between native and British quarters is striking.

16 Bird's-eye of Soweto in South Africa, one element in the string of new settlements built to relocate the black population out of Johannesburg, in pursuit of the official policy of *apartheid*. Note the personalized facades on the standard units, and the two user-built houses in the left foreground.

at all clear how the space can be reorganized to make it fit with society again. When the South Africans gain control of their country, what will they do with Johannesburg?

While the planted city is usually built for obvious reasons, it is more difficult to untangle the motives governing a more gradual development. How cities are reconstructed after major disasters gives us clues to this more general process, despite the complexity of rebuilding, and the inertia of the remains. We could analyze London and Chicago after the fire, Lisbon, San Francisco, Tokyo, Managua, and Anchorage after the earthquake, Atlanta, Halifax, and Warsaw after the human holocaust. The city is rapidly rebuilt, and motives are debated openly. As in surgery, much can be learned about normal city function and value by observing events when normal function is brusquely interrupted.

Reddaway

Burton

But the most difficult intellectual challenge is presented by the gradual development of cities, accomplished by many different, conflicting actors. The values inherent in this process are those closest to our own interests. Most relevant of all was that long, complex upheaval that transformed our cities into what is now their familiar form. It took place in the nineteenth century in Europe and North America and is still working itself out. Unlike first emergence, or most cases of deliberate plantation, this great change involved the reconstruction of a substantial existing fabric. The story is more intricate.

London and Paris are often-cited examples of this transformation—particularly London, where capitalism enjoyed its first strength. A small class built a new landscape to permit profitable production and the cumulative concentration of capital. Road, rail, and water lines to carry goods and workmen were driven through the old city. Efficient sites for production were created. New financial devices—such as deficit spending, building societies, and betterment assessments—and new public and private institutions were developed to build and manage the city. Work and residence were segregated by type and class, where possible—to some degree for greater efficiency, but more

Briggs
Evenson
Saalman
Sutcliffe
Weinberg

White

Warner 1972

Whitehill

See figs. 17, 18

particularly to control the threat of violence and disease, and to remove from the sight of the upper class the painful labor on which its profits were based. The dispossessed of the countryside flooded into the cities. Their cheap labor made profitable production possible, but their numbers, their diseases, and their grievances made life uneasy for those who profited. City evils appeared as a common literary theme. Gains could be extracted both from the production of goods and from the renting of sites for production and housing, and the two groups of capitalists, based on these two sources of gain, were often in conflict over the development of the city.

The story of the nineteenth-century transformation of London and Paris has often been told. But the same events were occurring in other European and American cities, if somewhat later. Look, for example, at the case of Boston.

The period after the American Revolution had been one of growth for the city of Boston, but it was still a mercantile town, both in its society and in its economic base. It was a center of world trade, a port of exchange. Its shipping dominated the South Atlantic, but it also traded in the Pacific and Indian Oceans, the Baltic, and the Mediterranean. Carrying goods about the world, buying cheap and selling dear, using its wits and capital to snatch at new opportunities, or to drop them once exploited, Boston was linked more closely to the navigable world than to its own rural hinterland. The port, in the curve of shore between Fort Hill and the North End, was the center of action, with the Long Wharf—and State Street, its inland extension—as its focus. Along State Street the great merchants lived and kept their countinghouses. At the head of the street stood the Old State House, which had only recently been replaced by the new capitol on Beacon Hill. Artisan and middle classes lived in adjacent areas, surrounding the core, producing goods primarily for local consumption in small, home-based workshops. A few Irish had arrived, huddled close to the edge of the port, but most of the transient, marginal people—the poor, the casual laborers, the sailors, prostitutes, and criminals—lived on the margins of the town, such as

17 Plan of the city of Boston in 1837. Landfills have begun around the original peninsula: in the Mill Pond and the South Cove to accommodate the new railway lines, and, along the edges of the Neck, to form the new South End. But the Back Bay is still open, and much of East Cambridge, East Boston, and South Boston remain to be made. The future airport has yet to engulf the Bird Island flats. (Fig. 19 shows the eventual extent of the filling.) Long Wharf, the extension of State Street is the heart of the harbor, and the new Quincy Markets are the black rectangles just north of it.

18 A bird's-eye view of Boston in 1850, looking from a point over the Back Bay, across the newly created Public Garden and the Common, to the harbor, crowded with ships. This is the mercantile city at the beginning of its transformation, still focused on its counting houses and its shipping, its wealth still at its center.

along the back side of Beacon Hill. Accustomed as we are to the poor at the center and rich on the outskirts, this mercantile city seems inside-out to us.

Mercantile Boston was transformed by two groups of people: the merchants, who stood at the center of the web of production, distribution, and credit, and who required a new habitat for a new economy, and the investors in land, building, and transportation, who sought to profit from this act of transformation. The process of change was a growth and differentiation of specialized land uses, which spread and shifted incrementally, moving painfully around obstacles of topography, prior occupancy, or symbolic sacredness, and always in competition with each other for the control of space. The process is marked by repeated efforts to improve the communication between various key activities, efforts marred by frequent failure.

The occasion for this transformation was the shift of the city's economy from a mercantile port of exchange to a center of industrial production, made possible by steam power and the flood of cheap Irish labor, and made necessary by the decline of the carrying trade after the depression of 1857. Merchant capital and organizing ability moved from overseas trade to investment in large, inner-city workshops. These shops were able to use cheap but unskilled labor, by means of a minutely divided process of production which reduced the worker's behavior to some routine, repetitive action. In particular, these shops produced ready-made clothes and shoes for sailors, slaves, miners, soldiers, and frontiersmen. The demands of the Civil War, and the opening of the west, gave great impetus to this industry.

Thence began a complex spatial quadrille, in which factories and warehouses shuffled among the restricted spaces and dense buildings of the peninsula. The first of these "rationalized" work-shops took over the old warehouses as the carrying trade declined and then were pushed out again when the traffic revived in such western staples as wool, leather, and wheat. Some industries, shoes and textiles in particular, were later successfully mechanized on a large scale, and jumped out to

See fig. 19

suburban locations, such as Brockton and Lynn, where spacious new plants could be built and a permanent labor force housed and controlled nearby. Other industries, such as clothing, were unable to mechanize, and in consequence were converted to sweatshop production in the adjacent tenement areas of the North End and the South Cove. The warehouses and markets themselves began to specialize and diverge: wool and leather on one side of State Street, the food markets for local supply on the other. While maneuvering outward, they had to maintain connections to the port for raw materials and to labor at walking distance, but, above all, to the supply of credit and of market information in the specialized financial district. This latter zone, whose origins lay in the former mercantile countinghouses of State Street, moved very little, only expanding southward as it needed space, while leaving the north side of the street to the food markets and the Irish.

Adequate space for offices, production, or storage was important, but access by adjacency was crucial, and access to credit and information was the most crucial of all. Growth was always incremental, invading some neighbor's space. Where necessary, substantial capital, or even public power, could be marshaled to clear and rebuild a needed ground, as occurred when Quincy Market was erected, the Broad Street wharves were laid out, Fort Hill was cleared and leveled, or Atlantic Avenue was cut through. The hilly, deeply indented peninsula of Boston was leveled and extended at great cost. Nine hundred acres were added to an original area of less than eight hundred. The developing city was compelled to thrash about in a narrow room, and as a result few early buildings have survived. The peninsular—almost island—site had originally been chosen for its defensibility, its harbor, and its water supply. The price of inadaptability and poor access that accompanied those assets was paid in the nineteenth century.

Simultaneously, repeated efforts were made to link up the port with the regional transport system. Eight independent railroads were brought into Boston between 1835 and 1855. None of them succeeded in reaching the port or the business center.

See fig. 20

Space for their lines and terminals could only be found in the marginal wetlands of the Mill Pond, the Back Bay, and the South Cove. One railroad reached deep water in East Boston, but it served a minor hinterland. The Cunard lines from Great Britain located at that point, but goods and passengers landed there had to be ferried across the harbor to the city center. Cunard soon deserted Boston for New York.

In the opposite direction, going outward from the city, one railroad had reached as far west as the Hudson River by 1842, but pushed no farther. Earlier ambitious plans for a canal across the Berkshires were abandoned. While struggling internally to reach deep water, Boston lost to New York the external race for access to the interior of the continent and never regained its original dominance. Thus, the Boston railroads served primarily to transport local passengers, especially commuters, and were interconnected only at a much later date. When the export of western staples by rail picked up, goods were transferred to ships at independent suburban railheads. The historic gulf between the city center and its port on the one hand and the rural interior on the other remained unbridged. Within the city, freight traffic between terminals, along with the converging horsecar lines, continued to congest the tangled central streets.

Meanwhile, the flood of Irish immigrants, which made this boom possible, had also to be fitted into that tangle, within walking distance of factory work and odd jobs. In one decade, the foreign-born in Boston increased from 15 to 46 percent of the city's population. They were packed into the old residential areas nearest to the docks where they had landed, along the margins of the North End and in the neighborhood of Fort Hill. Speculators built dense tenements and alley dwellings and converted old houses and their cellars. As a result, the Irish lived in numbing filth and crowding. In 1850 in the Fort Hill area there were, *on the average*, more than four families, or twenty persons, in every small apartment. Cholera broke out, redoubling the native fear and hatred of the Irish, on whom the economic machine now depended. The Fort Hill slums were acquired and cleared of tene-

See fig. 21

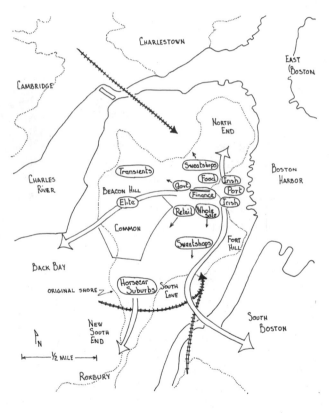

19 A diagram of the conversion of mercantile Boston to industrial Boston, showing the landfills, the penetration of the railways, and the movements of some of the principal activities and population groups.

20 Faneuil Hall, "cradle of the Revolution," at the left, and beyond it the long, granite Quincy Market, built and donated to the city by Josiah Quincy in 1828. The market was the centerpeice of Quincy's successful private speculation, which used public condemnation powers to redevelop the old town dock area for a new food market. This same area was rehabilitated once more, in 1978, to make a lively downtown shopping center.

21 Leveling Fort Hill in Boston, by pick, shovel, and horsecart, after the Irish tenements had been cleared away.

ments through public power and at public charge. The hill was leveled, and its inhabitants were pushed out to provide space for business expansion. The Irish went on to pack the South Cove, the North End, and South Boston, the latter a spatial cul-de-sac which they have continued to occupy.

The old South End (a region now part of the city's central business district, and not to be confused with what is called the South End today) was an elite residential area which first was converted to profitable slums and then cleared for business use. In other directions, residential enclaves held out against business pressures. Elite Beacon Hill stood firm, for example. It lay behind the State House and off the axis of commercial growth, which had been turned aside by the sacred Boston Common. In another direction, the working-class North End also held its ground. It was a dead-end peninsula behind the food markets, whose inhabitants manned those markets at early hours and had to be within close walk of them. The very constriction of the urban ground within which these elements battled for space and the tenacious resistance of some groups has resulted today in a variegated, multi-ethnic central city, quite unlike the empty speculative ring which surrounds the central core of most North American cities.

Firey

A breakout was effected to the south, however, through which the horsecar lines were extended beginning in the 1850s. Many of the affluent had already jumped out to country homes within 5 miles of the center, relying on the commuting railroads. A solid remnant stood their ground on Beacon Hill or took possession of the Back Bay as it was filled, but the well-to-do abandoned Tremont Street, the old South End, and then the new South End along the Neck to the oncoming waves of businessmen and Irishmen. That now familiar spatial segregation by social class began to appear, as well as a reversal of the old radial gradient of wealth, whose pinnacle had been at the center and was now shifting outwards.

Warner 1969

Railroads were too expensive for the great mass of the citizens. Workingmen walked to work. However, the new horsecars and their 5-cent fare suddenly made it possible for the lower middle

from political dominance to a reliance on economic power. In the 1880s, the immigrant tide rose once more, but now it was made up of French Canadians, Eastern European Jews, and southern Italians.

Merchant and speculative capital transformed the old mercantile city to house a new economic function and to absorb a stream of labor on which that function rested. But this was done only with great effort, within a resistant medium. The result was never an efficient locus for production, nor was an integrated transportation system ever attained. A severe price was paid in the health of the population. This struggle for territory left a powerful legacy of ethnic enclaves and exclusionist attitudes, as well as that diverse, tight center that seems so distinctive today. The horsecar expansion into Roxbury and Dorchester was a liberation for many families, a first step toward decent housing and a chance for social mobility. These early suburbs are also the areas with whose abandonment and decay Bostonians now must reckon. The motives of the transformation are clear—better access and space for production, an opportunity for profit in real estate development, and the control of space in order to control the productive process and its participants. Issues of health, of the dangers of violence or of fire, and of creating a setting better fitted to family life, all followed after these first three motives and as a reaction to the consequences of that initial transformation.

The values and the valuers who transformed Boston can be traced, overlaid as they are by the complexity of a great city and the vast inertia of its form. The city did not just "grow naturally," nor was it the inescapable outcome of impersonal historic forces. Neither was its growth a unique or incomprehensible tale. In the same fashion, one could look at the cities of some different culture, to see how variations in value affect city form. The medieval Islamic city, for example, with its emphasis on privacy, is markedly different from the cities we are accustomed to. Its dense, dendritic pattern seems at first very mysterious to us, until the underlying values are understood.

One might look for examples of the socialist city, built to fit the motives and circumstances of that new order of society. Few well-fitted examples are yet to be found. Many new towns have been built and old cities reconstructed in the USSR and Eastern Europe, but they are remarkably like the cities of the western capitalist world, although perhaps without that residential segregation by class which deforms the latter. Whether new forms are taking shape in Cuba or in China remains to be seen.

36
Socialist cities

Sawyers

Salaff
Towers

City forms, their actual function, and the ideas and values that people attach to them make up a single phenomenon. Therefore, the history of city form cannot be written just by tracing the diffusion of the rectangular grid street pattern. Peking and Chicago are not even superficially alike. Nor can that history be written solely by reference to the impersonal forces of the state and the market. Decisions are cumulative, leaving a strong legacy— valuable or encumbering—for each successive generation of inhabitants. The form of a settlement is always willed and valued, but its complexity and its inertia frequently obscure those connections. One must uncover—by inference, if no better source is available—why people created the forms they did and how they felt about them. One must penetrate into the actual experience of places by their inhabitants, in the course of their daily lives. Such an interpretive history is not the aim of this book. But some general themes are evident, even in the few examples cited: such persistent motives among city builders as symbolic stability and order; the control of others and the expression of power; access and exclusion; efficient economic function; and the ability to control resources. Even over this long span of time, some common physical strategies were used to these ends, based on human physiology and psychology and on the enduring structure of the physical world.

2

What Is the Form of a City, and How Is It Made?

Three branches of theory endeavor to explain the city as a spatial phenomenon. One, called "planning theory," asserts how complex public decisions about city development are or should be made. Since these understandings apply to all complex political and economic enterprises, the domain of this theory extends far beyond the realm of city planning, and it has been well developed in those other fields. So it has a more general name: "decision theory."

The second branch, which I call "functional theory," is more particularly focussed on cities, since it attempts to explain why they take the form they do and how that form functions. This is a reasonably thick theoretical limb—if not as robust as decision theory—and engages renewed interest today. I have summarized its leading ideas in appendix A, and there, from a safe distance, point to some of the more common blemishes on this limb.

The third branch, spindly and starved for light, but on which so many actions are hung, is what I would call "normative theory." It deals with the generalizable connections between human values and settlement form, or how to know a good city when you see one. This is our concern.

J. Friedmann 1960
Klosterman

As on any healthy tree, the three branches should spring securely from a common trunk. Unlike the branches of trees we know, they should not diverge. They should interconnect and support each other at many points. A comprehensive theory of cities would be a mat of vegetation, and some day the branches will no longer exist in separate form. While working perilously far out on the weakest branch, we must be aware of the other two and look for favorable places to insert a graft.

So this chapter scans planning theory and functional theory, the two companion branches to our own. It also sets forth what I mean by the "form" of the city. Otherwise, what are we talking about?

Almost all recent theories about the spatial form of urban settlements have been theories of urban function. They ask: "How did the city get to be the way it is?" and that closely related question, "how does it work?" One cannot ask, "What is a good city?" without some convictions about answers to those previous questions. Theories of function, in their turn, cannot be constructed without some sense of "goodness," which allows one to focus on the essential elements. All functional theories contain value assumptions—most often hidden ones—just as all normative theories contain assumptions about structure and function. Theoretical developments in one arena impose themselves on the other. A developed theory of cities will be simultaneously normative and explanatory.

As yet, there is no single theory of city genesis and function that brings together all the significant aspects of city life. These theories look at the city from quite different points of view, and some particular viewpoints are much more fully developed than others. Appendix A is a brief review of those reigning theories, grouped by the dominant metaphors by which they conceive of the city. These metaphors control the elements to be abstracted and shape the model of function.

The city may be looked on as a story, a pattern of relations between human groups, a production and distribution space, a field of physical force, a set of linked decisions, or an arena of conflict. Values are embedded in these metaphors: historic continuity, stable equilibrium, productive efficiency, capable decision and management, maximum interaction, or the progress of political struggle. Certain actors become the decisive elements of transformation in each view: political leaders, families and ethnic groups, major investors, the technicians of transport, the decision elite, the revolutionary classes.

From the standpoint of normative theory, these functional theories have some common deficiencies. Perhaps it is these very deficiencies which allow me (or is it the pervading dullness which motivates me?) to compress this extensive literature into a single appendix. If we had a compelling functional theory, no book on city values

Chapin 1964
Dowall

could be written without it. As it is, these theories depend on values which are unexamined and incomplete. Second, most of them are essentially static in nature, dealing with small shifts, balancings, or external changes which will be damped out, or lead to final explosions, or, at most, cause radical jumps that reach some new and endless plateau. None deals successfully with continuous change, with incremental actions that lead in some progressive direction.

Third, none of these formulations (except the historical, or "antitheoretical," view) deals with environmental quality, that is, with the rich texture of city form and meaning. Space is abstracted in a way that impoverishes it, reducing it to a neutral container, a costly distance, or a way of recording a distribution which is the residue of some other, nonspatial, process. Most of what we feel to be the real experience of the city has simply vanished. Fourth, few of the theories consider that the city is the result of the purposeful behavior of individuals and small groups, and that human beings can learn. The city is the manifestation of some iron law or other, rather than the result of changing human aspirations.

It surprises no one to hear that it is impossible to explain how a city should be, without understanding how it is. Perhaps it *is* surprising to encounter the reverse: that an understanding of how a city is depends on a valuing of what it should be. But values and explanations seem to me inextricable. In the absence of valid theory in either branch, concepts elaborated in the one must employ provisional assumptions from the other, while making that dependence explicit and maintaining as much independence as is possible.

In distinction to functional and normative theory, planning theory deals with the nature of the environmental decision process—how it is and should be conducted. This is a subject treated at length in many other sources. Since normative theory is intended to be useful in creating better cities, clearly it must be aware of the situations in which it is likely to be used.

Dyckman
Faludi

Cities are built and maintained by a host of agents: families, industrial firms, city bureaus, developers, investors, regulatory and subsidizing agencies, utility companies, and the like. Each has its own interests, and the process of decision is fragmented, plural, and marked by bargaining. Some of these agents are dominant, leading; others will follow those leaders. In this country, the leading agents tend to be the great financial institutions, which establish the conditions for investment; the major corporations, whose decisions as to the location and nature of productive investment set the rate and quality of city growth; and the large developers, who create extensive pieces of the city itself. On the public side, we must add the major federal agencies, whose policies of taxation, subsidy, and regulation merge with the actions of private finance to set the investment conditions, and the large, single-purpose, state or regional agencies which are charged with creating highways, ports, water and disposal systems, large reservations, and similar major chunks of city infrastructure. The basic patterns set by these form givers (to appropriate an egotistical term from architecture) are filled in by the actions of many others, in particular the location decisions of individual families and of firms of modest size, the preparatory activities of real estate speculators, small developers, and builders, and the regulatory and supporting functions of local government. The latter agencies, although unable to control the main currents, do much to set the quality of a settlement, through their fire, building, and zoning codes, by the way they service development with schools and roads and open space, and by the quality of those services: education, policing, and sanitation.

This process has certain marked characteristics. The leading agents, who have such a tremendous influence, do not control city development in any directed, central fashion. Typically, they are single-purpose actors, whose aim is to increase their profit margin, complete a sewer system, support the real estate market, or maintain a taxation system which generates sufficient revenue (and yet provides sufficient loopholes). These purposes are usually remote from the city form that

Braybrooke

they shape. No one takes anything like a comprehensive view of the evolving spatial structure, except perhaps the local planning agency, which is one of the weaker actors. When this is added to the great number of agencies who have *some* role to play in the game, and whose acts, however passively responsive, have great cumulative power, then we have a city-building process which is complex and plural, marked by conflict, cross-purpose, and bargaining, and whose outcome, while often inequitable or even unwanted, seems as uncontrollable as a glacier.

Yet it is controlled, if not with conscious purpose, by the leading actors we have named, and it can also be modified consciously by public effort, although with only partial (and sometimes with surprising) effect. Most purposeful public actions, beyond the single-minded decisions of public works agencies, are reactions to pressing difficulties, which are carried out with haste, poor information, and no theory, and which are designed to return the system to some previous condition.

Comprehensive theory might seem of remote value in such restrictive situations, and yet it is just here that a coherent theory is so badly needed. It is needed to make restricted actions effective, as well as to enlighten the inevitable political bargaining, or even to point to needed changes in the decision process itself. Thus structural theory guides the quasi-intuitional actions of a trained engineer in some emergency, and military theory illuminates the confused art of war. But theory must be of a certain kind, if it is to be useful. It must speak to purposes, and not about inevitable forces. It must not be esoteric, but be clear enough to be useful to all sorts of actors. It must be usable in rapid, partial decisions and in the constant "steering" of policy as the complex settlement changes. Indeed, as we shall see, various normative theories of the city have been used in just that way, however misguided they might have been.

Creating cities can be quite different in other societies. The power to decide may be highly decentralized but also egalitarian, instead of decentralized but unequal, in the United States. More often, it is more highly centralized. The motives of power may differ. The basic values of the society may not only be different from our own, but also more homogeneous and stable. Decisions may be made according to tradition, without explicit rational analysis. The level of material resources, of skill and technology, can be substantially lower, which changes the constraints and shifts the priorities. The rate of change may be faster or slower. All these variations in the dimensions of the decision process make varying demands on any normative theory. A general theory must be able to respond to those differences. At the same time, there do seem to be certain regularities in the contemporary decision process, at least within the large urban settlements which dominate our landscape today. We find plurality, complexity, and rapid change everywhere.

Whenever any significant actor, public or private, engages to make an important decision in this complex environment, that effort to decide has typical features. The first question is: "What is the problem?" The consciousness of a problem is always an integrated perception, however vague, that is simultaneously an image of the situation and its constraints, of the goals to be achieved, of who the clients are, and what kinds of resources and solutions are available. Problems do not exist without some inkling of all of these features, and the decision process is no more than a progressive clarification of this set, until a firm basis for action is found—one in which solution, aims, clients, resources to be used, and perceived situation all seem to match one another. To achieve this mutual fit may require modifying any or all of these separate features. But the initial concept of the problem is crucial. Often enough, it is wrong to begin with—the situation so poorly understood, the clients so restricted, the aims or the solution envisaged so inappropriate, that nothing can be done except to make things worse.

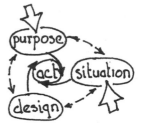

Some of the preconceptions that accompany initial problem definition are fundamental. One is the view of the basic type of response that is appropriate. For example: seeing a difficulty, one may not try to remove it, but simply seek to understand it and to predict its future course, so that one can adapt, survive, and prosper if possible. Grass bends to the wind, but the "street-wise" person does more: he takes advantage of the wind's momentary course and power.

At the other end of the scale, one may be convinced that a fundamental change in the rules of the game is essential. Society must make a radical shift. An environmental problem is the occasion for motivating others to that radical change. Nothing less than this great leap will do, and so a housing shortage is best converted into a confrontation and a revolutionary lesson. Or, following another alternative, one makes a persuasive model of a habitat or society which is radically better than the present one, but which can be realized gradually.

Between passive response and great leaps lies the strategy of making repeated changes in selected factors, in order to improve the whole piecemeal. One such gradualist approach is to change persons so that they can function better in an existing context. People's lives are enriched by learning to observe and understand their own city neighborhoods, and they begin to come to grips with their own life situations. Teaching children or the handicapped how to get about the city, or homeowners how to make a garden or repair a house, are other examples of this mode of intervention.

Alternatively, one may focus on modifying the environment, the better to fit the intentions of the person, which is the typical planning approach. The normative theory we have in mind is designed for use in this environment-modifying, piecemeal, and gradualist mode. However, it can also supply educative information, or the fuel for a more radical change. Changing minds, changing society, or even changing nothing at all, may in many situations be a more appropriate response than changing the environment. Most people are convinced of the eternal rightness of their own favorite mode. On the contrary, a well-formulated problem always entails prior consideration of the proper scope and mode of intervention.

It is also crucial to decide who the clients are. Who should make the decisions? In whose interests should those decisions be made? Are deciders and decided-for the same? The clients identified at the beginning of a decision effort usually exclude certain vital interests. Bringing in a new client, in the course of the decision, is delicate work, sure to be resisted by those already at the table and likely to impede any decisive action.

A highly decentralized decision process, in which the immediate users of a place make the decisions about its form, is a powerful ideal. It reinforces their sense of competence, and seems more likely to result in a well-fitted environment, than if they are excluded. The basic view is philosophical anarchism. But there are users whom we judge incompetent to decide: too young, too ill, or under coercion. There are indivisible goods, like clean air, that affect millions of users simultaneously. There are places used by numerous transient clients, such as a subway. There are conflicting interests, users who succeed each other, and distant persons whose interests are partially affected by some local use. There are unknown clients, people who are not there yet, or who have not yet been born. There are clients who are unaware of their own requirements, or of what they might value if they had the opportunity. All these difficulties, plus the political troubles inherent in any effort to shift control to new clients as a problem develops, give planning decisions their characteristic tone of ambiguity, conflict, and fluidity.

Bookchin
R. Goodman
C. Ward 1976

Other professionals hold a contrary view: all crucial decisions are inevitably, or even preferably, made by a powerful few. Since dominant interests cannot be suppressed, and since some professionals are uniquely endowed by their marvelous training and ability to solve environmental problems, those gifted ones should stand beside the seats of power. Problems are complex, values subtle, and solutions specialized and delicate. Find an expert who can grasp the situation, and give him room to work. Some of our more remarkable environments arose from heroic leadership of that kind, but few are well fitted to the purpose of their users. This model performs best when values are clear and common, and problems largely technical.

Professional planners take on many different roles in this complicated decision landscape. Most of them, perhaps, are project planners, working for some definite client, such as a corporation or government agency, and preparing a solution to some limited, well-defined problem, according to an explicit set of purposes. Here they are sheltered from most of the debates about the client or the mode of intervention. Those crucial decisions have been made for them.

Other planners consider themselves to be working in the public interest. Since they must work near some center of power in order to be effective, they are beset by the issues I have sketched out above: who is the client? who should make the decisions? how should goals be determined? are there in fact any common interests? how can I know them? how can power be effective without overriding those common interests with its own aims? At times, planners in this public interest role may try to avoid some of these dilemmas by attending primarily to the decision *process*—keeping it as open and equitable as possible—without attempting to set goals or to recommend solutions.

Retreating still further from decision, and in despair of discovering the public interest, many planners take on the primary role of informers (not spies!). They create accurate and timely information for public use: descriptions of the present state and how it is changing, predictions about coming events, and analyses of the results to be expected from this or that line of action. Actual plans and decisions are left to others, but presumably they will be better decisions because better informed. If these planners have strong beliefs about the decision process, they may shape their information especially for the use of certain groups: for decentralized users, for radical reformers, or for central decision makers. Alternatively, as I have mentioned above, they may think of themselves primarily as teachers, involved in educating, and so in changing, the public.

Lastly, some professionals are primarily advocates. They may be the advocates of some idea—such as new towns or bicycle paths or houseboats—in which case they must organize their own client base. These are pattern makers, who hope to be effective through the persuasiveness of their ideas.

If sufficiently radical, they create utopias: patent models for a new society.

More frequently, they will be advocates of some interest group—a social class, a corporation, a neighborhood—and press that interest vigorously, in competition with other contenders. Many professionals, of course, are advocates without being aware of it, while others take a more conscious position. They look on society as highly connected but irredeemably plural and contradictory. All decisions are made by struggle and compromise; few values are held in common. Inevitably, any professional works for one group or another. Some will add: but this system is unjust, since some groups have little power and no hired advocate. Therefore, a professional of conscience works for those poorly represented groups, advocating their interests as forcefully and as narrowly as a planner hired by a real estate developer.

Advocates, informers, project designers, and public planners—these are perhaps the predominant professional roles today. Their theories and models, usually implicit and unexamined, play an important part in environmental decision, amid all the customary confusion of that process. Unmanageable problems are made manageable by restricting the clients to be attended to, by taking a model of change and thus a type of solution for granted, by assuming a narrow set of operative values, and by controlling the supply of information. Information of a fairly broad range is often gathered while initiating planning studies. In the press of decision, only a small portion of that information is used, and that is the portion which accords with the models already in the decider's head. Developing a theory that is sufficiently concise and flexible to be used under pressure is one way of directing the attention of decision makers to one set of issues rather than another.

The process of decision (and of design, which is a subset of decision) is one of managing the progressive development and definition of a problem, to the point where situation, client, aim, and solution are sufficiently well-fitted to take action. This process, when applied to large environments at least, has difficulties which seem to be common throughout the world. It likewise poses some common issues: such as those about the nature of the client, the model of change and its management, and the nature of the professional role. It has consequences for the ethics of planning, as well. Planning, to my mind, has its own special interest in any public debate. I would characterize that special interest as one which is prejudiced in favor of five things (besides its focus on spatial form and form-associated institutions): the long-term effects, the interests of an absent client, the construction of new possibilities, the explicit use of values, and the ways of informing and opening up the decision process. These are professional counterweights to the de-emphasis of those considerations by other actors.

But what is this city, that we dare to call good or bad? How can we describe it in ways that different observers will confirm, and which can be related to values and performance? This simple step conceals unseemly difficulties.

Settlement form, usually referred to by the term "physical environment," is normally taken to be the spatial pattern of the large, inert, permanent physical objects in a city: buildings, streets, utilities, hills, rivers, perhaps the trees. To these objects are attached a miscellany of modifying terms, referring to their typical use, or their quality, or who owns them: single-family residence, public housing project, cornfield, rocky hill, ten-inch sewer, busy street, abandoned church, and so on. The spatial distribution of these things is shown on two-dimensional maps: topographic maps, land use maps, street maps with notations, utility networks, maps of housing condition. These maps are accompanied by population counts (divided into classes of age, sex, income, race, and occupation), and usually by maps showing the spatial distribution of population (by which is meant where people sleep). Then there are descriptions of the quantity of traffic on the various main arteries, and statistics on the principal economic activities (that is, only those human activities which are part of the system of monetary exchange), and data on the location, capacity, and condition of particular public or semi-public buildings or areas, such as schools,

Gottman

churches, parks, and the like. These descriptions are familiar, and they are infected with difficulties, which are also familiar to anyone who has handled them. Lay citizens are baffled by these maps, graphs and tables. This might be taken as a sign of the scientific sophistication of the field, except that professionals have the same troubles.

The fundamental problem is to decide what the form of a human settlement consists of: solely the inert physical things? or the living organisms too? the actions people engage in? the social structure? the economic system? the ecological system? the control of the space and its meaning? the way it presents itself to the senses? its daily and seasonal rhythms? its secular changes? Like any important phenomenon, the city extends out into every other phenomenon, and the choice of where to make the cut is not an easy one.

I will take the view that settlement form is the spatial arrangement of persons doing things, the resulting spatial flows of persons, goods, and information, and the physical features which modify space in some way significant to those actions, including enclosures, surfaces, channels, ambiences, and objects. Further, the description must include the cyclical and secular changes in those spatial distributions, the control of space, and the perception of it. The last two, of course, are raids into the domains of social institutions and of mental life.

The cut is not trivial, however, since most social institutional patterns are excluded, as well as the larger part of the realms of biology and psychology, the chemical and physical structure of matter, etc. The chosen ground is the spatiotemporal distribution of human actions and the physical things which are the context of those actions, plus just so much about social institutions and mental attitudes as is most directly linked to that spatiotemporal distribution, and which is significant at the scale of whole settlements. This choice is more fully discussed, and compared with conventional descriptions, in appendix B.

No one would claim that to describe these things is to grasp a human settlement in its fullness. We must see any place as a social, biological, and

Gans 1968
Guttman
Pahl

physical whole, if we mean to understand it completely. But an important preliminary (or at least a
necessary accompaniment) to seeing things whole
is to define and understand their parts. Moreover,
social and spatial structure are only partially related
to each other—loose coupled, as it were—since both
affect the other only through an intervening variable (the human actor), and both are complex
things of great inertia. For me, the acts and
thoughts of human beings are the final ground for
judging quality. These apparently ephemeral phenomena become repetitive and significant in at least
three situations: in the persistent structure of ideas
which is a culture, in the enduring relationships
between people which are social institutions, and in
the standing relations of people with place. I deal
with the last. While the social, or economic, or
political aspects of settlements are rather well-
defined—and often too narrowly defined—the
physical aspect is put so uncertainly that it is difficult to see whether it plays any role at all.

The cut I suggest seems to be the closest one
that can be taken, that still permits us to comment
on the contribution of spatial pattern to human
aims. Moreover, it is a coherent view, since its
common core is the spatial distribution, at a given
scale, of tangible, physical persons, objects, and
actions. It has the advantage of growing out of the
commonsense view of the environment, while reg-
ularizing and expanding it.

Building a full theory will be a long-range
effort, if it is to be a theory which deals with form
and process, and which is an understanding, an
evaluation, a prediction, and a prescription, all in
one. It will hinge on purposeful human behavior
and the images and feelings that accompany it. This
is the joint at which all three branches of theory
should grow together. Our particular subject,
which is normative theory, must be considered
with that possibility in mind. Such normative
theory as exists today is disconnected from the
other theoretical realms, but carries hidden
assumptions about function and process.

There are certain requirements, then, for any
useful normative theory of city form:

1. It should start from purposeful behavior and the images and feelings which accompany it.

2. It should deal directly with settlement form and its qualities, and not be an eclectic application of concepts from other fields.

3. It should connect values of very general and long-range importance to that form, and to immediate, practical actions about it.

4. It should be able to deal with plural and conflicting interests and to speak for absent and future clients.

5. It should be appropriate to diverse cultures and to variations in the decision situation (variations in the centralization of power, the stability and homogeneity of values, the level of resources, and the rate of change).

6. It should be sufficiently simple, flexible, and divisible that it can be used in rapid, partial decisions, with imperfect information, by lay persons who are the direct users of the places in question.

7. It should be able to evaluate the quality of state and process together, as it varies over a moderate span of time.

8. While at root a way of evaluating settlement form, the concepts should suggest new possibilities of form. In general, it should be a possible theory: not an iron law of development, but one that emphasizes the active purposes of participants and their capacity for learning.

Where shall we look for the material for such a theory?

3

Between Heaven and Hell

It would be reasonable to think that an examination of the form policies commonly proposed by public agencies, together with the reasons that are advanced to support those policies, would be a good way to begin any discussion of normative theory, just as a review of common opinions which explain why things work the way they do is a good first step in building a scientific theory. In doing so, we can conveniently divide most official proposals into two groups, one at the national or large regional scale, where actions concern systems of cities, national networks, and the regional distribution of population, and the other at the local scale, where one is concerned with intraregional patterns of development. Since we are primarily concerned with teasing out the values lying behind these policies, it is sufficient simply to list them here, without elaborating the proposals themselves, and without making any critique of their rationale. Nor need we comment on the historic rise and fall of some of these policies, which have waxed and waned as constraints and motives were transformed. I ask the reader's patience. The outline of an encyclopedia is bound to lack a little luster.

First, we find some common national spatial policies:

1. Controlling the size and rate of growth of the largest cities is usually advocated in order to reduce the social disruption of migration and rapid change, reduce service costs, improve the adequacy of housing and services, reduce pollution and crime, improve political control, and alleviate the discomforts of large settlements.

2. Discouraging migration from rural and depressed areas is proposed for similar reasons: to reduce social disruption and reduce the costs and improve the adequacy of housing and services, as well as to maintain certain agricultural and industrial activities and to improve the balance of equity between various regions.

U.S. Department of
Housing and Urban
Development

3. Attempts are made to create a balanced, hierarchical system of cities. The purposes are not so clear, but this is usually done in support of the first two policies, as well as to improve the equity of access and service, prevent the absolute dominance of a primate city, increase the choice of settlement type, spread an "advanced" culture to backward areas, improve productive efficiency, and perhaps because this is deemed a more "natural" system of cities.

4. New towns are built to exploit place-bound resources, to defend borders, or to populate "empty" lands, for better service efficiency, health, and amenity, to create a strong social community, to improve the housing supply, to help control the growth of large centers, and for profit.

5. The network of major infrastructure (roads, railways, airports, seaports, power grids, canals, aqueducts) is extended and thickened to improve transport and productive efficiency, increase interaction and access, open up new areas for use, to increase equity, for profit, and to promote the spread of some "advanced" culture.

6. Selected economic facilities are built to improve productive efficiency, for defense, or for profit.

7. The national housing supply is increased for better health, to support the family, to meet demand, to improve equity, or for profit.

8. Waste emissions, soil erosion, and the use of water and of energy sources may be regulated, in order to conserve resources for future use, or to improve health and comfort by reducing pollution.

9. Large "natural" areas are preserved because of their symbolic importance, to conserve resources, to improve recreation and other amenities, and to prevent ecological disruption.

Then there are a number of common urban policies at the local scale:

10. The size of the settlement may be limited— whether absolutely, or at certain thresholds, or by controlling the rate of growth—in order to reduce service costs, prevent social disruption, improve management, preserve community character and

environmental quality, reduce pollution, or prevent shortages.

11. The density of development is regulated below some maximum or above some minimum. This is done to reduce construction and maintenance costs, to improve the efficiency of infrastructure and services, to promote the compactness of a place, to support preferred styles of life, to improve community character and environmental quality, or to increase property values.

12. Increasing the supply of housing and social facilities is advocated to meet demand, for better health and education, to support the family, to improve equity, or for profit.

13. A mix of social class in residential areas is promoted for reasons of equity, better social integration, or social stability.

14. Different kinds of land uses are separated for functional efficiency, reduction of nuisance, improvement of health and safety, reduction of pollution, or to simplify planning.

15. Efforts are made to stabilize and rehabilitate declining areas, for a more efficient use of services and infrastructure, to protect the housing supply, prevent social disruption, maintain equity, maintain property and tax values, or to meet political pressures.

16. Old areas are redeveloped to provide for some new use, to strengthen a center or an area, to remove unwanted activities or people, for profit, to increase property and tax values, and to increase political prestige or control.

17. Residential areas are organized as neighborhoods, and a hierarchy of service centers is developed. The purpose is to strengthen social communities, to improve service and infrastructure efficiency, to increase the equity of service distribution, to reduce transport demand, to facilitate child rearing, and to simplify planning.

18. The infrastructure is extended or improved, in order to open up new areas, increase interaction and access, reduce congestion and transport cost, improve productive efficiency, or for profit.

19. A hierarchy of specialized routes may be developed or certain modal shifts be promoted for

reasons of transport efficiency, safety, health, the reduction of pollution, the conservation of energy, and planning simplicity.

20. The supply of open space may be increased for health, amenity, and to support child rearing.

21. Historic monuments and open areas are preserved for their symbolic importance, to prevent ecological disruption, to improve health and recreation, or to attract tourists.

Having made such a bare list of policies, it is interesting to look at the values, explicit or implicit, that lie behind them. Which values are more frequently cited? Which are more often achieved? Can their achievement be detected? Which seem to have a clear connection to city form, and which are doubtful? Are there hidden values behind some actions? Neglected ones? To that end, the objectives, so loosely cited above, can be reorganized into four groups: strong values, wishful values, weak values and hidden ones:

1. *Strong values.* By that term I mean objectives of city form policy which are frequently and explicitly cited, whose achievement is detectable and is clearly dependent to some significant degree on city form, and which can be achieved in practice, or, if not, the reasons for failure are apparent. Among them I would list such aims as:

meeting the demand for services, infrastructure, and housing
providing space for wanted uses
exploiting resources or new areas
reducing pollution
increasing access
maintaining property and tax values
improving safety and physical health
improving defense
reducing nuisance
preserving some existing environmental character or quality or symbol.

These, along with some of the "hidden" values cited below, are the principal engines and achievements of city form policy, its rational core today.

They are important—but also disturbingly narrow in scope.

2. *Wishful values.* Then there are the objectives which, although often cited, detectable, and probably linked to city form, like those above, are yet rarely achieved. This failure may be due to the difficulty of shaping city form to these ends; or perhaps the aim is only a pious cover, never seriously intended. I would put in this group such objectives as:

improving equity
reducing migration
supporting the family and the rearing of children
conserving material and energy resources
preventing ecological disruption
increasing amenities.

3. *Weak values.* Here I would group a list of frequently cited aims whose dependence on city form is doubtful or not proven, or whose achievement is very difficult to detect or measure. Thus they are rarely achieved, or we don't know if they are, or any achievement may be due to other causes. To call them "weak" does not deny their importance. It is only that their present role in policy is primarily decorative—a decoration sometimes confusing, sometimes hopeful and suggestive. Much more knowledge is needed to separate the useful aims from the false leads. I would put many (even most) of the values of current form policy here, including:

improving mental health
increasing social stability
reducing crime and other social pathologies
increasing social integration and creating strong communities
increasing choice and diversity
supporting a preferred life style
reinforcing an existing area or center
reducing the dominance of a primate city or region
increasing future flexibility.

4. *Hidden values.* Finally, there are a group of aims which are as "strong" as the first, but less often articulated, or at least less often cited as a

primary purpose. Yet they may be as fervently
desired, and as clearly achieved. Often enough,
they are the prime movers of policy, overlaid in
public with a delicate screen of weak and wishful
purposes:

maintaining political control or prestige
disseminating an "advanced" culture
dominating a region or a people
removing unwanted activities or persons, or isolating them
making a profit
simplifying the process of planning or management.

5. *Neglected values.* In addition to all the above,
it is possible to think of many potential values
which are now commonly neglected, whether because some aim is not thought important, or because its connection to city form, at least at the large
scale of public policy, seems dubious, impractical,
or obscure. Among such neglected values one can
think of discarded ones, such as the magical power
of city patterns, but also some more tangible qualities, such as the fit of environment to human
biology and function, the quality of the symbolic
and sensory experience of cities, or the degree of
user control.

If we confine ourselves for the moment to the
values which motivate actual form policies, or are
said to do so, we still have an instructive list before
us. Instructive because of the evident division between strong and weak aims and because of the
many loose ends which suggest numerous directions for research. Even as a sample catalog, the list
has some value as a description of current policy. At
the same time, this list is an uncomfortable starting
point for theory. It refers to so many scattered
regions of human concern, and its items are connected to city form by so many separate yet overlapping mechanisms, that convergence seems dubious. The workings of these mechanisms will,
moreover, vary substantially with culture and
situation, as will the definition and relative importance of each aim.

One also has the intuition that good theory
uses concepts and methods which are particular to

the thing theorized upon. The aims we have cited here and their half-understood linkages with form are a collection swept up from economics, sociology, psychology, ecology, politics, warfare, physics, and a host of other fields, intermixed with a few considerations which are peculiar to large physical environments. A theory which grew out of them would be less than likely to be centered in its own domain.

If current spatial policy does not lead us into the heart of our subject, however much it may illuminate its margins, why not turn to more dramatic material, to proposals for ideal or pathological cities? Dreams bring up deep feelings.

Utopian thinking displays some persistent flaws, such as a disregard for the process of development and an exceedingly narrow and static set of values. Serious thinkers put such schemes aside as foolish, or, worse, as fantasies which divert us from acting effectively in the real world. If carried out, they would lead straight to perversity. That danger may not be serious, since most utopias have had few immediate effects. Nevertheless, they play their part in social thought, and for our purpose, at least, they could expose some new values of environmental form, or confirm those already expounded.

To our dismay, then, we find that the great majority of utopian writings—at least those in the classical tradition—pay very little attention to the spatial environment; their principal concern lies with social relationships. The utopian physical environment may simply be an imitation of some contemporary setting, brought into the story to add realism, or modified in a few minor ways to support some desirable social shift. Clearly, the physical environment had to be dealt with whenever utopians actually sought to realize their dreams. But the visions themselves did not make much ado about it, at least up to such nineteenth-century proposals as those of James Silk Buckingham, Robert Owen, and Charles Fourier. Even then, although the spatial environment was illustrated in some detail, it was less than central to the proposal.

Choay
Lang
Reiner
Riesman

Fourier, for example, proposed a "phalanstery" as the material shell for his utopia, a paradise to be based on the manipulation of what he called the natural human passions. The phalanstery was a single, large, multistoried building housing all the activities of the colony, set in a rich farming region. With its symmetrical wings and arcades, it resembled a great palace of the nobility. The emphasis was on comfort, easy access, and prideful group identity. Nevertheless, the form had rather little to do with Fourier's intricate social proposals, except that the inhabitants were to take joy in improving and admiring their environment, and its maintenance was to be the chief care of groups of children, organized in "little hordes." As in most utopian proposals previous to his time, the environment was still primarily a *setting*—either a pleasant background or a symbolic expression of the perfection of the new society.

58
Nineteenth-century
utopias

See fig. 25

Fourier

Only later in the nineteenth century do we begin to find utopian writings in which the environment is a major concern: William Morris's *News from Nowhere*, Ebenezer Howard's *Garden Cities of To-Morrow*, and, in the present century, such proposals as Frank Lloyd Wright's Broadacre City. Morris was an artist and craftsman of talent and a convinced socialist. Thus his utopia is a rare example of a physical system and a social system which are fitted together. And yet, like Howard and Wright, he describes what is in many ways a backward-looking world, focused on the small, balanced, ordered community, whose members are in direct relation to the natural environment and to each other. The city is dissolved or reduced to small size. Individuals or small groups control the land, and the local community is relatively self-sufficient. These proposals follow the organic metaphor (of which more to come in chapter 4), emphasizing cellular order, balanced diversity, good health, intimacy, stability, interdependence, and a return to the "natural" world. The garden, the mixed farm, and the small town are their models. Even the buildings are traditional in style.

Howard
Morris
Wright

See figs. 26, 27

The physical proposals for Broadacre City are also rather routine, surprisingly so for an architect such as Wright. His individual buildings are hand-

Cambridge Institute

Conrads
Collins 1979
Cook
Major

Calabi
Le Corbusier
Miliutin
Wiebenson

See figs. 28, 29

See fig. 30

some, and his "air cars" are delightful fantasies, but his settlement is a simple derivation of open suburbia. Howard, the nonarchitect, is more inventive—for example in his proposal for a circular, glassed-in shopping arcade, leased by individual merchants who could be displaced by consumer vote. But it is only in Morris's work that one senses the quality of the whole landscape in any vivid and circumstantial way.

While most of these social utopians (Wright excepted) sought a supportive physical background for a communitarian society (and even Wright raged against private greed), a group of futurist designers followed a different line of thought. They focused primarily on the physical environment, rather than on the social one, and were fascinated by the new technical means that could be applied to it. Although we might cite Leonardo as a forerunner, these are mostly twentieth-century men—brilliant and at times inhumane, concerned with novelty, change, power, and esthetic complexity. Their physical proposals are works of art, within which the social structure remains unchanged, or perhaps has been forgotten. Their blind spots are the opposite of those in the communitarian eye.

Eugène Hénard's proposals of 1911 for traffic circles, level separations, and underground cities are early products of this line of thought, as is Tony Garnier's design for a new industrial town. Le Corbusier's "Radiant City" is a well-known example. N. A. Miliutin designed a linear city like a production line.

Antonio Sant'Elia drew a brilliant series of views of the future city before his death in World War I. These sketches are charged with speed, communication, power, and change—an apotheosis of dynamic motion. "We must invent and rebuild the modern city, like an immense and tumultuous shipyard," he writes, "active, mobile, and everywhere dynamic. . . . Elevators must no longer hide away like solitary worms in the stairwells . . . but swarm up the facades like serpents of glass and iron. The house . . . rich only in the beauty of its lines, brutish in its mechanical simplicity, as big as need dictates, and not as zoning rules permit, must soar up from the brink of a tumul-

25 An imaginary view of a Fourierist "phalanstery," drawn by Victor Considérant, Fourier's disciple. The utopian settlement is ordered and centralized— a combination of a factory and a palace of the nobility.

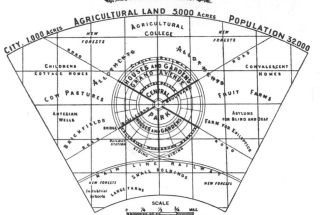

26 Ebenezer Howard's diagrams for his ideal "garden city," published in 1898, a satellite town meant to house 30,000 people. The more general diagram shows the relation of the new town to its greenbelt, and to the road and rail connections linking it to the central city and to other satellite settlements. The greenbelt contains farms, and space allotted to convalescents, the deaf, the blind, epileptics, and children. The diagram of one sector indicates the park and the cultural institutions at the center, the industries around the periphery along the rail line, the shops on an inner ring within a "crystal palace" or glass arcade, and the housing between these two circles, focused on a circumferential grand boulevard.

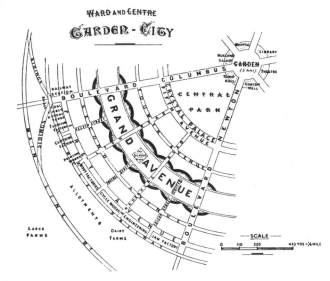

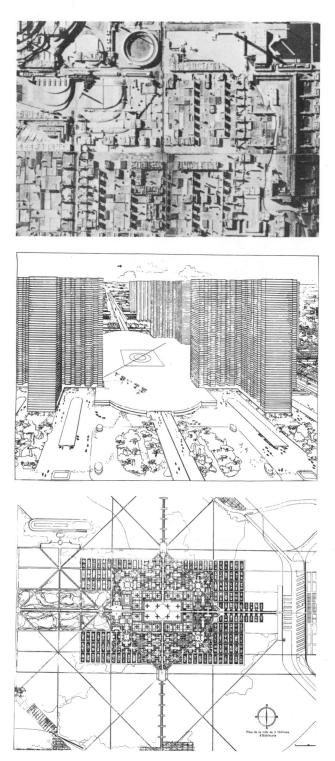

27 Looking down on the model of Frank Lloyd Wright's Broadacre City, presented in 1934. Houses, small farms, and other uses are widely dispersed and would be dependent on the automobile, while the industries form a linear concentration along the major highways. The natural setting is preserved and enhanced, and a colony of architects occupies the highest point.

28 Plan and view of Le Corbusier's 1922 project for a contemporary city of 3 million inhabitants. Skyscraper offices occupy the center, with an airport in their midst, under which is a railway station. The affluent live in the tallest, most central apartments. Farther out are six-story linear residential blocks, or four-story duplexes, while "garden cities" for industrial workers lie out of sight beyond the greenbelt. Public institutions and a romantic park are located at one edge of the core city, and factories at the other. The enormous buildings have no major approaches or any apparent effect at ground level, which is all parkland. The city is an expression of a clear, static, centralized order.

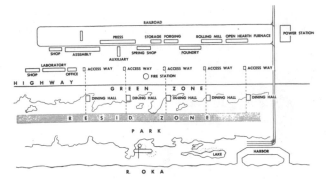

29 Diagram of a linear city for the Nizhni Novgorod auto plant, by N. A. Miliutin, 1930. River, parkland, housing, institutions, factories, and rail lines all run parallel to each other, in this ideal setting for a socialist society, like a coordinated set of production lines.

30 A 1914 sketch for Antonio Sant'Elia's imaginary new city, a futurist fantasy of towers and dramatic transportation.

tuous abyss; the street will no longer lie like a doormat at the thresholds, but will plunge storeys deep into the earth . . . connected to metal catwalks and high speed conveyor belts . . . the fundamental characteristics of Futurist architecture will be its impermanence and transience. Things will endure less than us. Every generation must build its own city."

Bletter
Scheerbart

Paul Scheerbart imagined a wonderful new world of light: hovering, transparent, intricate, and mobile. "We can talk in all seriousness of floating architecture . . . buildings can be juxtaposed or moved apart . . . every floating town could look different every day."

See fig. 31

Hans Poelzig, Eric Mendelsohn, Hans Scharoun, Kurt Schwitters, Ivan Leonidov, Buckminster Fuller, the Japanese "Metabolists"—a long line of inventive designers are caught up with the new technical possibilities. In his *Alpine Architecture*, written just after the terrible destruction of World War I, Bruno Taut proposed that men turn their energies to rebuilding the earth into a magnificient artificial landscape: carving the Alps and the Andes, reshaping the archipelagoes of the Pacific. People would come together to make a cathedral of the entire planet by means of vast engineering works. "People of Europe! Fashion a holy artefact . . . the Earth would deck herself through you!" Mountaintops were to be cut into shapes like jewels or flowers, and water, lights, and clouds would play about them.

See fig. 32

Taut

Soleri

In a magnificent series of drawings, Paolo Soleri proposes cities for wilderness sites: cities marvelously compact and intricate. The large community and its high-fashioned shell become a coherent superorganism, replacing the individual as the organized, living entity. The Archigram group in England imagines similar intricacies, in which machines come alive and the whole environment is mobile or demountable.

See fig. 33

In contrast to the older organic utopias, these forms are rich and fascinating. They play with adaptability, the technical aspects of access, and on the visible expression of function. But above all they are obsessed with the expression of an intricate but coherent man-made world which is orga-

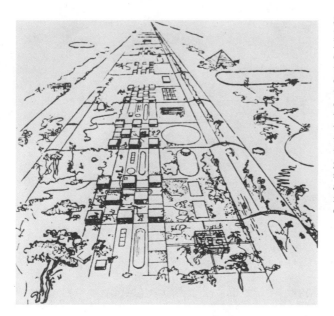

31 Bird's-eye sketch of the proposed settlement of Magnitogorsk, USSR, drawn for a 1930 competition by Ivan Leonidov, one of the most imaginative designers in the early days of the Russian revolution, whose dreams were never built. The two-story house blocks of this linear city are grouped in fours around small common courts, alternating checkerboard fashion with parks and communal buildings.

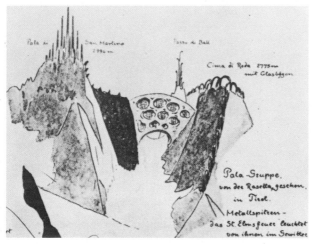

32 Bruno Taut's dream for remodeling the Alps. The rock is hewn in crystalline forms above the tree line, while glass arches and trellises run over the snow, or spring across the chasm. In a storm, St. Elmo's Fire caps the metal pinnacles, and a wind harp sounds on the bridge.

33 Two proposals for megaform cities by Paolo Soleri: Babel II D (in elevation), and Stonebow (in section). Babel II, 1950 meters high and 3000 meters in diameter, would hold a population of 550,000 in a cylindrical skin of apartments shaped like a giant cooling tower. Factories and services occupy the base, and fourteen "neighborhood park" levels fill the central tower. (To one side, an outline of the Empire State Building at the same scale gives a sense of this tower's size.) Stonebow houses 200,000 people in a linear structure spanning a gorge. Its center is at the midpoint of the bridge, where the section shown here has cut the city. The main highway is enclosed below the bridging wall of housing.

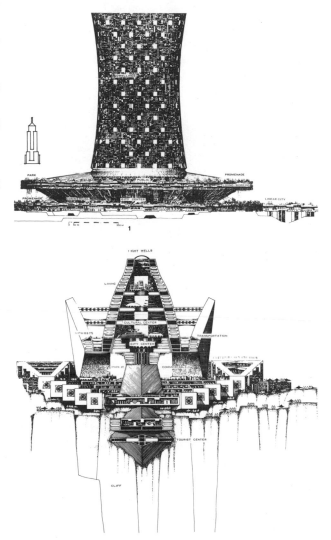

nized at a very large scale. When one considers the social organization which would be necessary to create and maintain these wonderful forms, or their impact on the ecological systems of the earth, the consequences of such schemes are terrifying. The necessities of control have been totally neglected. Or perhaps control is not neglected at all, only disguised. It may be that these are dreams of absolute mastery.

The proposals of Aldo Rossi are a very recent example of this focus on form. For him, architecture is an autonomous discipline, eternal, outside of time, creating form typologies which have an independent existence, like Platonic ideas. The city is a permanent structure, which, through its monuments, "remembers" its past and "realizes itself" as it develops. Architecture is divorced of function; it is collective memory, a pure, sophisticated formal game. Physical structure is abstracted from social structure, and becomes a thing of fascinating, independent possibilities. These attitudes unfold into monstrous, seductive flowers. Yet, far below, they are rooted in the same false idea: that man and his habitat are completely separate entities, linked only, if at all, by some mechanical, one-directional causation.

Few utopian proposals deal with place and society together. The dream of William Morris is one exception. Another is the set of "paradigms" described by Paul Goodman and Percival Goodman in *Communitas*. Three imaginary societies are created, along with their appropriate environments: one a world of overproduction, splendid consumption, and periodic voiding; another of freedom and biological security achieved by means of a dual economy in which one may choose wealth and anxious labor, or leisure and bare maintenance; and a third which is based on small, self-sufficient communities where production and consumption are fixed. While the first two are somewhat tongue-in-cheek, each has an inventive spatial structure that reinforces its social aims. The last paradigm, and presumably the preferred one, is the familiar organic metaphor. As seems to occur in any truly hoped-for paradise, the spatial setting is now less imaginative. The new community inhabits a small Italian hill

Moneo

P. Goodman

town, romantically viewed, with its piazza and its public life.

The "patterns" of Christopher Alexander are part of his larger system of thought, which centers on the process of environmental decision. Nevertheless, they are fragments of a utopian vision that is primarily concerned with spatial form. Unlike the others, however, each proposal is linked to its human consequences. Each is meant to be a very real piece of the world, based on an imagined human way of relating to that world which is underlying and stable. Thus, while the system as a whole is concerned with how decisions are made, the substance of the patterns is a long, richly illustrated disquisition on the match of form with behavior. Much of its emphasis lies on the complex variations of access.

When utopian communities become real experiments, then, at least, they are forced to deal with their physical environments. For many of them, this was a brutal awakening. Costs and difficulties the settlers never imagined intruded on the perfected society: crops failed, buildings burned, supplies or markets could not be reached, daily discomforts mounted, the assignment of household chores became a superchore. Others surmounted these small disasters, but failed to look to a new spatial order for support or inspiration. Taking over old buildings, perhaps temporary or discarded ones, some communities seemed more interested in spatial decoration than in spatial organization, as if making a big fuss over the physical world were unnecessary, even undignified. Yet there have also been utopian experiments that have dealt more explicitly with the environment and drawn strength thereby.

The Shaker communities of the United States, the longest-lived of all these real-world paradises, paid great attention to their architectural setting. The world was literally to be transformed into heaven, a perfect architecture of environment and society. Each community was a "living building." Space and behavior were channeled into regular, rectangular patterns, except in the ecstasy of the dance, when those restraints were deliberately thrown off. Loitering, waste, and disorder were swept away. The layouts of buildings and the form of equipment were prescribed and carefully detailed. Buildings were color-coded by use. From this attention to form and this intense practicality came the fine Shaker things that we so admire today, as well as many useful mechanical inventions.

The Oneida community (1848–1880) held the conviction that men and women could be brought to perfection within a well-tuned, free, communistic society. Community development and continuous development of the person were their aims, and they were a joyful process. Members in their eighties would begin a study of algebra or Greek. This group worked through many social experiments: joint ownership, work rotation, faith healing, vegetarianism, group marriage, and community eugenics, among others. The setting was to be perfected as well as its inhabitants. Loving attention was paid to rooms, decorations, and the surrounding garden landscape. The entire community participated in the design of buildings and additions. Sketch proposals could be made by anyone, and they were heatedly discussed until all were in accord. Places were given a particular form, and that form was thought important. Most of all, Oneidans were anxious that space and its furniture should encourage informal social encounters.

These successful built societies placed emphasis on the environment as a visible symbol of the community. It should have definite boundaries and a special character. It should be possible to overlook the whole. Order and cleanliness were considered valuable characteristics. The underlying natural world should be present to the senses. The spatial support of social encounter was a critical item, particularly as it affected the face-to-face meetings of small groups. Spontaneous versus regulated contact, or community versus privacy, were much-debated issues. Good access to persons, services, and places was sought for. Control and participation were important issues, although the level at which control should be exercised was a matter of disagreement, and the issue might be hidden, rather than open.

See fig. 34

Moos

In most utopian societies, the more direct and obvious criteria of comfort, good climate, a workable fit of form with function, and an easy access to economic resources were less often a matter of conscious debate. Yet they proved to be important in the real history of these communities. The careful environmental practicality of the Shakers and the firm industrial basis that the Oneidans were able to create were crucial factors in the longevity of these communities.

See fig. 35

Hell is more impressive than heaven. When a group of young boys from Cambridge, Massachusetts, were asked to describe their ideal world, they were baffled and even a little bored. When then requested to portray the worst environment they could imagine, they responded with glee and imagination. They agreed that police and adult gangs were to be assigned to separate, hostile territories. Doors and windows were blocked. Fences crossed the streets, which were deep in garbage, mud, and broken glass. All services were burned out. The air was foul, the noise deafening. It was very hot or very cold; and so on. In the same way, "cacotopias"—imaginary descriptions of horrifying worlds to come—have always been much more specific about their physical settings than have the utopian writings. *Gulliver's Travels* is spatially articulate.

White

Works of science fiction are replete with such descriptions. Their typical backdrop is an overgrown city of the future, enormously polluted, unresponsive, dense, and chaotic, in which life is precarious, personal communications are impossible, and every action is externally controlled. The descriptions of rooms and landscapes and machinery is marvelously detailed. As another example, look at those brilliant fantasies created by the team of designers called Superstudio: perfect geometric environments in which every person is isolated from every other, and no one controls any fragment of his life. Such cacotopias, billed as nightmares of the future, are written to expose the injustice of the present.

Superstudio

Real cacotopias occur as the result of diffuse malice or neglect, but they have also been built deliberately. Prisons and concentration camps are made to control others or to break them down. Interrogation centers use specific physical means to destroy the resistance of those from whom they want information or acquiescence. These means include direct physical pain, but also isolation, continuous stress, loss of privacy, disorientation in space and in time, noise, glare, darkness, pervasive discomfort, and similar physical strategies. From these perverse devices we may also learn something about the positive values of environment, just as a study of pathology informs our understanding of health.

See fig. 36

Fortunately, the heavens and hells we build do not last very long. When they disappear, they seem only to leave a few scars or nostalgic memories. Yet they are not ephemeral. They are valid expressions of deep human needs and feelings, and so they can be guideposts to environmental values. They can be consulted as environmental experiments, although that is rarely done. Unexamined as they are, they are nevertheless part of our cultural store, exerting a hidden influence on many practical decisions, and even on such major policies as those which opened this chapter. That influence should be open. Some of these utopian motives, along with those from many other sources, are compiled in appendix C, which is the lumber room in which the value dimensions to be proposed below were constructed.

In contrast to the stated motives of practical policy, the utopian and cacotopian themes cover a great range and respond to strong feelings that we have about the places we inhabit. Moreover, they often connect with spatial features in a very concrete way. Those connections may of course be illusory. They are fictions, and practical people stand clear of them. Their very style of expression— verbal or graphic—sets them off from the official reports. But they convey insights and passions which could electrify those listless public documents. Effective policy (or effective design) works on the boundaries between dream and reality, linking deep needs and obscure desires to open experience and test. City policy must be general, explicit, and rational, and yet also concrete and passionate.

34 A view of Hancock, Massachusetts, one of the prosperous Shaker settlements of the nineteenth century. The environment is productive, peaceful, and pragmatically designed. It matches the carefully ordered way of life of this celibate utopia. The round barn on the right is an innovation of Shaker design.

35 Hell is vivid and specific, while heaven is noncommital: a portion of the mosaic under the dome of the Baptistry of Florence.

36 A shameful American memory: the concentration camp at Poston, Arizona, built to intern Japanese-American citizens during World War II, as it looked when ready for use. The layout of the barracks was designed for economy, rapid erection, and effective control of the inmates.

The leading normative theories, which we explore in the next chapter, are powerful (whether they are true or false) because they make that bridge. I will attempt the same.

In Italo Calvino's *Invisible Cities*, Marco Polo describes one fantastic city after another to the great Kublai Khan. Each city is a society that exaggerates the essence of some human question, and for each there is a form, brilliantly and surprisingly conceived, that fulfills and informs that question. Polo talks of desire and memory; of diversity and routine; of the temporary and the permanent, the dead, the living, and the unborn; of images, symbols, and maps; of identity, ambiguity, reflections, the seen and the unseen; of harmony and discord; of justice and injustice; of mazes, traps, and endlessness; beauty and ugliness; metamorphosis, destruction, renewal, continuity, possibility, and change. The dialog is a great panorama of utopia and cacotopia, which explores, in a wonderful, circling fantasy, the relations between people and their places. At the end, he says: "The inferno of the living is not something that will be; if there is one, it is what is already here, the inferno where we live every day, that we form by being together. There are two ways to escape suffering it. The first is easy for many: accept the inferno and become such a part of it that you can no longer see it. The second is risky and demands constant vigilance and apprehension: seek and learn to recognize who and what in the midst of the inferno, are not inferno, then make them endure, give them space."

4

Three Normative Theories

If I have implied that there is little normative theory to be found, this is misleading. The form that a city should take is an ancient question. And if by normative theory we mean some coherent set of ideas about proper city form and its reasons, then there are a number of such theories. Each group of theories focuses on some comprehensive metaphor of what a city is and how it works.

As we have seen, it appears that the first cities arose as ceremonial centers—places of holy ritual which explained the risky forces of nature and controlled them for human benefit. Peasants supported the cities voluntarily, attracted by their sacred power. A redistribution of power and material resources to a ruling class went hand in hand with the growth of cities from these religious beginnings. In the process of building the structure of human power, while stabilizing the order of the universe, religious ritual and the physical form of the city were principal instruments—psychological rather than physical weapons. The design of this awesome and seductive instrument was based on a theory of magical correspondences.

This theory asserts that the form of any permanent settlement should be a magical model of the universe and the gods. It is a means of linking human beings to those vast forces and a way of stabilizing the order and harmony of the cosmos. Human life is thereby given a secure and permanent place; the universe continues its proper, sacred motions. The gods are upheld, chaos is kept off, and, not incidentally, the structure of human power—of kings and priests and nobility—is maintained. All of this may seem sheer superstition today, but the theory has had a tremendous historic influence. Moreover, it turns out that we enlightened ones still abide by many of those same ideas. There may be reasons for their tenacity that go beyond superstition.

The two best-developed branches of cosmic theory are those of China and of India. The Chinese model has had enormous influence. It controlled the conscious layout of almost every major city in China, Korea, Japan, and much of southeast Asia. This magical form is clearly exemplified in Peking, but also in what were once provincial copies, such as Kyoto and Seoul. The model includes meanings and colors assigned to the cardinal directions—north being dark and unpropitious, for example, a direction against which one should erect a defensive shield. The city was to be divided, subdivided and sub-subdivided by progressively finer grids of streets and ways: boxes within boxes. Representatives of the hierarchy of religious and civil power had their proper locations, proper colors, and proper building materials. Space was symmetrically divided into left and right, and this was mirrored in the organization of government. Enclosures, gateways, and approaches had magical protective functions. A whole series of city-founding and city-maintaining rites complemented these spatial arrangements. As the *Li-Chi* (Record of Rituals), a compilation of the second century B.C., stated: "Rites obviate disorder as dikes prevent inundation."

These ideas blossomed into the complex pseudoscience of geomancy, which studied the local currents of the "cosmic breath" as it was influenced by topography, water bodies, cardinal directions, and hidden veins in the earth. This science led to recommendations for favorable sites for towns, tombs, and important structures, and for ways of improving sites by means of symbols, earthwork, and planting—inviting favorable currents and blocking or guiding away unfavorable ones. One happy by-product of these religious preoccupations was the great care taken with siting, which produced many well-fitted settings.

The Indian theorists, while they may have influenced fewer actual towns, were even more explicit in the connections they made between gods, men, rites, and city plans. There was a series of texts on city planning, the Silpasāstras, which indicated how the earth could be parceled out and the evil forces of chaos enclosed and controlled. The typical form was a mandala, a set of enclosing rings divided into squares, in which the most powerful point is at the center. Enclosure and protection reinforces holiness, and the key movements

74
Chinese theory

See fig. 37

Meyer
Wheatley
A. Wright

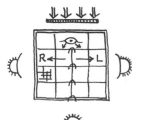

Dutt
Shukla
Smith

See fig. 38

See fig. 39

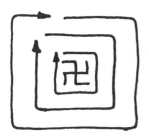

See figs. 40, 41

are from the outside in, or circling the sacred enclosure in a clockwise direction.* The earth is sacred and safe to inhabit, once these rites and spatial divisions are accomplished. The yearly religious processions follow the same encircling routes, and residents organize the city in their minds in the same way. Madurai in India is a striking example of this model, in which, even today, the city shape, the temples, the rites, the mental images of residents, the locations of activities, the main roads and even the bus routes are all matched to this symbolic form.

While China and India furnish us with the most developed examples of the cosmic model, the basic idea was widespread. Elaborate ceremonial centers in South and North America, in Asia and in Africa, are mute testimonials to it. Articulate theories are recorded in Egypt, the Near East, Etruscan Rome, and many other localities. The use of site and form to symbolize and reinforce power has been carried through Western civilization and survives today. The radial perfection of the ideal cities of the Renaissance was meant as a symbol of the orderly, mathematical universe. The influential baroque model of the city—an interconnected set of diverging and converging axes—was an expression and an instrument of power and order. It was only because he was heir to such a well-developed model that Pierre L'Enfant was able to survey, lay out, and commence constructing the city of Washington in such record time.

Each of these cosmic theories took a single, comprehensive view. By myths, they explained how the city came to be. They demonstrated why the city worked as it did, and what could go wrong. Thus they told one how a city should be: how to site it, improve it, or repair it. If these tenets were followed, they enhanced earthly power and gave people feelings of security, awe, and pride. They were complete and operative theories of the city, both functional and normative.

These theories use some common form concepts. Among them are the axial line of procession

*Note the similarity to the Christian ceremony of clock- wise, or "sunwise," circum- ambulation of a church.

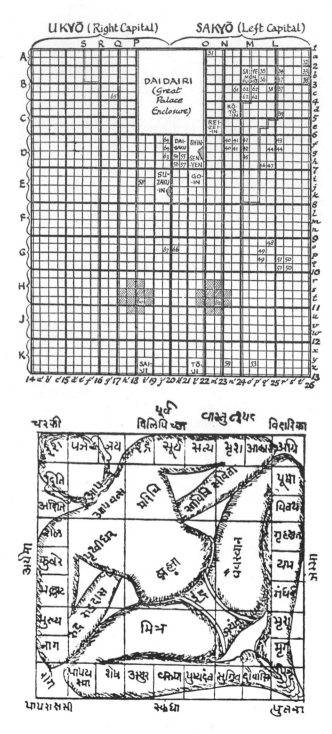

U KYŌ (Right Capital)   **SAKYŌ** (Left Capital)

DAIDAIRI
(Great
Palace
Enclosure)

37 Plan of the new imperial capital of Kyoto, Japan, founded about 800 A.D. and patterned on the prestigious Chinese model (see fig. 7). Beyond the limits of the illustration, an arc of mountains to the north protects the site while water flows on the east, west, and south. The city is regularly divided. The emperor looks south from his palace enclosure over his lords and priests to his symmetrically divided people. Even the central markets divide into left and right. The city subsequently grew eastward, abandoning the west market and leaving the old palace at its edge.

38 A vāstu-purusa ("dwelling of the spirit of the site") mandala of Indian planning theory, the model of ideal city layout. The purusa-demon is pinned down within nesting squares, each devoted to a god. Brahma is assigned the central square, surrounded by Ādityas, surrounded in turn by 32 Pada-devatas.

39 A plan of central
Madurai, India, as it is today. Note the central temple, the major encircling
streets, and the indirect
radials or capillaries
which run between them.
The plan coincides with
the encircling processions
which take place on spe-
cial holy days. Although
the city was established
earlier, this plan dates
from the sixteenth and
seventeenth centuries.

40 Imaginary scene of an
ideal city as depicted by a
painter of the Central Italian School, 1490–1495.
Order, precision, clear
form, extended space,
and perfect control: the
Renaissance ideal of the
city as a well-managed
stage for upper-class life.

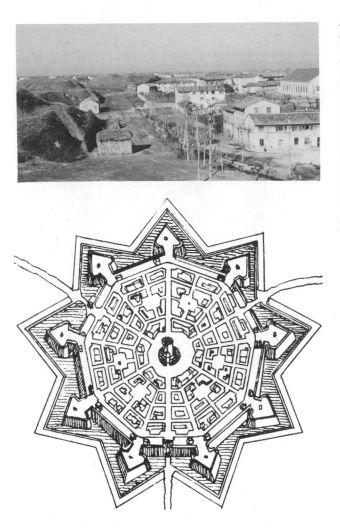

41 The original plan and a contemporary photo of Palmanova, Italy, a new city built in 1593 to defend the frontiers of Venetian territory, whose designer (perhaps Scamozzi) followed the Renaissance precepts of ideal radial symmetry. Today, the city straggles unsymmetrically along its streets, lost behind its cumbersome military earthworks. The central square is a great emptiness.

See fig. 42

and approach; the encircling enclosure and its protected gates; the dominance of up versus down, or
of big versus small; the sacred center; the diverse
meanings of the cardinal directions, due to their
relations to the sun and the seasons (the north is
cold and the south warm; the east is birth and
beginning, the west is death and decline); the regular grid for establishing a pervasive order; the device of organization by hierarchy; bilateral symmetry as an expression of polarity and dualism;
landmarks at strategic points as a way of visibly controlling large territories; the sacred nature of mountains, caves, and water. These similar features of
form were reinforced by similar institutional features: regularly recurring religious rites, the organization of government, the disposition of the social ranks, the dress and behavior of city people,
and so on. Space and rite are stabilizers of behavior
and serve to bind human beings together, just as
they do for many other animals. Institutions and
forms, acting in support of each other, have a
powerful psychological effect and were thought
invincible in reality, so that an actual disaster could
be attributed to some careless flaw that had crept
into those dispositions. Behind these concepts lie
certain primary values: order, stability, dominance,
a close and enduring fit between action and form—
above all, the negation of time, decay, death, and
fearful chaos.

Well, that's past and gone, of course, part of
the superstitious ages superseded by our enlightenment. Yet we are still affected by those devices of
rite and form. Power is still expressed and reinforced
by the same means: by a boundary and gates, a
parade route, a dominant landmark, the use of
elevation or size, bilateral symmetry, or regular
order. Capital cities are designed with monumental
axes, judges look down on prisoners, offices are
made "impressive," corporations vie for the tallest
building. These things still work on us today.

Even if we accept the psychological efficacy of
these forms, we may still reject them. They are the
cold devices of power, used to make some persons
submit to others. They will therefore no longer be
seen among us, once arbitrary power has been
abolished. Yet it is also true that these symbolic

42 "Front" entrance and "trade" entrance, on Beacon Hill in Boston. The physical environment expresses social dominance by big and small, up and down, prominent and retiring, elaborate and plain.

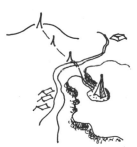

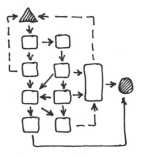

forms are attractive (and so they "work" for the purposes of the powerful) because they speak to deep emotions of anxiety in people. They do indeed give us a sense of security, of stability and continuity, of awe and pride. So they can also be used to express pride and affection for a community, to relate people to it, to reinforce a sense of human continuity, or to reveal the majesty of the universe.

In any case, while the magical rationale of the theory may be discredited, the psychological power of these devices cannot be so easily dismissed. These axes, enclosures, grids, centers, and polarities are functions of common human experience and of the way our minds are built—of how our cognitive apparatus took and takes its form, in order to operate successfully in the real world that we inhabit. Therefore these influences are realistic impacts of the form of cities, for good or for evil, and must be taken into account in any normative theory. Stones, water, old trees, the marks of time, the sky, the cave, up and down, north and south, axis, procession, center, and boundary—are all features that any theory must deal with.

The cosmic model upholds the ideal of a crystalline city: stable and hierarchical—a magical microcosm in which each part is fused into a perfectly ordered whole. If it changes at all, the microcosm should do so only in some rhythmical, ordered, completely unchanging cycle. Thinking of the city as a practical machine, on the other hand, is an utterly different conception. A machine also has permanent parts, but those parts move and move each other. The whole machine can change, although it does so in some clearly predictable way, as by moving steadily along some predetermined track. The stability is inherent in the parts, and not in the whole. The parts are small, definite, often similar to each other, and they are mechanically linked. The whole grows by addition. It has no wider meaning; it is simply the sum of its parts. It can be taken apart, put together, reversed, its pieces replaced, and it will run again. It is factual, functional, "cool," not magical at all. The parts are autonomous except for their prescribed linkages. It does what it does, no more.

To call this a machine model may be misleading on two counts. First, we think of machines as modern things, things which are intricate, powered by steam, gas, or electricity, and made of shining metal. But a wagon is a machine, and so is a well sweep, a windmill, or a skid on rollers. The metaphor of city as machine is not a modern conception, although it seems triumphant today. Its roots go far back, almost as far as those of the cosmic model. Second, for those who join the current chorus against technology, the very word "machine" may evoke overtones of inhumanity. I intend no such judgment.

This model has been particularly useful wherever settlements were temporary, or had to be built in haste, or were being built for clear, limited, practical aims, as we see in so many colonial foundations. The typical aim was to allocate land and resources quickly and to provide well-distributed access to them. To this might be added defense, or perhaps speculation in land. The city form is a way to get on with it, so as to set the stage for other, more important, activities, and so as to be able to change parts and their relationships without much fear for remote consequences. A few simple rules of layout allow one to deal with new and complicated circumstances in a quick and efficient way.

We have seen how the Greek colonies (but not the mother cities) of the fourth and fifth centuries B.C. used the standard *per strigas* layout of long, narrow blocks and sometimes imposed it on very accidental terrain. The defensive walls, in the meantime, follow the shape of the ground over which an attack will come, and their trace is quite independent of the repetitive block pattern. The Egyptian work camp of Kahun (c. 1900 B.C.) is an even earlier example of such a town, set up to get a pyramid built by furnishing houses for workers and their overseers.

See fig. 43

See fig. 44

The regular plan of the Roman military camp is well known. *Cardo* and *decumanus* cross between four gates set in a regular square. It could be thrown up for a single night's halt, and yet serve for the layout of a permanent town. The plan underlies the layout of the centers of many European cities. Less well-known, perhaps, is the fact that most medieval

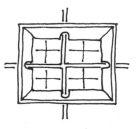

See fig. 45

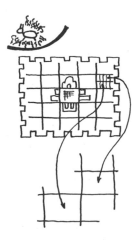

See fig. 46

Le Corbusier

new towns—and there was a great burst of such foundations in the twelfth and thirteenth centuries—also used simple, regular, rectangular block and lot divisions. Although we imagine that medieval towns were irregular, picturesque, and "organic," the kings and burghers built quite regular, practical settlements when they had the opportunity.

This medieval experience led to the proclamation of the Laws of the Indies of 1573, wherein the Spanish emperor gave directions by which the new cities of Anerica were to be built. These prescriptions governed the founding of hundreds of towns over a period of 250 years. The laws gave rules for site selection, the layout of an orderly square grid of streets and blocks, their orientation, the form of the central plaza (which was to be surrounded by public buildings and the houses of the wealthy), the segregation of noxious activities, the form of the wall, the disposition of common lands, the distribution of city lots and farms, and even the uniform style of the buildings. It was not a piece of magic, but a practical handbook. Each provision had a reason, and the model could be executed rapidly.

The grid towns of the United States, motivated by land speculation and land allocation, are only too familiar to us as examples of the same genre. The report of the commissioners who in 1811 laid out New York City above Washington Square is a lucid statement of the motives of that design. Compare just one of their statements with the cosmic doctrine: "[We] could not but bear in mind that a city is to be composed principally of the habitations of men, and that strait-sided and right-angled houses are the most cheap to build, and the most convenient to live in. The effect of these plain and simple reflections was decisive."

The machine model is not simply the application of a grid layout (indeed, grids were also essential features of the magical Chinese model), but rather a characteristic view about parts and wholes and their function. It underlies Le Corbusier's Radiant City, which at first appears to be so different in its form. A city, this model says, is made up of small, autonomous, undifferentiated parts, linked up into a great machine which in contrast has

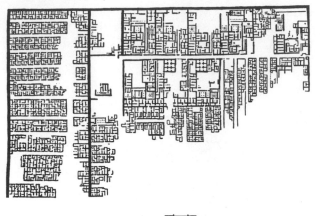

43 Plan of the Egyptian town of Kahun, built about 3000 B.C. to house workmen and supervisors for the construction of the Illahun pyramid. This was a planned town, rapidly built. Note the control of access and the separation of two classes of residents.

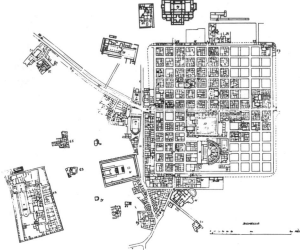

44 Plan of Timgad, a Roman colony founded by the emperor Trajan about 110 A.D. for veterans of the Third Legion. It was intended to help hold the Roman conquests in North Africa and to "civilize" the Berbers. The city is a square, 350 meters on a side, and planned, like any Roman military camp, with *cardo* and *decumanus* crossing at the center. Note the later growth on the fringe and the blocking and shifting of the southern entrance. The Berbers destroyed Timgad before 535.

45 Vertical air view (1958) of the "bastide" town of Sante Fé, near Granada, Spain, founded in 1492 as a siege town in the final attack on the Moors. When they had the opportunity, medieval town planners used regular geometrical forms. These experiences in new town planning led to the influential Laws of the Indies.

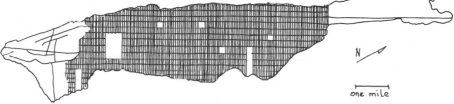

46 The Commissioners' 1811 plan for New York City, which guided the entire future development of Manhattan Island. This mechanical plan, vast in extent and heedless of topography, was motivated by the need to provide for future streets and to clarify land titles after the Revolution.

clearly differentiated functions and motions. The machine is powerful and beautiful, but it is not a work of magic or a mirror of the universe. It is itself (although it may also use some of the familiar devices of size, dominance, and axiality to emphasize the power of speeding machines or of the business corporation).

In a much more liberal and humane form, this machine model appears also in the work of Arturo Soria y Mata, who was concerned with health, open space, cheap housing, and easy access for people of moderate means. In fact, the linear form that he advocated is an excellent mechanical form, which seems to preserve its character despite infinite extension. One sees it in Edgar Chambless's Roadtown, in the work of Le Corbusier, and in its fullest form in Miliutin's ideal cities. His Sotsgorod is a very clear expression of the machine idea, extreme almost to the point of caricature, although it was seriously intended. He likens a town to a power station, or again to an assembly line. He focuses on transportation, the orderly separation of activities, the processes of production, and the health of the workers, who are key factors in that process. Simplicity, economy, good health, good order, autonomous parts. Children are to be separated from adults. Double beds will not be allowed, or "dirty rags" at the windows.

Collins 1968

See fig. 47

Chambless

Miliutin

The machine idea is still alive—in the daring ideas of Archigram and Soleri and Friedman, however distinct the particular forms they employ—but also in the powerful concepts of systems analysis, which models the world as a set of distinct parts linked by well-defined dynamic connections, like a giant aeroplane. In less sweeping terms, the machine model lies at the root of most of our current ways of dealing with cities: our practices of land subdivision, traffic engineering, utilities, health and building codes, zoning. The motives articulated are those of equity of allocation, good access, broad choice, smooth technical function, productive efficiency, material well-being, physical health, and the autonomy of parts (which means individual freedom, but also the freedom to exploit space and to speculate in it). These motives, arguable but surely not contemptible, fit easily into the

Cook
Y. Friedman

See fig. 48

47 The linear suburb commenced by Arturo Soria y Mata in 1894, which ran between two major radials of the city of Madrid and was originally intended to encircle the entire town. Each block shown contains about twenty lots for small houses and gardens. Local services are placed along the tree-lined central boulevard, through which ran a private streetcar line, connecting to lines to the city center. The suburb was to provide cheap and sanitary housing for people of modest income. The managing company operated successfully until the Franco regime, and the idea was popularized by a vigorous linear city movement.

48 Yona Friedman's 1958 proposal for an elevated grid city to be built over an old city below. Growth is accommodated and a new habitat created without uprooting existing residents. The drawing is sunny, the idea chilling.

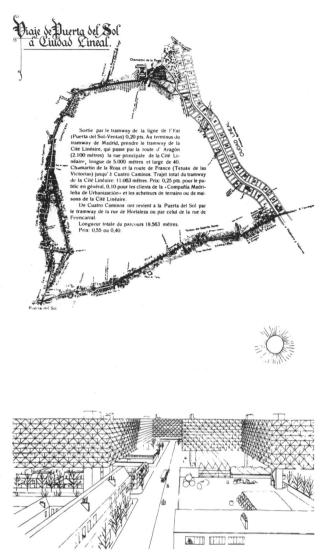

machine conception. Moreover, the machine, with
its divisible parts, can be analyzed and improved piecemeal, with great economy of effort.

Explicit rationality, with all its glories and its dangers, is here at its best. One wonders, of course, whether there might be more to cities than this. Is it any less misleading to think of the city as a machine—a device made up of rigid parts which transmit force and motion (and information, we would add today) in order to do work—than to think of it as a cosmic symbol? But the idea has its advantages, particularly for the rapid and equitable division of space or for managing the flow of goods and people. Grid layouts (in three dimensions as well as two) and linear forms have many useful characteristics for particular situations. Preserving the autonomy of parts preserves freedom and adaptability (and alienation, perhaps?). The piecemeal, analytic mode of thought is a powerful strategy for comprehending complex entities.

A pressure for standardization accompanies these advantages, a tendency to isolate, which is less than humane. Le Corbusier's Radiant City or Soleri's Babeldiga would be alien places. The separations, the oversimplification, the pure esthetics of the working machine, seem cold and repellent if we imagine ourselves actually living in these ideal places. They are founded on a conception of the city which seems basically wrong. Yet even when we put aside our social, psychological, and ecological qualms, still what remains—the built environment even in its most practical and functional guise—is only rarely an assembled machine, made for a single clear reason. Moreover, the machine metaphor often masks a form of social dominance which is simply less visible than the open display of power in the cosmic city.

The third great normative model is much more recent, even if it is already two centuries old. This is the notion that a city may be thought of as an organism, a notion that came with the rise of biology in the eighteenth and nineteenth centuries. It was one expression of the nineteenth-century reaction to the stress of industrialization, gigantic new cities, and the unprecedented leaps in technology.

The force of this current persists, as evidenced in the spreading political influence of the idea of ecology or in the academic struggles over subsuming human culture into the new field of sociobiology. While the organic model has actually influenced the building of fewer settlements than the two preceding doctrines, it is the view that is most prevalent among planning professionals today, and the enthusiasm for this outlook is spreading daily among lay citizens. If I end by being critical of this view, I must also admit to a long attachment, and to some regret that the world may not be so.

If a city is an organism, then it has some characteristic features that distinguish living creatures from machines. An organism is an autonomous individual with a definite boundary and of a definite size. It does not change its size by simple extension or swelling or limitless adding of parts, but reorganizes its form as it changes size, and reaches limits, or thresholds, where the change in form is a radical one. While it has a sharp external boundary, it is not so easy to divide it internally. It does have differentiated parts, but these parts are in close contact with each other and may not be sharply bounded. They work together and influence each other in subtle ways. Form and function are indissolubly linked, and the function of the whole is complex, not to be understood simply by knowing the nature of the parts, since the parts working together are quite different from the mere collection of them. The whole organism is dynamic, but it is a homeostatic dynamism: internal adjustments tend to return the organism to some balanced state whenever it has been disturbed by any outside force. So it is self-regulating. It is also self-organizing. It repairs itself, produces new individuals, and goes through a cycle of birth, growth, maturity, and death. Rhythmic, cyclical action is normal, from the life cycle itself down to heartbeat, respiration, and nerve pulsation. Organisms are purposeful. They can be sick or well or undergo stress. They must be understood as dynamic wholes. Emotional feelings of wonder and affection accompany our observation of these entities.

This concept of the biological organism is relatively new. It developed in the eighteenth century but received its first full statement in the work of Ernest Haeckel and Herbert Spencer in the nineteenth century. The application of this image to human settlements was a new insight which seemed to explain many earlier puzzles, an insight which reinforced many previous normative precepts that seemed intuitively correct. Many of the ideas that were brought together by this model had earlier antecedents: in utopian thought, in romantic landscape design, in the work of social reformers, naturalists, and devoted students of local regions. Giants created the organic theory of settlement in the nineteenth century and carried out its development in the twentieth: men like Patrick Geddes and his successor Lewis Mumford; Frederick Law Olmsted, the American landscape architect; the socialist reformer Ebenezer Howard; regionalists like Howard Odum and Berton Mac-Kaye; Clarence Perry, who set forth the neighborhood unit idea; Artur Glikson, the ecologist who dreamed of human communities and regional landscapes as harmonious wholes; and a number of designers who applied these ideas in detail, such as Henry Wright and Raymond Unwin.

90
Application of organic theory

Geddes
Glikson
Mumford 1938
Saarinen

See fig. 49

Their writings and their projects are still the classic basis of training in physical planning, although too often in some second-hand, well-watered form. And even as these texts begin to seem slightly old-fashioned in the "foremost" schools, the ideas contained in them spread more widely and deeply elsewhere. They were central to the English new towns, the greenbelt towns in the United States, and indeed to most modern new towns throughout the world—a lip service, at least, if nothing more. The model achieved a developed form in the Finnish new town of Tapiola, in the earlier Bedford Park and Hampstead Garden suburb in Great Britain, and in Radburn and Chatham Village in the United States. It has been reinforced by the recent application of ecology to public affairs. Its basic ideas are implicit in most public discussions of city form, and have even influenced such nominally antithetical examples as Chandigarh and Brasilia.

See fig. 50

Hertzen
Stein 1951

The first tenet is that each community should be a separate social and spatial unit, as autonomous as possible. Internally, however, its places and people should be highly interdependent. The organic model emphasizes the cooperation that maintains society, in contrast to seeing society as a competitive struggle. The form and function of each internal part should be fused together, while each part is itself clearly differentiated from other internal parts with other functions. A place where production goes on should look like that, and should be distinct from, and located elsewhere than, a place for sleeping. The community should be a whole, both apparently and in reality. It will have an optimum size, beyond which it becomes pathological.

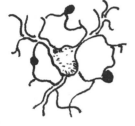

Inside, the healthy community is a heterogeneous one. There is a mix of diverse people and places, and that mix has some optimum proportions, a "balance." The parts are in constant interchange with each other, participating mutually in the total function of the community. But these parts, being different, have different roles to play. They are not equal or repetitive, but are diverse, and support each other in their diversity. The nuclear family is often taken as a model, with its differentiated supporting roles (and also its inequalities). In general, the internal organization of a settlement should be a hierarchy—a branching tree—with units that include subunits, which themselves include sub-subunits, and so on. Like living cells, each unit has its own bounds and its own center, and these are linked together. The "neighborhood unit," or small residential area including those supporting services which are in constant daily use, is a key concept in town organization. There are higher and lower functions.

Settlements are born and come to maturity, like organisms. (Unlike organisms, however, they should not die.) Functions are rhythmic, and the healthy community is stable by virtue of maintaining its dynamic, homeostatic balance. Societies and resources are permanently conserved by this uninterrupted cycling and balancing. If extended growth is necessary, it should occur by budding off new colonies. The optimum state is the stage of ecological climax, with a maximum diversity of elements, an efficient use of energy passing

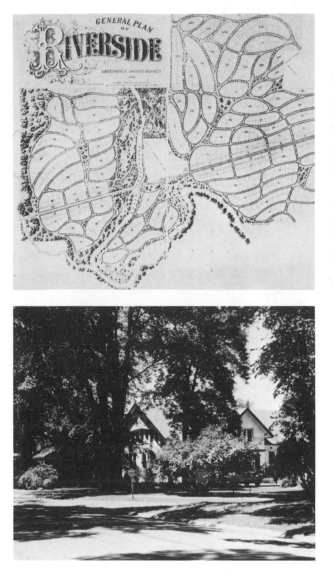

49 Original plan and contemporary photograph of the residential suburb of Riverside, Illinois, as laid out by Frederick Law Olmsted in 1869 for a firm of land developers, to be located where the Burlington Railroad crossed the Desplaines River, on the outskirts of Chicago. The planted streets curve in romantic fashion; the houses are set back from the street. There is a park along the river, and small parks at the road junctions.

50 The plan of Greenbelt, Maryland, in 1937, when it housed about 2800 persons in two-story row houses and three-story apartments. The curving superblocks fit the terrain and cradle the community center. This was a successful experiment in modest, subsidized housing, but its surrounding greenbelt was later sold off to developers.

through the system, and a continual recycling of
material. Settlements become ill when the balance
breaks down, when the optimum mix degenerates
to homogeneity, growth breaks its bounds, recycling fails, parts dedifferentiate, or self-repair ceases.
Illness is infectious, and it can spread if not treated
or cut out.

Certain physical forms are matched to these
ideas: radial patterns; bounded units; greenbelts;
focused centers; romantic, antigeometrical layouts;
irregularly curving, "organic" shapes; "natural"
materials (that means either traditional materials,
or ones close to their unprocessed state); moderate-
to low-density housing; visible proximity to earth,
plants, and animals; plentiful open space. The tree
is the admired model, rather than the machine. In
some crude expositions of the theory, the city parts
are even seen as explicitly analogous to animal
functions: respirations, circulation of the blood,
digestion, and the transmission of nerve impulses.
Human services, craft production, or activities
which are traditional, carried on in the open air, or
early in the chain of materials processing are more
highly valued than large-scale, automated, highly
synthetic production. There is a strong nostalgia for
the rural countryside and the small community of
the past. Historic landmarks should be preserved.
Irregularities or special character in a landscape are
something to rejoice over and respond to.

Since we have here crammed together an entire
set of ideas that cluster around the organic model of
settlement, we inevitably do injustice to some
aspect of each contributor's thought. Nevertheless,
it is a remarkably coherent and self-supporting
group of concepts, whose primary values are
community, continuity, health, well-functioning,
security, "warmth," and "balance," the interaction
of diverse parts, orderly cycling and recurrent development, intimate scale, and a closeness to the
"natural" (that is, the nonhuman) universe. It is not
only a massive prescription for cities, but also a
partial explanation for their genesis and function
(or rather for their failure to function). It has had a
lengthy and profound intellectual influence in plan- Stretton 1971
ning. Although it has been repeatedly attacked and
partially discredited, no other generally accepted

theory has appeared to take its place. It still rules
town design and public policy about cities—in the
form of policy rhetoric, if not otherwise. While at
the last one must be critical of many of the leading
ideas of this theory, yet there is much that is illumi-
nating in it.

The central difficulty is the analogy itself. Cities
are not organisms, any more than they are
machines, and perhaps even less so. They do not
grow or change of themselves, or reproduce or
repair themselves. They are not autonomous entities, nor do they run through life cycles, or
become infected. They do not have clearly differentiated functional parts, like the organs of animals. It is easy enough to reject the cruder forms of
the analogy—that the streets are arteries, parks
lungs, communications lines nerves, sewers the
colon, the city center the heart that pumps the
blood of traffic through the arteries, and its offices
(where businessmen, officials, and we intellectuals
cluster) are the brains. But it is more difficult, and
more important, to see the fundamental ineptness
of the metaphor and how it leads us unthinkingly to
cut out slums to prevent their "infectious" spread,
to search for an optimum size, to block continuous
growth, to separate uses, to struggle to maintain
greenbelts, to suppress competing centers, to prevent "shapeless sprawl," and so on. Sometimes, in
some places, these actions may be justified, but the
justification depends on reasons other than the
"organic" ones, which simply cloud our vision.

If we knock out the central metaphor, many
ideas remain, even if no longer set in such a coherent structure. Some of them, such as the superficial conservatism, the nostalgia for an unreal past,
can rather easily be stripped away. So can the
automatic preference for "organic" shapes. The use
of curves has visual consequences quite remote
from reminding us about organs or animals. Individual analogies with particular organic forms can
be useful clues to new ideas for the structure of
buildings or the function of hydraulic or aerody-
namic systems. So can crystalline forms. Neither is
indiscriminately useful.

Other organic concepts must be taken more
seriously, however. The idea of hierarchy, for exam-

ple, which seems such a natural and inevitable way of organizing complexity, and which can be seen in some patterns of trees and other organisms, is not a grand rule of nature. It is a common pattern of social organization among animals and insects, where it maintains the coherent action of a small unit in the face of predictable stress. It is used by kings, generals, and corporate presidents to maintain control over large human organizations, if with somewhat less success. Informal social networks often develop to subvert it. It is a way of imaging which is convenient to our minds—like dualisms or boundaries—a mental device based on a long evolutionary development.

But it is difficult to maintain hierarchy in very complex organizations such as cities. It is harmful to the easy flow of human interactions, wherever it is forcibly imposed. There are no "higher" and "lower" functions in cities, or at least there should not be. Elements and subelements do not rest within each other. Reaching someone or some service by passing up and down the branching lines of a hierarchy is laborious, unless all relations are extremely centralized and standardized. Hierarchy is primarily useful for indexing and cataloging. It is painfully maintained in certain formal authoritarian organizations, where the major branch points in this formal communications net are master keys of control. At the city scale, hierarchy keeps relapsing into disorder, or a different order. Lacking alternative conceptual schemes, we find it difficult to discard this "obvious" model.

Even the principle of clear, separable parts, which gives us such intellectual relief when creating a settlement design, may have grievous results. Few of the more complex elements of a city are separable organs with sharp boundaries. Melting transitions are a very common feature, and ambiguities are important, for reasons of choice, flexibility, or the evocation of complex meanings. Imposing a sharp boundary often reduces access, or serves to enhance social dominance. Boundaries must be maintained with effort. Our penchant for these separations has had severe consequences.

It is generally true that the small residential community (but it is one much smaller than that commonly prescribed) has an important role to play in city life, and that there are also larger functioning communities, usually political ones. But no communities are autonomous today, nor could they become so again, without severe losses of security, freedom, and well-being. They do not fit neatly within each other; they are not sharply defined; few lives are largely contained within them; many lives escape them completely. Social or economic autarchy can hardly be recommended as a contemporary ideal. Indeed, hierarchy and autonomy are in their essence antithetical concepts, even if both are prominent in organic theory.

Optimum city size also seems to be an elusive concept. No one has been able to confirm it, and the accepted figure shifts about (it usually rises). It is true that environmental qualities change with an increase or decrease of scale, and so, presumably, forms should change as well. There are important values in smallness (a family garden), as well as in bigness (an extensive wilderness). But the subject is complicated. There are more likely to be thresholds (such as a density that requires sewerage) which call for a new strategy of development, rather than any absolute limits. Unfortunately, different thresholds do not occur at the same point of growth, so that their composite effect is blurred. A better understanding of particular effects at thresholds of scale, and particularly of the importance of the *rate* of growth, is likely to be more important than the traditional search for an optimum size. This subject is taken up again in chapters 13 and 14.

Stable cities—even if we mean a dynamic, homeostatic stability—seem to be a will-o'-the-wisp. Cities change continuously, and that change is not just an inevitable progression to maturity. The ecological climax does not seem to be an appropriate analogy. Rather than being communities of unthinking organisms which follow an inevitable succession until they strike some iron limit, cities are the product of beings who can learn. Culture both stabilizes and destabilizes the habitat system, and it is not evident that we would want it otherwise. A climax state is not patently better than any other. A stable climax has never been maintained, in recent centuries, at any rate.

The affection for nature and the desire to be close to natural, living things are sentiments very widely held throughout the urbanized world. Settlements built according to the organic rule are attractive to us chiefly because they allow for this close contact. It is less tenable, however, that nature is what is nonhuman, and that the farther one gets from people and civilization, the more natural one becomes. By that rule, wilderness is more natural than hunting camp, hunting camp than farm, and farm than city. But people and their cities are as much natural phenomena as trees, streams, nests, and deer paths. It is crucial that we come to see ourselves as an integral part of the total living community.

Above all, perhaps, it is this holistic view which is the most important contribution of organic theory: the habit of looking at a settlement as a whole of many functions, whose diverse elements (even if not strictly separable) are in constant and supportive interchange, and where process and form are indivisible. This idea and the accompanying emotions of wonder and delight in diversity and subtle linkage are an enormous advance over the models of eternal crystal or simple machine. The model might be even more apt if it could divest itself of its preoccupation with simple plant and animal associations, with limits, stabilities, boundaries, hierarchies, autarchies, and inevitable biological responses. Incorporating purpose and culture, and especially the ability to learn and change, might provide us with a far more coherent and defensible model of a city.

5

But Is a General Normative Theory Possible?

While theories about the origin, development, and functioning of cities are in course of lively development, and while the theory of the planning process (decision theory) is well along, we have no adequate contemporary normative theory about the form of cities. There is dogma and there is opinion, but there is no systematic effort to state general relationships between the form of a place and its value. It we have some ground for understanding what cities are, we have practically no rational ground for deciding what they should be, despite a flood of criticism and proposals.

The dreams of utopian cities seem to come from nowhere and to go nowhere. Revolutionary theorists have little idea of what the city should be, once the revolution is achieved. "Scientific" planners put all that nonsense aside. They focus on how things change now and how one should maneuver to survive in the present context. And yet their formulations are also laden with unexamined values. Professionals propose workable solutions of modest range to the physical problems directly in front of them. They rarely have the time to think through the rationale of any solution. If it is suitable to one particular time, place, or culture, it may soon be misapplied to some other one. City design models look for small gains.

These limitations might be inevitable. It may simply not be possible to create a connected normative theory. There are a number of reasons why this could be so, and it is well to state them explicitly, thus allowing an explicit rejoinder. Many of these doubts have at one time or another been my own, as these ideas developed, waxing and waning, over the years. Here, then, is my position today.

Objection 1. Physical form plays no significant role in the satisfaction of important human values, which have to do with our relations to other people. One can be miserable in an island paradise and joyful in a slum.

Appendix A

No one can deny the crucial role of social relationships or of individual character in attaining satisfaction. Nor can anyone deny the role of some extreme physical conditions, such as an absence of oxygen or a lack of a flat surface on which to stand. Objectors will retort that these extreme conditions, while obvious, remain irrelevant because they so rarely occur. The physical alternatives about which we make decisions in real cities are much more narrowly spaced. Step by step, however, as one cites more realistic conditions—a lack of sun, cold, cramped dwelling space, difficult access, the absence of plants or water—this sweeping objection of irrelevance dissolves into one of the following, more cogent arguments. It is rather easy to demonstrate that we are made miserable or joyful by physical conditions as well as by social ones, although the effects are sometimes obscure.

Objection 2. More precisely, physical form by itself has no important influence on human satisfaction. Unless you specify the particular social circumstances of the people who occupy a place, you cannot judge the quality of that place. Eskimo families (perhaps we must now say traditional Eskimo families) live contentedly in quarters whose size would be intolerable to North Americans. A house in poor physical condition, but which you own and which gives you secure social status, has an entirely different meaning than a similar house to which one is forcibly exiled.

This argument is more telling. Once again, extreme physical conditions can be cited in which form has its influence independent of social context; but, in the great majority of realistic cases, the influences of social and physical form are difficult to disentangle. If one wants to change the quality of a place, it is usually most effective to change physical setting and social institutions together. There is a corollary to this argument, incidentally, which these same objectors will find more peculiar: most social patterns also have no significant independent influence, beyond extreme cases. To understand the effect on a person of some social institution— say the nuclear family—you must have a notion of its typical spatial setting.

Given this intimate linkage, it is still important to study the effect of varying one feature while holding the other constant, to come to an understanding of the whole. Social investigators rarely realize this fact and analyze social patterns as if they occurred at spaceless points. Spatial investigators are more timid, and hardly dare to neglect people in analyzing space. Yet it is evident that physical patterns have important effects on people, given a set of social patterns, and that an analysis of these physical effects is important to understanding the whole. It seems at least possible that some physical effects are broad enough to apply despite some moderate variation in social pattern, or even to be general in their application, because of certain regularities in the nature of human beings and their cultures. This leads us to:

Objection 3. Physical patterns may have predictable effects in a single culture, with its stable structure of institutions and values. But it is not possible to construct a cross-cultural theory. It is even dangerous, since it will inevitably be used to impose the value of one culture on another. Each culture has its own norms for city form, and they are independent of those of any other.

The linkage of preferred settlement form to particular cultures is evident. There are two ways of answering this objection. First, as noted above, certain effects are probably species-wide, and their disentanglement from culturally bound norms would surely be useful. Second, it may be that certain *concerns* about form transcend particular cultures, while the solutions to those concerns are special. A clear definition of those concerns and of how form affects them would then be of general use. This will be the general tack that we take below. Nevertheless, the danger remains, as in any theory dealing with human values, that a handsome general formulation cloaks an ethnocentric bias. Being aware of this danger is one defense against it.

Objection 4. Regardless of any influence it may or may not have, physical form is not the key variable whose manipulation will induce change.

Our physical setting is a direct outcome of the kind of society we live in. Change society first and the environment changes as well. Change environment first and you change nothing, if in fact the change can be made. Studying city form may have some value for understanding one of the more remote impacts of the social system, but it is otherwise irrelevant to changing the world.

But to cite the attenuated influence of physical change on social form is no more surprising than to show that a social change, even a revolutionary one, has just as often little direct influence on the physical pattern of a city. Social and physical patterns have inertia, and they work on each other over a lapse of time and through an intervening variable, that is, through the actions and attitudes of persons. It is not surprising that these secondary effects are obscure and slow to appear. Since the source of value (at least for me) is the satisfaction and development of the individual, then it is enough to show first that physical changes will have an impact on him or her, even if they may have very small *social* influence, and, second, that such changes can often be made independently of a major social change. The creation of public parks in this country is one example that comes to mind. They did not change our society, but they brought pleasure to many people.

In addition, physical change can sometimes be used to support, or perhaps even to induce, social change. The form of New Delhi supported the dominance of British colonial power and the internal structure of its social hierarchy. Outward Bound camps depend on danger in the wilderness to change the ways small groups of adolescents behave toward each other. Oneida and the Shaker communities made settings of a particular form in order to build a perfect society. To argue an absolute priority for one or the other of these kinds of change is foolish, in the absence of a specific situation. It is sufficient, in order to make its study relevant, to show that a change of physical form can often be made and can have an influence on persons, independent of social change.*

Objection 5. Well, perhaps. But physical form is not critical at the scale of a city or a region. The shape of one's home or workplace or neighborhood, where most people live out their lives, has something to do with the quality of life. But the shape of a city is irrelevant to it. At this and larger scales, economic and social considerations take over.

This is a common view, one held even by most physical planning professionals, and reinforced by the history of the design professions and by the nature of normal regional decisions. It is a reflection of the way things are. We will try to show that this consignment of physical concerns to a purely local influence is a false boundary. It may be that the features that have been *thought* to comprise large-scale city form are indeed irrelevant phenomena. On this point, the reader is asked to hold his breath and suspend his judgment.

Objection 6. But even if there were a demonstrable connection between city form and value, it would be inapplicable, since there is no such thing as the "public interest," even within a single culture and a single settlement. There are a plurality of interests, all in conflict. The only proper role for a planner is to help clarify the course of that conflict by presenting information on the present form and function of the city, predicting future changes and explaining the impact of various possible actions.

While the clash of interest is only too apparent, I must confess to believing in that outworn heresy, the public interest. The ground for this outmoded belief is the thought that the human species has certain basic requirements for survival and well-being, and that in any given culture there are important common values. This peculiar view can be supplemented by certain abstract notions about justice, the care for future generations, and an interest in the development of human potential. Admittedly, these abstract ideas can be connected to concrete issues in many diverse ways, and it is

*However, its effect will rarely be *predictable* without taking the social pattern into account, and the impact of either form of change is heightened if the changes occur together. This returns us to objection 2.

not always clear who has the best insight into them. Professionals, in any case, cannot claim a monopoly. Yet these notions can be rationally debated, and in that debate a public planner should hold certain general biases which narrow the range of alternatives he can espouse. Even if this were untrue, a normative theory would still be useful to any struggling group (and to its professional advocates) in order to make clear to themselves what they want, as well as being essential for any neutral planner who indifferently, amorally, and scientifically predicts the outcome of whatever outrageous proposal is submitted to him.

Objection 7. Normative theories—that is, explicit, commonly understood rules of evaluation—may be possible in regard to purely practical objects such as foundations or bridges,* but are inappropriate for esthetic forms. Here we rely on the inscrutable inner knowledge of the artist or the critic, or we retreat to "I know what I like." The beauty of a great city is a matter of art, not of science—an intensely private affair, uncommunicable in prosaic language.

My first answer is that cities are, of course, also very practical objects, whose multiple, explicit functions can be the subject of clear, external discourse. Moreover, collective decision, when it extends beyond the very small group, demands such discourse.

My second and more fundamental answer is that "practical" and "esthetic" functions are inseparable. Esthetic experience is a more intense and meaningful form of that same perception and cognition which is used, and which developed, for extremely practical purposes. Theory must deal with the esthetic aspects of cities, even though it may be a more difficult part of its task. Indeed, it must deal with function and esthetics as one phenomenon. Some of the complex, subjective qualities of places will escape us, others can be discussed and even agreed upon. Critics of art do not merely grunt and point when they identify a fine painting. They talk at length about it, even if the

*But are bridges, or even foundations, purely practical objects, unless they cannot be seen?

talk is at times difficult to fathom (and perhaps not
always preferable to grunting).

Objection 8. Even then . . . city form is intricate and complex, and so is the system of human
values. The linkages between them are probably
unfathomable. Not only that, cities are so complicated that, while you can design a house, you can
never design a city. And should not. Cities are vast
natural phenomena, beyond our ability to change,
and beyond our knowing how we ought to change
them.

The fundamental answer to this can only be an
empirical one, plus the belief that partial knowledge will be useful, even when a full understanding evades us. Attempting to design a city as one
designs a building is clearly misleading and dangerous, and this will be elaborated upon in succeeding
chapters. However, we do intervene in complex,
large-scale, "natural" phenomena, with some
knowledge, and do not inevitably incur disaster.
Whole regions have been laid out and cleared for
stable agriculture and ranges of hillsides terraced
for rice and corn. Huge artificial ports have been
successfully built and maintained. The Grand Canal of China was dug 1400 years ago and operates
today. There is a middle ground which is worth
exploring, in the tangle of links between form and
value. It is to this middle ground that I would now
like to turn.

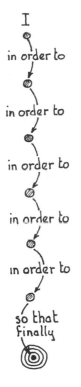

At first, it seems logical to think that each
action we take, at least each rational action, occurs
at the end of a long chain of considered values and
goals. We walk toward the telephone in order to
pick it up in order to make a call in order to reach
some person in order to arrange a meeting in order
to be able to persuade some people in order to have
a regulation passed in order that restrictions will be
placed on the spacing of septic tanks and wells in
order that future wells and tanks will never be too
close together in order to reduce the chance of
disease organisms passing into well water in order
to reduce the likelihood of disease among residents
in order to prolong their lives in good health in
order to allow them to be more productive and

happier. Each link in the chain is an intermediate aim and can be examined by testing the strength of its connection either up or down the chain. We ask either, "What do I want to do this for?" or "Will this next step really carry out my purpose?"

However logical, it is clear that this is a very unreal picture of human action. No one would stop to go through such a long and upsetting chain of reasoning before going to the telephone. The lower ends of such chains are submerged in habit, while the upper ends are lost in the clouds, to be revealed only on oratorical occasions. We stop to think only about the middle links of the chain: "Is calling a meeting the best way of getting that regulation passed?" Even when controversy develops, the entire chain is never inspected. Opponents will not question that the use of a telephone is a good way of arranging a meeting, and they will grant you that preventing disease is a worthwhile objective. They will focus on what they think are better ways of accomplishing disease prevention, like drinking wine instead of water, or installing purification plants. Or they will point out some serious additional consequences of a rule on well spacing, such as the resulting inability of people of modest means to acquire small, inexpensive lots.

Not only is the chain of aim and action long, and in places insecurely linked, but different chains merge and diverge in confusing ways, so that single actions spring from multiple values and have plural consequences, which in themselves are linked back to other values. The result is a thicket rather than a chain, or more exactly a thicket whose roots and branches interlace and are grafted onto each other. When we add to these difficulties the fact that different people hold different values and have different images of consequences, and further add that the changing context of any problem causes values and consequences to shift with time, it is at first hard to believe that we can ever act with any rational purpose, particularly on public questions. Yet, in spite of its failure to follow aerodynamical theory, the honey bee can actually fly.

In practice, we manage these obscurities by restricting our rationality to narrow bounds. More general aims are usually agreed upon, but not ex-

amined either in themselves or for their linkages.
More specific actions are instinctive, culturally determined, or habitual to the individual and so are
performed "unthinkingly." We confine our explic-
itness to very circumscribed regions of the thicket
of value. We will focus on one or two consequences
or reasons and neglect the rest; we shut our ears to
heretics; we leave the details to specialists. Fierce
opponents willingly accept an upper and a lower
bound, in order to battle within a definite space
(and thus the ability to win a political battle depends very much on the skill of choosing bounds).
While initial public arguments are at times wide-
ranging, they are usually only an introduction to
that crucial moment when someone says: "Well,
since we must decide, let's accept that. . . ."

Since decisions about the form of cities affect
many people, they must at least *appear* to be explicit
and rational. More than that, since rationality,
however cumbersome, is the only means we have
for making better decisions, public decisions
should be rational in fact. If one looks at most
physical planning reports, one sees a consistent
strategy for dealing with this. They first state some
very general public aims, such as health, well-
being, a good quality of life, a high standard of
living, the highest and best use of the land, the
conservation of resources, a stable and integrated
society, a maximum of opportunity, and the like.
These are difficult to disagree with, in this general
form, and their implications are likely to be
obscure. The report will then leap to proposals at a
much lower level: a subway line should be built
because it will shorten the travel time between *A*
and *B*; further suburban development should be
resisted to prevent "sprawl"; for safety's sake, all
buildings over two stories high should have two
means of egress in case of fire; and so forth. The
connections to the broad aims lie unexamined, and
indeed they are probably unexaminable. The proposals may be reasonable, but they are specific and
fixed. As specific solutions, they might have some
unwanted consequences, such as forcing a shift in
the commercial center or causing a shortage of
moderate-priced housing. So one would like to start
with the aim just preceding these concrete spatial

proposals, to see whether it could be done differently. One may even have the idiocy to ask: "Why not *lengthen* the travel time between A and B?," "What's wrong with sprawl?," or "Would it be worthwhile to increase the risk of death by fire, just a little, in order to reduce building costs?"

The linkages of very general aims to city form are usually incalculable. Low-level goals and solutions, on the other hand, are too restrictive in their means and too unthinking of their purposes. In this dilemma, it seems appropriate to emphasize the aims in between, that is, those goals which are as general as possible, and thus do not dictate particular physical solutions, and yet whose achievement can be detected and explicitly linked to physical solutions. This is the familiar notion of performance standards, applied at the city scale. The proper level of generality is likely to be just above that which specifies some spatial arrangement. For example, neither "a pleasant environment" nor "a tree on every lot," but "the microclimate should fall within such and such range in summer" or even "some long-lived living thing should be visible from every dwelling."

It looks as if performance characteristics of this kind might be a foundation on which to build a general normative theory about cities. Developing a limited and yet general set of them, which as far as possible embraces all the important issues of form, will now be our aim. This will be our alternative to the dogmatic norms that customarily guide discussions about the goodness of cities.

II

A THEORY OF GOOD CITY FORM

6 Dimensions of Performance

Performance characteristics will be more general, and the easier to use, to the degree that performance can be measured solely by reference to the spatial form of the city. But we know that the quality of a place is due to the joint effect of the place and the society which occupies it. I can imagine three tactics for avoiding the necessity of taking the entire universe into account in this attempt to measure city performance. First, we can elaborate those linkages between form and purpose which exist because of certain species-wide or human settlement-wide regularities: the climatic tolerances of human beings, for example, or the importance of the small social group, or the very general function of any city as a network of access. Second, we can add to the description of the spatial form of a place those particular social institutions and mental attitudes which are directly linked to that form and repeatedly critical to its quality, as I have already done at the end of chapter 2. Both of these tactics will be employed below.

Third and last, however, we must realize that it would be foolish to set performance *standards* for cities, if we mean to generalize. To assert that the ideal density is twelve families to the acre, or the ideal daytime temperature is 68°F., or that all good cities are organized into residential neighborhoods of 3000 persons each, are statements too easily discredited. Situations and values differ. What we might hope to generalize about are performance *dimensions*, that is, certain identifiable characteristics of the performance of cities which are due primarily to their spatial qualities and which are measurable scales, along which different groups will prefer to achieve different positions. It should then be possible to analyze any city form or proposal, and to indicate its location on the dimension, whether by a number or just by "more or less." To be general, the dimensions should be important qualities for most, if not all, persons and cultures. Ideally, the dimensions should also include all the qualities which any people value in a physical place. (Of course, this last is an unbearably severe criterion.)

For example, we might consider *durability* as a performance dimension.* Durability is the degree to which the physical elements of a city resist wear and decay and retain their ability to function over long periods. In choosing this dimension, we assume that everyone has important preferences about the durability of his city, although some want it evanescent and others would like it to last forever. Furthermore, we know how to measure the general durability of a settlement, or at least how to measure a few significant aspects of durability. A tent camp can be compared to a troglodyte settlement, and, given the values of a particular set of inhabitants, we can tell you which one of them is better, or people can make that evaluation for themselves. They can also decide how much durability they are willing to give up in return for other values. Perhaps we can show that very low or very high durabilities are bad for everyone, and so we identify an optimum range. Although the linkage of durability to basic human aims is only a chain of assumptions, we believe that the assumptions are reasonable. Correlations of durability with preference exist, and people are content to use this idea as a workable intermediate goal. Meanwhile, its connection to city form—to such concrete physical characteristics as building material, density, and roof construction—can be explicitly demonstrated.

To be a useful guide to policy, a set of performance dimensions should have the following characteristics:

1. They should be characteristics which refer primarily to the spatial form of the city, as broadly defined above, given certain very general statements about the nature of human beings and their cultures. To the extent that the value set on those characteristics varies with variations in culture, that dependence should be explicit. The dimension itself and its method of analysis should remain unchanged.

*But we won't. This is a red herring.

2. The characteristics should be as general as possible, while retaining their explicit connection to particular features of form.

3. It should be possible to connect these characteristics to the important goals and values of any culture, at least through a chain of reasonable assumptions.

4. The set should cover all the features of settlement form which are relevant, in some important way to those basic values.

5. These characteristics should be in the form of dimensions of performance, along which various groups in various situations will be free to choose optimum points or "satisficing" thresholds. In other words, the dimensions will be usable where values differ or are evolving.

6. Locations along these dimensions should be identifiable and measurable, at least in the sense of "more or less," using available data. They may be complex dimensions, however, so that locations on them need not be single points. Moreover, the data, while conceivably available, may for the present escape us.

7. The characteristics should be at the same level of generality.

8. If possible, they should be independent of one another. That is, setting a level of attainment along one dimension should not imply a particular setting on some other dimension. If we are unable to produce uncontaminated dimensions of this kind, we can settle for less, if the cross-connections are explicit. Testing for independence will require detailed analysis.

9. Ideally, measurements on these dimensions should be able to deal with qualities which change over time, forming an extended pattern which can be valued in the present. More likely, however, the measurements will deal with present conditions, but may include the drift of events toward the future.

There have been many previous attempts to
outline a set of criteria for a "good city." The dimensions I propose below are not original inventions. Appendix C indicates some of my sources. Previous sets have always broken at least some of the rules above. They have at times been so general as to go far beyond settlement form and to require a complex (and usually impossible) calculation which involves culture, political economy, and many other nonformal features. Or they refer to some particular physical solution that is appropriate only in a particular situation. They may mix spatial and nonspatial features, or mix levels of generality, or mix the scale of application. Frequently, they are bound to a single culture. They do not include all the features of city form which are important to human values. They are often given as absolute standards, or they call for minimizing or maximizing, instead of being dimensions. The qualities are sometimes not measurable, or even identifiable, in any clear way. They frequently overlap each other.

The list that follows is an attempt to rework and reorder the material in a way that escapes those difficulties. The presumed generality of this list lies in certain regularities: the physical nature of the universe, the constants of human biology and culture, and some features which commonly appear in contemporary large-scale settlements, including the processes by which they are maintained and changed.

But some view of the nature of human settlements, however unclear or general, is necessarily assumed in making any list. Unfortunately, it is much easier to say what a city is not: not a crystal, not an organism, not a complex machine, not even an intricate network of communications—like a computer or a nervous system—which can learn by reorganizing its own patterns of response, but whose primitive elements are forever the same. True, somewhat like the latter, the city is interconnected to an important degree by signals, rather than by place-order or mechanical linkages or organic cohesion. It is indeed something changing and developing, rather than an eternal form, or a

Moos
Odum

mechanical repetition which in time wears out, or even a permanent recurrent cycling which feeds on the degradation of energy, which is the concept of ecology.

Yet the idea of ecology seems close to an explanation, since an ecosystem is a set of organisms in a habitat, where each organism is in some relation to others of its own kind, as well as to other species and the inorganic setting. This system of relations can be considered as a whole, and has certain characteristic features of fluctuation and development, of species diversity, of intercommunication, of the cycling of nutrients, and the pass-through of energy. The concept deals with very complex systems, with change, with organic and inorganic elements together, and with a profusion of actors and of forms.

Moreover, an ecosystem seems to be close to what a settlement is. Complicated things must in the end be understood in their own terms. An image will fail to stick if it is only a borrowing from some other area, although metaphorical borrowings are essential first steps in understanding.

Apt as it is, the concept of ecology has its drawbacks, for our purpose. Ecological systems are made up of "unthinking" organisms, not conscious of their fatal involvement in the system and its consequences, unable to modify it in any fundamental way. The ecosystem, if undisturbed, moves to its stable climax of maturity, where the diversity of species and the efficiency of the use of energy passing through are both at the maximum, given the fixed limits of the inorganic setting. Nutrients recycle but may gradually be lost to sinks, while energy inevitably escapes the system or becomes unavailable. Nothing is learned; no progressive developments ensue. The inner experiences of the organisms—their purposes and images—are irrelevant; only their outward behavior matters.

An evolving "learning ecology" might be a more appropriate concept for the human settlement, some of whose actors, at least, are conscious, and capable of modifying themselves and thus of changing the rules of the game. The dominant animal consciously restructures materials and switches the paths of energy flow. To the familiar ecosystem characteristics of diversity, interdependence, context, history, feedback, dynamic stability, and cyclic processing, we must add such features as values, culture, consciousness, progressive (or regressive) change, invention, the ability to learn, and the connection of inner experience and outer action. Images, values, and the creation and flow of information play an important role. Leaps, revolutions, and catastrophes can happen, new paths can be taken. Human learning and culture have destabilized the system, and perhaps, some day, other species will join the uncertainty game. The system does not inevitably move toward some fixed climax state, nor toward maximum entropy. A settlement is a valued arrangement, consciously changed and stabilized. Its elements are connected through an immense and intricate network, which can be understood only as a series of overlapping local systems, never rigidly or instantaneously linked, and yet part of a fabric without edges. Each part has a history and a context, and that history and context shift as we move from part to part. In a peculiar way, each part contains information about its local context, and thus, by extension, about the whole.

Values are implicit in that viewpoint, of course. The good city is one in which the continuity of this complex ecology is maintained while progressive change is permitted. The fundamental good is the continuous development of the individual or the small group and their culture: a process of becoming more complex, more richly connected, more competent, acquiring and realizing new powers—intellectual, emotional, social, and physical. If human life is a continued state of becoming, then its continuity is founded on growth and development (and its development on continuity: the statement is circular). If development is a process of becoming more competent and more richly connected, then an increasing sense of connection to one's environment in space and in time is one aspect of growth. So that settlement is good which enhances the continuity of a culture and the survival of its people, increases a sense of connection in time and space, and permits or spurs individual growth: development, within continuity, via openness and connection.*

These values could, of course, be applied to judging a culture as well as a place. In either case, there is an inherent tension as well as a circularity between continuity and development—between the stabilities and connections needed for coherence and the ability to change and grow. Those cultures whose organizing ideas and institutions deal successfully with that tension and circularity are presumably more desirable, in this view. Similarly, a good settlement is also an *open* one: accessible, decentralized, diverse, adaptable, and tolerant to experiment. This emphasis on dynamic openness is distinct from the insistence of environmentalists (and most utopians) on recurrence and stability. The blue ribbon goes to development, as long as it keeps within the constraints of continuity in time and space. Since an unstable ecology risks disaster as well as enrichment, flexibility is important, and also the ability to learn and adapt rapidly. Conflict, stress, and uncertainty are not excluded, nor are those very human emotions of hate and fear, which accompany stress. But love and caring would certainly be there.

Any new model of the city must integrate statements of value with statements of objective relationships. The model I have sketched is neither a developed nor an explicit one, and I retreat to my more narrow concern with normative theory. But the surviving reader will see that these general preferences—for continuity, connection, and openness—underlie all the succeeding pages, even while the theory makes an effort to see that it is applicable to any context.

Given that general view and the task of constructing a limited set of performance dimensions for the spatial form of cities, I suggest the following ones.† None of them are single dimensions; all refer to a cluster of qualities. Yet each cluster has a common basis and may be measured in some common way. I simply name the dimensions at this

*The bias of the teacher is now unmasked.
†At the end of appendix C, the curious reader will find some of the excess baggage which I discarded while developing these magic five.

point. Subsequent chapters will discuss each dimension in detail.

There are five basic dimensions:

1. *Vitality:* the degree to which the form of the settlement supports the vital functions, the biological requirements and capabilities of human beings—above all, how it protects the survival of the species. This is an anthropocentric criterion, although we may some day consider the way in which the environment supports the life of other species, even where that does not contribute to our own survival.

2. *Sense:* the degree to which the settlement can be clearly perceived and mentally differentiated and structured in time and space by its residents and the degree to which that mental structure connects with their values and concepts—the match between environment, our sensory and mental capabilities, and our cultural constructs.

3. *Fit:* the degree to which the form and capacity of spaces, channels, and equipment in a settlement match the pattern and quantity of actions that people customarily engage in, or want to engage in—that is, the adequacy of the behavior settings, including their adaptability to future action.

4. *Access:* the ability to reach other persons, activities, resources, services, information, or places, including the quantity and diversity of the elements which can be reached.

5. *Control:* the degree to which the use and access to spaces and activities, and their creation, repair, modification, and management are controlled by those who use, work, or reside in them.

If these five dimensions comprise all the principal dimensions of settlement quality, I must of course add two meta-criteria, which are always appended to any list of good things:

6. *Efficiency:* the cost, in terms of other valued things, of creating and maintaining the settlement, for any given level of attainment of the environmental dimensions listed above.

7. *Justice:* the way in which environmental benefits and costs are distributed among persons, according to some particular principle such as eq-

uity, need, intrinsic worth, ability to pay, effort expended, potential contribution, or power. Justice is
the criterion which balances the gains among persons, while efficiency balances the gains among
different values.

These meta-criteria are distinct from the five
criteria that precede them. First, they are meaningless until costs and benefits have been defined by
specifying the prior basic values. Second, the two
meta-criteria are involved in each one of the basic
dimensions, and thus they are by no means independent of them. They are repetitive subdimensions of each of the five. In each case, one asks: (1)
What is the cost (in terms of anything else we
choose to value) of achieving this degree of vitality,
sense, fit, access, or control? and (2) Who is getting
how much of it?

I propose that these five dimensions and two
meta-criteria are the inclusive measures of settlement quality. Groups and persons will value different aspects of them and assign different priorities
to them. But, having measured them, a particular
group in a real situation would be able to judge the
relative goodness of their place, and would have
the clues necessary to improve or maintain that
goodness. All five can be defined, identified, and
applied to some degree, and this application can be
improved.

Now, is this really so? Do the dimensions really
meet all the criteria which were given at the beginning of this section? Do they in fact illuminate the
"goodness" of a city, or are they only a verbal
checklist? Can locations on these dimensions be
identified and measured in a concrete way? Are
they useful guidelines for research? Do they apply
to varied cultures and in varied situations? Can
general propositions be made about how optima
vary according to variations in resource, power, or
values? Can degrees of achievement on these
dimensions be related to particular spatial patterns,
so that the benefits of proposed solutions can be
predicted? Do our preferences about places indeed
vary significantly as performance changes? All that
remains to be seen.

First, it is necessary to elaborate on each
dimension, in order to expand its various sub-

dimensions and to explain its probable connections to particular forms and more general values. In doing so, we can review what evidence there is and indicate some gaps in our knowledge. However, it will shortly be obvious how much of this evidence is speculative.

7 Vitality

Cappon
Hinkle

An environment is a good habitat if it supports the health and biological well-functioning of the individual and the survival of the species. Health is surprisingly difficult to define. Many aspects of health (and even the definition of good health) depend more on social structure than on environmental structure. We will focus on those aspects of health which are relatively clearly defined, which depend to an important degree on the nature of the spatial environment, and which are rooted in universal characteristics of human biology, so that they are similar across different cultures. There are perhaps three principal features of the environment which are conducive to health, good biological function, and survival in this sense, that is, which make it a vital place, an adequate lifeground:

1. *Sustenance.* There should be an adequate supply of food, energy, water, and air, and a proper disposal of wastes, i.e., the "throughput" must be adequate to sustain life. Sustenance is affected by the physical systems of supply and disposal, the density of occupation relative to sources, the location of settlements, the effect of buildings and landscape on insolation and air movement, and the way space, soil, and vegetation are conserved and are adapted to produce the required supplies. Crop lands, greenhouses, soil conservation, managed forests, sewer systems, wells, coal mines, stream control, interior ventilation, food markets, aqueducts, latrines, and site dispositions are some of the spatial devices used to achieve this.

2. *Safety.* A good settlement is one in which hazards, poisons, and diseases are absent or controlled, and the fear of encountering them is low. It is a physically secure environment. The attainment of safety involves problems of air and water pollution, the contamination of food, the presence of poison, the suppression of disease and disease vectors, the reduction of bodily accidents, defenses against violent attack, the prevention of flood and fire, the resistance to earthquake, and the treatment available to someone who has been exposed to any

Burton
Grandjean 1976
Neutra
Rainwater

of those hazards. The list is long, but the aims and
physical means are relatively definite, since they all have to do with the avoidance of some specific problem.

3. *Consonance.* Lastly, the spatial environment should be consonant with the basic biological structure of the human being. It should be conducive to the maintenance of internal temperature. It should support natural rhythms: sleeping and waking, alertness and inattention. It should provide an optimum sensory input: neither overloading a person nor depriving her of adequate stimulus. She should be able to see and hear well. This may be especially important to the normal development of the child. Elements in the environment, such as steps, doors, rooms, and inclines, should all be fitted to human size and powers—to such characteristics as height, reach, jointing, handedness, forward vision, and lifting power. These are the base data of ergo- Grandjean 1973 nometrics, or human factors engineering. The setting should encourage the active use of the body, so that no parts of the body degenerate for lack of exercise. Some of these issues are well defined, others—the support of body rhythms in particular—are less clear, but their implications are developing.

Perhaps only a few bands of hunter-gatherers or some small settlements of agriculturists in favored regions have ever in the past enjoyed a sustenant, secure, and consonant lifeground. Except for defense in war, these vital requirements have not usually been the real, driving motives of city builders. Recurrently, they were forced on official attention by plague, fire, or famine. But sustained attention to the city as a living habitat is perhaps a relatively recent phenomenon.

These three requirements are common to everyone: poison sickens us all, in Hackensack as in Soweto. These are the problems usually referred to in public discussion as "the environmental issues," using environment in that misused, wrongfully narrow sense. But the degree of value placed on health and individual survival or the absence of hunger or fear may vary from place to place. Vitality is not an absolute good, except for the survival of the species itself, which is biologically built in. A life

Esser
Hosking
Leff

may be sacrificed for other ends, and its prolongation traded for better living. Some risks are acceptable. Would we want a perfectly healthy environment even if it were possible—a world in which there was no injury, no illness, no stress? A short and painful life may be accepted as a natural, even as a proper, thing as long as each generation can rear the next. In any case, individual death is unavoidable.

Biological health and function are the issue here, not comfort. A soft chair, a convenient trip, an equable climate, an easy death, or a pleasant dinner may be irrelevant to health, or even inimical to it. Some conditions for health may run counter to instinctual drives, and certain hazards may be hidden or not part of common knowledge. Thus experts may "know best" for those who are actually at risk. This raises ethical issues of acting on behalf of others, or even against their will. Should people be forced to drink fluoridated water?

Good health and well-functioning may be felt and enjoyed, yet they are difficult to measure and define, particularly if we speak of mental health. Ill-health and frustration are much easier to identify. Effective environmental rules are therefore likely to focus on a threshold of avoidance, rather than on some optimum. We look for reasonable levels of risk, not a total absence of it. Criteria can usually be set as ranges of tolerance and measured as the likelihood of stress, disease, reproductive failure, or death. At times, individuals will seek out risks, to test themselves and enjoy danger. The basic rule is group survival, followed by individual well-being and the opportunity to use and develop inherent human powers. The growing child, for example, should be able to extend its range gradually, confronting more and more of the world, exercising its powers with greater and greater responsibility, and yet always be able to retreat to a protected nest. Clearly, these precepts are the foundation for those to come, since biological survival underpins all other human values. Vitality is a conservative, as well as a very general, rule—a passive, supportive feature. It emphasizes continuity, yet provides the opportunity for individual development. Since the basic aim is species survival, these rules have special importance for their bearing on the reproduction and rearing of children.

These issues have enjoyed a long history in theoretical texts of environmental planning, however little they may actually have been followed. Vitruvius laid down rules for the siting and design of healthy settlements in the first century before Christ, and he was compiling a much earlier knowledge. In the same way, the ancient Indian texts speak of rules of health in settlement design, and so do the Laws of the Indies. Most of these rules deal with climate and visible pollutants. Armed with new knowledge about an invisible world, the English sanitary reformers of the nineteenth century brought on an enormous undertaking of drainage and water supply, which converted the urban sinks of their day into the relatively healthy settlements of the present developed world.

Yet the issues of vitality remain crucial. In many areas where we have certain knowledge, that knowledge has yet to be applied. The great metropolises of the developing world are almost as dangerous to life as were the western cities of 100 years ago. Malnutrition and disease are still endemic in the poorer areas of the affluent cities. New threats to survival have appeared: a world shortage of food, water, or of energy (at least until solar power becomes economically feasible); nuclear disaster; or global contamination of the atmosphere or of the seas. Fresh hazards are created as technology develops. Even our systems of pollutant removal may cause pollution to reappear in new forms.

New ways of living, the removal of previous threats to health, and the development of knowledge all uncover threats not perceived before, or convert old, accepted fates into soluble (and thus anxiety-provoking) problems. For example it is becoming apparent that prolonged exposure to the narrow spectrum of artificial light may be depriving us of the necessary stimuli provided by wide-band sunlight, and may be disturbing our built-in body rhythms, which are based on the solar day. The removal of gross threats to physical health such as cholera and rickets shifts attention to the possible role of environment in heart disease or cancer, or to even more subtle spatial predisposers to mental illness. When earthquakes can be predicted, then one must consider how and when to evacuate a threatened city. Thus, although there has been much success in improving the living habitat, it is a more difficult issue today than it was. Because of our rising expectations, it seems even farther from realization.

Vitality comes as close to being a pure public good as any on our list, since health and survival are values very widely held, and threats to health are often indiscriminate in their incidence. In this realm, we are more secure in making judgments for others, especially for the generations to come, since we can predict that they too will wish to survive. Like most public goods, however, vitality tends to be honored in the breach, since the cost to anyone to increase it (or to refrain from decreasing it) may have little connection with his own benefits. Downstream drinkers swallow upstream pollution. The warhead in our silo is salutary, since it will radiate someone else's city. Threats to health seem almost to increase, just as we come to realize the importance of a good fit between our animal nature and our physical setting.

Large dollar costs may be incurred by a new sewage system, the denial of a plant expansion, a prohibition of tobacco or automobiles, or the closing of a war industry. When making a "rational" analysis of these issues, one is plagued by the problem of computing the dollar value of life and of comparing diffuse future dollars to well-defined present ones. Of course, there are second-order costs imposed on the economic system by poor vitality, but these are hard to identify. Thus measures to increase or protect this quality are often imposed rather arbitrarily by a public authority, and application lags behind knowledge.

The earliest ways of modifying the world to make it more habitable had to do with simple shelters, the domestication of crops and animals, and the location of settlements near sources of food, fuel, and water. While long-range transport and modern food production have apparently freed those of us in the more affluent nations from some

Meier 1976

of these early constraints, they have also raised the possibility of shortages due to world-wide losses of sustenance. In consequence, people are reconsidering the value of local autonomy in regard to some basic resources.

At another period in history, much of the expertise in settlement design had to do with defense against human attack: the siting and design of fortresses, walls, and outworks. Most of this is outmoded today. We live in the shadow of weapons against which there seems to be no physical defense, although underground facilities are still being built, and we make hare-brained evacuation plans. Using city form to defend against attack now turns to discouraging local criminal assault, or to ways of living with the automobile our comfy killer. Much of traffic planning is concerned with the relation of physical patterns and the rules for their use to motor accident rates.

Newman

Structures are sited and designed to avoid damage from fire, flood, and earthquake, and this knowledge is substantial. The spatial organization of rescue, relief, and control services is also a factor in the defense against natural disaster. However, we are just beginning to study how people behave in such disasters. Similarly, we have substantial knowledge about the suppression of infectious disease and its vectors, the supply of pure water, food, and drugs (however little that may be regarded in the commercial world), on matters of waste disposal and cleanliness, and on the spatial organization of medical care.

Burton

The debilitating effects of poor microclimates are well-known and commonly resented, but less often managed, except for technical solutions applied indoors: air conditioning and central heating. Arranging structures to create a more pleasant and healthy microclimate is a known craft, but little practiced. The regulation of city form to provide solar access to all building sites is now an important issue. The control of climate on a larger scale escapes us yet. That may be our good fortune. The impact of city air pollution is now widely studied, and the first effective steps are being taken to control it. What is just now being realized and nowhere dealt with is that indoor air pollution is far more

Lynch 1971

Knowles

Grandjean 1976

Goldsmith

critical, especially in a country such as the United States where 95 percent of our time is spent indoors.

The implications for health of city noise and city lights are only beginning to be appreciated. Noise has been considered simply a minor nuisance and lighting a mere convenience, to be increased in intensity as quickly as money allows. It is now clear that both emissions have direct effects on bodily health and important indirect ones as well, since they can reinforce or disrupt body rhythms: harass our sleep or desynchronize the normal fluctuations of internal function. The notion that city life may impose an alien structure of time on us should have consequences for the temporal organization of city activity.

While popular interest in daily exercise is rising, traditional settlement design has always sought to reduce physical effort: to shorten distances, avoid human portage, abolish level changes, introduce mechanical lifts and vehicles, multiply labor-saving devices. The memory of hard human labor has been too fresh. Recent studies in one North American suburb have shown that the average adult there moves his or her body somewhat less than someone permanently bedridden. Designing to promote, rather than to avoid, the use of the body may be on its way: not simply by providing space for athletics, which are indulged in by no more than a minor portion of the population, but by arrangements which encourage bodily action in everyday life, or even compel it.

Dubos

We are still some distance from understanding the degree to which man-made settings should duplicate the natural environments in which the human species evolved and to which the species is presumably adapted; or to what degree our health declines or improves when we depart from those primitive features. But we know a good deal about the details of a vital environment, and our greatest difficulties lie in applying that knowledge. The value is clear and widely held. There is a substantial literature on the subject.

The money costs involved in converting the city into a vital place and the difficulties in apportioning them have already been mentioned. There

are other costs, as well. Since much of the knowledge about health is "invisible" or arcane, experts
will dominate the discussion. Improving vitality
tends toward central control, and coercion as well,
since diffuse costs must be carried back to their
agents. Suppressing drugs requires police, and encourages mugging and smuggling. Suppressing
smoking will call out an army. To be deprived of the
drug of your choice is hard to bear. When environmental controls must be applied on a world scale,
this necessary and dangerous power is inflated.
The potential monotony and oppression of a completely safe, managed world is a common theme in
science fiction. An ideal climate might be boring. It
is even possible that there could be a long range risk
to the species, if its individuals need no longer cope
with stress and risk. However, these dangers seem
rather remote to us today.

We can move from questions of human health
to the health of other species, or of the entire
biological community. This is a direct extension of
human concern if we speak of the species on which
we are economically dependent. We are obviously
concerned about cattle disease and crop failure. We
should also be concerned about maintaining genetic diversity among plants and animals of value
to us. A human interest in the health of the entire
ecological community can be justified on the
grounds that we depend on the entire web of life,
and may suffer when that web is torn. Thus the
relative stability of the local ecological system
should be a measure of some importance to us.

Should we go further, and attend to the health
of the total living community, or perhaps just the
health of other selected species, because we grant
their own rights to live? Many people might be
ready to extend their concern to those mammals
which have been historically close to man, with
whom we have developed emotional ties, and with
whom we think we can communicate in some degree. Thus a concern for the good health of pet dogs
and horses might be accepted as a reasonable criterion in an affluent town, although it has rarely been
publicly mentioned. Few argue for the health of
rats, cockroaches, or even of such pleasant and
harmless species (harmless in the human view, of

course) as butterflies. So far (but this may change) our principal values center on ourselves. We concern ourselves with human health, with the health of those species on whom we are directly dependent, and with the general stability of the entire biological community on which we indirectly depend.

In summary, there are a number of performance dimensions for city form that group themselves under this heading of vitality:

a. *sustenance:* the adequacy of the throughput of water, air, food, energy, and waste;

b. *safety:* the absence of environmental poisons, diseases, or hazards;

c. *consonance:* the degree of fit between the environment and the human requirements of internal temperature, body rhythm, sensory input, and body function;

d. for other living things, how well the environment provides for the health and genetic diversity of species which are economically useful to man; and

e. the present and future stability of the total ecological community.

While measures *a*, *b*, and *d* are often considered, the others, if widely discussed, are more rarely applied. Nevertheless, the measures seem general in their application and valid for long-range planning.

8 Sense

By the sense of a settlement, I mean the clarity with which it can be perceived and identified, and the ease with which its elements can be linked with other events and places in a coherent mental representation of time and space and that representation can be connected with nonspatial concepts and values. This is the join between the form of the environment and the human processes of perception and cognition. Too often ill-defined and so passed over with a few pious regrets, this quality lies at the root of personal feelings about cities. It cannot be analyzed except as an interaction between person and place. Perception is a creative act, not a passive reception.

Sense depends on spatial form and quality, but also on the culture, temperament, status, experience, and current purpose of the observer. Thus the sense of a particular place will vary for different observers, just as the ability of a particular person to perceive form varies for different places. Nevertheless, there are some significant and fundamental constancies in the experience of the same place by different people. These constancies arise from the common biological basis of our perception and cognition, certain common experiences of the real world (gravity, inertia, shelter, fire, and sharpness, to name a few) and the common cultural norms that may be found among those who habitually use any particular place. Places have a greater or lesser sense, and so do events. Activities and celebrations associated with a location support its perception to the extent that they are themselves perceived as vivid and coherent.

The simplest form of sense is *identity*, in the narrow meaning of that common term: "a sense of place." Identity is the extent to which a person can recognize or recall a place as being distinct from other places—as having a vivid, or unique, or at least a particular, character of its own. This is a quality often sought by designers and warmly discussed among them. It has an obvious, almost banal, practical function, since the ability to recognize objects is the foundation of effective action. But is has much deeper and more interesting meanings than that.

Most people have had the experience of being in a very special place, and they prize it and lament its common lack. There is a sheer delight in sensing the world: the play of light, the feel and smell of the wind, touches, sounds, colors, forms. A good place is accessible to all the senses, makes visible the currents of the air, engages the perceptions of its inhabitants. The direct enjoyment of vivid perception is further enlarged because sensible, identifiable places are convenient pegs on which to hang personal memories, feelings, and values. Place identity is closely linked to personal identity. "I am here" supports "I am."

Relph

See fig. 51

Intense familiarity will create a sense of place, just as will special form. One's home or one's childhood landscape are usually very identifiable settings. When form and familiarity work together, the emotional result is powerful: "I am the citizen of no mean city." Tourism is based on a superficial exploitation of this same sense of place. Not many of us, however, experience that abiding pleasure (and occasional irritation, but at least heightened sensibility) of daily life in a distinctive environment—a Venice, a mountain intervale, an island town.

Events can also have identity; this is the "sense of occasion." Special celebrations and great rituals have it in heightened degree. Occasion and place will reinforce each other to create a vivid present. The result is an active involvement in the immediate, material world and an enlargement of the self.

See fig. 52

The identity of a place or event can be analyzed and crudely measured by simple tests of recognition, recall, and description. Such tests are now reasonably well developed. People may be asked to recognize photographs or other representations and to recall places verbally or graphically. The quickness and intensity of recognition and recall can be quantified roughly, as can the number of interviewees who are able to do so. These tests should be complemented by field descriptions, which identify and describe the places and events recalled, and provide a basis (along with an under-

Lynch 1976

51 In the Park Güell, in Barcelona, Gaudí conferred a unique identity on an old prototype—the formal baroque staircase—through a wildly imaginative use of form and material.

52 A memorable physical setting reinforces a special event: dancing the Sardana on the steps of the old cathedral in Barcelona.

standing of the culture and individual experience of the interviewees) for analyzing the reasons for the degree of identity encountered. But to rely on field description alone, as many designers are wont to do, is to neglect one major element of the interaction which gives rise to sensibility. It is a substitution of the analyst's perceptions for those of the people who actually live there. It is equally incorrect, of course, to rely solely on how people respond, without studying the locale which is the subject of their responses. But this is not such a common sin.

The next element of sense is formal *structure*, which at the scale of a small place is the sense of how its parts fit together, and in a large settlement is the sense of orientation: knowing where (or when) one is, which implies knowing how other places (or times) are connected to this place. Orientation may be an inarticulate memory of the act of navigation ("follow me"), or a more or less structured mental map (ranging from one which is a vague topological network to a scaled geometrical representation), or a remembered series of sequential images ("turn left at the beech tree beyond the green house"), or a set of verbal concepts ("wealthy suburbs surround the center-city slums"), or some combination of these.

Lynch 1965
Peets

The practical significance of orientation is clear enough: poor orientation means lost time and wasted effort, especially for strangers. It is crucial for the handicapped—the blind, in particular, but also for those crippled, retarded, or deaf. Sensible structure must be extended as the scale of daily living extends. Today, many of us are called on to understand the structure of a large urbanized region.

There are other aids to navigation than environmental form, of course, including maps and other persons. Yet the fear and confusion that attend poor orientation, and the security and pleasure evoked by its opposite, connect environmental form to deep psychological levels. In addition, good orientation enhances access and so enlarges opportunity. Local structure makes it easier for us to identify a place by perceiving how its parts fit together.

See fig. 53

Appleyard

Lynch 1972

See fig. 54

While good structure may be highly prized by some, others are more indifferent to it, except as they move along their accustomed paths. People use many different clues to establish structure—the recognition of a characteristic form or activity in areas or centers, sequential linkages, directional relations, time and distance, landmarks, path or edge continuities, gradients, panoramas, and many others. Tests for structure are easy to make, by means of sketching and mapping exercises, route descriptions, interviews while traveling, distance and direction estimates, and other techniques. Such tests have been carried out in many localities throughout the world, and we now have some knowledge of the relations between large-scale form and image structure—how it varies with culture and situation, and in what ways it seems to be invariant. We know much less about how the environmental image develops, however. Nevertheless, composite maps of structural strength and failure can be generated for certain populations in regard to certain places—just as they can be made for identity.

There is also an orientation in time. It includes that grasp of clock time which enables us to order our day, know when events occur, and coordinate our actions with those of others. It also includes the deeper emotional sense of how the present moment is linked to the near or distant past and future. This deep sense of orientation in time is very likely more important to most people than is the corresponding sense of orientation in space. Moreover, since our internal representation of time is poorer than our internal representation of space, we are more dependent on external clues to keep us temporally well oriented. Thus, environmental forms and sequences are very useful for anchoring and extending our temporal orientation: clocks, natural processes, activity rhythms, signs, lighting, historic preservation, celebrations, ritual, and the like. Orientation in time may be analyzed by asking people to describe temporal linkages, to make estimates of time or duration, or to describe past or future. But the techniques are not as well developed as those of analyzing spatial orientation.

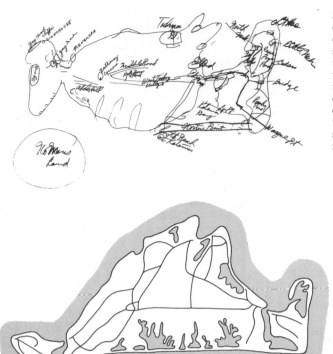

53 A resident of Chappaquiddick, on the eastern end of Martha's Vineyard, sketches her concept of that island. Compare this with a normal outline map: familiar places are enlarged and names are clustered, yet the characteristic features are preserved, especially the natural ones.

54 On the Piazza dell'Olio
in Florence, the facade of
San Salvatore al Vescovo
(about 1220) is imbedded
in the Archbishop's
Palace (about 1580), and so
makes visible the historic
leap in urban scale. In a
Greek squatter settlement,
on the other hand, the
sequence of construction
makes the future visible

Identity and structure are those aspects of form which allow us to recognize and pattern space and time in themselves. Next come those qualities which help us to connect settlement form with other features of our lives. The first level may be called *congruence*: the purely formal match of environmental structure to nonspatial structure. That is, does the abstract form of a place match the abstract form of its functions, or of the features of the society which inhabits it? For example: Are residential buildings family size, if residing is done by families, or do they contain many unrelated families? Is a locality of strong visual character inhabited by a distinct group of strong social character? Are ownership and social dominance matched by visible divisions and dominances in the world of things? Is city form most intense at the peaks of activity? Are big places associated with big groups and main channels with main flows? Is the rhythm of visible activity congruent with the rhythm of social activity, or with the rotation of the earth or the rhythms of the human body? Take one banal example: the large parking lot is an ugly, uncomfortable, often disorienting convenience. It has the deflated meaning of a storage yard; its massed cars are so many empty shells. But the parking space by the house displays the family car, a machine with personality, by which neighbors recognize the presence of its owner.

Congruence is the perceptual ground of a meaningful environment, which in its full sense is a much more complicated subject. Congruence can be tested for by abstracting or diagramming the parts, links, and intensities of a place and seeing how they match up with similar abstractions of the function, economy, society, or natural process of that place. Such tests may be confirmed by asking local people to describe the formal match between place and function.

Transparency or "immediacy" is another relatively simple component of sensibility.* By this I mean the degree to which one can directly perceive the operation of the various technical functions, activities, and social and natural processes that are

*Using "sensibility" in its now obsolete meaning of "capability of being perceived by the senses."

See fig. 55

occurring within the settlement. Can one actually see people at work? hear the waves strike the shore? observe the course of a family argument? see what a truck is carrying or how the sewage drains away? touch what is for sale or see when the parking lot is full? watch the transfers of money and messages? Some of these processes are important, some interesting, some trivial, others abhorrent. They convey a "sense of life" in any settlement, and, with congruence, are the direct perceptual basis for deeper meanings. Functions presented immediately to our senses help us to understand the world. Thus we gain practical competence and maturity. Certain processes are basic, and the ability to sense them is a fundamental satisfaction: for example, the action and movement of persons; the processes of production; the evidence of maintenance, care, and control; group conflict and cooperation; the rearing of children; human affection; birth and dying; the transformations of plants; the motions of the sun. Other processes must be visible to allow us to carry out our normal daily functions. Still others are best left hidden. A common complaint about the modern city is that it is opaque, impersonal, lacking in immediacy. Yet motives of privacy, prudery, and control may urge us to maintain that opacity. The subject can be sensitive, but our culture seems to be shifting toward a greater openness. Transparency can be analyzed by field observation and by asking strangers and residents (including the blind) to describe the processes that are apparent to them as they look at the city, listen to it, touch it, smell it.

The urban environment is a medium of communication, displaying both explicit and implicit symbols. flags, lawns, crosses, signboards, picture windows, orange roofs, spires, columns, gates, rustic fences. These signs inform us about ownership, status, group affiliation, hidden functions, goods and services, proper behavior, and many other things which we find it useful or interesting to know. This is a component of sense that we might call *legibility*: the degree to which the inhabitants of a settlement are able to communicate accurately to each other via its symbolic physical features. These systems of environmental signs are almost entirely

See fig. 56

55 A fisherman mends his nets in a peripheral street of Venice. A basic economic activity is immediately presented to the senses, a rare occurrence in the contemporary city.

56 Citizens converse, using the surfaces of the city. But one must know the symbols to understand the talk.

a social creation and are often unintelligible to the cultural stranger. But they can be analyzed for content, accuracy, and intensity by any familiar observer, and those findings can be confirmed by interviews and photographic simulation tests conducted with the inhabitants of the place. The signage of a place may be rich or lean, accurate or false, important or trivial, open or dominated. It may be *rooted*—that is, located in the same space or time as the activities, persons, or conditions to which it refers—or it may be free-floating and only abstractly related. Environmental form may be manipulated to suppress and control this spatial talk, or to make it freer, less in conflict or more expressive, as well as rooted, accurate, or useful. Environmental forms may be created, or combined in new ways, to elaborate the language and thus to extend our capabilities for spatial communication.

Preziosi

Semiotics, which deals with the structure of meaning in symbolic communication and developed out of studies of language and of cultural anthropology, has recently turned to the meanings of settlements. Out of that effort, we may hope for more precise knowledge of how environmental symbols are employed. For the moment, however, the effort suffers from the difficulties of translating its concepts from the verbal languages—which are pure communication systems and employ separable, sequential symbols—to the environmental language, where neither condition holds.

Rowe

Some contemporary architects, attracted by these fashionable ideas and in flight from previous "functional" theory, are engaged in designs which manipulate applied symbols in a free and eclectic way, meaning by such allusions to deepen the symbolic resonance of their buildings. Under the fond illusion that meaning resides in the object, they play an esoteric game, whose messages may shortly be exhausted or become incomprehensible once the shock is over.

Congruence, transparency, and legibility are components of sense which describe explicit connections of settlement form to nonspatial concepts and values. But there is a deeper level of connection, one much more difficult to specify and measure, which we might call the expressive or symbolic *significance* of a place. To what degree, in the minds of its users, is the form of any settlement a complex symbol of basic values, life processes, historic events, fundamental social structure, or the nature of the universe? This is the holistic meaning of a city, as opposed to the series of meanings conveyed by its separate symbolic elements. At times it may be the backdrop of existence, at other times only a rhetorical reference.

Whether a settlement should be designed to *mean* in this sense is a matter of disagreement. At times this has been the supreme function of a great city. Then it was the first task of a city builder to see that a city was a vivid symbol of his society's conception of itself and of the universe. The Islamic city, for example, was intended and widely understood as an expression of the fundamental religious concepts of that society. At other times, such an attempt has seemed ridiculous. Any deep symbolizing is left to the fancy of the individual, operating on the accidental characteristics of form. Nevertheless, we find that some symbolic connections are always made between a person's environment and her central beliefs. She may choose to focus on the symbols of home, or on those of nation, neighborhood, nature, divinity, history, or the life cycle, but the security and depth of these symbolic associations enrich her life. So I risk a general proposition: a good place is one which, in some way appropriate to the person and her culture, makes her aware of her community, her past, the web of life, and the universe of time and space in which those are contained. These symbols are culture-specific, but also draw on such common life experiences as cold and warm, wet and dry, dark and light, high and low, big and small, living and dead, movement and stillness, care and neglect, clean and unclean, freedom and restraint.

The significance of a place is difficult to specify and varies among persons and cultures. Yet common meanings do exist and are communicated. Inevitably, they are an element of settlement design. One must have an understanding of them, in order to analyze the impact of a place on its people. Standard interviewing devices have been developed to tap these connections, including the

Crane
Jackson
Strauss
Tuan

Bianca 1976

Bachelard

semantic differential, the repertory grid, thematic apperception, story completion, and other techniques which proceed from surface characterizations to underlying structures of meaning: to such dimensions as potency, activity, goodness, and the like. Those techniques which allow respondents to set their own dimensions are the more sensitive ones. They all rely heavily on conventional verbal responses, and, in the search for standardized replication, suffer from a certain shallowness. These meanings may better be explored in extended discussions with inhabitants, or by living with them, or to some extent by empathy. A content analysis of tales, myths, art, and poetry or a study of individual memoirs or photographs are also avenues to understanding.

Identity and structure are the "formal" components of sense. Congruence, transparency, and legibility are specific components which connect environment to other aspects of our lives. All of these can be analyzed in some rather direct and objective way.* Symbolic significance, on the other hand, the deepest level of legibility, can be intuited but is at root elusive.

None of these characteristics, however important, are absolute desiderata—qualities to be maximized. No one would want to live in an infinitely vivid place, where everything is patently connected to everything else. We do not seek an absolute one-to-one correspondence between form and society; we don't wish to live in a goldfish bowl; we would be overwhelmed by a multiplicity of evocative signs. Human cognition has its limits, and the  process of cognition is of greater value than the resulting mental structure. There are pleasures (and there is food for development) in puzzles, ambiguities, and mysteries. We want definable elements rather than defined ones, complex connections, regions remaining to be explored, and some freedom to camouflage. Privacy—the ability to deny information about personal beliefs and actions—is a sensitive issue and a shield against tyranny.

*"Objective," of course, in the sense that the analysis is open to replication and criticism. The material being analyzed is quite properly subjective.

So there are two important qualifications to the ideal of good sense: first, that there are limits at which individuals may wish to deny further knowledge of their affairs, or beyond which the human mind is overloaded, and second, that a settlement should permit an *unfolding* creation of meaning, that is, a simple and patent first order structure which allows a more extensive ordering as it is more fully experienced, and which encourages the construction of new meanings, through which the inhabitant makes the world his own. It is not so clear how this quality of unfoldingness can be measured, or perhaps even identified. How does one evaluate a place in these terms, or determine what degree of unfolding is wanted? How can it be achieved for the great diversity of people who use a modern city? Intuitively, it seems right and important, but it is difficult to specify as a workable measure. Nevertheless, a city which invites ordering is surely better than an orderly city.

Sense is an important functional concern, since the ability to identify things, to time behavior, to find one's way and to read the signs, all are requisites of access and effective action. It is also a basic component of the emotional satisfaction of living in favored places, and for that reason people compete for sensibility. It is bought and sold. It is dealt with explicitly in situations where severe disorientation is likely, or in small places, where builders hope to create or retain characteristics which will attract affluent people. Yet its application is in fact universal. It is a strong support for group identity and cohesion. Its connection to the mental development of the person may well be its most fundamental value, since a city can be a deep and comprehensive education. Creating order is the essence of cognitive development. Sensibility is useful for maintaining the continuity of adult personal identity, and the stable meanings of a culture. Perhaps it is far more useful to the growing child, who is less deeply immersed in abstract verbal notions and more open to the immediate sights and sounds of the world about him. A rich, sensuous world, full of diverse meanings and characterized by an unfolding order, is a fine growing medium, if the child is free to explore it and can at times

Hart

Scruton

withdraw from it into some quiet and protected place. The survival of the species depends on rearing competent children. If we add our concern for the development of fully realized human beings, we have before us our two primary values.

Granted that a highly sensible world may also be an inadaptable one. The structure may be too clear and fixed to be rebuilt easily. New ideas come into focus at fuzzy margins. But if strong sense may interfere with changing something, it can also support its continued usefulness. Roger Scruton comments that since the streets which Pope Sixtus cut through Rome had an esthetic aim as well as a direct functional one, "the journey through them remains satisfactory even in an age without religion."

Sensibility has often been used to impose and maintain some permanent, dominant position, as by building a monumental setting of power, or the religious center of a theocratic state. Yet it may also be effective in pluralistic and dynamic situations, where the image created is one of linked multiplicity and of process rather than stasis. Since we comprehend change only with some difficulty, special devices can emphasize underlying rhythms, express the current drift of transformation, or compress history. Since different people have different strategies of structuring, the visible organization of a settlement should not be closed and unitary. Diverse clues should overlap and penetrate each other, to make a more intricate and redundant network. Making change and plurality comprehensible may well be the most challenging application of sensibility today.

The economic cost of producing a highly sensible settlement can be enormous, as in some monumental cities. The costs are not only those direct ones of construction and maintenance, but also the disabilities that a highly developed formal order may impose on routine functions. At the same time, sense can often be achieved at very small cost, or even at zero additional cost, beyond the time and effort required for thoughtful design. This is especially true when working with modest materials, at the local level, and when the achievement of sensibility is integrated with other ends.

The sense of place is not dependent on high finish, exotic materials, or totalitarian control.

Since sense is a matter of knowledge and attitudes, its indirect political and psychological costs may be high for particular groups. For example, while more often used to maintain social dominance, it can also be employed to extend revolutionary consciousness. It can express values congenial to one group but abhorrent to another. Therefore it will be a battleground, even when its material and functional cost is low. And because it is not often recognized as an explicit value, the battle can be obscure, or seem to be fought on some other terrain. Clearly, one crucial feature of sensibility is the degree to which the image of a place is widely shared.

If it has only infrequently been an explicit issue, nevertheless we have had long experience with the sense of settlements. We can draw on a treasure house of fine historic cities and landscapes, existing and remembered. These examples have been studied frequently, but usually only as isolated visual objects. They are infrequently seen through the eyes of their own inhabitants. While certain famous locales repeatedly draw our attention, we rarely consider the legibility of those ordinary settlements where most people pass their lives. It is particularly unusual to study the image of those large urbanized regions where most citizens of the developed world now reside.

Cullen
Kutcher
Sitte

Since the quality is a join between mind and setting, the means of achieving it naturally divide themselves into two operations: changing city form on the one hand and changing mental conceptions on the other. Designers have focused on the first of these, and the list of devices is lengthy.

One may work to clarify the circulation system as the key to settlement structure by making understandable street patterns, heightening the identity of streets and destinations, making intersections intelligible, or creating vivid spatial sequences along some important path. The baroque avenue was one classic example of this emphasis. Achieving a clear layout of streets in a subdivision is a more recent and modest example.

See figs. 57, 58

Knowles

One may also make districts which have a strong visual identity or endow them with visible boundaries; build active centers of special character; create visible and audible landmarks at strategic points and times; exploit and intensify natural features; or conserve and enhance an existing urban character.

Orienting buildings to the apparent movement of the sun makes the compass directions legible and increases our sense of the structure of time. One may try to make the environment more transparent in the activities it shelters, or more congruent with them. Good maintenance and visible care may be promoted. Community celebrations may be encouraged or sights and sounds be provided which dramatize the time of day or season.

Although there have been frequent attempts to control or suppress the legibility of places, efforts to develop and enhance it are less frequent. While historic conservation is used to make connection with the past, less thought is given to make connection to the future. The perceptual requirements of special groups have yet to be routinely considered: the blind, the deaf, the aged, the retarded, children, those in wheelchairs.

It is also possible to increase sensibility by improving the human ability to perceive the environment, and this is less often thought of by designers trained to focus on things. One may educate users to attend to their environment, to learn more about it, to order it, to grasp its significance. "Environmental education" is just now

Goodey

coming out of the woods and fields to explore the cities we live in. As it does so, it touches on social issues, which make its work more dangerous and more hopeful.

Names, signs, recordings, symbolic codes and other similar devices can increase the level of available information and make the setting more intelligible. By their symbolic manipulations, artists and writers create new environmental meanings and teach us new ways of looking. Paris became more legible after the Impressionists had painted it, and for this generation the scrap metal of a junkyard is no longer shapeless. Dickens helped to create the

57 An accidental visual sequence may have a powerful effect. On a walk through the narrow streets of Córdoba, the space draws one forward as it twists and opens out.

58 A visual sequence meant to be experienced in motion can be explicitly designed. This sketch for an imaginary highway progression deals with its turns, its movement up and down, the opening and closing of adjacent space, the forward views, and the succession of objects that will pass alongside.

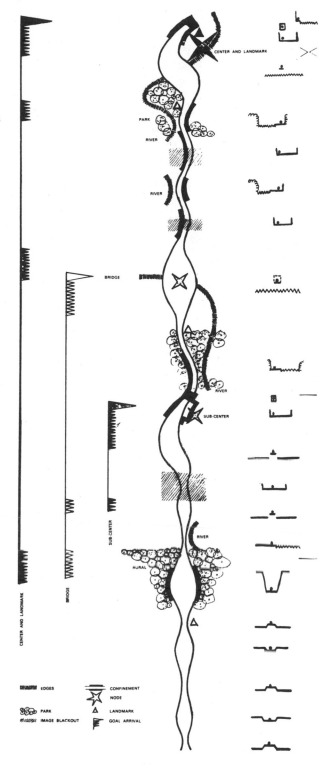

CENTER AND LANDMARK

PARK

RIVER

RIVER

BRIDGE

SUB-CENTER

SUB-CENTER

RIVER

RURAL

CENTER AND LANDMARK

BRIDGE

SUB-CENTER

EDGES

CONFINEMENT

NODE

PARK

LANDMARK

IMAGE BLACKOUT

GOAL ARRIVAL

London we experience as surely as its actual builders did.

Indirectly, sense is affected by the nature of
control and by the fit of form to behavior. Local
ownership tends to strengthen the mental sense of
connection. A good functional match usually
means a more congruent landscape, and often (not
always, by any means) a more transparent, significant, and identifiable one.

In the past, the consideration of sense has been
based solely on an analysis of the physical environment. Concepts such as harmony, beauty, variety,
and order have been thought of as attributes of the
thing itself. Designers have unconsciously relied on
their own implicit values and perceptions, project-
ing them on the physical world as if they were
inherent qualities. Not so—one begins with the
images and priorities of the users of a place and
must look at place and person together.

It could be explicit public policy to increase
certain types of sense for certain groups of people,
measuring achievement by some of the "objective"
tests mentioned above. The sense of one settlement
can be compared with that of another, for a given
group. Policy issues would revolve around the relative importance of sensibility in relation to other
ends, and who stands in most need of it, and what
limits need to be imposed on it. The plurality of
users in any large settlement will always pose technical problems. Thus sensibility will be easier to
attain in more stable and homogeneous societies.
It is likely to be important both in rich and poor settlements, since human perception is a constant, but
the means for achieving it will differ. There is
always a danger that sense will be used as a device
to gain dominance or to fix the status quo. But this
is not inherent in the quality, and perhaps the most
interesting questions of design have to do with
achieving sensibility in societies which are plural,
dynamic, and relatively egalitarian. Identity, structure, congruence, transparency, and legibility are
aspects of sense which we can analyze explicitly.
The qualities of significance and of unfoldingness
remain to puzzle us.

9 Fit

The fit of a settlement refers to how well its spatial and temporal pattern matches the customary behavior of its inhabitants. It is the match between action and form in its behavior settings and behavior circuits. So we may ask if a factory building, the machines within it, and the way those spaces and objects are put to use are a good system for achieving the production to which it is devoted. How smoothly do work actions and work objects fit together? From the viewpoint of management, this will be mirrored in productive efficiency—from the standpoint of labor, in feelings of well-working. Similarly, one asks if a classroom is a good teaching place, or if a new stadium is a first-class device for putting on a football spectacle. The personal correlate of fit is the sense of *competence*—the ability to do something well, to be adequate or sufficient.

Fit is linked to characteristics of the human body and of physical systems in general (gravity, inertia, the propagation of light, size relations, etc.). This context is universal. But since fit is the match between place and whole patterns of behavior, so it is intimately dependent on culture: on expectations, norms, and customary ways of doing things.

Places are modified to fit ways of behaving, and behaviors are changed to fit a given place. Fishermen learn to deal with the sea, even if fishermen from different cultures deal with it in different ways. The modification of action has been most striking in the case of games, where behavior is plastic. Court tennis is a game which evolved from the arbitrary characteristics of a particular room. Step ball is a creature of the city stoop.

Suburban housing is matched to affluent, middle-class, North American adults and unsuitable for poor Navajos just in from remote sheep pastures. The newly housed Navajo will begin to change the suburban house and his way of living in it to increase the fit. But the misfit will persist, and he will be discontented. In contrast to a measure such as vitality, it is not possible to evaluate fit if one is ignorant of the culture of the occupants, although it is possible to see the evidence of mismatch without perceiving the cause. The archaeologist suffers from the same dilemma in a more acute form. He looks at the remains of an ancient city and wonders: "How did it work?"

The term fit is loosely related to such common words as comfort, satisfaction, and efficiency. These words shift in meaning as expectations shift. Moreover, a comfortable place may also be an unhealthy one. Like health, fit is easier to identify in its absence. Mismatch is relatively easy to spot. One takes less note of places that work well. Nevertheless, a superb match of place and action—a well-tuned instrument expertly played in a fine hall, a skilled sailor in a good boat—conveys an exhilarating sense of competence. Good training and good thing-making are both required to attain it.

Much of the bread and butter of city design and management deals with fit, if at levels far below those heights, and aiming to satisfy no more than overt, current ways of behaving. This is referred to as the "functional aspect" of some design, as though one could distinguish it from some other qualities of form which are not functional.

Simple quantitative adequacy is the elementary aspect of fit. Is there enough housing of standard quality? a sufficiency of playgrounds? room enough for the factories that will be built? Unfortunately, the qualitative basis of these numbers is often neglected. We forget that the number of available dwelling units depends on our definition of standard quality, the adequacy of the industrial zone on the type of factory process assumed, and the count of playground space on a view about play and how dense it can be.

Chapin 1979

We are attracted to numerical data, which are so much more precise, firm, and impressive than the soft, subjective stuff of patterns and feelings. The numbers that stand for traffic congestion outweigh the frustrations of pedestrians who cross the street. The square foot requirements of a room (itself distantly derived from feelings of adequate size) override the characteristics of patterns for easy social intercourse. Planners will strain to increase the quantity of open space and forget to monitor its

Lerup 1972
Perin 1970
Whyte 1980

See fig. 59

quality. The amount of something is one of its important characteristics (and there can be too much of it, as in the case of public plazas too large to seem active and inviting). But the key test is the behavioral fit.

There are two ways of observing that fit. The first is to watch people acting in a place, in order to see how well overt actions match the characteristics of a location. Is movement hindered? Can people easily carry out the actions they attempt, such as lifting something, opening a door, or talking to another? How many apparent misfits can be seen: hesitation, stumbling, blockage, embarrassment, accident, evident discomfort?* Is there congestion, or, on the other hand, a lack of use? Are there incongruities of use and form: abandoned autos on a front lawn, or worn dirt paths which short circuit the paved walk system?

Note that most of these questions deal with problems rather than with benefits. Yet the overt clues to discomfort may be slight and fleeting: a momentary check, a frown, a sigh. The observer must be quick and have an empathy for the values and life experiences of those he is watching. To that degree, these cannot be neutral, "factual" observations; already they are interpretations. But they can be documented by photographs or audial recordings so that other observers can verify that interpretation.

The second method is to ask to users themselves, whose sense of the appropriateness of a place is the final measure of its fit. They can be asked for a judgment: how well does the place work for what you try to do in it? what problems and difficulties do you encounter there? More concretely, they can be asked to recall what they did in a place yesterday and what troubles arose then. Indirectly, if they are hesitant to expose themselves, the question can become: what problems do other people meet with here? Or (but this is less reliable), what would you like to do there, that you cannot do now?

Fit deals with place and actual behavior, or, at most, behavior consciously desired. Unconscious

*Here is a new measure for the quantity-minded: "observed misfits per person-hour"!

needs are slippery, unless a firm link to health can be demonstrated. Even conscious desire is a poor predictor of future satisfaction, unless the person has had past experience with the wanted fit.

Systematic studies are made of environmental preferences, expressed in the abstract, or in reference to simulations, such as photographs. Correlations of these preferences with environmental, personality, or social characteristics are being investigated. In our culture, some common feelings have emerged, such as an attraction to parklike landscapes and to small towns. But there are bewildering complications. These preferences are the complex product of numerous personal and physical factors, in which the symbolic significance of a place may override its actual fit. The causal links are poorly explained. Building theories about the stable value dimensions of the environment is a prerequisite to building theories about preference. For the moment, the methods of preference investigation are more useful than any general findings. Where preference is based on imagination or common report, rather than on personal experience, it is unreliable. The most telling methods are those that deal with immediate experience. The firmest ground is the here and now, place and the actual action in it, the round of repeated daily behavior, the common ground of experience.

One should test any proposed new form to see if it is adequate for the actions likely to take place in it: working, resting, eating, loving, dying, teaching, curing, storing, exchanging, communicating, reading, running. The "program" for a structure or settlement is properly the set of desired behaviors and the spatial qualities appropriate to them, rather than a statement of quantities of space by type. The plan may then be evaluated by imagining the programmed behavior and predicting the fit. Once the settlement is built, the same test can be applied in reality, in order to confirm or deny the prediction, and so to improve subsequent predictions.

This is all very rational. Alas, the programmed behavior may never take place. What is more certain, it will change in the near future. A program should focus on general and predictable behaviors,

Michelson

See fig. 60

Hack

See fig. 61

59 A visible misfit. The bench at the base of Boston's Public Library is a favorite spot in which to sit and sun. It is handsomely proportioned to the facade above, but not to the human frame.

60 A typical "preferred landscape" which is elicited in interviews. It is parklike, and features water, trees, and hills. This is the Mount Auburn Cemetery in Cambridge, Massachusetts, a forerunner of the park movement in the United States.

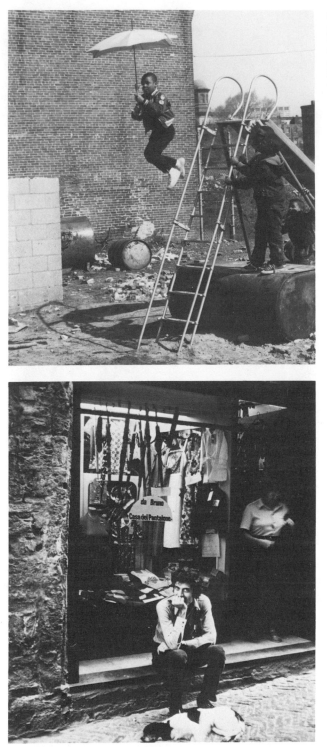

61 Umbrellas become parachutes and stone sills become seats: the environment and its objects may be used in ways that had never occurred to their builders.

such as movement or social intercourse, rather than on the fine details of action. Behavioral flexibility becomes an attractive feature in any new place (with all *its* puzzles, as will be discussed below).

Moreover, these programmatic devices overplay the behavioral side, since they assume that action is given, while space is the dependent, responding variable. But action also adapts to space. Programs might emphasize a mutual accommodation of place and action. They could include the training and the management needed to make a designed place work well. They could be concerned with that ongoing process of fitting which will commence once the place is occupied. Indeed, since human behavior is so very variable, one might argue that fit is an inconsequential issue. Given spaces of sufficient quantity, which are adaptable, substantially made, and matched to such basic human requirements as warmth, light, dryness, access, and body scale, then in a reasonable time a good fit will appear. Action and place will have adjusted to each other. People can accommodate to almost anything in the normal range of physical environments.

Unfortunately for this simple answer, the process of adaptation is costly and sometimes painful. It requires time to accomplish. Once achieved, an apparent fit may conceal continuing difficulties, invisible to the casual observer, but real enough for those who deal with them.

Space suggests action as well as constraining it. Discontents and mismatches appear in existing places which were once acceptable, because expectations have changed in response to possibilities opened up by new places elsewhere. A new kitchen in one house devalues the old one in another; the recently-acquired telephone creates a sense of isolation for those who do not have one. A new game on a new field enlarges the range of competence in its players. People play with things and find new uses in them. Fit is not a rigid link between action and place. Happily, the latter does not determine the former, nor can the former mechanically be translated into specifications for the latter. Fit is loose; it has turning room; it is subject to creative surprises. Environmental programs should therefore also be concerned with inventing *new* behavior settings, innovations in behavior and setting working together.

It is obvious that places should be fitted to what we want to do, and so our discussion began. Now we stumble over some ethical issues, like old stones in our path. How *should* we act in the world? To whose actions should the fit be made? Shall we consider whether our places should be fitted to the actions of other species as well as our own, or whether we should act differently toward these others or toward ourselves? But let us bury those stones and agree that fit is the match between place and the overt or intended behavior of present human users. It is created by the adjustment of either place or action or both and can be achieved by creating new behaviors in new places.

Customary behavior has inertia and can override the characteristics of a new place. At the same time, places are relatively slow to change, and, if well matched, will reinforce customary behavior. Enduring place stabilizes our expectations of action and so reduces uncertainty and conflict. It tells us how to behave, just as culture does. We hush in a church and sprawl on a beach. The *stability* of behavior settings is thus an element in the goodness of their fit.

"Does this place work well?" is a common-sense question. The response tends to be superficial, particularly at larger scales. For convenience in thinking about a myriad of places and activities, they are classified into stereotypical groups, in which physical form and human behavior are fused Shapiro in such a way that it is quite difficult to analyze the fit and difficult to think about rehousing the one or reusing the other. "Single-family housing" is a type of structure in a typical context occupied by a standard social unit living in a normal way. The actual diversity of the family unit, its way of living, or its spatial configuration cannot be seen on the land use map. Creating new forms and behaviors is difficult, since expectations and regulations are categorized by these same mental fissures. Standards are developed for these typical settings, and the analysis of fit becomes a matching against standards. "Does

Perin 1977

Barker

Girouard

it work?" dwindles to "is the side yard large enough?" or "is it occupied by more than one family, related by blood and marriage?" The analytical convenience of classification becomes a way of seeing the world and then a moral. People *ought* to live in single-family houses in a single-family way, separated in space and time from other kinds of behavior settings.

Evaluating large, complex wholes is impossible without classes and standards. But in describing a class it is important to maintain the distinction between form and behavior in order to judge how well they are integrated. The complete analysis of a settlement would entail its decomposition into the mosaic of all its behavior settings—that is, those locations where spatial form and behavior are repeatedly associated—followed by a grouping of those settings into classes of similar associations. Roger Barker described a small town in Iowa in this way. The description is tedious, and yet it evokes the character of that town as no land use map or statistical summary could ever do. Once having built a classified mosaic, one could then test the fit of a representative sample of its parts.

For a large city, this would be an overwhelming task. In place of such an elephantine approach, one must choose a few settings which, in that culture, are felt to be typical, important, and problematic. In our urban world, we might choose some characteristic settings for family life (suburb, tenement), some common work and goods distribution environments (office, factory, supermarket), some familiar scenes of commutation (bus trip, driving on an arterial), some haunts of children (school, street corner, vacant lot), and some places of illness, age, and dying (hospital, nursing home). Observation and interview in these selected places, plus use of the substantial literature already available on behavior in these localities, will furnish a good initial view of the quality of a city. The questions are: "Is there a good fit here between behavior and form?", and "Is this match sufficiently stable and in accord with the expectations of participants?" Studies could include the design and management of these prototypical settings. The analysis of prototype is a powerful way of understanding complicated phenomena. The creation of a prototype is a powerful way of influencing them.

While it proves difficult to build firm generalizations about the interrelation of form and behavior because of the wily plasticity of the human being, the methods of observing place behavior are blossoming, notably in environmental psychology. A settlement manager may fail to find general predictions that will illuminate her problem, but at least she can find ways of learning about her particular case. The methods were mostly developed in studies of houses, schools, and hospitals, but they are general methods. Indeed, our concern for the fit of settings has been too narrowly focused. Relatively little work has been done on the workplace, the sidewalk, the bus ride, or the vacant lot, to name a few.

Analysis is complicated, particularly in public places, by the conflicting intentions of different actors. A plaza may be a delight for tourists and a frustration for the locals. A playground may provide for the competitive games of adolescents and not for the imaginary adventures of younger children. Public spaces and most semiprivate ones are occupied by different people doing different things. Analysis must deal with this variation. Design must provide for overlapping territories, shifting use, and rules of tolerance.

Many settings deliberately favor some dominant group. Imperial cities, financial districts, and other power centers are laid out that way. Analysis will uncover this; design is unlikely to cure it. There may also be conflicts between legitimate and illegitimate behavior. As isolated nighttime place may be well-matched to criminal activity, for example.

Since fit is specific to activity and culture, forms universally conducive to it could hardly be found. Perhaps the only general formal device is that of compartmenting: the division of an area into many smaller settings, so that different behaviors may flourish without conflict in settings proper to themselves. These specialized settings must be protected from one another, but not be so sharply or so completely divided that they are not in some mutual communication. Transitions and overlaps help people to learn from one another. Ambiguity

See fig. 62

Browne

See fig. 64

at the edge—some permeability of the membrane—is needed so that a person can move at will from one setting to another, or linger while deciding to do so. Doorways, stoops, and the margins of activity areas are sensitive and necessary places.

Activity schedules may also be manipulated in order to compartment behavior in time. By custom or deliberate arrangement, an open square will serve in sequence as a transport terminal, a vegetable market, a children's playground, and an adult meeting place. Like the spatial edges, the time boundaries are important elements. Scheduling may reduce peak loads and so increase the quantitative match of facilities to use. The infamous "hot beds" of the slums, in which immigrants slept in rotation, are one example; the staggering of work hours to even out the demand for space on the roads is another, more palatable, one. Many of our physical facilities are congested while in use, and yet are grossly underused. Here is an obvious opportunity for increasing fit without increasing cost.

The most useful devices for increasing fit have more to do with generalities of process than with generalities of form. Careful programming is the heart of it—a formulation of the behaviors and spatial characters that are desired, considered as an integrated whole. Programming should be the first step in the design of any new place and the first in managing any old one: "How does what we want to happen here compare to what is actually happening?" Once explicitly formulated, the program is not only a guide to management and design, but also a plan for the repeated testing of the place, to see how well it is performing.

Repeated monitoring of the function of a place, based on a hypothesis of how the place is intended to be used, allows that continuous fine tuning which is the secret of good match. Even in an alien culture, we are quick to notice that evidence of care and attention which is the sign of well-functioning. A landsman will remark on a well-kept ship and a visitor note a tidy community. Monitoring and tuning can be elaborate procedures carried out by a central bureaucracy or the simple, half-conscious attentiveness of a resident owner.

62 The chain of central squares in St. Petersburg (now Leningrad), after their reconstruction in 1840. The superhuman scale was designed to display power.

63 Any transition, especially a doorway, is a place to linger and talk. One can be in two domains at once, able to enter either one at will.

64 The evidence of care for a place is immediately apparent, as in the front yard of this cottage in the Camp Meeting Ground, Oak Bluffs, Massachusetts.

Fit may be increased by changing behavior to fit place, as well as vice versa. People "get used" to a place, or "learn to like it." They can also be trained to use or appreciate it. One of the side effects of the contemporary effort at environmental education has been to show people how to exploit a forest or a city more successfully. Designers neglect the opportunity to demonstrate to future users how they might act in a new place. They assume that behavioral fit will be automatic and immediate, if only the form is right. New behavior does develop, but it can also be guided and opened up, without coercion. Inventing and communicating new forms of place behavior can be as creative an act as inventing and building new physical forms. Fit can increase most dramatically when place and action develop in tandem. A family might rehabilitate its housing and reshape the way its own members relate to one another, in a simultaneous process. Discussing the redesign of the house is an exploration of family behavior. A new cult, as another example, creates its setting and its ritual concurrently.

A case could be made for deliberate experiments. Volunteers might conduct extended try-outs of some setting in which place and action have been modified in an explicit way: a new mode of living and working underground; a communal family life in a house and grounds designed for the purpose; a new way to organize factory work or to ride a bus, with workshop or vehicle to suit; a new form of dense, inner-city living; a new way of rural life with limited resources. As the test progressed, these experimental settings would be tuned and managed by the volunteer subjects themselves. If successful, the setting could be tried out by others in order to communicate the new possibility. If we had an explicit method of inventing and testing behavior settings, we might acquire many such possibilities. Sporadic trials of this kind, spurred by faith or necessity, have been made and abandoned. They have never been planned and monitored as experiments from which others could learn.

Perhaps the most powerful way of improving the fit of our environment, however, is to put the control of it into the hands of its immediate users,

See fig. 65

See fig. 66

Boudon
Fairbrother

who have the stake and the knowledge to make it function well. We look forward here to one of our dimensions to come. If users are in control, rather than some remote owner, and if the setting is sufficiently flexible for them to reshape it to their requirements, then a good match is more likely.

I have discussed fit as a present phenomenon and yet most city buildings other than houses are being used in ways for which they were not originally designed. Even the continuous residential use of an old house, stabilized as it is by the persistence of the human family, changes in many ways, since the family is not the original family, or it has multiplied, or at least it has grown old. Actions change: the physical setting persists. This lag gives our lives a semblance of stability, but misfits are a natural consequence. We expend our energies reshaping the structure which has been handed down to us, or we reshape our actions.

The great defensive walls of the old cities encumbered the land for generations after they had lost their protective power. Since they strangled the communications between center and periphery, they were finally dismantled at great cost. Once down, however, they released the space for fine boulevards and parks. Our elevated expressways may soon be even more cumbersome, and as difficult to remove. Will they leave as useful a trace? Old factory areas typically decline to partial abandonment and marginal use—not because workers and management wear out, but because the old structures and roads become obsolete. It is less costly to move to an untouched site than it is to rebuild.

The merchants and builders of Boston struggled for half a century to connect their seaport with the terminals of the continental railroads through the physical chaos of the old center. Their failure contributed to the shift of economic dominance to New York. Of course, when cities slow down, it is not due to physical obsolescence alone; other factors, such as shifts in markets, supplies, skills, or capital, are likely to be more critical. But physical obsolescence and the psychological attitudes that accompany it play their role. The condition of old productive plants in the northeastern United States

65 An old form adapted to a new use: the Back Bay fire station in Boston becomes a museum of contemporary art.

66 Model of "Motopia," an ideal city by G. A. Jellicoe, in which traffic and parking occupy the roofs and the ground is devoted to parks. But since the buildings take their form from the roads, how can the town be rebuilt, once it is discovered that traffic circles do not work?

has surely reinforced the present shift toward the "sunbelt."

The loses of obsolescence cannot simply be reckoned as the costs of rebuilding, or even the difficulties endured by those left behind. They may also include the exhaustion of resources which cannot be replaced: space, pure water, soil, energy, building materials. Science fiction is crammed with gloomy references to a future running down of the globe. At the same time, planners are well aware of the difficulties of accurate prediction, even in the medium run, and of the (fortunate!) improbability of their control of the future. Thinking of the incessant changes that will assault their designs, they pray that they will be flexible and so continue in use. Flexibility, then, is a frequent slogan in planning—a way of dealing with uncertainty and a way of placating the future generations. It seems obvious, if we want to survive in a changing world, but also if we wish to repair our frequent mistakes or accommodate our more frequent changes of heart, that a good settlement should be an adaptable one. A flexible world is one which is open to development.

Lynch 1964

However frequently flexibility is invoked, its meaning remains unclear. No one knows quite how to attain it. It differs from the other dimensions in that we have very little evidence about achieving it. Some thought has been given to the adaptability of hospitals and to rates of obsolescence in such things as automobiles and telephone poles. There is a new literature on the aftermath of environmental disaster. But the cause and cure of urban obsolescence is mostly hearsay and the invocation of adaptability primarily decorative.

Cowan 1963

A well-adapted place is one in which function and form are well fitted to each other. This may be achieved by adaptation of the place to the activity, or vice versa, and also by a mutual adaptation. In discussing future fit, however, I speak primarily about the first—the ability of a place to be adapted easily to some future change in function. Clearly, adaptability in the more general sense is also achieved by the presence of adaptable persons, and often more easily and effectively.

We think of things that have survived for a
long time in active use under changing conditions as being admirable. The Roman street grid still functions at the center of many European towns. There are agricultural areas in France that have See fig. 11 been farmed for more than a millennium. The layout of New York City was planned to allow flexible shifts of activity, and so it has. The regular connections and modular spaces of the main buildings at the Massachusetts Institute of Technology permit an ever-changing pattern of offices, laboratories and classrooms, just as they were designed to do, even if the change must be accompanied by construction noise and academic politicking. But what is the value of these survivals? A contribution to sensibility certainly, if the physical survival makes us aware of our past. What else?

Other than as a landmark of the past, a survival has value only if it is a present resource which cannot be duplicated at less than the cost of its present maintenance, that is, if its survival and adaptation allow people to do what they wish to do at less cost than its demise would permit. Otherwise, the survival of things might mean no more than a growing dominance of activity by its setting. The true question is whether the cost of bringing the fit to an acceptable standard by adapting an old setting to some new use is lower than either making a new setting, or adapting the use to the old setting as it stands. An environment in which things do not survive but are rapidly replaced by new forms may in fact be a highly adaptable one.

The society and the territory of the United States have been highly adaptable in this particular way. The size of the land and the nature of its ownership, as well as the outlook of society and the institutions of a capitalist economy, have encouraged a fluid migration of labor and capital, a rapid consumption of things, and social approval for the ability to meet new situations quickly. A substantial human price has been paid for this mobility, however, including the rupture of social ties and a loss of reference to time past. Resources have been depleted, and this may presage a loss of long-run adaptability. But short-range adaptability has been achieved.

Callahan

The costs inherent in adaptability and its relations to other environmental values can be discussed only after we are clear about what we mean by it. Maintaining a sense of place and past (which is an aspect of sensibility), or maintaining social ties, are values which are quite often in conflict with adaptability. But not necessarily so, as we will try to unravel.

When we speak of adaptability to future change, what future do we mean? Whose future is one question: the general who can shift standardized regiments easily, as the battle develops, or the foot soldier who is caught in an inescapable round of discomfort and fear? Are we concerned with the near future, in which adaptability may be the ability to cut trees at will, or the longer future, in which the life chances of future residents may be restricted by deforested land? How far into the future do we care? It seems right to think about tomorrow, next year, and our children, or even our grandchildren. Some people concern themselves about water supplies or the supply of farmland a hundred years from now. But the difficulties of predicting far future events and of imagining the interests of future people multiply at such a rate that remote anxieties of this kind must narrow down to avoiding actions that would probably endanger the survival of the species: issues of vitality rather than of the other dimensions, since it is the vital requirements that are most stable and general. Even at that, no one worries in any effective way about the coming demise of the sun, although we can be sure that that worry will come. Since our species will then already be extinct, the issue is obscure.

Our culture (and particularly our middle-class culture) is future-anxious. Other cultures, living more completely in the past or present, or with different views of coming events, may be unimpressed by our anxieties and our tenderness for flexibility. They live as they always have, or they foresee an apocalypse. Indeed we always live in the present, not in the past or future. Our memories and anticipations are part of the present. Yet no human being, other than an ill or incompetent one, is completely mindless of the future. Survival and the actions necessary to meet anticipated need are built into the species. Adaptability is a concern for all cultures. But the span of concern depends on cultural values and knowledge.

Degrees of adaptability might be measured as the reciprocal of the future cost, discounted to the present, of adapting the spatial system of form and activity to possible future function. Alas, this is an impossible measure—impossible, that is, unless we can specify what costs we speak of, to whom, and what functions we mean, and when, and what level of future performance we require. I can make a guess about how many dollars it may cost the owner of a movie theater, five years from now, to convert his building into a concert hall which is the equal of the one down the street. This is a limited measure of his theater's present adaptability. But it neglects the costs to movie-goers. And what if a concert hall isn't what is wanted five years from now? How much more difficult this calculation becomes for an entire settlement, and all its inhabitants!

There is a circularity between adaptability and prediction. If prediction is very good, then adaptability is rather trivial, since it is reduced to the relatively simple technical feat of planning for some present use, to be superseded at a known time by another known use. Yet if prediction is poor, then how can adaptability be measured, since one is ignorant of what one is likely to have to adapt to?

So this proposed measure is most useful in special situations of partial foreknowledge, such as knowing the limited set of replacement activities that are likely. A place or a plan can then be analyzed to estimate the discounted cost of those predicted adjustments. For example, we may ask of a planned housing development: Could a specified increase in the number of families of decreased average family size be housed there, ten years from now, and what would be the cost of this to whom? The calculation hangs on this prediction of demographic change, and the answer will be limited in scope and time. The answers will be multiple, if there are different actors or different probabilities to consider. It could be refined by weighting the answers by the relative probabilities of change or the relative importance of the actors, but now we are climbing the beanstalk to a methodological heaven. The measure may be useful in special cases, where knowledge and control are extensive, for example, in planning for the physical setting of a sophisticated medical institution. It is less likely to be generally useful, particularly in view of our known incompetencies at prediction.

We live in the present forever, and measures which require extended foreknowledge are difficult to apply. But we are also aware that change is forever. We have survived by virtue of our ability to respond creatively to change as it occurs. On that account, we want an environment that leaves us free to act and whose development will not lead us into some irreversible dead end. We may therefore reformulate adaptability into two more modest measures:

The first is *manipulability*: the extent to which a behavior setting can presently be changed in its use or form, in an easy and incremental fashion, and whether that ability to respond is likely to be maintained in the predictable near future. Thus one might set arbitrary limits of time, cost, and political power, and ask what degree of change could be effected under those limits and whether that degree of change is likely to decrease or increase as successive changes are made. To what extent can a moderate-income family modify its dwelling within a year, in ways that are likely to be of interest to it (such as by expansion, room rearrangement, modified access, or a new external finish, on the one hand, or by relocating the eating place, and shifting room assignments, on the other), when we compare a small apartment with a large, free-standing house? Will that advantage of manipulability subside, as the family continues to tinker?

While particularly important as a criterion for the maneuvering room of small groups, manipulability can also be a concern of larger, more powerful institutions. They will ask the same basic question: how much change can we now effect in a brief time, at moderate cost, and will such change reduce the openness for the next round of change?

Here we have a general criterion, measurable in the present, which speaks to the fact that a creative response to change is the ultimate guarantee of survival. It also measures the present openness of a setting to its inhabitants, and so, indirectly, it is a measure of their control over it. High manipulability presumably would result in a better present fit, since fitting is more easily accomplished. A manipulable environment is also one that increases opportunities for learning by doing, and this in itself increases creativity and control.

But the permitted manipulations should not make later manipulations more difficult. An "open plan" may only allow first comers to establish their chosen boundaries. "Floating zones" in planning go aground with the first developer. The danger of incremental muddling through is not that it is inefficient but that it might lead to some muddle without escape. A steady maintenance of environmental responsiveness is desirable.

Thus the second restricted measure of adaptability is concerned with the avoidance of future dead ends, and might be called *reversibility*, or, less clumsily, *resilience*. If past moves into future through a net of diverging possibilities, then if one can retrace the net to an earlier state, one has another chance to undo a mistake (or even to repeat it, if one wishes). Thus we may ask of some feature: what is the cost of undoing it?

Cowan 1969

There is no beginning, and nothing is completely reversible. Time's arrow flies in one direction. Places carry the scars of every recycling, however efficient. But approximations are possible. We could estimate the cost of removing an office district and of restoring the topsoil, forest cover, and native fauna of its original site. This would be a gauge of the costs imposed when such offices, once developed, closed other pathways into the future. One need not calculate the cost of return to some mythical pure beginning, but only to some relatively unoccupied and ecologically stable state which is similar to that state with which urban development began there. That earlier state may well be less desirable in human terms than the present one. We are only judging the cost of the rollback. The Acropolis as it was before Athens is hardly preferable to its present glory, ruined and encumbered as that present state may be.

It is also possible that a previous state may be more restricted than the present one or than some intermediate condition. A rocky swamp, once drained and leveled (but not yet built upon), may present more opportunities for human use at little cost than did the earlier state. An "original" condition which is assumed for an estimation of reversibility must be chosen with care. It should be stable, so that it can be held in reserve at low cost, and also be a form that permits many alternatives of new development.

Reversibility could be an interesting measure of a city. We might find, for example, that the maligned low-density suburb, which is regularly accused of "eating up" the farmlands about a city, is rather easily reversible. Even the airfields of World War II in Great Britain have successfully been restored to farm use. In contrast, modifications of topography and water pattern, the erosion of soil, wastes laid down in the earth, or the accelerated eutrophication of lakes will be far less reversible. It could be enlightening to announce the cost of demolishing a new skyscraper along with the cost of its construction, or to introduce the cost of eventually restoring a park, once it has been taken for a highway, into the debate about permitting the highway taking in the first place. What would be the cost of undoing a new settlement, or a pedestrian mall, or the reuse of some historic building, should they prove mistaken?

But it would only be a curiosity to compute the cost of returning Boston's Back Bay to the old tidal swamp, including the costs of relocating its present population. The cost of refilling a mine with coal would be astronomical and of no interest, since no additional future branchings are allowed by the refilling. The repacked coal could only be used again, while the empty mine might have alternative uses. On the other hand, computing the cost of restoring the disturbed ground surface of a surface mine is a useful calculation.

Reversibility may be more deeply affected by institutional rigidities—such as a fragmentation of ownership—than by the physical pattern itself. Buildings come and go, but patterns of lots and access are persistent. Lands which have doubtful title or belong to an absentee owner may block a rollback far more effectively than rocks or ruins.

A particular and practically important type of reversibility comes into play after a disaster. Here we are concerned with what it would cost to bring a settlement back, not to some undeveloped state, but to its normal form and level of performance, after some severe disruption such as earthquake, fire, attack, plague, or flood. Structures are often tested for their ability to resist such dangers, but less thought has been given to the conditions at city scale which are favorable to recovery. Calculations of this kind might be useful in civil defense planning. Development could be discouraged that would make future recovery difficult. However, recovery seems to depend primarily on three actions: rescuing the human resources, distributing fresh material resources quickly, and establishing a clear reconstruction plan rapidly. Reversibility of this kind may therefore have more to do with the social system, with the planning process, and with abundant access than with other physical elements of settlement. Creative, future-oriented action is a human ability and not an environmental one. But it may be supported by good access and indirectly by manipulability, if the latter encourages a taste for the creative act.

Manipulability and resilience are dimensions, not absolutes. No one wants an infinitely manipulable world, nor a completely reversible one. Sometimes we seek to fix the future or to prevent a return, as when the Romans sowed the site of Carthage with salt. A totally adaptable environment, in which each person could surround himself on the instant and without effort with the setting of his choice, would be a fairy-tale nightmare. Place would be meaningless and the pattern of life dissolve in conflict and chaos. The stability and resistance of the large-scale physical environment may be one of its chief assets, as I have noted above. An adaptable place can be a characterless and disorienting one. Think of the "all-purpose" room or the reserve spaces of an industrial district. The conflict between adaptability and the stable meaning of place is an inherent conflict. So any desire for increased manipulation must be limited at least by two qualifications: never so easy as to threaten psychological continuity or so broad of range as to unleash unmanageable social conflicts.

The devices of adaptability must deal with these tensions. One may compensate for the psychological ambiguities of a shifting landscape by establishing fixed symbolic landmarks. One may reduce future choices to a small number in order to ease the future decision process. The stability and the manipulability of present fit can be mutually reconciled in concrete cases. Yet in the abstract they bicker.

People have different tolerances for change. Some are hungry for novelty and delight in being at the forward edge of any new wave. Others are desperate for tranquillity and old custom. In complex and heterogeneous settlements, planning could make it possible for people to sort themselves out by such preferences. Some areas might be highly adaptable places where experimental forms and ways of life were applauded. Others might be traditional, fixed in form. In the latter, new techniques or customs might be prohibited until thoroughly tested elsewhere, perhaps even until no one who had ever been unfamiliar with them was left alive. Beyond the basic manipulability and reversibility needed to insure survival of the whole community, such "time zoning" would provide a range of adaptabilities, a choice between the archaic and the zany.

People can be trained to use the adaptability of their environment and to be comfortable with it. Our ways of thinking and perceiving incline us to see things as unchanging until they undergo some abrupt and dramatic shift. The old house is just as it always was, and then suddenly it goes to ruin. We often dramatize a gradual change by some ceremony that seems to condense it into one pivotal shift: we lay cornerstones, conduct initiations, and hold grand openings. Slow drifts make us uneasy, but this unease can be dealt with, not merely by the illusory devices of physical stability, but also by training people to perceive the change that encompasses them. Change has its own constancies—of direction and rate, of the mode of transition, of history. If one grasps those constancies, then meaning and stability can be preserved, even as the river flows. What's more, designers might strive to make those constancies more legible in the environment, without incurring any sacrifice of adaptability.

Although adaptability has rarely been analyzed carefully, we have a little anecdotal evidence about some ways of providing it. Some of these means are a matter of settlement form, others of activity pattern, and others have to do with how form and activity are managed.

One formal means is to provide excess capacity: a framework strong enough to take extra stories on top of a structure, the provision of extra space to grow in, or sewers large enough to handle population growth. Many older houses of the well-to-do are easy to convert because they have excess space in halls, stairs, and rooms—the "loose fit" of the current vogue for flexibility. It is not difficult to add a room to a house on a large lot or even to build a second house in the rear. Similarly, new houses are built with expansion space in the attic. Materials can be stockpiled for an uncertain future, just as we are now pouring oil into underground caverns at substantial cost. The street right-of-way can be made broad enough for some future highway. The settlement may be laid out as a "growth form," that is, as a linear pattern, a star, or a checkerboard, all of which provide growth room close to every previously developed point.

There are several difficulties in applying this common means. One is the sheer cost of providing and maintaining the unused resources. The technique is most effective when the excess is of a kind that is cheap to supply initially and which requires no care while it is being held for use. Building a scattered town, or a bridge strong enough to take twice the traffic, can be very expensive, and the increased population or traffic may never come. It is more sensible to leave room for a second bridgehead or a second town. Reserving alternate vacant lots or wide rights-of-way can incur serious costs in the name of an uncertain future: present costs of extended utility lines, extra maintenance, and a loss of spatial cohesion. There have even been paradoxical cases in which the reservation of space for future

Lynch 1958

See fig. 67

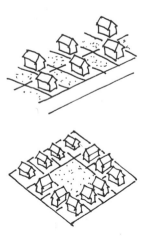

See fig. 68

growth so scattered a settlement that future growth was discouraged. Leaving unserviced open space in the centers of large blocks which are developed on their margins, on the other hand, is a clever idea, since that space is cheap to begin with and need not be serviced or patrolled until needed.

Secondly, excess capacity is likely to fill up as its flexibility is exploited. The rear lots are built upon, the stockpiles consumed, the extra stories added. The adaptability has been real but temporary. Certain strategies avoid this "silting up" by providing for a continuous replacement of the excess capacity. One classic example is the Shinto temple at Ise, Japan, where there are two temple sites, and the old one is cleared each time the new one is built upon (although in this case the flexible process is used to preserve a traditional form). An analogous urban device would be to allow the building of new structures in rear lots along an interior street right-of-way, provided that front-lot structures were then razed and the previous street lots were in their turn returned to interior reserve space. The revolving fund in finance is a similar model for retaining surplus capacity. It is rarely imitated in spatial design, apart from the long-range, uncontrolled processes of decay, abandonment, return to waste, and eventual reuse.

Excess space also results in perceived ambiguity and formlessness. The vacant lots of a development which is only partially complete are depressing. Once more, concentration of the unused excess, and its removal from direct view, is one solution to this psychological difficulty.

Another prime means of increasing adaptability is to improve access, thickening and extending the web of communication and transportation (which is itself a performance dimension to be discussed in chapter 10). If it is easy to obtain information and to bring in resources, then I can change my activity quickly and with small effort. An electric bus bar allows me to set my equipment wherever I want it. A good street system means that I can obtain a special tool or a particular material at a moment's notice. Or, if my present quarters are unsatisfactory, I can move to another. Recovery from disaster is notoriously dependent on rapid

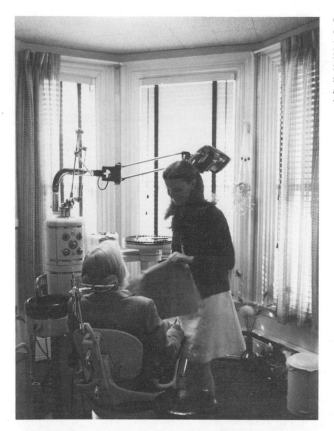

67 Old houses are easily converted to small professional and commercial offices. The interior spaces have a scale suitable for many uses, and retain their sense of warmth.

68 The alternate sites for the Naiku Shrine, at Ise, in Japan. Every twenty years, a new temple is built upon the empty site, in exact replica of the standing structure, which is in its turn demolished, and whose site stands in wait for the next twenty years. Thus the form, but not the substance, of the ancient temple has been preserved for some 1300 years.

information and a quick deployment of resources. In history, it has been the large, complicated, highly accessible cities that have survived the shock of change, for all their apparent vulnerability. Small isolated villages are regularly wiped out by famine, flood, and war.

Good access, like excess capacity, is expensive. Unlike the latter, however, transport gives good service in the present as well as in the future. Moreover, good access does not "silt up" or convey a sense of waste or ambiguity. Thus it is one of the more powerful devices for adaptability.

A third and commonly advocated measure is to reduce the interferences between parts, so that a change to any one part will not force change on another. An architect employs wide-span structures, assuming that uses and partitions can be moved about within those spans without touching the few columns on which the loads are concentrated. If dwellings are separated into single-family houses, and the family is the social unit most likely to decide on environmental change, then each family can modify its house without disturbance to its neighbor. If children are spatially separated from adults, then changes in child rearing can be accomplished without disturbing the elders (however much that separation may damage the social fabric in other ways). In a hospital, if the ever-changing operating rooms and special laboratories can be separated from the wards, whose functions are more nearly constant, then the tumult of the former need not infect the latter. Urban designers have hold of a similar idea in their notions about "megastructure," in which the main supporting and transportation framework would be fixed, while allowing constant variations in the individual buildings attached to it. Unfortunately, they have it backward, at the city scale. It is the individual buildings (the dwellings, especially) which are relatively fixed in form and function, while the main transportation system is in constant flux.

Still another variant of this strategy is to organize the activities of a settlement around fixed focal points, rather than dividing them by fixed boundaries. The assumption is that the diverse activities can grow and shrink in the ambiguous territories between the foci, with minimal disturbance to each other. Nevertheless, an adjacent use must be ready to shrink when another expands, unless there is excess space at these margins.

All these examples of reducing the interferences between parts depend on a prediction of the social units by which decisions to change the environment are likely to be made, plus an ability to distinguish those environmental parts which are likely to change from those unlikely to do so. Megastructure plans fail because of a false prophecy of the latter kind. Should the family ever lose its importance as a social unit, and so its power of decision, then the present flexibility of single-family housing will also falter.

A fourth general strategy is the "modular" one, in which standard units are used repetitively, either because experience has shown that those units are peculiarly apt for diverse functions or because such standardization will permit easy connections between parts and thus easy repatterning. The army submerges individuals in standard, replicable units. Room sizes in a certain limited square foot range were found usable for many purposes in remodeled hospitals, while larger or smaller rooms were far less adaptable. Presumably, then, a hospital consisting primarily of that range of room sizes would be easy to reuse. Many "modular" plans miss this point about evidence from experience, however. They assume that any array of standard pieces assures flexibility, while in fact it may assure the reverse.

Cowan 1963

Standard screw threads and electric plugs are examples of the value of interchangeable connectibility. Examples at the city scale are more difficult to find, although a standard lot may allow builders to put up a routine structure almost anywhere, and a regular street grid may facilitate speculation and the shift of activities, as the planners of New York declared in 1811. Very likely, the use of rectangular buildings, set in a common orientation, will facilitate additions, and a standardization of floor levels may do even more.

Standardization has clear advantages in production and for the stocking of repair parts. It is less clear that it is a useful path to flexibility in anything so complex as a city. Certainly it implies other problems, such as monotony, or the difficulties of large-scale implementation. The link between flexibility and the use of modules is often illusory. One must be able to predict, from substantial experience, that the module in mind is usable for a great diversity of functions and that it will continue to be so usable. The possibility of easy connection and reconnection of the modular parts must be demonstrated, and the continued availability of these connectible parts must be guaranteed. One suspects that the most useful modules are not standard neighborhoods, megastructures, or building systems, but modest things like bricks, pipe threads, and lumber dimensions.*

Finally, of course, there are particular materials, tools, and building technologies that are relatively easy to manipulate. Light wood frames are easier to change than reinforced concrete. Small power tools, sheet materials, shingles, light blocks, earth, plaster, and the trim to cover joints are all the resources of the small patchwork builder. Wood, brick, and stone can be reused, while many synthetics must be discarded. Mass-produced precision plastics, metals, and concrete panels may have advantages of initial speed and cost but will occasion serious future losses of adaptability. In the same vein, are there special types of activity patterns which are inherently easy to change?

Features of the environmental management process can be even more important means for increasing adaptability than the form of things and activities. The first, most important, and most obvious device is to increase the information available at the point of decision—whether by a regular monitoring of changes as they occur, or by good forecasting. Information is expensive, of course. It can be more efficient to shift the point of decision to that group which already has the best information—the people on the spot, perhaps. An alert and well-informed management is surely the key to rapid adaptation.

*But see how the mills shave their lumber down, as the years go by!

There are planning devices which deal with uncertainty. One of them divides development into stages and makes contingency plans for each stage. Army general staffs while away peacetime hours by exploring such contingencies at exhausting length. Dead ends may be foreseen and avoided and a quicker emergency response assured. But full-scale contingency planning is an elaborate affair, and often it is just make-work. Its effectiveness is more likely to be restricted to the next jump and a few possible emergencies.* Good prediction is needed once more.

In a similar vein, actions and decisions may be prepared, but deferred until the last possible moment, so that they can take advantage of last-minute information. Deliberate trials are made early to reveal unexpected complications. This is a familiar procedure in engineering, in which full-scale mockups of innovative parts and processes are a normal thing. It is less common to design the first sections of a new settlement as experiments and to make a plan for learning from them.

Still another device borrows the familiar financial trick of amortization: in addition to accumulating the capital to replace the old investment, one may accumulate the funds to pay for reversing the site to some "original" condition, so that new development will take place without the burden of abandoned structure. Reversibility is paid for, along with maintenance.

The control of space can be a serious obstacle to adaptability. Ownership may be fragmented, unable or unwilling to act, or subject to rigid controls. To circumvent this, one turns to devices which allow the periodic recapture and reassembly of ownership or development rights by some group able to act, such as a public agency or a well-capitalized development group. Long leases, life tenure, and periodic renewal are some of the known devices of this kind. We need to explore other flexible forms of ownership: temporary pos-

*The contingency plan for Three Mile Island missed the contingency of a hydrogen bubble, you remember. Quick access to trained people and special equipment, plus the ability to devise new procedures rapidly, was more effective.

sessions, holdings with vague or overlapping boundaries, and ownerships of partial rights. Areas of lax control—the backlands and abandoned places which are the institutional counterparts of the natural wilderness—provide space for new ways.

Public bodies can shift from control by rigid specification to performance codes, which allow a range of forms as long as a given level of performance is achieved. The much-discussed transferable development right is another attempt to increase the flexibility of settlement patterns. So is the "floating zone," which sets the standards of control, but does not fix their location until a concrete proposal arises. We are beginning to think about controlling the rate of change itself, as in the suburban "growth rate" ordinances. An action is not prohibited, yet its rate of occurrence is regulated. It is slowed down, or equalized, or confined to set periods, so that there are intervals of security. In some states, for example, the designation of historic landmarks may be made only at certain recurrent but well-separated periods.

All of these are ways of reducing the rigidities of place control without losing the basic objectives of that control and without introducing so many uncertainties that confident midrange predictions become impossible.

These process means have their costs, just as do the formal means. They raise ambiguities as well. The "blueprint" plan, the precise development control, the parceling of land into distinct and eternal ownerships all make us feel that our future is secure. Many of the complexities which are written into performance controls, development rights, or long leases are compromises between these conflicting desires for adaptability and certainty. Such intricate rules and procedures exact their own costs of time, money, and administrative energy.

Effective adaptability depends on the dissemination of information, so that decision makers can take advantage of the adaptability that in fact exists. People must be taught how to adapt places to their purposes: how to remodel a house, redecorate a room, or reshape a park. Opportunities may be provided to experiment with new patterns or try out patterns developed by someone else. The perception of adaptability is itself important, and perceived adaptability may have psychological value, even if the quality itself is never used.

Accurate information and sophisticated control are expensive goods. As they become more complex and specialized, they foster a technical centralism that is itself a threat to free manipulation by actual users. Central controls and central information should be confined to securing basic reversibility, or aimed at increasing manipulability for the direct user. Training users how to monitor and modify places can be more important than generating information at the center about current change, except as that information will reveal basic threats to reversal or to general manipulability. Fine-tuned performance controls may daunt the small builder more than rigid but simple prescriptions do.

Much of the above and much of the reasoning that lies behind attempts to be flexible is sheer speculation. We need analyses of actual experience. How are cities adapted during abrupt transformations, such as disasters or social revolutions? What were the typical sequences of adaptation in an urban district, and to what extent were they blocked or diverted by physical rigidities? Can people be taught how to adapt their settings more effectively? What has been the actual experience with buildings and areas that were designed to be flexible? What new devices for adaptability might be used, both physical and administrative? How can adaptability be measured, and how do different places compare when so measured? How effectively can the inherited physical fabric of Havana be used, after the Cuban revolution?

Systematic measures of adaptability could be useful in programming, in design, in management, in control, and in cost-benefit evaluations. Incremental comparisons could be made: which alternative is more manipulable for this particular group, or will have the lowest cost of reversal? Is that reversal cost provided for? How will this area recover from a flood? Can we increase the existing manipulability? Controls might set a required threshold level for these qualities. Programs might even state more specific physical rules, such as "for every unit of 10,000 square feet of floor space, it must be possible to add an additional 2000 square feet without disrupting adjacent units," or "it must be possible to remodel any interior space without using specialized labor, tools, or materials," or "the cost of a complete furnishing of the open space is to be allowed for in the budget, but the expenditure is to be deferred until users have had a year's experience in the place, and can participate in planning for it."

Lowry

In times of extreme stress and confusion, when the evaluation of public action is most unclear, one may even be justified in narrowing all the value dimensions of settlement policy to a pessimistic version of "Lowry's rule":

1. Avoid the most obvious difficulties: patent present unfitness or clear threats to present or future vitality.

2. Maintain the sense of the environment and encourage a flow of information about it, so that everyone concerned is aware of its present state and of changes as they occur.

3. Maintain manipulability and reversibility so people may make their own adjustments, and so that society can draw back from catastrophe when it threatens, or even after it has occurred.

Retiring from that pessimistic view, let us summarize the general criterion. The measure of present fit is the degree of congruence between daily behavior, overt or intended, on the one hand, and the spatial setting on the other. It can be achieved by the modification of place, or behavior, or both. The means of analysis are the observation of actual behavior in some setting coupled with a discussion of problems and intentions by those who use that setting. Empathy and a sharp eye are the best analytic tools, and an intimate sense of the culture is the necessary background. The perceived *stability* of the match is important. Conflicts between different actors must be taken into account. The creation of new, well-matched settings and the education of users to use places properly are matters of interest, as well as the improvement of existing settings. Compartmenting in time and

space, user control, and careful programming,
monitoring, and tuning are universal ways of increasing present fit. The criterion and its methods
of analysis are general, but other prescriptions are
specific to particular cultures. Stereotyped classifications and standards, the multiplicity of
behavioral settings, cultural variations, conflicts
between users, and our bias for quantitative data
are some of the difficulties encountered in applying this criterion at the settlement scale.

A flexible provision for future fit is a more
puzzling criterion. It is difficult to define as a general measure. Two more limited rules have been
suggested: *manipulability*, or the degree to which
use and form can be presently changed under specified limits of cost, time, power and a sense of
continuity, without narrowing the potential range
of the next round of change; and *resilience*, or the
present cost of restoring a place either to some
previous "open" state or to its present state after
some assumed disaster. Both measures are general,
operational, and significant. They express the conservation of two goods which will predictably remain valuable: the ability to respond and the ability
to recover. There are some general formal means
for achieving these ends, such as excess capacity,
good access, the independence of parts, the use of
modules, and the reduction of recycling costs.
There are complementary process means: better
information at the point of decision, flexible planning procedures, and the loosening and renewing
of the patterns of control. All of these means have
their own peculiar costs. The stability and manipulability of present fit are to some degree at odds
with each other, but there are ways of reconciling
them in concrete cases. People can be trained to
cope with change, and their diverse preferences in
this regard can be provided for. All these various
measures of fit can be used in programming, design, management, control, and evaluation.

10

Access

Cities may have first been built for symbolic reasons and later for defense, but it soon appeared that one of their special advantages was the improved access they afforded. Modern theorists have seen transportation and communication as the central asset of an urban area, and most theories of city genesis and function take this for granted. Activities are assumed to locate according to the relative cost of reaching materials, customers, services, jobs, or labor. Other values are simply subsidiary constraints in this struggle for access. A high degree of personal mobility was once a privilege of the rich, or something forced upon poor vagabonds or migrants. Now, in the more affluent countries, thanks to cars and other transport devices, voluntary mobility is widespread among the social classes (but not among the age grades). The personal car is our image of freedom, and tourism is a commonplace. The valued end is greater access, although increased mobility may not always increase access, and it generates costs of its own, as we shall see.

Alonso
Wingo

Access has been well worked over in planning texts. Measurements of access (to open space, to services, to jobs, to markets, etc.) appear frequently in reports. An entire branch of engineering is concerned with the analysis and manipulation of access via new roads, new modes of travel, traffic controls, and so on. Many economic enterprises and some households choose their locations primarily on grounds of access. The ideal city is imagined by some as being a great center where one has easy access to an enormous variety of goods, services, and other people. Conversely, traffic congestion and the difficulties of reaching jobs, stores, schools, parks, or hospitals are a frequent source of urban complaint.

Blumenfeld 1967, 1977
Paquette

Thus we have substantial information on which to base this particular dimension of performance. Even so, while many of the obvious measures are well developed, there is a gap between them and some of those felt qualities of access which citizens prize. Systematic attention to the entire range of the dimension is lacking.

Access may be classified according to the features to which access is given and to whom it is afforded. Most basic, perhaps, is access to other people: to kin, to friends, to potential mates, and to a variety of more casual acquaintances. Human beings are social animals, and frequent contact, at least between members of a primary social group, is fundamental to their well-being. Primitive societies group their dwellings by this rule, and so do modern ones, although electronic communication is a growing substitute for physical proximity. Journeys to visit other persons are still a substantial component of urban trips.

Next in importance is access to certain human activities. The key activities for many adults may be work and residence, but we must also include certain important services—financial, medical, recreational, educational, and religious. These activities either represent opportunities for the person to do something—to work, worship, learn, or recreate, for example—or they supply a valued service— as does a hospital or a bank. The greatest number of recorded city trips is still the commutation from home to work. On the other hand, the journeys of children are rarely counted, unless the child is shipped by car. Moreover, the peak demands on the highways in this country have shifted from the rush hour of the working day to the rush hour of the vacation weekend.

Access is also required to certain material resources: food, water, energy, and various other goods. This requirement overlaps our first criterion of vitality when these resources are the prerequisites of survival. For many city people, this may mean no more than convenient trips to the store. But urbanites are supported by a hidden supply system, which gives them access to out-of-state water, transcontinental lettuce, and Iranian oil (or it did). Disturbances in this system remind the city dweller of what the countryman has never forgotten: that his dependence on access to certain resources is vital and may be precarious.

People also want access to places—to shelters, to open space or even to wasteland, to centers and symbolic places, to fine natural environments. In the more developed countries, we find a growing emphasis on access to particular landscapes, whether because of their sensuous quality, their symbolic meaning, or the opportunities they offer for recreational activity. Not only are household locations within city regions affected by this criterion, but households and firms now use it to distinguish the city they choose to move to. For this reason, they may opt for a small town or a rural location, rather than a large city. Recent dramatic shifts in population in this country seem largely conditioned by this particular access motive.

Finally, we want access to information. Today this has become a key requisite. It has long been a prime requirement for certain economic activities that depend on accurate, fresh news—activities such as central banking, the direction of corporations, or the manufacture of fashion goods. But it is also important to neighbors who gather for the latest gossip, professionals who cluster in special office areas, or young people who gather about a university. The acquisition and processing of information, the management of credit and decision, are the prime economic functions today. The persistent growth of the central business district, in the teeth of a more general decentralization is the outcome of that primacy. Head offices and advanced commercial services are held close by the fine threads of personal communication, and the presence of these sophisticated, affluent office workers downtown is the motive for the heavy investments there. Mass media, conferences, and the telephone have usurped the primacy of fixed spatial proximity as a basis for the exchange of information, but these substitutes remain ineffective for the more subtle and protracted forms of discourse. The signs and symbols of a city, discussed in chapter 8 under "legibility," is a special aspect of this access to information. Access to information may be an emergent key to the quality of the environment. Richard Meier has built a theory of cities on this base, and Melvin Webber considers that the present shift in the mode of communication is a prime determinant in the reshaping of our urban patterns. A mapping of the flow of information within and between re-

Meier 1962
Webber 1967

gions is one index of underlying urban patterns.

Access is unequally distributed. A woman may be confined to her household and another to the range of her wheelchair. The spatial range of small children is sharply restricted and may be narrowed even further by adult prohibitions or by the nature of the environment. People too poor to own a car cannot reach distant jobs. Jews or blacks may be excluded from desirable places. The world of the aged shrinks as their powers of locomotion fail. In analyzing access, one computes how the selected measures vary by area, but also how they vary by different groups of the population.

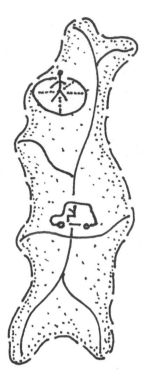

Moreover, access will vary by time of day and by season. People may be cut off at night or in winter. The wartime invention of the snowmobile opened up vast stretches of winter forests to vacationers to the detriment of the common ear. If one's rhythm of life diverges from the standard rhythm, one can be effectively isolated. One advantage of a big city is the 24-hour services available there. Thus a rearrangement of schedules is an important way of affecting access. When the Sunday blue laws were lifted, access to shopping goods was dramatically improved, at the expense of the clerks in the stores.

There are many variations in the mode of access, which have consequences for the value of that access. Physical transportation is one thing, visual or aural access is another. Information can be transported faster and with less energy than material bodies, so we find communications substituting for many grosser forms of travel. Transportation itself appears in many guises: pipeline, boat, automotive vehicle, steam railroad, shoeleather, bicycle, traveling belt. Each mode carries certain things—fluids only, or adults but not children—and has an appropriate speed and carrying capacity, or potential rate of flow. One mode may be under public control, another be furnished by a private company, still another be composed of independent vehicles.

The channels of movement are as much a part of a mode as are its vehicles. Some channels are highly specialized: a gas pipe carries only gas. Others are very generalized: along a street flow many types of goods, people, and information. While most modes permit a two-way exchange, some limit the flow to one direction: a one-way viewing screen, or television, for example. The raft floats down the river; the coal car comes back empty. Modal characteristics are an obvious modifier of access quality. One mode may be more efficient than another, have a longer reach, or be more responsive to its user, even while imposing more serious inconvenience on its neighbors. Thus transportation policy is centrally concerned with the optimum modal mix, or with how to reduce modal conflict, or how to promote a shift from one mode to another, or how to facilitate transfers.

Access is not simply a quality to be maximized, although many urban location theories take that as axiomatic.* To have everything instantly available is no more desirable than it would be to live in an infinitely adaptable world. Moreover, access cannot be measured by the sheer quantity of things that can be reached at given levels of cost and expenditure of time. Mere quantity loses its meaning once a satisficing level is attained. Value then turns on the degree of choice offered among accessible resources. Presumably it is better to be able to reach five food stores which handle goods of different quality and type, than five stores which are all alike. One is then more likely to get the precise food wanted and may be encouraged to enlarge the range of food enjoyed. This is the principle of diversity, so often mentioned in discussions of city quality. It applies to the entire range of accessible things. A diversity of people, of food, of jobs, of entertainment, of physical settings, of schools, of books, are all desirable. Variety among the available behavior settings means that it is easier for any individual to find one that is congenial to him, or to

*Indeed, that outspoken critic of the great city, William Cobbett, wrote in 1826: "[I] am convinced that the facilities which now exist of moving human bodies from place to place are amongst the curses of the country, the destroyers of industry, of morals, and, of course, of happiness. It is a great error to suppose that people are rendered stupid by remaining always in the same place." Just the same, Cobbett's greatest pleasure was to ride through the English countryside, observing the state of the land and its people. He could only have been referring to travel by others.

become competent in new ways. Fit is thereby improved.

It turns out to be difficult to measure diversity, however. All things are to some degree like and to some degree unlike each other, and these infinite differences may be unimportant or may be critical. What is similar or dissimilar depends on the needs and perceptions of the observer. The monotonous scrubland of the tourist is an encyclopedia of information for the skilled tracker. A sparkling variety of high-fashion clothing stores is of little interest to someone on a scant clothes budget. A home buyer is intrigued by some permutation in the front entrance of her newly acquired house, which she later ignores as she wrestles with some deadly arrangement of internal space. Much of the valued diversity of modern consumer goods seems trivial when examined. However desirable in the abstract, diversity cannot be identified or measured until one knows how people perceive differences, and in which features variety is important to them.

See fig. 69

Not only that; we find that diversity is a limited good. We are able to make choices among no more than a restricted set of alternatives. As the number of choices rises, we resort to self-limitations—arbitrary rejection, a lumping of choices in broad classes, or a withdrawal of attention. Too many choices paralyze the ability to choose. Some of the stress of urban life lies in the abundance of offerings, the constant pressure to choose and decide. One desirable quality of access, therefore, may be kin to that of "unfoldingness," discussed in chapter 8. A good environment is a place which affords obvious and easy access to a moderate variety of people, goods, and settings, while this variety can be expanded if a person wishes to expend further energy—an *explorable* world, whose vast diversities can be sought out or ignored at will.

Thus the use of diversity as a criterion depends on knowing the levels of choice that people desire and can tolerate. It is true that this level may rise with experience or training, and that people may cope more easily with choice making, and come to value diversity more highly, the longer they live in a stimulating and varied environment. But as the level of choice continues to rise, people begin to

value seclusion, simplicity, and the control of access. Thus a common fantasy of the ideal environment is one in which the level of access is itself variable at will. Many people, when asked what they imagine would be the best place to live, think of a house in a secluded garden, which is but one step from the center of a great city. The ability to exert control over access—to shut off flow when desired—is therefore a value in itself. We like telephones that can be unplugged, remote locations reached by fast private vehicle, and a secretary who screens the incoming calls. At a larger scale, control of the access system is essential to maintaining economic or political hegemony. Mapping who controls the main communication channels, and the extent to which they can exclude certain people from the use of these channels, is therefore a significant analysis of a place, as we will see in the chapter to come.

The access that can be achieved at a given cost in one settlement, or the costs of achieving a given level of access there, may be compared to their counterparts in another settlement. When we speak of person transport, the cost is usually assumed to be the time consumed. Other measures may be more important for bulkier, less perishable goods of lower value. Yet even in the case of personal transport, which is normally the most important type of carriage, there are other costs: money, energy, bodily effort, personal danger, or the unpleasantness of congestion and an ugly roadside. These plural dimensions prevent us from deriving a total cost, unless everything can be melted down into dollars. As a best substitute, we use time as the basic measure, constrained by certain limits in the other dimensions. Thus one may measure the time-cost of reaching a choice of twenty employment opportunities of a given kind, assuming that one cannot pay for the use of a private car and cannot enter areas which are unsafe or unknown. Unfortunately, the analysis of access and its costs is usually confined to those movements documented in official statistics, that is, the movements which are highly visible and money-consuming. Cars are more planned for than feet, adults than children, motion on the streets than that within a building.

Time itself is a variable cost: commuting times under twenty minutes may be indistinguishably good, while those over an hour rise steeply in their burden. Waiting and transfer time will seem far longer than time in motion, so that people choose to drive slowly, rather than to wait for a fast bus. Time costs may even reverse themselves. People will prefer to be ten minutes from their work, rather than live above the shop. The energy costs of travel have only recently been recognized. There are social costs as well, which are only partially paid by the traveler—increased air pollution and noise, the invasion of privacy, the expense of providing streets and parking space, or the burden of travel accidents and death. Numerous urban struggles now center on *reducing* the access to local areas in order to improve their safety and quiet.

The common emphasis on the cost of travel reflects the underlying assumption that travel is sheer waste time, an unproductive factor like leather trimmings or coffee breaks. Supposedly everyone hates it, unlike the coffee break. Yet driving for pleasure is the most common form of outdoor recreation in the United States. A pleasant trip in good company through a fine landscape is a positive experience. We might think of travel as a pleasure, rather than a brief and necessary evil. It is possible to provide fine roadscapes, pleasant vehicles, and opportunities for work, entertainment, or companionship en route. Walking, cycling, or jogging can be encouraged for reasons of health and enjoyment. The arbitrary division that our culture makes between work and pleasure appears in transportation, just as it does elsewhere. Any comparative measurement of access must account for the benefits of moving, as well as just arriving.

See fig. 70

There are various means of improving access, many of them well developed and rich with accumulated experience. Automatically, one thinks of improvements to the system of routes. Channel capacity or speed may be increased by widening, realigning, and paving a road, or deepening a waterway, or lengthening an airport runway. Routes may be extended into new territory, or their texture be thickened. The existing pattern may be revised to make it safer or more efficient, by creat-

Paquette

69 Multiple choice can be nearly meaningless.

70 Transportation is not pure cost. Parades and joyrides are old familiars. In Philadelphia, when the electric streetcar was new, long evening rides to the suburbs in illuminated cars were a form of entertainment. Some outings were masquerades, with bands to provide music.

ing a hierarchy of routes, by redesigning or reducing intersections, or by rationalizing the local road
pattern. Major terminals such as railroad stations
and airports are first brought closer in, often by
means of extensive clearances, in order to improve
access to the center and then pushed farther out
again, as congestion, noise, and pollution build up
around them. There is an endemic tension between
easy access, vitality, and good fit.

The designer of a new settlement is always
conscious of (and at times obsessed with) these
connections between route layout and good access.
Barriers to movement may be removed, whether by
bridging a river or by cutting wheelchair ramps into
high curbs. Signs and landscaping may be used to
make orientation easier, or even to improve the
quality of the moving experience. These are the
familiar devices of the transportation engineer, and
their accomplishment absorbs substantial sectors of
the public budget.

Access may also be improved by modifying the
mode. Cars, boats, and airplanes are made faster,
safer, more capacious or less disturbing. New or
neglected modes may be brought into use—the
bicycle, the dial-a-bus—which promise savings in
cost, convenience, or safety. Shifts in the distribution of trips by mode may be encouraged, to
achieve a more efficient or more vital mix. Thus a
congested central city will improve its public transit
at some expense to the individual car, or convert
downtown streets into pedestrian malls.

One may also attempt to manipulate the origins and destinations of travel. This is thought to be
the more fundamental aspect of the travel phenomenon (is that really so?), and is frequently discussed in the planning literature. It is less often
implemented, save in some new settlement or
when a single plant or office is consciously relo-
cated.

Origin and destination can be brought closer
together by increasing the general density of
occupation of a settlement, or at least by packing
common destinations more tightly together,
although, at some limit depending on the dominant
mode of travel, the increased density so increases
congestion as to cancel out the advantages of prox-

imity. The grain of the uses may be made finer, in the hope that the home-to-work journey will be shorter because homes and workplaces are mixed together. Inadvertently, then, we may reduce access when we reduce density, separate houses from factories, or segregate income groups. But unlike the first set of policies, which take travel for granted and seek to speed and increase it, these operations on the pattern of origin and destination have effects on access which are not well understood. To be certain about minimizing trips, you must build company towns, provide company stores, and house workers next to the plant. You might also imprison people.

A redistribution in space is not the only way of reducing the load on the access system. One may redistribute in time as well. The staggering of work hours or individually planned adjustments in the timing of weekend travel are common practices. Experiments are now being made with "flextime" in the workplace and with longer, marginally staggered, vacation periods. Both will presumably reduce peak congestion.

Autonomy is another strategy. If one works at home, or grows the family vegetables, or heats by the sun, then one enjoys access to employment, food, and energy at less transport cost.* National autarchy is the same ideal at a larger scale. The counterargument is that increasing autonomy may increase the cost of insecurity of supply, and may decrease the advantages of widened contact between persons. The self-sufficient family farm is a persistent American ideal, but it was an isolated and a risky life. The increase in global transport and communication has been associated with rising standards of living. It remains true, however, that if the measure of access is the *ability* to reach things, then a reduction in actual transport demand on a heavily loaded system may increase that potential ability, as long as the reduction of load does not lead to a decay in the transport system itself.

Access to information may be substituted for access to persons and things. The telephone replaces routine business trips, and television, a trip

*But not at zero cost. One must move about within the home site, too.

to the movie palace. Improving the communication system is a low-cost way of increasing the access to information, and, vicariously, to other persons and resources as well. Telephones, television, radio, computer links and the mails are the key connectors, but, as volume rises, improvements to information processing become even more important than the connections themselves. These devices have had powerful effects on the general quality of life, and their effects continue to augment. Their impact on the physical form of urban settlements is not entirely clear, however. While they substitute for many previous routine trips, they cannot replace more subtle dialogues, and furthermore they seem to stimulate demands for new trips. It is clear that the telephone has greatly increased the rate of communication between distant persons, and yet not at all clear that it has brought about that spatial dispersal of activities that might have been predicted, if it simply substituted for previous person movements. It has not reduced the volume of travel, surely.

The dramatic jump in the technology of communication produces problems of its own: of information overload, of threatened privacy, or an excessively passive reception of one-way messages. If one's measure of the goodness of a city is simply the *rate* of communication within it, then these new devices have made a spectacular improvement. But if the measure is the *ability* to reach things of the type and in the variety desired, then the improvement, while real, is more modest.

We are not yet through with our list of improvements, since one may tamper with more than technology. One may modify the management of transport or communication, as when the mails or a transit authority is reorganized, or traffic controls are imposed. Travel rules and police reduce the incidence of accident and delay. The fear of the dangers to be encountered while traveling is itself a severe constraint of access: many elderly are trapped in their city apartments by the fear of assault, and children fenced in for fear of using public transit.

Public subsidies may be employed to increase access. This is a politically visible way of increasing the availability of public transit service and a less visible way of extending the reach of the automobile. Public roads are now considered a matter of course, and perhaps it may not be too long before we are ready to consider the whole transportation system as a public utility, whose costs are apportioned between users and society as a whole, following social policies of desirable use. Suggestions have been made for fareless subway systems and for providing public bicycles. Cuba has experimented with a free telephone system. Low-cost fares for children and the elderly are commonplace, and so is the provision of free seeing-eye dogs for the blind. The contrary strategy is to shift all costs of access as far as possible to the immediate user, via gasoline and vehicular taxes, toll roads, higher transit fares, steeper mail charges, and pay television (could we add toll bikeways and sidewalks? shoe taxes? taxes on signs which command the view from public roads?). The advantage is that those who benefit bear the costs, and presumably there will be a less wasteful use of the access system. The disadvantage is that access will be graduated even more sharply by income, and that basic requirements may be beyond the reach of some. Where people have equal income and are able to make an informed choice, then we incline to the direct levy of cost, if such levy is possible and not too costly to administer. When these conditions are absent, then equity argues for the public utility approach, at least for basic access.

Finally, the traveler herself may be trained to increase her access. She may be taught to orient herself in unfamiliar territory, to overcome barriers, to operate vehicles, or to use the route system or the communication network. Many people are shut in by their own fears, ignorance, or inability. Training children, the blind, or the retarded to use public transport is one way of enfranchising them.

While access is important in any settlement, it is especially so in unstable conditions, when the ability to move or to shift operations is critical for survival. Thus good access is a strong component of adaptability, as we have noted. Socially, it will be important in complex, plural societies, especially if they are threatened by an estrangement of whole sectors of their population. In poor societies, the access to work, to kin, and to basic resources is a preeminent need. In wealthier ones, more attention will be paid to variety, to the access to information, and to reaching specialized activities. The access system may be a strategic element in increasing the sense of the environment. The equity of access among groups of the population is always important, and so is who controls the system. Rapid and ubiquitous access has unwanted side effects, in the form of accidents, noise, and unwanted intrusions. User control of space is usually at some odds with the criterion of access, as will be explained in chapter 11. Achieving wide access to wanted features while preserving local privacy and control requires some agility in shaping the physical and institutional pattern.

There are numerous ways of measuring the components of access. More general measures, which encompass the accessibility of whole settlements, for whole sectors of the population, are less easily found. There are a number of puzzles in this. One, which is common to the other dimensions, is that meaningful access is not an absolute, but depends on what people want access to. The "objective" measure is contaminated with wishes and may vary for different groups of people. But we can compare the access to commonly desired things. We can also generalize by considering access to those fundamental resources, such as other persons, or information, which can be turned to many different purposes. But we cannot exclude "subjective" values.

There is the further puzzle of defining diversity, as we have discussed above. Once again, the definition will depend on perceived and desired differences. And there are technical difficulties, such as how to draw a generalized time-distance map.* Representing the "attractiveness," or negative cost, of a route is another sticky problem.

Savigeau

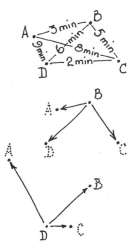

*Distorted maps showing the time-distance from any one place to all surrounding points are often made. The problem arises when one wants a general time-distance map, readable between any combination of points. This will turn out to be a bewildering, three-dimensional network of time-proportional travel lines, taut or looping, which pass over and under each other. Even this intricate

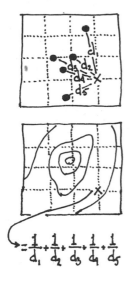

$$-\frac{1}{d_1}+\frac{1}{d_2}+\frac{1}{d_3}+\frac{1}{d_4}+\frac{1}{d_5}$$

The time-distance map, with all its difficulties, is one way of representing generalized access. Another is to map those areas that are open or closed to various groups, or that they feel to be so. Linkages which are present or absent between localities can be shown, and they can be analyzed by graph theory. Areas (or groups of people) which are above or below some given standard of access (within two blocks of a park, within ten minutes' drive of a choice of twenty jobs of a certain kind) can be indicated. Quantitative levels of access can be analyzed statistically by population group.

Potential maps can be drawn, in which the quantities of any type of feature accessible from a point, divided by their distance or time-distance from that point, are summed, and the resulting quantities displayed as a contour map. The most common unit in such maps of potential is persons per minute or per mile, since the proximity to persons is presumed to be a general surrogate for all other kinds of access. But potential maps can refer to other things than people: acres of park per minute, for example, or jobs per minute. The diversity of access can even be brought in, that is, one could locate the nearest five schools that are all different from each other by some defined rule (different in size, or tuition, or social integration, or academic quality, for example) and sum up the reciprocal of their total time-distance from the point. The resulting spatial distribution of these quantities is a contour map of the relative accessibility of a diversity of schools.

Maps and statistics of these kinds can further be compared for different people—those with and without a car, the sighted and the blind—in order to analyze equity. Or they might be compared at differ-

---

model requires that the rate of travel along any one line through any very small elementary area be the same in both directions along the line. In other words, it is not permissible (as it may be in the real world) for anyone to move faster through an area than someone else can, just because he is going downhill rather than up, or is on the expressway, or is flying over, or has a fast car. A general time-distance map on flat paper is possible only if the rate of travel in different directions and between area and area is constant or varies only very gradually and regularly, as on a windless ocean or a trackless plain.

ent hours, to show variations at night or in the commuting rush.

To be more specific about measures requires a more specific context. One might guess, for the North American city today, that three types of analysis might typically be most useful: a map of the general potential of access to persons, maps of substandard access, and a map which compares possible reach with the range actually used. To be more specific, an analyst might:

1. Compute and map the variation in population potential in a settlement, in terms of persons per time-distance, by modes generally available. One might further show how this field varies if persons are weighted by income or if the only available modes are public transit or shank's mare. One might also compute the access potential of certain things very generally desired, such as jobs or open space. One could analyze the peaks, hollows, and sudden slopes in this field and on whom they are incident. Potential maps are unusual in planning analyses, but they are powerful, compressed representations.

2. Set standards of minimum access to certain activities and places that are considered basic to a normal life by the people that presently occupy the settlement. These could be features expected to be available at a regional scale, such as shopping, medical services, schools, open spaces, city centers, or job opportunities matched to capabilities. In such cases, the maximum time-distance would be measured by the mode generally available to the persons in a locality. On the other hand, access may be desired to features at a local scale, such as a nursery school, a local shop, a transit stop, a given range of housing types, a private outdoor place, a vacant or waste place, a meeting place, or a minimum number of persons of different social class. In these cases, maximum time distance would be measured by foot travel. In either case, a spot population map of the settlement can be made, showing the distribution of persons who have less access than the given standard. They may also be analyzed by class. These analyses of substandard access, while rarely done systematically, are familiar in planning work.

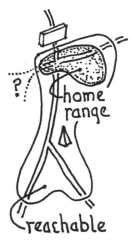

3. For selected groups in some particular localities of the settlement, map the territory they consider "reachable," that is, which they believe is accessible to them, at a reasonable cost and within a reasonable time, and without danger, discomfort, or a sense of exclusion. [The analyst may also note the routes which they enjoy traveling, that is, where the cost may be negative.] Compare this mental territory with the objective barriers to movement, the areas actually exclusive or dangerous, the regions which are in fact too distant or costly to reach. Compare it also with the territory actually used by these people, whether for pleasure or by necessity. Thus one can analyze whether the "home range" of different groups is constrained by choice, by objective obstacles, or by mental ones.

These analyses of access not only are fundamental to a study of settlement quality, but have an obvious utility in studies of social equity or of the regional economy. Access is one fundamental advantage of an urban settlement, and its reach and distribution are a basic index of settlement quality. No one wants maximum access, but only some optimum level, although that should be a level which can be increased, if one is willing to explore. It is a matter of potential reach, and the obstacles to it may be physical, financial, social, or psychological. Access to what and for whom must be analyzed, as well as the mode and the cost (which may be negative). The three important subdimensions of access are the *diversity* of things given access to, the *equity* of access for different groups of the population, and the *control* of the access system. The latter is a prime means of enforcing social control. Sharp variations in access, if under the control of the individual, may be very desirable features.

There are well-known devices for improving access, including the provision of new channels and modes, the rearrangement of origin and destination, the abolition of social and physical barriers, a heightening of system legibility, a substitution of communication for transport, the modification of management and control, subsidy, and the training of the traveler himself. There are numerous ways of measuring access, including time-distance maps, linkage diagrams, maps of potential, plots of substandard access, "home ranges," and the mental map of reachable territory. Access is central to studies of the productive economy, but also for an understanding of the social system and for analyzing the psychological impact of the city.

11　Control

See fig. 71

Space and the behavior associated with it must be regulated. Man is a territorial animal: he uses space to manage personal interchange and asserts rights over territory to conserve resources. People exercise these controls over pieces of ground, and also over volumes that accompany the person. Our subject is the former, however. Spatial controls have strong psychological consequences: feelings of anxiety, satisfaction, pride, or submission. Social status is buttressed, or at least expressed, by spatial dominance. A principal motive of war has been the struggle for place, and governments are land-based units. These are pervasive phenomena.

I shall speak here of the control of human space. The rat knows another territory, through which human beings wander like dangerous erratics. Human ownerships are underlain by a denser network of animal ownerships. This complexity may someday be an element in the evaluation of a settlement. For the time, we will ignore it, as it has been ignored. Still, we must admit that we do not own the earth. Ownership is a human convention that allocates present control, sufficient for human purpose, among existing people. It is neither permanent nor total.

We are accustomed to one particular form of space control: the legally defined ownership of a sharply bounded area, which includes all rights not explicitly excluded by law or contract, which is held "forever," and is transferable at will. It seems most peculiar to us that other cultures may have different notions. Even among ourselves, moreover, informal controls overlap these legal ones.

The first spatial right is the right of presence, the right to be in a place, to which may be added the further right of excluding others (indeed, much of our sense of property returns lovingly to the pleasures of throwing other people out). In normal circumstances, I have the right to be on any public sidewalk, but I cannot keep others off of it.

The second right is that of use and action, of behaving freely in a place or of using its facilities

71 People set invisible territories about themselves. Elsewhere, territories are explicitly marked (and sometimes violated).

without appropriating them. This may be restricted within certain explicit or commonly understood limits, or be expanded by some power to limit the acts of others. I can regulate sidewalk behavior to some degree, as mine is regulated. All of us may walk and pull our carts along the pavement, but none may be too noisy or too violent, or block the passage of another.

The third right is appropriation. When I have that, I can take the resources of a place for myself or use its facilities in some way that prevents their use by others. If I wish, I spread my grain on the walk to dry, or cut the grass at its edge for hay. To greater or less degree, I may monopolize the benefits of the place.

Fourth is the right of modification. Now I can change the place as I see fit, however permanently. I can even destroy it or prevent others from doing so. I may break up the pavement for fill. In the extreme, I am free to do that no matter what the external consequences. I may break it up at night with a jackhammer, even if the noise awakes my neighbors, or I may sow it with land mines. Two restraints should have been laid on me: the prohibition of nuisance to others not on the property and the prohibition of permanent damage. Do what you wish with that path of yours, but do it quietly, and remember that others will want to walk there in the future.

Fifth is the right of disposition. I can give my rights in the walk to whomever I please. My control is then permanent and transferable, like a piece of money.

We think of all these as being aspects of one thing, which is true ownership. But these rights are separable, and not inevitable. In some cultures, land belongs to whoever is using it at the time. This means only the rights of presence, use, and appropriation, and these rights are extinguished when active use is abandoned. Other controls, in the sense of rights to transfer, modify, or exclude, rest with the tribe or with the gods. Control may be explicit and codified, or implicit, informal, and even illegitimate, as when an adolescent gang controls its turf. It may be effective or ineffective; continuous, temporary, or recurrent.

How do variations in control affect the goodness of a place? One primary dimension is surely the *congruence* of use and control, that is, the extent to which the actual users or inhabitants of a space control it, in proportion to the degree or permanence of their stake in it. Do families own their houses? Do shopkeepers own their stores? Do students and teachers control the schools, and workers the workplace? Tenant management, factory work teams, producer's cooperatives, "free schools," and the community control of neighborhood facilities are current proposals for increasing this congruence of spatial control. User congruence has two advantages: the better fit that flows from control by those most familiar with place use and most motivated to improve it, and the greater security, satisfaction, and freedom to operate which is thereby afforded them.

Cambridge Institute
Turner

This rule must be modified in a number of ways. In the first place, it should somehow be expanded to take account of future and potential users, as well as actual ones. User control must not deny others the basic opportunities that the owners themselves enjoy. Regulation by present users often entails the exclusion of those who are elsewhere, but who may have a legitimate interest in the use of the place or of some similar place. Local sovereignty in the suburbs may deny the freedom of all classes and races to have the suburban home they desire. Some external authority representing potential users must then determine how outsiders may have access to a place, and how they may join in its use and control, if a denial of this will deprive them of equal opportunity. For example, it is not necessary to rule that any person should have the right to join any family in its own house, since that person is free to establish another family in another house. But if she is excluded from an extensive residential area, she has lost an important freedom. One looks for controls which achieve local ends without complete and extensive exclusion, such as the English right to free passage in the countryside, but not near a house or with damage to crops. One thinks of small areas of local control, laced with public access and with open lands which are subject to very lax control. The management of all but very small areas must thus be tempered by the participation of potential users elsewhere.

Indeed, the inquiry may be turned upside down. Instead of looking at spatial settings to see whether they are regulated by their users, one may look at the typical entities in any society—individuals, families, work groups, peer groups, religious bodies, self-identifying ethnic or class groups—to see whether they have a "land base," that is, a place which they control. One maps the range of space that is open to these groups, and to what extent the territory within which they carry out their daily activities is under the control of others. In any good settlement, there should be places that are intensely private to persons and strong primary groups, and also some form of free or "waste" land within their reach which no external power effectively controls.

The issue of the future user is even thornier. Once more, some external authority concerned with long-range interests will be required, especially when present users have no emotional ties to those that are to come. But how does one speak for the interests of someone not yet in existence? We are forced back on the more general and enduring values, which the unknown future user is highly likely to share. Therefore, a good control system will include ways by which local control, however congruent, is constrained to maintain future vitality, manipulability, and resilience.

One further complication remains, and this is whether the users of a place may be competent to exercise control. In some cases, a setting is used by people who are so heterogeneous and transient that user control is improbable. A subway system whose stations were owned by the community living above them, whose trackmen disposed of the line, and whose cars were managed by their riders would have predictable difficulties. In other cases, since control requires effort, local users may voluntarily cede certain functions to the management of specialists, when aims are clear but the techniques complex, as in the case of sewerage or fire control.

In still others, immediate users may be (or may appear to be) less informed or less caring or less capable than others more remote. This is the caretaker situation, familiar to us in the nursery, prison, and hospital. It appears in less total form when some specialist has better data about a particular function (or during a temporary period) than those directly engaged. The airport tower controls the incoming aircraft (or so we trust); the board of health supervises the plumbing of a house; and civil defense takes command in a disaster. Quite often, the very scale of the problems in a place (or which a place causes) transcend the capabilities of users to address them. A family is competent to control the plants in its backyard, but helpless to maintain the purity of that yard's air.

In discussing these limitations of congruence, we must distinguish between the cases where users are by their nature, or the nature of the situation, incapable of effective control, and those where they might become capable. In the first class are those whom society judges to be constitutionally incapable: too parochial, too old, too young, too ill, or too malevolent. (But society should take care in making that judgment. Many provincials, prisoners, patients, and children are more capable of place management than society thinks, and the very exercise of that capability might help cure them of their illness or their youth.) In this same group are the areas used by transients and the problems that transcend local power, such as air pollution. (Take care once more. It is possible that the form of the setting may be the source of the discrepancy. Skyscrapers and subway systems are hard for local users to manage. Houses are easier, and so are small buses, since they are separable from the supporting street system.)

In other situations, the discrepancy between problem and local capability may be only apparent or may be soluble. Management should be exercised by those with the best information, yet information includes values, feelings, and experiences, as well as facts and techniques. Local users are rich in the former. Ceding fire control to specialists is painless, since the value is clear and widely shared, while the technique is intricate. Ceding the management of children raises more substantial questions. Giving local users more information, or changing the scale of a setting, may at times dimin-

C. Ward 1977

ish the discrepancy between user and problem congruence.

The balancing criterion to congruence is therefore *responsibility*: those who control a place should have the motives, information, and power to do it well, a commitment to the place and to the needs of other persons and creatures in it, a willingness to accept failure and to correct it. It is commendable to increase both congruence and responsibility, by means of education and the system of management. This suggests that place control should devolve upon its users step by step, as they build their competence to exercise that control. Training people to be place managers is a useful social task, and so is reshaping the setting in order to open up opportunities for place management. Indeed, progressive responsibility for place is an effective means of general education, both intellectual and moral.

A final dimension of control is *certainty*, the degree to which people understand the control system, can predict its scope, and feel secure with it. This is not the same as saying that control should be unchanging, since shifting situations or values may require change. But conflict and ambiguity mean waste and confusion. If there is no consensus about spatial rights, or much illegitimate use, then people are insecure and must devote their energy to self-defense. In a good settlement, spatial rights are notorious, accepted, and clear, and correspond to the reality of control. The smoothness with which control can be transferred is this same measure, extended in time. Conflict is normal, however, and I will discuss some of the means of dealing with it below. High certainty and low congruence are oppression.

There are many possible variations on our concept of normal land ownership which might tailor it more closely to the requirement of good settlement. Could we accept fuzzy boundaries, where rights overlap and are transitional? Is it possible to allow a transient ownership of certain public spaces, in a way which corresponds to what so often is a social reality? Could the ownership of most land be nontransferable, reverting to some public body or trust when the owner dies or moves, as we sometimes achieve by the device of life interest? Could ownership exclude the right to modify permanently (as under a conservation easement), or be compatible with some right of public passage or some non-damaging presence or use by others?

The prevailing mode of transferring control is an important feature of settlement. Does it accompany an exchange of money, or follow a traditional line of inheritance? Does it rest in the hands of some permanent community? Is it the result of force, passing from one violent hand to another? Does ownership shift as casual users move in and out? Or is each change made at the will of some central agent, which explicitly redistributes space at intervals (which was the ancient feudal theory)?

Determining the future controllers of a place is a matter of interest to present users. Yet their stake in this may be less than their interest in present use and behavior. Since transfers of control have large-scale effects and long-term impacts, the larger community may be justified in asserting a right to manage them. The system of transfer has much to do with the adaptability of any settlement. Security of tenure is not incompatible with a denial of the right to dispose of it.

The dynamics of control go beyond the issues of transition. The degree and nature of control shifts continuously: new groups assert themselves; permitted behavior changes, and so do the resources which are to be protected or exploited. These changes must be monitored to detect undesirable shifts: a growing inequity or incongruence, rising exclusion, or increasing incompetence. Moreover, control will sometimes enter a self-destructive spiral: perhaps downward—as when behavior begins to escape any regulation and control groups lose their confidence—or perhaps upward—as when a threatened control progressively rigidifies, prescribing actions and rights more and more minutely. These instabilities will also require intervention. Once again, the ideal state of congruence must be balanced by external regulation.

There are numerous physical means by which control may be allocated and secured. One is the marking of boundaries: by hedges, fences, signs, and landmarks. Another is to increase one-way visibility into the space for the controlling group, so that monitoring is easy. These are the devices discussed in Oscar Newman's *Defensible Space*, which is a book about spatial control by physical means.

Space is also controlled by manipulating access. Walls and other barriers to movement are erected. The act of entering is concentrated at the gates, where it can be supervised and, if necessary, repelled. Roads are built within a settlement, or between settlements, to permit the rapid movement of troops or police when control is threatened. Other roads are dead-ended or diverted, to increase the privacy of a place. Islamic cities made exceptional use of many of these means, since private control was so important a value and so often at risk.

If territories are relatively small (garden or house versus park or apartment building, for example), and if they can be modified or maintained with modest effort, then it is easier for individuals or small groups to achieve control. Conversely, large forms, or those which require special resources to maintain, make for control by large organizations. An ocean liner, a jet aircraft, a strip mine, a subway station, and a solar power satellite all induce a different social organization of command than does a small fishing boat, a hot air balloon, a peat bog, a bicycle, or a solar panel on the roof. Recent publications about future colonies in space analyze their technical requirements at length, with hardly a thought for the strict spatial control that will be required and its eery implications for that small colonial society.

Symbols can be used to assert control. Symbolic barriers and pathways are created, such as low hedges or the painted lines of highways. Periods of time can be controlled, as well as chunks of space. Behavior may be marked off audibly, and so constrained to particular times. In the factory during working hours, between the whistle blasts, the worker's actions are regulated by management. Similarly in classrooms at classtimes, or in church on Sundays.

Size, elevation, and spatial distancing are frequently employed, whether by kings on thrones, or chief executives high up in skyscrapers. The act of approach may be designed to increase submission, as was done so expertly in Peking, and in such a lesser way in the modern office. Uniforms and passes are devices of spatial control, used at times in individual factories, and at others to control the movement of whole populations. But physical means must be matched by social conventions to be effective. There must be laws regarding the rights of ownership, common understandings about group territory and personal space, education in proper spatial behavior, a record of spatial rights.

One way of lessening spatial conflict is to clarify and enlarge the social consensus about rights in space, so that everyone knows who controls a place and how to act properly there. Some traditional societies have been able to control their ground rather easily, since they possess a large body of custom with regard to the land, which is reinforced by religious dogma. But custom also resists change, or breaks up in the face of it. Is it possible to create stable yet evolving custom about the control of space?

Today, we depend primarily on central authority to mediate conflict and to look out for the interests of absent and future users. The police are charged with that task, supported by legal and planning institutions. Otherwise, diverse people in one place may attack one another, mutually interfere, or find another's behavior bizarre or offensive. Yet we prize freedom and wish to act in freely chosen ways. What's more, the spectacle of human diversity is one of the attractions of the great city. Applying that minimum of unobtrusive control which is necessary to keep heterogeneous users at peace with each other, and yet feeling free, is a delicate art.

Tolerance supports that art—learning ways of coexisting in space and time. One controls a minimum area, in a minimum way, and tries to remain indifferent to the strange actions of one's neighbors. The tolerant cosmopolite is not easily aroused by what other people do, but observes them with amused and calm detachment. Psychological and social fragmentation acts in place of police, or of a parceling in space and time. Along with tolerance may come indifference, however.

The fourth means of conflict reduction is the
division of space into relatively small parcels,
clearly marked off, so that there is little mutual inter-
ruption. This is the technique of compartmenting,
already mentioned in the discussion of fit. We use
bounded offices, private rooms, houses whose insides are well defined from their outsides, ethnic
ghettos, and railroad yards. The boundary of the
special area is insulated (a wall which deadens
sound, a greenbelt), and external effects such as
pollution and access are regulated. Since most uses
are intermittent, this may produce an underutilized
settlement space.

To avoid such waste, ownership can be divided
in time as well as place. Different vacationers may
occupy the same cottage, week by week, and pro-
fessors follow each other through the same classrooms. We do not consider this to be a form of
ownership, and yet it is. Formal ownership of
place, for specified, recurrent time periods is now
being instituted in some second-home developments. In this case, there must be regulation of the
time boundary (the moment of transition), and the
"external" impacts of use, in addition to effects on a
spatial neighbor, are taken to include the condition
in which the place is left for a successor. This
requires a super-owner once more: whether it be a
lessor, or some larger group which monitors the
transitions between temporary owners. Nevertheless, formalizing the control of a succession of uses
in a place may be a good way of reducing spatial
waste. Scarce and desirable places can thus be
rationed: wilderness camps or waterside cottages,
in-town apartments, sacred locations (as occurs
today in some of the holy places of Jerusalem),
hunting grounds, workshops, meeting halls.
Where the temporary control of use is permanently
recurrent rather than ephemeral, then each owner
·will take greater care. By neglecting time, we waste
our spatial resources. Extensive areas lie long unused. Idleness is succeeded by congestion.

Instances of the joint control of a large area,
which depends neither on ancient custom, nor
on the overview of some superior authority, nor on
mutual accommodation in a tolerant society, nor on
a careful parceling in time and space, are relatively

Browne

rare. Certain cooperative communities (such as the
Oneida Community) achieved it, but the circumstances were special. True cooperative control
requires expending much energy in group communication and decision.

Force achieves place control, and place control
is used to display and augment force. The form of
any colonial city is an example. Elevation, distance,
barriers, access, grandeur, style, regularity, hierarchy, even place names and planting confirm the
dominant power. Modern societies are also marked
by great inequities in the control of the space which
the different classes enjoy. Thus one telling evaluation of any settlement is an analysis of the places
controlled by the various social groups.

King

The obverse of this phenomenon is the persistent role of fringe areas in history—regions of low
control, where small groups can maintain their
independence and the forces of change or of resistance may collect themselves. Revolts are mounted
in the mountains, the deserts, and great forest
areas. Christian heresies survived for centuries in
the Alps and the Pyrenees. These places shelter
relict societies, whose special ways of living may be
useful later, if the prevailing context shifts. In that
way, a failure of spatial control at the margins may
promote long-term adaptability. In like manner, the
waste lots of the city shelter native plant and animal
associations and afford children an escape from
adult control. At this moment, new wastelands are
opening up in the center of the metropolis.

See figs. 72, 73

Control requires effort, and a well-controlled
settlement (in our sense of the term, and not in the
sense of an oppression) will always demand a large
degree of skillful political energy, particularly when
place issues become as large and complex as they
are today. The price of such control is education,
committees, discussions, and the tireless maintenance of political organization. Indeed, not controlling may have values beyond the mere saving of
effort. One sign of maturity is the ability to enjoy
the development of others—to allow them to act
in their own way while maintaining one's own vital
conditions with a minimum of effort. Often
enough, we control space too closely: trimming the
grass, driving off small children, keeping loiterers

72 The flood plain of the Arno River, at the very center of Florence. This unkempt no-man's-land is a pleasant relief in the stony intensity of a great city. How many users can you find?

73 Wastelands are fine playgrounds.

on the move, painting, dusting, rearranging to perfection. A more selective control reduces costs and increases spatial openness for others.

Unfortunately, mixing uses or allowing them to succeed each other in time will require more intricate layers of control. Even the conservation of "uncontrolled" waste land demands control. The degree of control may not be the main issue, after all, but rather the selectivity and quality of control, and by whom it is exercised.

The control of space is important to environmental quality in any social context: rich or poor, centralized or decentralized, homogeneous or heterogeneous, stable or fluid. But it is particularly critical in a changing, pluralistic society, where power is unequally distributed and problems are large in scale. In an authoritarian society, decentralized place control will be an escape valve, even a possible wedge of change (although revolutionaries will argue this point).

Political control is still largely area-based, even when many political functions are aspatial or have a very extended radius of influence. The destructive ideal of nationalism, which assumes that the entire world should be divided into land units associated with independent military and civil powers, threatens us with a holocaust. Our equation of politics with land units may be an obsolete cast of mind. We are unable to think of political control apart from place, or to establish place control at the scale of the problems of world pollution, corporate enterprise, nuclear catastrophe, and the shortage of water, food, and energy.

The metropolitan region is an area within whose confines interdependencies are high. In the United States, we have no effective control at that level and little sense of community on which an effective control could be based. We do find resurgent feelings of identity in the local community. Unfortunately, while these local feelings are often potent, and while the local community may be able to take over certain tasks of environmental maintenance, the more serious issues are beyond (or even beneath) control at that level. Making community control of community space a reality will require drastic changes in our economy, political power, and way of life. The effective units of space control, commensurate with current issues, may likely be the family (even if it is a family modified and enlarged), the very small residential neighborhood or small workplace, where association by propinquity still maintains, the political community of moderate size, in which representative politics can still be face to face, the great urban region, and thence up to very large regions of the world. Control of place is a necessity. Properly constructed, it offers psychological benefits. But not all public power should be place-bound.

There are two ways of analyzing the dimension of place control in any settlement. First, identify the typical behavior settings and the major communications systems, and in prototype cases, ask:

Who owns this place or system? Are there diverse sets of ownership within it?

Are there ambiguities and conflicts of control? informal or illegitimate controls?

Who can be present here, and who are excluded?

Who regulates whose behavior?

Who can modify or maintain the place or system and use its resources?

Do those in control have the information, motives, and ability to do it well?

Are there control intrusions by outside groups, or problems which escape control?

Is there a consensus among users about the reality and the rightness of control? Do they feel free to act as they wish, and as they think proper for the place?

Is the control pattern changing? how is control transferred?

Are groups excluded from control who might have a legitimate present or future stake in it?

Such an analysis of the most important settings and communications channels will be a fundamental description of any settlement. It might be mapped, in condensed form, to show such things as the variation in scale and type of control, the degree of congruence or competence, the presence of conflict or change, and so on.

A second approach to analysis is to look at the crucial groups in the society, and ask similar questions about what places typical members of that group control, and where they must submit. Again, there could be summary maps, showing the spaces they actually control (their "land base"), the areas and channels open to their presence or use, the spaces and times where they are controlled by others, and the "free" areas—the wastelands—that may be accessible to them.

In summary, a good settlement is one in which place control is *certain, responsible,* and *congruent,* both to its users (present, potential, and future) and also to the structure of the problems of the place. The relative importance of these dimensions and their level of adequacy will depend on the social and environmental context of the settlement. Positions on these dimensions can be identified in the field. There are some common dilemmas and some common ways of meeting them. The ideal state, to express it in vague, general (and perhaps even contradictory) terms, is one of responsible, capable, and certain local control, which is open to potential users and conservative of the future, and which is interspersed with areas of low control, tolerant of diversity and deviance. The continuity of any human society depends on good control of its living space, but responsible control is also critical to the development of the individual and of the small group. In our minds, control is associated with status, power, and dominance.* It can be subverted, however, to the purposes of an open and egalitarian society.

*Just as the sensibility of places has usually been associated with kingly or theocratic power.

12 Efficiency and Justice

Efficiency is the balancing criterion: it relates the level of achievement in some performance to a loss in some other. Efficiencies of settlements can be compared only by seeing which achieves the best level in some one dimension, given a fixed amount of other values expended or achieved. Since the values which enter the calculation are not objectively commensurate with each other (dollars versus a clear environmental image, for example), "objective" comparisons of efficiency can be made only when all types of costs and benefits but one are held constant.* Subjective comparisons among more complex variations can always be made. Such choices are made every day. We can make those necessary choices explicit, but not measurable.

In making comparisons, the costs and benefits of creating and maintaining a system must be considered together, at least over some moderate span of time. We are prone to consider only initial costs and ongoing benefits, while neglecting the ongoing costs, and, at times, the immediate benefits of the act of building as well. It is as though making something were pure pain, and using it thereafter were pure pleasure. On the contrary, we should evaluate a *stream* of values and costs. In our case, unfortunately, most values cannot be quantified except in the crude sense of more or less, and so one cannot explicitly discount them to the present. One must simply express a preference among futures whose values decline, increase, strike a plateau, fluctuate, or vary in other ways. One may be driven to an even more restricted evaluation: simply that of an ongoing present, with its sense of direction into the future.

Many of the more critical costs of achieving a good settlement will be losses in other, nonspatial realms. Reckoning such costs is a first step in analyzing how much to invest in the qualities of settlement in relation to attaining other human ends. These costs are likely to be expressed in such wide-

*Except, of course, in the rare case when one alternative is better than another on *all* counts.

spread values as money, an expense of energy or
material resources, political effort, or psychological
stress. A theory of city form will necessarily dwell on
how some of those costs may be reduced. What is a
cheap city, for example, or an energy-saving one?
But the theory says nothing about how those nonspatial costs should be assessed and compared. It
can only look for ways of reducing those external
costs to attain its peculiar ends, without being able
to judge whether that reduction is important or
trivial. It costs fewer dollars to build row houses
than high flats of comparable spaciousness, for
example. But extended row houses require more
energy for heat and for transport to and fro than do
dense apartments with central steam plants. Form
theory will look for patterns that are *both* cheaper
and less energy-demanding than either of those
alternatives but can offer no wisdom on balancing
dollars and calories. Nor does the theory deal in any
central way with *productive* efficiency, which is
often what people mean when they use the general
term of efficiency. The productive efficiency of an
economic system is affected by the access and fit of
the settlements in which it operates, but clearly is
not wholly, or even perhaps largely, determined
by them.

The theory may in time be able to say something more about costs which are internal to its own
universe, however, just as economics can speak
with more confidence when efficiency is measured
solely in economic terms. In this narrower sense, an
"efficient" city is one that offers a high level of
access without any loss of local control, or one that
has a vivid and legible image and yet is very adaptable to future change. It may be useful, then, to list
some areas where performance dimensions are
likely to be in conflict with each other. These could
be the elements regarding which it would be important to make calculations of efficiency (in this narrower sense, internal to the theory), and where
innovative, more "efficient" spatial forms might be
most useful. Where possible, theory would go
further and show how to assess the relative significance of these conflicting values in any particular
cultural, political, and economic context.

Certain interdimensional conflicts are readily apparent:

1. A vital environment will often conflict with decentralized user control, since many biological effects are invisible, at least to the layman and in the short run. Moreover, settings which are preferable to the direct user may easily be detrimental to the health of others, if not to his own. The conflict can be dealt with by accepting a loss on one side or the other (imposing central controls on fireplaces, for example, or choosing to breathe polluted air), or by incurring "external" nonspatial costs, such as those of expensive air conditioning or massive propaganda campaigns to decrease the user preference for open fires. However, an "efficient" solution, in our limited sense, internal to the theory, would be a cheap, attractive, open fireplace that emitted nothing but unpolluted warm air (an open fire burning hydrogen, for example?). A more mature theory would also explain why unhealthy air might properly be accepted at some one point in political development, in order to encourage user autonomy, but not at some later stage.

2. The ideal of a vital environment will often conflict with a well-fitted one, when by good fit we mean comfort. A well-designed, push-button setting makes no call on our muscles, our hearts included. Therefore, push buttons degrade performance in another dimension and are inefficient, even if they make a comfortable fit. An efficient setting would make it fitting for us to run. Even further, that which is conducive to the immediate good health of the individual may not always be ideal for the survival of the species. An environment which is stressful to some degree may have evolutionary advantages. Perhaps this is not an immediate worry, however.

3. Sense is frequently in opposition to adaptability of fit. A vivid, structured, meaningful place may easily be a rigid and inadaptable one. A flexible place, apt for many uses, can seem shapeless, gray, and ill-defined. "Efficient" solutions at this particular crossing are those which create sensibility while imposing small restraints on the future, as by relying on focal points to organize an area, rather than by using sharp district boundaries. Alterna-

tively, adaptable space may be relegated to the interiors of blocks, while the settlement image is composed by the more permanent main avenues. Beyond this, in the face of an inescapable choice between the two criteria, there are certain situations of uncertainty and transition in which adaptability is always key, and others in which it is crucial that people feel secure.

4. Present and future fit are often contradictory to each other. To be adaptable usually implies being loosely fitted to the present, and vice versa. What one might call a "well-fitted loose fit" is hard to come by, except through providing rather costly reserves of excess capacity. (Of course, this costly dodge *is* efficient in our limited sense, even if it may be inefficient in the more usual, economic meaning of the word.) A high level of access in a region may be a more generally efficient solution. Another may be the conservation of reserve capacity which is cheap to supply and to maintain, such as unserved waste space or wilderness. Still another is a good present fit which is also highly manipulable.

Since the typical conflict here is all within one general dimension (of fittedness), it may also be possible to construct a rationale for balancing present and future fit. That is, one could investigate how variations in resources, powers of prediction, environmental or social mutability, the stability of values, or cultural orientation toward time all affect the relative importance one places on providing for future fit.

5. Good access for all often clashes with local control of territory. Under what circumstances should one be favored, rather than the other? Are there efficient ways of satisfying both demands?

6. High levels of personal access may cause serious health problems, as when our beloved automobiles pollute the air and kill more victims than the most desperate of wars. Wouldn't hydrogen peroxide, or electric cars, or bicycles be a more efficient solution? Surprisingly enough, subway systems, unless modified in costly ways, are not efficient in this peculiar sense, since while they improve safety, they decrease personal mobility. Needless to say, subways may still at times be the most rational solution. They may even be more

efficient than other systems in the normal economic sense, that is, they may move people at less dollar cost per person-mile when settlement is very dense. But that is not our measure of efficiency.

While efficiency deals with how costs and benefits for any one group are distributed among the several types of value, justice is the way in which benefits and costs of any one kind are distributed between persons. What is considered to be a just distribution will vary in different cultures. In some, justice means conformity with custom or precedent. Goods may be distributed according to people's hereditary or acquired rank, which is thought to be a reflection of their intrinsic worth or ability. In other societies, and to some degree in ours, distribution is based on comparative power, although that is not likely to appear just to us, unless power is legitimized by rank or money. For us, while these other rules have some force, the principal basis of distribution is the ability to pay, a fact which does not usually offend us, unless it shuts off some basic goods such as political freedom or the resources essential for survival. Since it is our official conviction that cash on hand derives from a combination of individual ability and productive effort, the money rule seems just to us. Moreover, distributions according to money simplify the management of distribution and free the individual to choose the goods he wants. Goods are priced according to the degree of general desire, and by that means they are rationally allocated.

But distributions by price will be quite unequal unless everyone has an equal money income, which he expends as he wishes, in some world where all goods have money equivalents. Distributions of particular goods might then safely remain unequal, because of individual valuations and the resulting prices and patterns of spending, while the general ability to choose would be equitable. For equity is most often espoused as our ideal of a just distribution, whether it is meant to be applied to all distributions, or just to certain key enabling powers, such as income. As it did to our forefathers, equity seems self-evident. It is presumably the only rule to which all parties might agree, if they had equal bargaining power and were equally ignorant of future events when they sat down to write a constitution for the distribution game. This is the classical "voluntary contract" hypothesis.* Not only does equity seem obviously fair, it attracts us by its intellectual simplicity, and it reflects a moral view which sees intrinsic value in every person, however weak or imperfect. Equity also appears easier to apply than other rules, at least in theory, since it eliminates the necessity of measuring relative rank, need, or worth.

Everyone is aware of how far away all modern societies, even the socialist ones, are from this egalitarian ideal. Most of us would be pleased if we could only begin to reduce present inequities. But there are theoretical puzzles, even within this ideal. First, should *all* goods and costs be equally distributed (3 pounds of potatoes, 37 square feet of floor space, and 27 hours of heavy labor to everyone), or just certain "essential" goods, such as food, health care, and education, or just an equal "start in life," or just some general enabling powers such as money and free speech? Moreover, how does one deal with need? Surely a handicapped or ill person requires more than a healthy one? How about intrinsic ability: can a child cope with the same amount of goods that an adult can? What of potential contribution: should a person of high native intelligence receive a special education and be excused from hard labor, or be asked to make specially intense intellectual efforts? Indeed, the old utopian slogan, "from each according to his means, and to each according to his needs" appears to me to be a higher ideal than pure equity. Yet it is a very difficult one to implement.

Among these classic stumbling blocks, we look for bits of justice, poking about with various simplifying devices. One device is to set some minimum or satisficing thresholds of equity: "everyone should have at least 12 years of education," or, "no one should be more than 30 minutes away from shops for daily necessities." Here, justice concentrates on what are deemed to be the minimum

*Note the inevitable circularity of this "objective" reasoning, which must assume equality at the hypothetical beginning.

essentials. A second device focuses equity rules on goods which seem to be the keys to obtaining other goods. In our case, we might be particularly concerned about equities of vitality, of access, or of territorial control, just as, in other domains, one speaks of income, free speech, and the vote. A third device is to focus on the least-favored group, and to insist that any changes must at least improve that group's situation. This is the "maximin" strategy of decision theory, or the "difference principle" so thoroughly expounded by John Rawls.

We are light-years away from a just world. Many deep changes must precede our approach to it, changes in actual distributions of goods and power, in our focus on self, and in our attitudes toward those of different age, class, race, and sex. A truly just system might be a world so arranged that all its people have an equal opportunity to unfold to their own latent potentials, while reaping the benefits of the development achieved by others. This is clearly a complicated guide to apply. It is a just rule, but not a directly equitable one.

The rules of distribution must *seem* just, since justice lies in the mind. The rules must be clear enough that everyone can understand them; they must be stable, predictable, and continuous with past and present experience. A distribution made according to some clearly understood and long accepted rule of hereditary worth may leave everyone far more satisfied than a division based on a poorly comprehended and shifting basis of need. If this hereditary rule can also assure basic necessities to everyone and encourage their growth as persons, it may indeed be the appropriate rule of justice in that case. But equity, tempered in some way by need and potential, is a thought that sticks in the Western mind.

What does justice have to do with our performance dimensions? Because these dimensions are qualitative and complex, we cannot expect to generate any such simple guide as the equalization of income. But we can spot some critical points.

Clearly, every person should have a right to the basic vital requirements—enough food, clean air and water, a reasonable protection from hazard and poison. Never argued in the abstract, this principle is frequently circumvented in reality. The cost of environmental protection can be large, and it can fall unevenly on different interests. It is often difficult to trace the source of an environmental hazard—or the source (like the automobile) may be so widely dispersed and so well entrenched as to be difficult to control. The obligation of preserving the habitat for the future generations is particularly hard to meet, since hazards may only be accumulating slowly, without causing any apparent present ill, while the future generations are mute. Yet this is the most important environmental benefit that we owe to the future.

If we consider sense, issues of justice may seem less critical, since here we deal more with emotional and intellectual satisfactions than with sheer survival. Yet surely a bare modicum of good orientation must be available to everyone. Since that quality is most often either an indivisible good, produced by means that benefit large sectors of the population at the same time, or is something that can be achieved at small scales by granting local territorial control, problems of equitable distribution will come up more rarely with this than with other goods. They may appear, however, when we think of the city as a symbolic communication device, which can be manipulated to express one set of cultural values and not another, since the freedom of thought and communication is indeed an important issue of justice. In addition, sensibility plays an important role in the childhood environment. Since the significance of a city is an important ingredient of its educative value, here is one area where we might plead that the just distribution be an *unequal* one, to be based on need. Specially gifted children may justify special opportunities of enrichment. Specific qualities of identification and orientation are of particular importance to the handicapped. Unless this is attended to, they will have a very unequal share of access to other goods.

Equal access, indeed, is second only to vitality as a pivotal issue of environmental justice. The lives of the handicapped, the young, the old, the poor, the ill, the subjugated races, classes, and genders are severely diminished when their access to other people, areas, services, and activities is curtailed.

Exclusion may be an expression of privilege, or a deliberate device of oppressive control, or simply an unintended consequence of other choices, as has happened to the teenager in the North American suburb. The ability to range safely over a city has an important part to play in the development of early adolescence. Substantial equity of environmental access, at least up to some reasonable range of space and diversity of setting, must surely be one fundamental characteristic of a good city. Implementing that particular principle of justice entails some public subsidy of transport and communication, as well as special efforts to free those whose movements is restricted by some personal characteristic. Free movement and free communication are a fundamental component of that freedom of thought and of person that we prize.

When we consider the relation of justice to fit, we face a more complicated picture. The banner of equity has most often been raised precisely in this realm, particularly in regard to housing, schools, and parks. Surely there is a basic minimum of such spaces that should be available to all, and we are dismayed to compare a Newport mansion with a tenement apartment. But once vital requirements are assured, that basic minimum of space may change markedly as social resources and styles of life change. A good environment exhibits a quantitative and qualitative fit between form and intended behavior, but those characteristics of form need not be evenly divided among all persons. We may be more ready to accept an inequality between the physical facilities provided to individuals, as long as some very simple social minimum is met (as is considered essential by that society for any normal life), and as long as individuals have some rough equality of means whereby they can acquire goods of various kinds. In this particular realm, then, the simplifying criterion of equalizing income and power, rather than trying to equalize a great array of desired facilities, seems to be the more cogent rule. Understood, of course, that baseline minimums may have to be set higher for disadvantaged people, and that some thresholds of manipulability and reversibility may also need to be set, in justice to the future generations.

Last, we come to control. A just distribution of one type of spatial control can be considered critical, since the ability to maintain a private territory (and perhaps also to have access to some "wasteland" where behavior is open) is another important component of freedom. Justice may require that all people should be able to participate in the control of those activity settings in which they have a vital interest and to which they are willing to devote substantial effort (as long, that is, as such control does not unduly constrict the access and participation of others). Thus teachers and children might claim a voice in school management as a matter of justice, workers in workplace management, and so on. The analysis of participation in spatial control by various social groups would be, like the mapping of equity of access, basic evidence in the analysis of justice.

I conclude that essential equities of vitality, of access, and of the control of private and small group territory, including the conservation of the future habitat and the provision for childhood growth, are the most crucial areas of environmental justice. To that we might add satisficing minimums of the basic behavior settings, as tempered by individual need and social norms. Special individual requirements may be of some importance in allocating sensibility. A just allocation to future generations is the most critical issue of all and the most difficult to analyze.

The spatial environment is a pervasive influence, with great inertia. It is like genetic endowment and social structure in the persistent way in which it distributes life's chances. The justice of that distribution is therefore one of the more critical aspects of environmental value. The comments above are clearly culture-bound and cannot be defended as eternally just. They reflect Western preoccupations with equality and freedom and the author's preoccupation with individual development.

Let us now peer back into our thicket of values, to see how well they have met the general criteria set forth at the beginning of chapter 6. On most counts, they do reasonably well. They are general, and at the same level of generality. They are explicitly connected to city form, assuming that we allow perceptions and control institutions to be considered as features of city form. They can be connected to important goals which appear in the vast majority of cultures, if not in all of them. Whether they cover all the features of settlements that are relevant to all cultural goals will appear only later. It is likely that they do not, but it also seems likely that they cover a substantial majority of aims, and nothing in the theory sets a limit on the eventual list. They are dimensions of performance, measurable by obtainable data. On two counts, however, they may be weak, and this is worth some discussion.

First, to what extent are they independent of each other? Where does a setting on one dimension entail fixing performance on another? To the degree that there is such interdependence, analysis is more difficult, although the dimensions are not thereby rendered completely useless. Interdependence will appear only after detailed study, but our suspicions are aroused. There would seem to be a connection between access and sense, for to be accessible a place must also be sensible. The reverse is not necessarily true, however. In addition, one valued subdimension of access—the degree to which local inhabitants can open up or close off communications at will—is clearly only a particular aspect of the general dimension of control. Here we find a direct overlap. A more confused tangle of dimensions is associated with adaptability and control than in other cases. If a place is highly manipulable and locally controlled, then one would expect that it would be well fitted and sensible as well. Independence is difficult to imagine, in this case. But a place can be well controlled and not manipulable, and vice versa. Everywhere else, however, independence at least seems thinkable. We can recall well-fitted places which are poor vital habitats, for example, or controlled places which are either accessible or inaccessible, or adaptable places which are sensible or insensible, and so on. Of course, achievement in one dimension may support or conflict with achievement in another without losing possible dimensional independence. Thus, good access is one of the devices useful for achieving

adaptability, or for increasing sustenance, but an
accessible place need not be adaptable or sustenant.
Local user control may frequently conflict with
general access or with safety, but not by necessity.
Good legibility is one way of increasing access to
information, yet is not requisite to it.

The second and more difficult issue is the relation of these dimensions to cultural variation.
Clearly, different cultures will value positions along
these dimensions differently; the dimensions are
designed to allow for just that. But would these
cultures *define* them differently, so that no analysis
of position on any dimension could be made until
the culture was specified? Vitality seems independent of cultural definition, since it is based on
human biology. So do access and adaptability to
future fit, to large degree, once technology, control
institutions, and place attitudes are defined as part
of environmental form. Sense is not independent of
culture, when one is talking of complex meanings.
But in most of its subdimensions, as I have laid
them out, it is primarily related to form, common
experience, and the nature of human perception
and cognition. Control can also be specified mostly
by reference to form (because we have defined form
to include the institutions of spatial control, which
are clearly a part of the culture, too). Fit is the
maverick. Since it is the match between behavior
and form, it can be described only at a superficial
level of misfit, if one simply observes the activity in
a place. When we inquire into the appropriateness
and difficulty of fit as it is felt by users, we are in the
midst of all their customs and attitudes. Even the
definition is culture-dependent, and thus few
generalizations can be made about the features of
form which are effective for achieving good fit, such
as can be made for the other dimensions. We are left
with a focus of concern and a generalized method of
observation.

If desirable positions on these dimensions vary
with situation, it would be comforting to state some
general hypotheses about *how* they vary. There are
several fundamental differences among societies
that might be expected to be critical for our purpose:
the level of resources available, the homogeneity of

values, the degree to which power is concentrated, and the relative stability of society and setting. The matrix below displays some first speculations as to how valuations on these dimensions might be expected to vary with social situation. The variance of situation is expressed as a crude polar opposition.

These are crude guesses, only the first steps in developing testable hypotheses. We might summarize this guessing matrix by saying:

1. As a society becomes richer, there is a shift in interest. Sensibility in particular may become more highly valued, but fit and control remain important. Many dimensions may become less critical—not because they are less highly valued, but because it is easier to find a substitute for them or to pay the costs of failure.

2. Vitality is important in any case, but in a homogeneous society, many of the other dimensions are either less critical or easier to achieve.

3. The stability of society and setting makes a fundamental and clear-cut difference. All dimensions are either less critical or easier to achieve in a stable situation.

4. A centralized society (or at least those who are at its center of power) are likely to value and use these dimensions for different purposes than other societies or persons, rather than more or less. I would guess, however, that access may be more critical for such a society and that it is less likely to achieve good fit.

Perhaps an even more global and misleading guess can be made: except for sense and vitality, a rich, stable, homogeneous society is less dependent on the quality of its environment than is a poor, unstable, plural one. But these guesses (or hypotheses, to be more dignified) refer only to general tendencies of valuation in any society. Persons and small groups within that society will set their own goals and thresholds along these dimensions, according to their own deep values and situations. A poor migrant to a third-world city will emphasize access to jobs, services, and basic vital resources. A tourist will focus on the sense of place. A child may be most concerned with manipulability, freedom,

		Vitality	Sense	Fit	Access	Control
Society is:	rich	important for both, but	generally more highly valued	easier to achieve but more complex; future fit less critical	substitutes available; diversity is valued	important for both
	poor	more critical where margin is narrower	but symbolic meaning valued even when poor	simpler but more critical	crucial, especially to basic resources	
Society is:	homogeneous	important for both	easier to achieve	easier to achieve	less important?	less important?
	heterogeneous		more difficult, but richer	more complex	important, to avoid alienation	important
Society is:	stable	easier to accomplish	easier to achieve	easier to achieve	less important	less important
	unstable	more difficult to maintain	more difficult	present fit more difficult to maintain; future fit is crucial for survival	crucial for survival	crucial
Society is:	centralized	easier to attain via standards and technical knowledge	used to express and support dominance	less likely to be achieved; formal adaptability is valued	critical for control	local control suppressed
	decentralized	more difficult to achieve except via stable customs and widespread knowledge	expresses diversity	more likely to be achieved; manipulability is valued	less critical	local control favored

Some hypothetical variations in
the achievement and valuation
of the performance dimensions,
in relation to variations in
social situation

safety, and a world which reveals its significance to him as he searches out its secrets. The dimensions are constructed to allow these variations to be made explicit.

Even for such particular groups, we cannot develop a single index of goodness, since that would require that all dimensions and subdimensions be quantified in some common unit. Although our values are measurable, at least in rough degree, their integration must be left to personal and social judgment. Moreover, I speak only of the formal qualities of the city. The goodness of any human settlement, considered as an entity, depends on much more than its form.

So what is good city form? Now we can say the magic words. It is vital (sustenant, safe, and consonant); it is sensible (identifiable, structured, congruent, transparent, legible, unfolding, and significant); it is well fitted (a close match of form and behavior which is stable, manipulable, and resilient); it is accessible (diverse, equitable, and locally manageable); and it is well controlled (congruent, certain, responsible, and intermittently loose). And all of these are achieved with justice and internal efficiency. Or, in the more general terms of chapter 6, it is a continuous, well-connected, open place, conducive to development.

III SOME APPLICATIONS

13

City Size and the Idea of Neighborhood

Having come up with some fine words, can we apply them to practical problems? Do they help us understand, even a little better, any prevailing controversies over urban form? Certain grand questions have preoccupied these debates. Some of them are persistent questions, some are emergent, others fading, still others have faded once and now reappear. More are probably waiting in the wings.

The great-grandfather of all those questions has been that of city size. The insufficiency of very small settlements and the oppression and confusion of very large ones, as well as the pangs of growth and decline, have led to the idea that a city, like an organism, has a proper size, at which its growth should be stabilized. This idea goes well back in intellectual history. Plato proposed that the good city should have a population of 5040* landholders or citizens, a number which would be maintained by emigration and by rules of inheritance. He failed to explain why this peculiar number should be the right one, but we may guess that he thought a factorial number ideal because it could be divided so flexibly into various equal groups (and perhaps also for more mystical mathematical reasons) and that factorial 6 (or 720) was in his judgment too small, while factorial 8 (or 40,320) was too large. Aristotle, in the *Politics*, was more careful to say that "ten people would not make a city, and with a hundred thousand it is a city no longer." It should be big enough to be "self-sufficient for living the good life after the manner of a political community," but not so big that citizens lose personal touch with each other, for "to decide questions of justice, and to distribute the offices according to merit, it is necessary for the citizens to know each other's personal characters." The total population of the Athens of his day may have been about 250,000, both free and slave, of whom perhaps 40,000 were citizens. But most Greek city states had 10,000 citizens or less.

*5040 is factorial 7, which is $1 \times 2 \times 3 \times 4 \times 5 \times 6 \times 7$.

There is a vast literature on the subject of city size. It seemed to peak a generation ago, but recently it has gained in volume once more. Our anxiety on the subject is recurrent. The size generally considered optimal rose from Aristotle's 5040 to 20,000 and then progressively higher, until it now stands somewhere between 250,000 and 500,000 persons. Attempts to act on this belief in an ideal size go back at least to the futile attempts to stop the growth of Elizabethan London, which had the effect of raising the price of housing and of affording favorable opportunities for corruption. The reduction or stabilization of city size is now a commonplace of national policy in most of Europe and in the socialist countries, and it is at least an item of faith in much of the rest of the world.

Until recently, most efforts to halt the growth of the largest cities have had little effect, including the well-known program in England and the much more severe measures taken in the USSR. More recently, however, it appears that the strong measures applied in Cuba, in Vietnam, and in China—which in varying degree have included the tying of food rationing to locality, the diversion of investment to the countryside, and the induced or forced emigration of students and adults from the city—have at last begun to brake the growth of the big urban areas. And now, under a new regime, the disaffected backwash of that involuntary emigration to the Chinese countryside is surfacing again in the big cities. The antiurban policy of the recently defeated government of Cambodia has been even harsher, causing the virtual depopulation of Pnom Penh and the destruction of all its services, utilities, and equipment. Meanwhile, in the most highly developed countries, such as the United States, there is evidence that the tide has turned on its own account, and that the biggest cities and metropolitan areas are now losing population.*

The concept of a limit size is of course an integral component of the organic model. Arguments for optimum size are based on its effects on social intercourse, on political and social control, on the vitality of the environment because of accumulated

Appelbaum
Elgin
Gilbert
Kracht
Pinchemel
Richardson 1973

*Or is it possible that our urban regions are now becoming so vast that they outrun our census divisions?

Hoch 1973, 1976
Real Estate Research
Stone

pollution, on tolerable levels of social and perceptual stimulus, on travel time, on economic production, and on the costs of maintaining cities of different sizes. For the most part, these are different ways of stating our previously defined dimensions. But, while there are acres of such literature, it is very thinly sown with evidence. The greatest density of information can be found in the recent work of Irving Hoch, of the Real Estate Research Corporation, and of P. A. Stone in Great Britain.

In summary, there is evidence that some types of air pollution (an aspect of vitality) are positively correlated with city size, and that so is the travel time to work (a component of access). Otherwise, most quantifiable factors show no correlation, or at least their connection is doubtful. In addition, real incomes and productivity are higher in large cities. Many economists therefore conclude that large cities are economically more efficient than smaller ones, even if perhaps more unpleasant to live in. This unpleasantness is compensated for by higher real wages, and so people choose to live in bigger places. No major limiting factors in city size can be discerned. Public policies to restrict city size involve hidden costs and should be avoided.

These conclusions reflect the normal outlook of the economist: an emphasis on quantifiable factors which can be converted into a common index ($), the use of the concepts of equilibrium and of informed choice in a perfect market, the idea that a city is like a firm in competition with other cities, and so on. There is less attention to who pays and who benefits in large cities (justice), to the actual freedom of choice of location, and to those social and personal values which cannot be converted into dollars (sensibility, for just one example). It is ironic that these attacks on city size theory are developing just as the theory is becoming a basis for policy in most other nations, and just as trends away from large cities are appearing in our own country.

U.S. Department of
Housing and Urban
Development

Unfortunately, the evidence that there is general optimum city size is weak indeed. May it be that this great question is, after all our mental labor, only an empty one? Many effects that we attribute to city size, such as congestion, are more correctly associated with the general *density* of a city, and particularly with the density of its employment centers, when many people must converge into a relatively small area each working day. Congestion need not appear in extensive, multinucleate cities of low density, even if they are extremely large.

There are modifications to that question that might give it more substance. First, of course, any single city might have an optimum size—based on its geography, culture, economy, political system, way of life, etc.—even if there is no general optimum. Or an optimum might be applicable to all cities within one strong, homogeneous culture. But this has yet to be shown, except under such severe restrictions as those imposed by a very limited site. If such diverse optima were to be included in a general theory, they would have to be associated with a general method for deriving the particular optimum. No one has yet proposed such a method.

An intermediate position, and one that is closer to the pattern of real settlements, is to assert that, while there is no such thing as a single size optimum, there is a preferred *system* of settlements, made up of a series of places whose sizes are distributed in some optimum way. Central place theory, through its investigation of how marketplaces of different sizes would be distributed in a uniform region, has come to such a hierarchical ranking. Approximations of this ranking can be found in real cases where conditions are relatively even and stable. Therefore, this is the right pattern. It *should* exist, as a matter of policy. One wonders a little at the leap from *does* exist to *should*, and whether an efficiency for marketing (given a long list of equalities and assumptions) should be the key rule in city form.

Berry 1970
Christaller

Most likely, if a basis for optimum size can be found, it will be in the form of a series of sizes, for different functions and especially for the different preferences of residents for such dimensions as identity, access, and control. But it seems less likely that this will develop into a single prescribed series, or even that much can be accomplished in prescribing a series, until progress has been made

Malisz

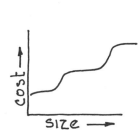

in connecting size and value dimensions in particular kinds of cities.

Another possibility is that no one size is an optimum, even for a single city, but that there are a series of thresholds at which certain major benefits and costs (particularly the latter) are encountered, as growth crosses those limits. These costs then level off as growth rises toward the next threshold of size. At some particular point an expensive new sewage plant will be required, for example, to maintain a vital habitat, and that adequacy will then be maintained through an entire cycle of growth. Knowing these thresholds, policy should try to keep just below them, or, if growth cannot be restrained, to jump over them rapidly and by a wide margin.

This seems intuitively reasonable. When settlements are small relative to the size of public works needed for their development, and when the works required are either few or tend to have similar thresholds, this seems a sensible thing to analyze as a basis for public policy. But when the settlement is large and complex, it is likely that the threshold costs of the many services and facilities required will so overlap each other that no clear steplike pattern can be found. We have too often based city form policy on single factors when a whole complex was at work: we have used a preferred classroom size to set the proper population for a neighborhood, and indices of land value to determine the "highest and best" location of activities. Only in smaller settlements may it be reasonable to look for a coincidence of thresholds. But the idea does point to the more general possibility that the rate of change in size may be more important than size itself.

Moreover, there is some confusion about how size is to be measured. There is general agreement that the key variable is the number of the resident population, rather than, say, the number of workers, or the geographical extent of settlement, or the square footage of floor space, or the dollar volume of production. But the residents of what unit? Do we speak of the commuting region, for example, the area within which no smaller boundary can be drawn that would not be crossed by substantial numbers of people commuting daily to work? If so, these regions are of very large extent in the developed countries and are steadily growing larger, to the point where they escape the conventional definitions of the metropolitan region (indeed, this breakdown of the definition may explain some of the apparent recent population losses of these regions). Since both the diversity and range of access appear to increase as a commuting region increases in population, there should be advantages in larger size, both for reasons of economic productivity and of personal satisfaction. Sustenance might be more secure. Adaptability should also be enhanced, since there would be more alternative locations, jobs, bases of production, sources of service, etc. There is no apparent reason for an increase in costs, at similar levels of service, nor for a poorer fit to desired behavior.* Despite our deep-seated fears about "endless" cities, there is no necessary reason why sense should suffer in a large commuting area. Such a region could (at least in theory) be as various, as satisfying, as meaningful as (and no more "suffocating" than) an extended farming area or a large wilderness.

There are serious problems of political control as size goes up, and it is possible (but not inevitable) that certain kinds of air and water pollution will be harder to control. There is likely to be a greater dependence on exotic sources of energy and material, and a more extensive problem of waste disposal. But none of these seems at first glance insurmountable (except perhaps the political issue, for which see below). Like many other effects, they may be more closely connected with density than with size itself.

The likelihood that we will find an optimum size for a commuting region seems dim. Moreover, as communications improve, more and more people may be enabled to work at home, at least part of the week, and still be active members of large-scale productive systems. If so, the critical living space becomes a communications, rather than a commuting, region—that is, a region within which any smaller boundary would interrupt a significant flow

*Note that I am speculating here about size alone, at comparable densities and mixes of activity. High densities or sharp segregations of activity will have effects of their own.

of daily messages. At that point, the issue of regional size seems to dissolve before our eyes. As cities become less and less like tangible, bounded objects, the old conundrum can no longer be posed, much less solved.

But there are smaller groupings whose size might be analyzed for optima. These are the service regions for various facilities which are important for access, and the various ranks of political units which are so crucial for control. Indeed, it is probably the latter size that most people have in mind when they say that they abhor the big city because it is "uncontrollable," and why opinion polls in the United States regularly uncover strong preferences for living in suburbs and small towns.* It is in governmental units of 20,000–40,000 people that ordinary citizens can be active in politics if they wish, feel connected to an identifiable political community, and sense some control over public affairs, constrained as small town moves may be by regional, national, and corporate decisions. The requirements that Aristotle had in mind when discussing city size were precisely these political ones. In any given political economy, there may be optimum sizes for political units, ranging from regions to towns and even localities. But these considerations refer more to political than to spatial organization, except that political structure can be reinforced by providing a legible identity and by the way in which localized services are distributed. The scale of interdependent settlement is extremely large today and demands a political unit at a regional level, to manage spatial resources which are of necessity regional systems. Thus we may want to strengthen *both* regional government and small, self-governing "towns" within a single urban region, while dissolving the "big city" which lies between them in scale. Further, in the search for better control, we might consider devolving certain simple political functions to small local districts, as will be discussed below.†

*If they are within a reasonable drive, that is, of some larger urban center—no one is about to give up modern standards of access!
†There is another issue that arises here. We are accustomed to a world where government is always a territorial unit, except for a few special purpose authorities, while private centers of power are

The issue of physical size may indeed be meaningful, and even generalizable, at the scale of the *very* local unit, within which people are personally acquainted with each other by reason of residential proximity, and where size—plus other features such as social homogeneity, street pattern, identity of boundaries, and common services—may play a definite role in promoting control, present fit, and sensibility. Neighborhoods of this kind are probably no larger than 100 households at the most, and more likely 15 to 30. They are a good deal smaller than that "neighborhood" which in classical planning doctrine is sized to fit an elementary school.

This idea of the urban neighborhood has ridden a professional rollercoaster. In the first quarter of this century, it was a unit of social analysis used by pioneers in urban sociology. The idea then grew that the neighborhood was the proper territorial base of a socially supportive group, among whom there would be many personal contracts. Planning theorists, reassured by their organic models, picked up the idea of the neighborhood as the basic building block of a city. It was to be a defined spatial unit, free of through traffic and as self-sufficient in daily services as possible. The unit was sized to the catchment area of the typical elementary school, and the catchments of other services were to be adjusted to this module, or to integral multiples of it. This idea is still influential in city design throughout the world. It has advantages of simplicity for design; it provides quiet streets; it insures some fit of services to demand.

Later, the social assumption of this idea was thoroughly debunked. It did not correspond to conditions in most North American cities, where social contacts might be territorially based at the smallest scale (such as within a single block), but were otherwise dispersed across large sectors of the city. These connections were based on kinship, or work, or interests, rather than on place. This spatial

Park

American Public Health Association
Dahir
Perry

Isaacs

often functionally, rather than spatially, defined. Is this matching of turf and public power always the best way to organize government? I am glad to slip by this question, since a new answer would have disturbing consequences for us.

Sims

dispersion seemed to hold for all but a few low-income residents of ethnic ghettos. The bounded spatial unit did not fit the network of social interaction. When the neighborhood idea was actually applied in city design, moreover, it produced a run of stereotyped units. The catchment areas of various services could not easily be fitted to any single module, and they kept changing. Adult friendships were not based on children's attendance at the elementary school, and the administratively efficient sizes of these schools distorted the urban fabric, if they were taken as a fundamental measure. Access suffered.

Just after the neighborhood idea had been thoroughly demolished at the highest intellectual levels* it flared up again from below. Various threats to existing local areas—threats of urban renewal, school busing, new expressways, institutional expansion, or an ethnic invasion—raised a surge of resistance, organized principally at the neighborhood level. People demonstrated that, while their jobs and even their friendships did not follow neighborhood lines, they could nevertheless join hands at that level when it was necessary to defend themselves. These neighborhood organizations were issue-oriented and change-resistant, rather than change-generating. They have since become politically effective at higher, more formal levels of government. Ward politics has reappeared. The neighborhood idea proved useful as a weapon of control.

Recent investigations of how people conceive of a city in their minds show that the named local community is often an important element of that mental structure. The neighborhood may not be essential to their social relations, but it is, along with the main routes, an essential piece of their mental equipment. So, from being an ideal unit of social organization and an organizer for access to public services, the neighborhood idea becomes a concept of control and, less critically perhaps, a concept of sensibility. It is no longer a space within which people know each other because they live next door, but a space which is commonly defined

*Naturally, I refer to our
graduate schools of planning.

and given a name, and within which people find it relatively easy to band together when things get dangerous. These communities exist in the minds of city dwellers, and there is often fair agreement about their boundaries and their stereotyped characteristics. That agreement is reinforced by word of mouth and by the media. City agencies use it as a basis for setting up local liaison, and this further cements the structure.

Since the basic issue is one of control, the question for city design is, first, whether this type of community organization can, and even should, be reinforced by spatial form, and, second, what elements of the settlement might properly be placed under community control, and in what way. It seems evident that settlement design can reinforce an agreed-upon image of community by means of separations, the placement of local centers, the diversion of main trafficways, the exploitation of irregularities of terrain, and other differentiations of physical character. As long as these visual compartments do not block general access patterns and do not constrain social contacts or service areas, they increase legibility, decrease the noise and danger of fast traffic, and increase the possibility of local organization and control, all without major cost.

But if barriers to movement are erected, or if people are directed to shop in one place and work in another, or to use a particular service, then access and adaptability decline. Moreover, if efforts are made to increase the social homogeneity of a place, which is much more powerful than physical design as a way of inducing a sense of community, then all the issues emerge which will be discussed below under the heading of "grain." Planned social and physical homogeneity are certainly defensible at the level of the much smaller, "true" social neighborhood,* since they improve social cohesion, fit, control, and sense without seriously damaging anyone's access. But they are more dangerous at the community scale. Apart from that, the pleasures of living in an identifiable district which has quiet, safe streets and daily services easily accessi-

*Below a size of 100 households.

ble nearby, and within which one can organize politically when the need for control arises, are surely a legitimate feature of good settlement. For certain age groups, moreover, particularly the young child, a place-based social community is quite important. Identifiable local residential areas also allow individuals to participate in improving their immediate surroundings.

The argument for the neighborhood* goes further than this. Advocates of smallness and of decentralization would insist that this local district should be able to control its own living space and, to some degree, its own economy and public services. Any approach to self-sufficiency in such factors as food, energy, and construction, is commendable in that view. Local corporations should provide local jobs and retain profits locally, instead of "losing" them to others outside. A local polity could run the school, manage the open spaces, and patrol the streets.

There are two difficulties in this position. The first is that it runs counter to the scale of the present political economy, both in the capitalist and the socialist countries. In the United States, for example, locally controlled businesses, which rely on local labor, resources, and capital, have difficulty in surviving, much less in equaling the productivity of firms which are nationally or regionally based. Self-sufficiency is a dream of the past. Disadvantaged groups which depend solely on community action may be locking themselves in with their disadvantages, destroying their own access. They are merely camping on the lower slopes of power. Furthermore, many environmental issues, such as pollution, transportation, housing policy, or public finance, simply cannot be tackled at this level. They are incongruent with that scale. But local food gardens and energy supplements, locally managed housing, parks, day care centers, and street patrols can be useful and satisfying. The confidence and organization gained in supplying local services can be a step toward reaching for citizen control of

*Perhaps local district is a better word to use, reserving "neighborhood" for that very small area within which people are acquainted simply because they live next door and "community" for the coherent social entity.

larger events. Thus local management can improve vitality and control and be one path to better control at more critical levels. But it will surely be a mistake to restrict, or even focus, strategy on the local level, as the key to social change.

The second difficulty in local control is an ethical one. Control of the local turf slips easily into exclusion or expulsion of the unwanted. Exclusion may not be a serious issue at the small scale of the true neighborhood, but at local district levels and above, it becomes an important deprivation of access. Local control of the suburbs, extensively employed, results in trapping lower-income groups in the inner city, or in shunting them into a few less favored sectors of expansion. Housing costs rise in this restricted maneuver space. A legitimate aversion to imposing long trips to school on small children becomes a defense of school segregation. The quality of local services will vary widely when no overall set of standards can be imposed and paid for. Short-term interests may override long-term goals. Again, local control must be restricted to such functions and defined by such limits that these ethical difficulties do not arise.

Thus, while user control is admirable, control at the district level may lack the effectiveness of regional or national control, on the one hand, and the direct satisfactions and ethical simplicity of control by the very small true neighborhood or family, on the other. Nevertheless, limited district control, and especially the existence of a district framework on which political organization can be erected when needed, are two valuable features of any settlement. Legible local community areas, quiet streets, and convenient local services have a clear value. Building small, defined, and homogeneous clusters of dwellings may in cases support true social neighborhoods. It is the concept of the large, autonomous, sharply defined, and rigid neighborhood unit of standard size, to which all physical and social relations are keyed, that seems to be inappropriate to our society. In another economy— one communally organized and relatively coherent in its values, where small is really beautiful, local control might become a central feature of settlement design.

Cambridge Institute

Growth and Conservation

If the absolute size of a settlement is less important than we have thought, except perhaps at the neighborhood scale or in a political sense, we cannot be indifferent to the rate of change of size. Rapid growth means constant turmoil, facilities which are ill fitted to demand, and institutions whose capabilities constantly lag behind the need for them. The landscape is scarred with construction. Sense suffers, and access is confused. Events seem out of control, and decisions may be made badly under stress. Most serious, perhaps, are the constant breaking and remaking of social ties that is required and the political conflicts that arise between natives and newcomers.

Some of these problems are results of a growth in total size, while others derive from the movement of people, whatever the resulting net growth may be. Mobility and the growth of places are not the same. Much back and forth population movement can occur with little effect on aggregate growth rates. In the United States at present, gross migration is something like ten times its effect in net growth. Much of the world, and the United States in particular, is on the move: immigrants, refugees, job seekers, vacationers, tourists, travelers, and retirees. Where it is voluntary, this human flux, like the mobility of capital, has important advantages, since it brings skill and labor to places where they can best be used and people to places which they prefer. But much mobility is far from voluntary, and so moving entails serious costs, of which psychological depression is not the least.

There may be some environmental ways of coping with these emotional costs. One thinks of better communication and information, rituals of transition, training newcomers to understand new places, transporting artifacts other than furniture, the migration of whole communities, "sister" relations between exporting and importing places, second homes located in both, and so on. But considerations of that kind are rarely introduced into public policy, which simply offers, if anything, a subsidy to pay direct relocation costs. Population movement is a fact of our time, and there are ways to enhance its human qualities. But the consequences of rapid mobility are such that there are good reasons for policies that will moderate it.

To control the movement of people is to withdraw an important personal freedom, to restrict access in a most fundamental way. In theory this is unconstitutional within the United States, but any extensive local growth controls will have that indirect effect. The freedom of movement between nations has increasingly been restricted, just as (and because) migration has come within the reach of poor people. If equity of access is our aim, growth rate control at the settlement level should at least be accompanied by some rationing of relocation opportunity that does not discriminate by income. Even in highly controlled societies, severe measures have been necessary to block migration, or to direct it where economic plans would like it to go. We must wonder not only about what an optimum growth rate might be, but also about the best way of achieving it. Do we restrict the movement of persons, or stop house building, or prevent the expansion of jobs, or raise development standards so high that the costs discourage newcomers? Surely the more humane devices are those that encourage investment where people are, rather than those that prevent it where they wish to go or promote it where they are not. Apparent growth may also be caused by the replacement and enlargement of facilities. While this may consume (and also create) resources, it may have few of the negative consequences of a population shift. Keep in mind, moreover, that our concern is the growth of settlements, and not other changes that are vilified under the same name, such as growths in consumption, production, waste, or crime.

In any event, it is apparent that the growth in size of a place or a change in its function can often be too rapid for successful adjustment of the vitality and fit. While growth was once applauded, and still is in economics, we have recently come to see dangers in it, and some argue for "zero growth," just as Plato did. But absolute stability is hard to maintain. Moreover, since populations and places

252
Freedom of movement
and zero growth

L. Gordon

Rust

Thompson

age, the composition of the whole will change in a marked way when there is a transition from steady growth to permanent stability. This compositional change—the shift to older ages in a stable population, for example—may have its own unpleasant consequences. Secondly, a policy which focuses on stability may as easily precipitate a decline. Thus it seems reasonable to think that there is some moderate rate of growth which is an optimum. Despite all the talk, however, and the flurry of public measures, no serious studies have yet been made to see whether there are optimum change rates for places. At what rates can good fit, sense, and access be continuously provided?

Turn back for a moment to the second argument against zero growth, that of potential decline. We see the world through metaphors, and the metaphor here is that a settlement is an organism which, if it decreases in bulk, is about to die. Or it is an engine which either runs forward, stops, or goes in reverse; and who knows where it will go in reverse? All planners bewail decline. Our theories analyze growth, not loss. Yet, while rapid decline (like rapid growth) may be a catastrophe, there are also values in a moderate, negative rate of growth, including such things as good access to an abundance of space and facilities, low stress, increased adaptability and control, and strong historical legibility. Tourists and summer people seek out just such places, and natives will often remain in them by choice. Could we plan for decline, to realize those values?

Thus it is possible that there might be optimum rates of growth *or* decline in certain general situations. Public strategy might seek to keep within an optimum range of rate on both sides of the zero point, for reasons of cost, legibility, control, and political competence. Optimum rates might refer to changes in density as well as in size, or to rates of interchange of population. These optimum rates would be different at different scales of territory. A very rapid increase of decline in a local place might be tolerable if adequately supported, while large regions should stay much closer to stability. We have little information on such optima, however.

Controls based on rates of change, rather than on absolute limits, seem to have some advantages. Instead of setting a maximum allowable size or density, or a fixed use, they limit the speed at which that size or density or use could allowably change. For example, Knowles suggests rules for solar access which depend on the context of a site, and change as that context changes. The permissible density of a city would then grow smoothly, consistent with its existing density and its immediate past and future. Problems of too rapid a shift, so often confused for those of absolute magnitude, could thus be directly avoided. At the same time, adaptability would not be impaired, and public action would be guided by current reality, rather than by some doubtful, long-range prediction. Abandoning fixed limits may deprive people of a sense of security, but that is a false sense in any case. I have earlier suggested the value of looking for sensible constancies within change itself, and how environmental form might support that search. But the law will also have problems of its own with rules of rate. Those legal problems reflect the same psychological search for security.

Nevertheless, when we begin to look into it, we may find that the concept of an optimum rate of change is as elusive as optimum size itself. The "goodness" of a change may depend more on its form than on its quantitative rate: was it an abrupt leap succeeded by stagnation, a wild oscillation, a steady unending expansion, or an S-curve of growth from one plateau to another? Repeated oscillations, for example, may give rise to standard difficulties. Or the form and magnitude of change may have to be considered together. Yet even the effect of simple rate on our dimensions has still to be investigated. The forms of growth and decline are intrinsic features of urban form, with multiple and interesting consequences. They should not be sources of automatic satisfaction or alarm.

Throughout the developed world, many people are preoccupied with the conservation of the natural, or of the historic, environment. The two drives had separate origins, but now they are merging. Saving the environment has become a holy

Knowles

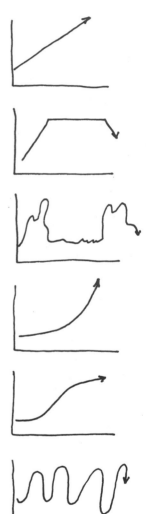

cause, and great energies are expended to this end. These efforts are usually last-minute rescue attempts, made in the face of some strong economic pressure to change. They are backed by a substantial sector of public opinion in the developed countries. Many people are convinced that rural areas, or the older sections of cities, are much more attractive than any possible area of new building.

Of these two attitudes, the admiration for the natural environment is the more widespread and deep-rooted. It goes back to the romantic reevaluation of nature in the eighteenth and nineteenth centuries. In that view, the wilderness was no longer ugly and dangerous, but beautiful and sublime. Lords and prosperous merchants began to build villas in the countryside, and the well-to-do to take rural vacations. Instead of threatening man, nature was threatened by his new-found powers. People (those who needed not labor there, that is) were healthy and at ease in the country, but tense and alienated in the city. The city itself was seen to be an unfortunate economic necessity, spreading without control over the countryside. Woods and small farms were being destroyed to make room for houses and factories, or the vast fields of agri-business. Water and air and soil were being polluted. This degradation might be irreversible and lead to some disastrous end: a man-made desert, oceans poisoned with waste, a sudden climatic shift, a wholesale elimination of species, or unbreathable air. Thus cities were seen to be a fundamental threat to our habitat. The developing science of ecology, while damping out some of the more extreme fears of this kind, also laid the intellectual groundwork for these attitudes, by demonstrating the interconnectedness of the living world and how its perturbations work themselves out in surprising ways.

Preservation of the countryside has also been used, whether consciously or not, as a means of class exclusion. Land takings for nature reserves and the imposition of minimum lot sizes have been effective devices for keeping low-income people out of the suburbs. It has therefore been asserted that the conservation of nature is simply an upper-class slogan, articulated by the well-to-do for their own purposes.

As far as I know, the last proposition is false. The preference for natural scenery is widespread among all classes, in the United States, at least. This preference may not be so general in countries where much of the population experiences or remembers rural poverty, but its near-universality in this country has been amply demonstrated. These preferences are rather specific: for the well-managed, productive landscape of the small family farm; for the shores of lakes and seas; and for park landscapes: places which are grassy and open, with scattered trees, small woods, water nearby, and a view of hills or mountains. The cult of the wilderness—places untouched by man—is a more restricted taste, but it is also a growing one. Unfortunately, few true extensive wilderness areas still exist, except in the polar regions, the shrinking tropical forests, and the great deserts.

If nature is the world untouched by man, then to preserve it, it follows that we must isolate the few remaining pure natural regions from human intrusion, including any intrusion by the wilderness lover himself. Should these unsullied lands then also be protected from other "natural" changes, such as erosion or forest fires set by lightning? The wilderness would be saved for its own sake, for scientific study, and for the mental satisfaction that it still exists, even if it is not accessible.

If we follow our impure preferences, on the other hand, and admit managed landscapes such as farms, parks, ponds, and woods to be parts of valued nature, then how can we exclude the city? If nature is the living system and its habitat, man is part of that living system, and a city is as natural as any wood or stream. So we are forced to explain what aspects of nature we prefer to protect or to suppress.

The city and the inhabited countryside have always been one unit. Sometimes it has been the unity of exploiter and exploited, but they have always been linked together, socially, economically, and politically. The country we have idealized has usually been the country with the labor taken out of it, as Raymond Williams demonstrates. The feeling for rural scenery in the United States may in part be explained by our present distance from hard

See fig. 60

R. Williams

rural labor. It is also true, however, that in some areas of this country, there was in the nineteenth century a limited period of rural prosperity, based on the family farm.* Most of our rural memories refer to this time, if not to the even briefer (and far nastier) age of the open cattle range.

None of this can debunk the strong contemporary feeling for trees, water, and rural scenery. The country may be idealized, but it is certainly enjoyed. It is a well-fitted and meaningful place, at least for a temporary stay, or more permanently when fortified with urban services and access. If this preference is used for class exclusion, that is only because some classes have greater means, and not because they are the only nature lovers.

The criteria of vitality are legitimate motives for the conservation of the rural environment. They are just as applicable to the inner city and are indeed more crucial there. The mental sense of connection with nature in the more general sense (that is, to the world in its entirety, and especially to the network of its living creatures) is a basic human satisfaction, the most profound aspect of sensibility. Rural scenery will convey that sense, especially if we understand it and have a functional part to play in it, but the urban landscape can also convey the same intuition. Whether in country or in city, this is not simply a matter of saving plants and animals, but of making their presence apparent. The movements of sun and tides, the cycles of weeds and insects and men, can also be celebrated along the city pavements. Once we can accept that the city is as natural as the farm and as susceptible of conservation and improvement, we work free of those false dichotomies of city and country, artificial and natural, man versus other living things.

Preservation of the historic environment had a political motive at its beginning. In the United States, the movement appeared just before the Civil War, a sign of the anxiety to prevent, and then to heal, that disastrous breach in national unity. Later, it was explicitly connected to the "Americanization" of the disruptive foreign immigrant. Other

*And a more recent period of prosperity based on corpo- rate agriculture.

motives were subsequently added: correct architectural restoration, archaeological investigation,
and then tourist promotion, as the enjoyment
of historic places became more widespread. Today,
this pleasure has become such a settled taste that
whole urban areas are preserved or restored to
some former condition, and this not simply for
tourists but on behalf of their permanent residents.

Most often, these are *new* residents, attracted
by the historic quality of the area. The market
responds to the influx with a rapid rise in property
values. Former residents of low or moderate income are replaced by those who can pay the inflated prices and for whom the historic quality is
worth the price. This is part of a more general
process of "gentrification," now familiar in many of
our inner-city areas. In contrast to its original political function, historic preservation is now fueled
by powerful class and economic motives.

This nostalgia for the past in an era of change is
diffusing downward through the economic classes,
just as the preference for the "natural" environment did in its time. Moreover, historic preservation embodies a similar intellectual puzzle. Just as
all environments are a part of nature, so all things
are historic—all have existed previously, all have
been connected with some events and persons, and
so all have a historic meaning. We must choose
what we would keep. The criteria employed have
been political, or are based on some esthetic qualities set by experts, or they simply rely on survival:
whatever manages to weather a certain lapse of
time is worthy to be preserved. Things are new;
next out of date, worn, and discardable; and only
later are they reborn as historic. The wave of redis-
covery follows after the present, at some decent
interval that allows for sufficient clearance. That
interval seems to be shrinking: it was once a hundred years, and now it is approaching thirty or
forty. As more and more of the existing physical
fabric becomes eligible for preservation, the issue of
what should be preserved and the struggle with the
forces pressing for environmental change become
sharper.

The struggle is made more acute by the widely
held notion (however curiously it may contradict

the parallel contempt for things presently new) that old things were best at some original moment, and have since then gradually decayed. The true believer restores the preserved thing to its state of first purity and hides any evidence of modern function, just as the nature buff will attempt to camouflage the presence of man. History stopped at some golden period; change is an awkwardness. Thus a whole body of expertise develops on the subject of proper restoration. Since current function cannot long be denied within extensive city areas, sharp limits are drawn: the outsides of buildings should be restored, while their insides are immaterial. Moreover, restoration should focus on a few historic districts.

Just as we delight in work-free rural scenes, we are pleased to see purified history, detached from change, free from the ugliness and stress of the past. We enjoy Williamsburg, as we enjoy a farmland, because we need not labor in it. Moreover, the history which is visible to us is a chosen history, selected from a multitude of things historic. The choosers are upper- and middle-class experts, with their own highly developed views of architectural correctness in building form.

One may therefore criticize the historic preservation movement on three related counts: first, that it too often displaces the people who live in the areas about to be restored; second, that it conveys a false, purified, and static view of history (vividly sensible, one might say, but falsely so); and lastly, that the values on which the criteria of preservation are based are narrow and specialist. Large-scale preservation, moreover, will impair the fit to new functions and inhibit future adaptation.

Once again, all of this does not serve to dismiss the strength and meaning of the preservation movement. Class-biased as it may presently be, the attitude is diffusing to other classes. The pleasures of restoration are real. People have begun to pay attention to their visible surroundings, to care for them and enjoy them. Inner-city neighborhoods, previously on the path to disinvestment and abandonment, are being restored to good use. Conservation can provide economic benefits, not solely as a tourist attraction, but by saving expensive physical resources that otherwise would be wasted.

The urban world thereby becomes more variegated and interesting.

If we think of historic conservation as a problem of sensibility—as a way of enriching our image of time—then some of the puzzling contradictions of the movement might fall away. We conserve old things, not for their own sake nor in a quixotic attempt to stop change, but the better to convey a sense of history. This then implies a celebration of change, and of the conflicts of values that accompany history. It means connecting the process of the past to present change and values, instead of attempting to detach it from them. Many things then become easier to accomplish: allowing for the presence of changing function, avoiding the dichotomy of inside and outside, choosing more openly between past forms that we admire or despise, modifying old things in a creative way, loosening up the "proper" forms of the specialist, and allowing for the diverse values of users. The environment can deepen the resident's perception of change and help him to connect the past with his present and his future. Conservation expert and resident or worker can then enter into a dialogue, to which each contributes an understanding of the place. In the process, each comes to see a deeper meaning there, to sense a stronger continuity. Users can take pride even in a formerly oppressive place, since they have labored in it and have survived it. Their modification of it can express both linkage and liberation.

Lynch 1972

In potential, at least, these two powerful conservation movements, those of nature and of history, may not only become one movement, but may also be connected to the conservation of human community, which also has a history and is a part of nature. Were that connection made, we would never attempt simply to preserve a place. Nor would we even try to conserve it, except when it could be shown that this conservation had a tangible value for us now or in the future. The aim, rather, would be to maintain *continuity*, both of the community itself and of the image of history and of nature that is held by its members. If the coalition of conservation movements can be forged on that basis, then the concept of local continuity will become a key idea in reshaping our settlements.

The internal *texture* of a settlement is probably more important to its quality than many of the gross map patterns that have usually attracted design attention. For example, in contrast with some of the more elusive issues we have just considered, the implications of settlement density—a feature so often confused with size—are quite substantial. The preferences of most (but not all) groups of the population of the United States is for a relatively low residential density. These preferences have been stable over a long period of time. The current "return to the city" seems to be a minor (and class-specific) countercurrent to the main flow, which picks up somewhat each time there is a fuel crisis, or when the cost of housing rises faster than incomes. But the great tide of desire is still outward, directed now toward the ex-ex-suburbs, or to small towns and the countryside which lie outside the official metropolitan regions. Moreover, this preference seems to be shared by majorities in most countries of the developed world, despite differences in culture, political economy, or in the doctrines of their leaders and planning professionals. Even in urban Japan, where a small house on a tiny plot costs five to ten times the yearly income of a middle-class family, where the land on which a small car parks may cost two or three times the price of the car, and where commuting from the suburbs may take two hours each way, on incredibly crowded trains, still the demand for the single-family house remains insistent.

This majority preference has some obvious bases: the enjoyment of nature, a liking for a clean and quiet environment, a desire to control one's own home—with the security, satisfaction, and cash savings that come with that—and a perception of low-density residence as a good place for rearing children. This density preference can be reinforced by the preferences for the size of social neighborhood and political unit I noted above, and by the status symbols of suburban living, or by the opportunity it affords to escape from other social classes or ethnic groups. The last is not a function of density, of course, but of the spatial segregation that in the United States has accompanied suburbanization.

While recent studies of the correlation of city size with various social problems have been inconclusive, the connection of increasing residential density with increasing pollution, noise, and poor climate is well established. Building costs are also closely linked with density. The capital cost of new housing in the United States—raw land costs and the quantity of enclosed living space being held equal—is close to a minimum for row housing at tight densities, if we compute all costs, including utilities, streets, and public facilities. It is slightly lower for dense three-story walkup units, and probably would fall lower still for higher walkup units, if people would accept living in them. Costs rise substantially as densities diverge from this low point in either direction—toward single-family housing on the one hand, or toward high-rise apartments on the other. There seem to be similar findings in Great Britain, where housing is built at least cost in the vicinity of 10 dwelling units per acre. In countries whose construction industries are organized differently, and where housing standards vary from our own, the least-cost densities will also vary. A squatter settlement may be cheapest, or a uniform zone of prefabricated high-rise slab apartments. The point is that—unlike the uncertain correlations with city size—capital costs, preferences, and environmental qualities (our dimensions again) vary markedly with residential density in any one culture and political economy, and this variation can be analyzed.

Ludlow
Real Estate Research

Stone

Of course, there is no such thing as a *general* optimum residential density. Not only are there substantial differences between nations, but also between social groups within nations: single adults, the elderly, urban sophisticates, child-rearing families, transients, and the various income classes. The preference for city-center living has persisted as a minority taste in this country and appears to be increasing a little as new housing

Baldassare
Schmitt

costs rise. But this is in the face of a continuing dominant preference for suburbia and rurality. However, no good city could ever be total suburbia, like Wright's Broadacre City, or entirely high-rise, as in Le Corbusier's model, or even be built all at "twelve to the acre," which was garden city dogma.

Some dimensions are not directly linked to density. Considerations of sense are often cited against low-density living. Suburbs are "formless" or "monotonous"; they lack the vivid sense of place that dense cities have. The point is doubtful, and it is certainly the view of an outsider. It can be tested only by evoking the sense of place of the inhabitant himself. What studies we have indicate that at any level of density there are dull and meaningless places as well as intriguing and meaningful ones. Sense depends on so many other things—visible form, social connectioms, sense of control, means of access, daily experience—that it probably can be attained or lost within any reasonable degree of residential closeness (although surely the means of attaining legibility will vary with density).

Inversely, there have been attempts to connect social pathology with high settlement density, on the premise that an increase in the frequency of stimulus and of encounter, particularly with strangers, coupled with a loss of the ability to control that access, will overload the human capacity to cope, thus bringing on crime, neurosis, stress, ill health, and social alienation. Analogies are drawn from some striking experiments on rats, but the data on human beings are far less conclusive. People can buffer a stimulus overload by many social and psychological devices. The psychological studies of crowding seem to find some connection between stress and being in a crowded room. But there is little to show for any effect of residential density, once the influence of class, social organization, and other factors are removed.

There may be some connection in the United States between health and the number of persons per room, but it is weak. Public housing in Hong Kong, built at incredibly high densities, is not accompanied by high rates of crime or of family breakdown, in all probability because of the social organization and values of the Chinese people who are housed there. Camps of the !Kung bushmen may contain less than 50 square feet of total camp space per person, and children spend their entire time within these extremely dense camps. Yet these desert settlements are dense by choice, and there are no signs of biological stress among their inhabitants.

Fears of social crowding have been reinforced by the concept of "carrying capacity," taken from ecology and animal husbandry. In any pastoral region, for example, there is a maximum number of cattle which can graze there, year after year. When this number is exceeded, the grass cover degenerates, erosion begins, and inedible plants take over the ground. By analogy, then, there is a maximum human population on the earth and, by a more tenuous analogy, a maximum urban density, a habitat limit. In the city case, at least, we have leapt not only from animals to human beings, but from local energy cycles to those of extremely large interdependent regions, and from static behavior to very dynamic technologies. A maximum carrying capacity of the earth in regard to the human species is conceivable, but it will vary in unknown ways with technology. When it is applied to a single urban area, the idea is quite dubious.

Despite these false trails, residential density has clear and discoverable relations with other dimensions: vital quality, cost, fit with desired behavior, control, and adaptability. The critique of the suburbs is especially directed at their effect on access, in the light of an energy shortage and on the behalf of those who cannot drive or who are not allowed to do so. The elderly, the handicapped, the poor, and the teenager suffer from special access disabilities at these low densities. In analyzing density and access, of course, the transportation mode must be taken into account. New modes of low-density travel would shift these consequences. Moreover, clusters of relatively high activity density can increase the level of access, even within a low average residential density. So the density of housing is always a fundamental decision in city design. It sets the framework for all the other features and has far-reaching implications.

The density of the workplace also has a great impact on the quality of life, as well as on costs, access, and the fit with production, yet very little is written about it. Activity densities of other kinds, such as of the service and shopping centers, are critical not only for access to those things, but also for sense and the facilitation of social encounter. Densities of this kind may be locally heightened, even while residential area averages are kept low, thus achieving the amenities of both density levels. The time pattern of density is also worth attention. A low spatial density of fixed facilities may be complemented by occasional temporary congregations, such as conventions, market days, and festivals.

Density, in all its various forms, is a complex but substantial issue, which has many connections with the value of a settlement. Plagued by numerous myths, it nevertheless has very real impacts on the performance dimensions, which must be traced out in any given situation.

The *grain* of a settlement is another fundamental feature of its texture, a feature often confounded with density. By grain I mean the way in which the various different elements of a settlement are mixed together in space. These elements may be activities, building types, persons, or other features. The grain of a mix is *fine* when like elements, or small clusters of them, are widely dispersed among unlike elements, and *coarse* when extensive areas of one thing are separated from extensive areas of another thing. An inverse measure of fineness of grain might be the average distance from all (or a sample of) the elements of one kind, to their nearest unlike neighbor. Fineness is the fundamental characteristic of grain, but sharpness is another, if less crucial, characteristic. A grain is *sharp* when the transition from a cluster of like elements to its unlike neighbors is abrupt, and *blurred* if the transition is gradual. A possible measure of sharpness might be made by dividing a region into an arbitrary set of small cells, and then by counting the number of pairs of adjacent cells between which the mix varies by more than some threshold percent. Thus a grain may be fine and

sharp, fine and blurred (what might be called a
"gray" mix), coarse and sharp (highly segregated),
or coarse and blurred; and these qualitative terms
can be quantified.

Grain is simply a way of making explicit a
spatial feature of cities which is often discussed and
is variously referred to by such words as segregation, integration, diversity, purity, land-use mix, or
clustering. In its many forms, grain is critical to the
goodness of a place. Take, for example, the grain of
residence of persons by their social class, that is, the
degree of social segregation in a city. This is a
pervasive problem in the United States. Indeed, it
may well be one of the most critical of all the issues
of spatial form in this country. The grain of residence by class in American cities is markedly
coarse, if sometimes blurred, and likely it is becoming coarser. To the degree that people can choose
their place of residence, they consistently opt for
places near their own kind. This choice is made for
reasons of behavioral conflict (especially over the
raising of children), because of fears of violence or
of sexual relations across class boundaries, as a
symbol of social status, as a means of protecting
a housing investment, in consequence of social
aspirations for self or for children, to gain access to
better services, or simply because people can more
easily find friends among their own. Since different
groups have very unequal opportunities for choice,
this preference results in a markedly coarse and
graded array. Once it appears, it will then be reinforced by the conscious exclusion of other racial and
economic groups.

Gans 1961

The motives that produce coarse grain are
powerful, and the preference for living near people
of one's own class is widespread, not only in the
United States, but perhaps throughout the world.
What groups will segregate themselves depends on
the culture. In the United States, segregation is
presently shifting from ethnic group to income
class. Whether that grain will be reinforced or suppressed is a feature of the political economy, since
the sorting of a capitalist market will exaggerate
it, while a centralized socialist economy can substantially mute it, as may be seen in Poland, for
example.

Grain has a profound impact on many other values than those directly sought by the resident. Coarse grain decreases the access to other kinds of people and other ways of life. Inequities of access to resources, and facilities are also likely to increase with spatial segregation. Violence and tension may increase, although if the grain is extremely coarse and sharp, the opportunities for intergroup violence may decline or turn inward. Regional coordination and control are more difficult in a coarse-grained settlement, while local control may in contrast be enhanced.

It is professional doctrine that the grain of residence by class should be fine and blurred. The organic model insists that each small area should be a microcosm of the whole. Yet this doctrine has largely been neglected in practice, or has been ineffective, except in some of the socialist nations. If one looks for equity, for communication between groups, and the ability to cross barriers, then one is led to advocating a much finer grain of residence than now obtains in this country. But the values that impel so many people toward segregation (such as security or easy primary relations) argue that within any mix there must be clusters of similarity which are relatively homogeneous and "pure," so that people may be at ease among their own. At the same time, for reasons of equity, the mix within large areas should be more balanced, and regional access should be high. There should also be zones of transition ("blurs"), within which status is more ambiguous, so that people may "cross over" if they choose.*

Whatever the value choice, the grain of residence is clearly a critical feature of any city. Reducing the grain of the North American city is an uphill battle. To be effective, it requires a substantial interference with the real estate market, as well as legal moves, the application of large housing subsidies, and regional controls on development. It may well require much more radical measures, such as socialization of the land, making housing a

Downs

---

*Ideally, one might hope to see, not a classless society, but one in which classes were numerous and were differentiated by chosen ways of life, rather than by a ladder of power and wealth, a ladder which only goes up or down. But that is another story.

free utility, or the restriction of ownerships to life tenure. The coarse grain of settlement has deep roots in our society.

Residential mix by class is not the only important granular characteristic. The grain of activity type is also significant: whether work and residence are to be separated, for example, and whether workplaces themselves should be located in large zones of similar productive activity. Like residential grain, activity grain is also steadily coarsening, because of the increasing scale of development and of the firm, and because of a more closely controlled market. Here, professional doctrine swims with the tide rather than thrashing against it. As planning operates at larger scales, it tends to sort out extensive areas of pure offices, pure warehouses, pure housing, pure recreation. A coarse grain of activity makes central control easier and the demands for service more predictable. Interactivity conflicts and nuisances are avoided. Large operations can be provided for, and space for future growth is easier to arrange. Transportation and utility systems can be laid out more efficiently when they serve one class of activity. Large profits are possible from large-scale manipulations of land. The coarsening of activity grain is even more marked in the socialist countries, with their strong central planning apparatus.

Nevertheless, incremental growth, as well as confusion, cross-purposes, and individual cussedness, all work to reduce the grain of our magnificently simple schemes. Some critics favor a finer grain of activity. Coarse grain means poor access and a long commutation. It reduces the chances for communication and education. Children may never see their parents at work, for example, and the construction of a new building may be the last exposed industrial process that most people can actually watch. Coarse grain reinforces the big institution, whereas now the virtues of smallness are being celebrated. As highly centralized planning loses some of its credibility, it may appear wiser to develop by smaller increments.

Coarse grain contributes to the prevalent fragmentation of life (although many delight in a

Kropotkin

separation of home and work). A world in which work, residence, and leisure are integrated has been an important goal for many social thinkers. To "urbanize the countryside and ruralize the city" is settled Marxist doctrine. In Cuba, vacant city lots are planted to tobacco, city people are pressed to work on surrounding farms, and isolated rural dwellers are gathered into small urban settlements. The proponents of neighborhood in the United States argue for city farms to produce food and solar panels to make energy just as the progressive urbanization of farm life is reducing the polarity of city and country at the opposite end of the scale. The delights of a landscape in which diverse occupations, residence, and leisure occur side by side are frequently praised in travel literature. These tracts are written by strangers, of course, and we would do well to inquire of the actual inhabitants, who may have diverse opinions. However, memoirs of childhood, at least, make it clear that a fine grain of activity is a beneficial growing medium.

Hart

As usual, no general rule can be set out, except to reduce the activity grain as far as possible, until serious costs of conflict or fit are encountered. A fine-grain, varied settlement is attractive in the abstract, although each type of activity will have its appropriate scale of clustering. At any rate, the mix of activity is a critical measure. The *scale* of settlement features is a function, or an adjunct, of the fineness or coarseness of its grain. A fine-grain place is made up of small buildings, small open spaces, and small enterprises. These smaller parts can be more closely fitted to the varying activities of occupants, more completely under their control, and more easily sensed as connected to individual values and experiences, than are the larger features of a coarser grain.

See fig. 74

Still other aspects of grain can be cited: the grain of density and access, for example. Many people, if asked to describe the ideal house of their fantasy, will sketch one from whose front door one steps onto a lively urban promenade, while at the rear there is only silent countryside. If a single door lies between excitement and serenity, the pleasures are sharpened on either side by the thought of what

74 Behind the elegant
house fronts of Beacon
Hill in Boston. A quiet
garden in the heart of the
city is a commonly valued
delight.

Alexander 1975

lies beyond. Childhood memories are full of these delights. Christopher Alexander's "patterns" return frequently to prescriptions of a fine grain of activity, density, and access.

The land market tends to destroy such anomalies, since land is valued and developed by generalized rules of access. Efficient large-scale planning has a similar effect . Most examples of a fine grain of density are the product of natural irregularities, or of inefficiencies of the access system, or of the deliberate action of wealthy owners. These sudden transitions appear where the land market has been circumvented, or where speculation and development has suddenly been halted—as in the arrested North American subdivisions of the 1930s or in socialist Havana today. "Cluster zoning" is a legal device for obtaining and preserving some of these advantages.

At the regional scale, access should be rather uniformly distributed for reasons of equity and adaptability, but there are substantial advantages in forms which produce a rather fine, sharp local grain of density and access. This may be achieved by dispersed pockets of open space, by clustering, by limited access routes, by "laceworks" (Alexander's term for linear fingers of development in a rural background), or by a variation of building and activity density, arrayed in small clumps close together. A fine grain of this kind is rarely seen in the modern city, but it has distinct advantages of diversity of setting, a choice of habitat, access between different life functions, and an interesting visible form.

There can be a grain of the *timing* of activity, as well. Thus some areas can be distinguished by being active throughout the day and night, while others are alive at some hours and quiescent in between. Places may be devoted to a single kind of activity throughout the day (coarse-grained in the temporal sense), or one activity may suddenly succeed another (a relatively fine, sharp temporal mix), or functions may succeed each other but overlap (a fine, blurred grain). A plaza may be a food market in the morning, a children's playground in the afternoon, and a place for adult gossiping in the evening, with all the opportunities for interaction (and conflict) afforded by the temporal boundaries of transition. The old and the new, the temporary and the permanent, may be juxtaposed or separated. The same considerations will hold for temporal grain as for spatial grain: a fine sharp mix has substantial advantages of access, diversity, and interest, within the limits that may be imposed by good fit and increased requirements for control. Most people speak with enjoyment of places where contrasting activities succeed one another. The periodic emptiness of single-activity space seems to be inefficient (but it may not be; that requires analysis). Our planning emphasizes spatial patterns and neglects the temporal organization of things.

Still other kinds of mixes may be identified, to which the concept of grain may be applied: a grain of control (large areas in one ownership versus a fine mosaic of public and private places, group commons, children's turf, and no-man's land); a grain of microclimate; a grain of ecosystems (vast prairie versus intricate garden); and so on. The grains of residence, of other activities, and of density and access may be the more critical parameters of settlement form, but many others can be considered. This characterization of the mix is very likely much more significant to settlement quality than many of the aspects of form that have preoccupied us, such as total size, settlement outline, or the two-dimensional pattern of the street system.

At an earlier date, the discussion of access systems was thought to revolve around choices of street pattern: linear, radioconcentric, or the rectangular grid. But the map pattern of streets hardly seems crucial in the large, developed city today, at least as a theoretical issue, although just where a street will go can, of course, be important in a particular case.

The more general debate now concerns the mode of travel. What mix of modes is preferable, and to what degree should the modes in that mix be segregated? (Another question of grain.) What subsidies or other devices are justified to achieve the desired mix? Obviously, the answers depend on settlement grain and density as well as on culture, political economy, and technical means. Vitality

Blumenfeld 1967, 1977

will be at stake, because of the pollution generated by various modes, and their accident rates. Control and fit are involved, since the individual modes are more responsive to the person than group transport, and some modes are better fitted to such behaviors as carrying packages or to such users as the handicapped. The performance dimensions shift the ground of the debate from "the car versus the subway train" (as though these machines were allegorical monsters locked in a mythical combat), or just from the energy requirements of these vehicles or their carrying capacity per lane-minute, toward the experience and values of those transported. Even when the modal mix is set, the performance dimensions can clarify the design of the elements. How can eight-year-olds roam a city region safely? Can cyclists piggy-back on the trains? Can public vehicles be endowed with the small-scale controllability of the automobile? How does a shopper with packages and two small children manage to ride the bus? Under what circumstances can people enjoy social contacts while riding, or delight in the moving view? How can local streets be made safe and quiet once again without blocking vehicular access to the dwellings fronting on them? And so on.

The private car makes our cities less habitable: it kills, it maims, and it loads the air with its noise and its exhausts. It consumes petroleum and is expensive to run. Any system which relies heavily on it is an inequitable system, since the access of those without cars is inevitably poorer than that of drivers. Yet it has obvious advantages of pride, direct access, and user control, which account for its tenacious hold. Equity suggests that we need two converging technical innovations: a public vehicle whose routes can be more finely and widely dispersed, and which can be more responsive to scattered individual destinations; and private vehicles which are less polluting, less dangerous and costly, and more easily used by those now unable to drive. Elaborate technical devices, such as subways, monorails, automated guideways, and "people movers," are unlikely to fill this vacuum. Refinements to older, simpler devices offer more hope—small buses with flexible scheduling and routing, weatherized bicycles, group taxis.

Adaptability will favor simple, plural means and nonspecialized channels. Not only should access be spread more evenly throughout an urbanized region, but also more evenly throughout the day (and night), so that individual choice and reach may be increased. This implies changes in density, grain, and the timing of activity, of course, as well as in the management and use of cheaper, more flexible modes of transport. And yet, even while increasing and equalizing the levels of regional access, a good settlement will diversify or even diminish access at the very local scale—allowing local residents to restrict the timing, type, or density of local traffic, if they wish.

The extensive low-density North American suburb has three glaring deficiencies: its coarse grain of use and of social class, its heavy cost of construction and maintenance, and its reliance on the private car, which leaves it vulnerable to fuel shortages and makes access difficult for outsiders or the young and the aged among its own people. Recasting the suburb for prolonged usefulness is a principal task of North American urbanism. Part of that task will be the invention of a public vehicle that can operate satisfactorily at suburban densities.

Travel can be a positive experience; we need not consider it pure cost. In potential, the access system is a prime piece of educational equipment. It enlarges an individual's reach, but in addition the act of moving through a city can in itself be an enlightenment. Taking advantage of that possibility, especially for children, means opening up the transport system, making it safer and easier to use, providing guidebooks, treating it seriously as an educational opportunity. Travel can be a pleasure, if we pay attention to the human experience: the visual sequences, the opportunities to learn or to meet other people.

Density, grain, and the access system—the internal texture of a city—are the principal features by which we may judge its performance. The nature of its growth and change are equally important, but we know rather little about those effects. A city's size and its outline on a map may be much less critical than we had thought. The concepts of local community, and of conservation as a maintenance of local community, are key organizing ideas in shaping city form. But they have a different impact and meaning than we are accustomed to give them.

The performance dimensions recur regularly among the reasons for choice between these form possibilities. At times, they transform the argument, once it is seen in their terms. Clearly, they are not the only reasons for choice. External costs—losses in values which lie outside form theory—appear frequently. In general, however, these issues can be discussed within a framework of performance dimensions, concepts of city form, and calculations of external costs. At present, this is a crude framework. Were the relations between forms, dimensions, and costs fully explicated, it would be a sufficient framework.

16 City Models and City Design

No discussion of city form can ignore the role of design in choosing among form possibilities, or refrain from wondering about the connection between cold theory and the warm enthusiasm of the creative process or between the latter and the actual decisions that shape a city. Design decisions are largely based on models in the head of the designer. Presumably, those models connect with more general theories, but models and theories can be surprisingly independent of each other. To begin with, the word "model" is ambiguous. In common talk, it is a three-dimensional physical miniature of a building, machine, or landscape, or it is this year's car, or it is a person who exhibits new clothes. I don't mean those. It is also the current academic word for an abstract theory of how something functions, in which the elements of a system, and the relations between those elements, are clearly specified, preferably in a quantitative mode. The city metaphors described in chapter 4 were, in one sense, grand models of that kind, but they were non-quantitative, and their elements were not clearly specified. At any rate, in this chapter I shall not talk of models in that sense.

Not long ago, *model* was an adjective meaning "worthy of emulation," and this is the tradition I shall follow. For our purpose, a model is a picture of how the environment *ought* to be made, a description of a form or a process which is a prototype to follow. Our subject is environmental form rather than the planning process, but models for form must take the creation and management process into account. The model statement may be precise and explicit, or vague and unthinking. It can be graphic, verbal, or mathematical in form, or even be communicated without language, simply by concrete example. Models range from detailed prototypes followed habitually, almost unconsciously —such as sidewalks at the street edge—to major patterns put forward for consciously developed reasons—such as the idea of the satellite town. I shall argue for their necessity, but also for their more rational use.

Criteria, standards, and performance dimensions are means by which models are evaluated, but they are not models in themselves, except where they become detailed enough to specify form (such as a prescribed setback). Policies and strategies may include models, but, since they are decisions about future actions, they must include much more, and they may not employ models at all. The process of design always uses models, although a basic model may be obscured by a surface innovation, or an alien model may be converted to some surprising new purpose. The use of models is not confined to the creation of new places, but is equally important in the management and remodeling (!) of existing places.

There are two ways of setting form rules: by prescription or by specifying performance. Models are more like the former than the latter: "make a bay window," rather than "make it possible for someone in the room to see up and down the street." But the distinction is not as clear as it seems. Both statements are only a piece of a much longer means-ends continuum. The bay window can be made in many forms and requires detailed instructions for its construction, while looking up and down the street is instrumental to other more general ends, such as sociability or security. Nevertheless, any particular prescription (or model) is instrumental relative to its associated performance statement, and usually the performance statement stops short of describing a recognizable environmental form.

Since performance statements are more abstract and general than models, they must be features of any general theory. They are also touted as the best way to write regulations and guidelines, since they hold fast to the underlying effect that is wanted, while leaving the means flexible and open to innovation. But performance standards may not always be preferable in realistic situations. They require rather elaborate, usually post facto, tests to see if they are being adhered to. By leaving room for innovation, they are likely to increase the uncertainty of design, and thus the time and effort it requires, as well as to increase the burden on those who will implement the new form. Even though a new form satisfies the required basic performance,

Baer

it may have unpredicted side effects, or fail to fit in with other elements of the environment. For example, if the degree of summer shade required is specified (instead of specifying trees), the unexpected solution may be a series of opaque metal panels which are ugly, cause a massive disruption of the land, and cast an unpleasant shade in the winter as well as in the summer. Customary prototypes are relatively easy to specify and construct, are likely to fit with other customary parts, and will have well-known consequences. Thus, while performance statements are the building blocks of general theory, they may or may not be useful as direct guides to action. They tend to be more apt in regard to key elements, where the gain in flexibility and innovation is well worth the cost and risk entailed in their use. In more routine design and evaluation, people work directly from a stock of implicit or fuzzy environmental models: culs-de-sac, fire escapes, foundation plantings, ranch houses, highway cross sections, civic centers, shopping malls, front yards, park landscapes, rear entrances, side-yard setbacks, suburban districts—the list is enormous and yet quite familiar. To be of any use, a theory must be able to connect its statements to these ordinary and indispensable mental pictures, while explaining the way in which their usefulness depends on the concrete situation in which any design finds itself.

The most useful model is one in which the dependence on the situation in which it is to be applied is carefully stated, and in which the expected performance of the model is also specified. Then the model is open to test and improvement. These are the characteristics embodied in the elaborate series of environmental models developed by Alexander 1975 Christopher Alexander, which he calls "patterns." Similarly, where public regulations or guidelines are prepared, the reasoning behind them should also be laid bare, so that they are fully open to political correction. A hybrid regulation may specify an acceptable, conventional form (such as a wall detail or a street cross section), and also specify the performance wanted, so that those being regulated may propose a new form for the purpose, if they are willing to suffer the detailed testing of performance that will be required.

Most models refer only to a completed form,
and for this they have been much criticized. They
take no account of the process by which the form is
achieved. A fence built by neighbors has quite a
different impact than one built by armed guards.
Even more, this emphasis on completed form
ignores the reality of continuous change, in which
no form is a permanent feature. This leads us to
think that the preoccupation with form is the mark
of a mind which focuses on things rather than on
their consequences for people. Some planners will
therefore eschew any serious consideration of
form. *Process* is the key. "It ain't what you do, but
the way what you do it." Never mind what it is
when finished; by what means were the decisions
made, and how will they be carried out?

The human consequences of any environment
are the measure of its quality, and not the form
itself. But not the process itself, either. Process
people can be as blind to human consequence as
form fanatics. A local playground, produced by a
genuine participatory process, but muddy and
shabby in its final form, is a failure just as much as a
handsome design imposed on the community—
and it might be a greater failure. In particular situations, sometimes form and sometimes process can
be the dominant consideration, but usually they
work together. How a feature got there, what it is
now, how it is managed and how it is changing,
must all be evaluated. Ideally, models will specify
form, creation, and management as one. Unfortunately, most models tend to fix on one and neglect
the others. But the necessary corrective is not a
neglect of form.

Some models are useful as regulatory devices,
and many of them are so used: setbacks, height
limits, land use mixtures, local street patterns, and
so on. Most of them, however, since they refer to
qualities that are less than precise, and because
their application depends so largely on the concrete
situation, are more useful as guidelines for design
and decision.

Look at the baroque axial network as one example of a model often used in the past to guide
designs for new as well as for old cities. This is a
coherent and well developed idea about city form.

See fig. 75

Sutcliffe

It states that one may organize any complex and extended landscape in the following way: choose a set of commanding points throughout a terrain, and site important symbolic structures at those points. Connect these foci by major streets, wide enough to carry arterial traffic, and shaped as visual approaches to the symbolic points, or nodes. The borders of these streets should be controlled to give them a sense of unity, by means of special planting and furniture, as well as height, facade, and use restrictions. Once that is done, a more intricate, less controlled pattern of streets and buildings of varied type can occupy the interior triangles between the linking arteries. The model has some particular advantages. It is a simple, coherent idea that can be rapidly employed in a great range of complex landscapes. Major L'Enfant, using the model at a time when it had been well developed, was able to survey, design, lay out, clear, acquire materials, auction off lots, and commence construction on the future city of Washington—all in nine months and with the aid of two surveyors. The model told him just what to look for and how to decide. If the resulting city is not as clear and vivid as he hoped, it is due in part to his ill-advised overlay of the baroque model with an unevenly spaced grid. Even more, it was due to the subsequent management of Washington's development, which never followed his model of powerful central control, and indeed could not have done so.

Given effective central control, the model works well in organizing extended, irregular landscapes, whether virgin or developed (for example, Paris under Haussman). It creates a memorable general structure without imposing control on every part and without requiring an unattainable level of capital investment. It is, in fact, a strategy for the economical application of central power. It produces strong visual effects and lays the groundwork for public symbolism. In other words, it is a useful way to achieve sensibility, and to apportion public and private control. In one respect, at least, it is a flexible form, since changes can occur within the blocks created by the linkage network without disturbing the general pattern in any way. Yet while local flexibility is achieved, more general

75 The plan for Washing-
ton, D.C., as drawn by
Major Pierre Charles
L'Enfant in 1791. A net-
work of radial streets,
which connect the prin-
cipal buildings and the
commanding features of
the land, was laid over an
irregularly varying rec-
tangular grid. This hybrid
plan, coupled with the
federal government's in-
ability to implement his
proposed controls, has
produced a city of fine
vistas and confusing in-
tersections.

changes in use and flow are difficult to make, since the nodes and their links are permanent, symbolic features, and they must retain their significance.

As an access system, it is a workable strategy for opening up an existing circulatory maze and performs reasonably well for traffic moving from focal point to focal point (tourists or processions), or for flows which are local, using low-speed, maneuverable, space-efficient modes, such as horseback, bicycle, or foot. However, the form is difficult to traverse by high-speed, long-distance, space-demanding vehicles. Extended movement must follow an erratic route from point to point, and each point is a peak of congestion, where many routes converge.

While visually quite powerful at the intermediate scale of a central city or a large park or garden, the irregular triangular network can be very confusing at more extended scales. The foci and all the links between them must be recognizable and memorized. General cognitive strategies of direction or overall pattern cannot be applied. Finally, while the model emphasizes certain uses, such as the symbolic public ones or the commercial activities which favor the arterial frontages, it has very little to say about ordinary houses or workplaces.

Thus this particular concept can be analyzed in terms of appropriate situation and expected performance along the various dimensions. It has a wide, but far from universal, usefulness. It is an idea which has developed over several centuries, first in the royal hunting forests (where the primary motives were the visual tracking of game and quick access to it), and then in the planning of papal Rome (where the motive was to enhance and control the processional movements of pilgrims). Subsequent to L'Enfant, Haussmann used the model in Paris to improve access in the central city, to create profitable new building sites, and to displace and control the working class. Historically, it has always been an elite model: a way of using the city as an expression of central power and a strategy for attaining visual magnificence and control within available means. For that purpose, it works.

Appendix D presents a catalog of such city models in some detail and gives some key references to them. The grouping used there is an arbitrary one. Some models refer to overall settlement patterns of outline or skeleton, such as the radial star, the linear city, the various grids, the "lacework," the baroque axes I have just discussed, the "capillary" form, the box-within-box of the sacred Indian city, the satellite city idea, or the megaforms, bubble covers, and underground and floating settlements of current invention. Other models focus on the pattern of central place, such as center hierarchies, multifocal or afocal patterns, linear centers or strips, neighborhood centers, civic centers, special-function or mobile centers, enclosed shopping malls, and so on.

Still other models prescribe something about the general texture of a city, whether it should be continuous or organized in cells such as neighborhoods, whether the grain of persons or activities should be fine or coarse, whether it should be sprawling or compact or even scattered, and what its basic spatial character should be. There are models for the circulation system: for modal composition and the separation between modes, for preferred channel patterns and the concept of channel hierarchy, for minimizing travel distances, and for the design of the channels themselves.

There are warmly espoused models for particular housing types: high slabs, towers, dense walk-ups, garden apartments, courtyard houses, town houses, and freestanding houses, as well as some recent innovations. We find even more models for ways of providing open space—patterns of distribution such as greenbelts, green wedges, green networks, and fine dispersions, as well as prototypes of kinds of open space: regional parks, city parks, plazas, greenways, playgrounds, adventure playgrounds, and "vest pocket" openings. Finally, there are models for temporal organization, for growth management, strategies of development, preferences for permanence, and ideas on the timing of use.

Since each of these is described in that lengthy appendix, it would be tedious to repeat their description here. These concepts are presented there as a disjointed list. They are building blocks which can be used in various combinations and for varying motives. Therefore, they cannot carry the conviction of the great normative metaphors discussed in chapter 4, which combine motive, form, and a view of the nature of human settlements in one connected statement.* Of course, the general normative theories themselves imply choices among the various elementary models. Each of these models has its advocates, uncompromising or reasonable as they may be.

While the list is surely not complete, it covers most of the concepts that are in people's minds as they discuss city form. As we summarize them, we get yet another view of the state of the art. The list groups most easily according to some very familiar categories of the physical features of a city: street and transportation systems, housing, open space, centers, general map patterns. But since that is not a logically inclusive system, it conceals the gaps in the series. There is little here about the workplace, for example, or about the marginal spaces of a city—the wastelands, fringe areas, transition spaces, vacant lands, dead storage areas, and underutilized places. The street system is a prominent concern, but not the remainder of the flow system: those flows of goods, wastes, energy, and information which are not carried in street vehicles. Thus questions of the conservation and management of material and energy sources, or of information, cannot easily be dealt with. The sensory aspects of the city, while implicit in some of the models, are not openly specified. Most of these models are models of physical form, and few of them deal with the associated institutional patterns

Alexander 1975

*Nor the conviction of Christopher Alexander's beautifully composed book, *A Pattern Language*, which is also a long, connected statement about the good environment. Indeed, it is for reasons of this very connectedness that I would quarrel with him, since those patterns are put forward as the "timeless" and "natural" ways of building, correct for all people, places, and seasons. Variations of culture, political economy, or individual values are submerged. The dogmatic form of these Tablets of the Law belies their humane content and his own convictions about user participation. Yet this is a most important book—the first contemporary attempt of which I am aware to be explicit about the good spatial environment as a whole, and the reasons for its goodness. The patterns themselves are full of much good sense, especially for our own culture and situation.

and processes. They are more often static concepts; few include the form of change. Temporary uses and mobile users are usually not considered. The progressive development of inhabitants or society, and how that must be allowed for or might be supported, is never mentioned. The transition from traditional to modern society, or the characteristics of cities proper to emerging new forms of society, are not reflected upon. None of these deficiencies can easily be supplied. They are the result of how our ideas about cities have grown up, including the problems to which professionals were drawn and the theoretical preconceptions which they brought to those problems.

Is it possible to think of a model which deals with form, process, and associated institutions in one whole? Examples are rare. The familiar model of an isolated dwelling, a nuclear family, and private land ownership connects form and institution, but not process. The trailer camp as a way of housing refugees or temporary labor connects form with process. But the form is not well developed, and the process is banal and truncated: no more than here today and gone tomorrow. So we are forced to imagine a model of this kind, even though it must be an unripe one. This imaginary model might be called an "alternating net":

The basic pattern is one in which the major arterials form an open, irregular grid, sufficiently widely spaced that there is ample open space within the interstices. The arterial frontage is occupied by a relatively dense and continuous set of land uses. Orthogonal to the arterial grid, and offset half an interval from it, is a grid of similar pattern which is restricted to pedestrians, cyclists, horsemen, boaters, and other slow and backward travelers. Its frontages are occupied by recreational uses, as well as by uses catering to these peculiar people. Both grid systems, while irregular in detail in order to be able to conform to the land and its history, are regular grids in the topological sense. That is, each grid consists of two sets of continuous, mutually intersecting lines, which maintain their sequential order with respect to each other. These rights-of-way were originally laid down by some regional

planning authority. In the blocks between these two grid systems, the land is farmed, wooded, waste, or occupied by small, relatively self-sufficient groups, who put a low value on access. This interior land is serviced by a shifting, maze-like system of low-capacity lanes, penetrating inward from one or the other of the two grids.

The arterial "fast" grid system is owned, and its immediate frontage is controlled, by a public body, while the fronting uses are individually held. The "slow" grid, while open to the public, is managed by local frontage associations. Both rights-of-way are permanent, although their structures and management are not. The interstitial land is individually owned, or is held by small communitarian groups, and is relatively free of public control, although the density of use must be kept low. Densities are moderately high along the arterials, and the uses, while regulated, are finely mixed. Uses along the slow grid are also mixed, but are low in intensity, and with a greater predominance of recreational activity.

Minor adaptations can easily be made along these lines, or shallow additions can be extended into the interstitial lands near their borders. On initiative of the regional authority, and by agreement of the majority of the fronting owners and frontage associations, a periodic reversal of the two grid systems can be made, to accommodate major changes. That is, a single "slow" line, or portion of it, can be taken over for public management as a new arterial. As this new channel is completed, the parallel arterial is closed down and ceded to local frontage associations. Uses on each old line are abandoned, or take up new sites on the appropriate renewed line. The old arterials are cleared for their new recreational use, while a few interesting landmarks are saved and reused. The ample open space along the old recreational way provides for a new order of movement and intensive use. Thus the settlement maintains a permanent reserve of circulation space and may gradually accumulate a "layering" of notable structures saved from successive epochs. However, any truly permanent symbolic features are located on neither line, but in the interstices just off the line, so that they can be maintained without disturbance.

This concocted model refers at once to map pattern, flow pattern, the grain of use and density, the distribution of control, and a cyclical pattern of change and how it is implemented. Presumably, these elements are fitted one to another. The motives are adaptability (albeit a somewhat convulsive one) and good generalized access, combined with a high degree of access to open space and a sharp grain of local access, as well as a wide variety of density and activity and a diversity of modal choice. An efficient means of central control is allied to a convenient way of escaping that central control. The model produces three widely different yet connected habitats (the arterial frontage, the "slow" frontage, and the rural interior), and a strong sense of time, via the cycling of the grids and the retention of the permanent symbolic locations. It seems to be suited to a low-density landscape, rich in land and in transport vehicles.

It has its antecedents in the street village, the "section" grid of the American midwest, the baroque axial network, and many exurban areas of the United States, whose new houses have reoccupied the roadsides of the old farming communities while letting the backlands return to forest. The trick of renewal via alteration has other precedents: I have already cited the periodic rebuilding of the Shinto temple at Ise. In the proposed model, however, the administrative difficulties in reversing the use of the two grid systems simultaneously might be formidable. Since the model is untested, its true performance is unknown, as well as whether it would be desired by any group, or whether it conceals destructive incompatibilities. Speculative as it is, and vulnerable to criticism (as it should be), it serves to illustrate what is meant by a model that deals with form, process, and management all working together.

Models of some kind *must* be used: one cannot manage complex, real problems, under the pressure of time, without employing prototypes already in the head. On rare occasions, gifted designers produce new models from more general metaphors, or by recombining old models or shifting their application in some surprising way. These new models must then undergo a lengthy period of development and testing before they are fully usable. Where models do not exist for some aspect of a settlement, that aspect is normally not attended to. When we look at planning proposals from all over the world, we sense the power of these familiar ideas: new settlements in Ghana, in Cuba, the United States, and the USSR look astonishingly alike and deal with similar features.

The difficulty is not that we use prototypes, but that our set is so limited, and so unrelated to purpose and situation. While performance dimensions may be valid universally, and performance standards may be generally applicable for any given culture and class of circumstance, form models must be thought of as an arsenal of possibilities. A more systematic analysis of precedent and an elaboration and analysis of new prototypes are most important tasks for city design. Indeed, we should be engaged in anticipatory design, creating prototypes which will be useful for those new situations and motives which are only unfolding today.

In practice, most designers and decisionmakers do not treat these concepts as possibilities among which to choose, but cling to some single set. They believe in an ideal city, even while understanding the impossibility of an ideal countryside or an ideal house. While the city ideal may have to be jiggered to fit some real situation, this is only a regretful compromise. The designer cannot shift to other models, or connect his model to the motives of the particular users.

No one creates form without precedent. But we should move more flexibly among our models. This means a change in our process of design. This also means that a broader array of models must be developed (which is hard work), and that explicit connections must be made between model and appropriate situations, clients, and performance (which is even harder).

Since these models are not neutral, but are closely associated with values (as was the baroque network that we cited above), value-coherent normative theories will tend to favor certain models over others, or (mistakenly, as I have tried to explain) to propose one set of models as the universal solution. Thus the "city-is-a-machine" view will be attracted to clear, repetitive patterns, made up of rather uniform, replaceable, separate parts: regular grids, isolated buildings, and the like. But it would be an error to think that the rectangular grid is the proprietary mark of the machine view. Grids were regularly employed by the cosmic theoreticians of China, for quite different reasons. To distinguish the presence of a working normative theory, one must see form, use, and motive together. Organic cities need not have winding streets. Regular, nonhierarchical street systems are not restricted to egalitarian societies.

The normative viewpoint that I have presented also favors particular models, although the choice is broader as a result of the greater generality of the theory. It prefers models which have a relatively fine grain of use and character, a high degree of access to places, persons, services, and information, a diversity of place, a close integration of work, residence, and leisure, and a low general density, set with open spaces and intense centers. Many particular models would incorporate these rather vague characteristics; others would not. The theory is general, but it is not indifferent to form.

Design is the playful creation and strict evaluation of the possible forms of something, including how it is to be made. That something need not be a physical object, nor is design expressed only in drawings. Although attempts have been made to reduce design to completely explicit systems of search or synthesis , it remains an art, a peculiar mix of rationality and irrationality. Design deals with qualities, with complex connections, and also with ambiguities. City design is the art of creating possibilities for the use, management, and form of settlements or their significant parts. It manipulates patterns in time and space and has as its justification the everyday human experience of those patterns. It does not deal solely with big things, but also with policies for small things—like seats and trees and sitting on front porches—wherever those features affect the performance of the settlement. City design concerns itself with objects, with human activ-

Alexander 1964
Lynch 1979
Montgomery
Reichek
Schlager
Wagoner

Boutourline

ity, with institutions of management, and with processes of change.

City design may be engaged in preparing a transit or a shoreline plan, a comprehensive regional access study, a development strategy, a new town, a suburban extension, or a regional park system. It may develop prototypes for houses or workplaces, a policy for bus shelters, or a neighborhood analysis. It may seek to protect neighborhood streets, revitalize a public square, improve lighting, planting, or paving, set regulations for conservation or development, build a participatory process, write an interpretive guide, or plan a city celebration. It uses techniques of its own: area diagnoses, framework plans, sequential strategies, conservation zones, illustrative designs, design liaison and service, development controls and guides, process rules, place monitoring, and the creation of new place institutions. Its peculiar features are the consequences of the scale and complexity of its domain, the fluidity of events, and the plurality of actors, as well as its imperfect and overlapping controls.

Having laid out this splendid array of subject matter and technique, I should also admit that city design is rarely practiced—or, more often, it is mispracticed as big architecture or big engineering: the design of whole towns as single physical objects, extended site plans or utility networks, to be built to precise plan in a predetermined time. True city design never begins with a virgin situation, never foresees a completed work. Properly, it thinks in terms of process, prototype, guidance, incentive, and control and is able to conceive broad, fluid sequences along with concrete, homely details. It is a scarcely developed art—a new kind of design and a new view of its subject matter. A well-developed stock of models which integrated process and form would be of immense value to it. These models and theoretical constructs must be sufficiently independent and simple, however, to allow for that continuous recasting of aims, analyses, and possibilities that is inherent in the conduct of city design.

17   A Place Utopia

I will make a more personal statement about the good environment, further to illustrate the theory. This is a position taken along the performance dimensions. Being personal, it can hardly please everyone, although I encompass as much diversity as I can. Perhaps no one would care to join me in this strange place, but it may illustrate how concrete proposals may arise from very general statements.*

Most utopian proposals lose track either of space or of society. There are brilliant spatial fantasies which accept society as it is, and social utopias which sketch a few disconnected spatial features, in order to add color and a semblance of reality. Their spatial proposals are as banal and conventional as are the architects' thoughts of society. Only in antiutopias can we find examples where physical oppression abets social oppression in a very direct and circumstantial way. Hell, at least, is vivid and convincing. Indeed, it is difficult to unfold a coherent vision of a desirable new society in a desirable new world.

I attempt something more modest here: without losing track of society, or accepting it as it is, I propose to leave it unaccounted for, except where it springs from some feature of place. I mean to show how utopian features might be generated from thinking about how people relate to their surroundings, rather than out of a self-absorbed technical fantasy, on the one hand, or as a mechanical consequence of a social prescription, on the other. Values can spring from the relation of people to things, as well as from the relation of people to each other. More exactly, values spring from our relations to people-in-place, and my recital is only one step toward that holistic view. This is not a denial of the importance of values socially generated, but simply a shift of attention to an aspect traditionally neglected. The spatial setting does not merely set limits; it is the source of satisfactions. Ask someone

*Or did the utopia write the theory?

how he would like to live, and the reply is usually replete with spatial detail. Ethical influences run from place to man, as well as vice versa; our ideas of what is right derive from the nature of things around us, as well as from the nature of ourselves.

Imagine an urban countryside, a highly varied but humanized landscape. It is neither urban nor rural in the old sense, since houses, workplaces, and places of assembly are set among trees, farms, and streams. Within that extensive countryside, there is a network of small, intensive urban centers. This countryside is as functionally intricate and interdependent as any contemporary city.

It flows over the old political boundaries and occupies, or is in the process of settling, many kinds of habitat now avoided: mountain slopes, shallow seas, deserts, marshes, the polar ice. In that sense, the world is more evenly inhabited, and even those places not permanently settled are more frequently used than before. Cities are no longer islands encircled by a barrier reef of suburbs, washed by a rural sea. Nor is that sea an emptiness to pass over, a mine of food and energy, or a remoteness in which to rest. Most people no longer think of "home town," but of "home region." Each region is developed in its own way.

This expansion of settlement has not come easily, since a good fit between men and place requires a modification of both. At the poles and on the open seas, there were serious difficulties of boredom, stress, and illness, until people learned how to respond to those places and found a way to endow them with human meaning. That discovery made them different people. Efforts to occupy the deep sea permanently, as well as the moon and the planets, have so far failed. We have not yet been able to domesticate ourselves to these alien places, nor them to us. But already there are labyrinthine underground environments, complete with gardens, cave birds, internal weather, intriguing lights, intimate and awesome spaces. People born to them are homesick on the surface.

While almost all types of terrain, and some waters, are somewhere successfully occupied, and while settlement is continuous in the sense of being interconnected, yet most of the world's surface is still rather lightly occupied by man. Large areas, in all types of ground, are given to extensive and shifting agriculture, forests, pasturage, open space, wilderness, and waste. These open lands and seas are also connected and so are interwoven with the occupied surface.

This did not come about in some cataclysm. The older urban areas were gradually rebuilt as community ownership took hold—opened out with gardens and recreations, their specializations diminished, their infrastructure converted to new uses. Private preserves were opened to the public; buildings were weeded, transplanted, and rebuilt. New centers were built in the outer suburbs and rural lands. Old village centers, once drowned in the tidal wave of metropolis, emerged. Scattered buildings were clustered, and productive activities brought into residential zones.

The old intensive urban cores have for the most part been retained, but have been radically rebuilt and reused. They are natural landscapes, of as demanding a type as a tropical rain forest or an alpine ridge. Special settlements and ways of living have been fitted to their peculiar characteristics. A few have been converted to wilderness, and a few preserved as historic monuments. Old cities are pruned and shaped to bring out their character, just as any landscape might be. Some specialized buildings—skyscrapers, tenements, luxury apartments, huge mills—have provided difficult to adapt and have been abandoned, or wrecked in some dramatic spectacle. But most old buildings, if still structurally sound, have found new uses. Each place has visibly evolved from what it was before, and this growth, overlaid on the diversity of land and of society, has resulted in rich variety. The history of human settlement is vividly inscribed.

The land (or rather, the space, now that there are settlements underground, in the shallow seas, and more recently in the air) is owned by those who use it. But this ownership simply means the right of present control and enjoyment and the responsibility of present maintenance. The impossible dream of eternal, absolute, transferable, individual possession has evaporated. People now accept that the

life span of any human owner is brief, while place
abides, and that the territories of many other creatures overlap their own. In the more permanent
sense, the intensively urbanized central areas and
major transport routes are held by local or regional
governments, while all the remaining space is in
the hands of special regional trusts.

These regional land trusts, self-perpetuating
but subject to public supervision, are in some sense
almost religious bodies. They conserve basic environmental resources, protect the variety of species, and keep the environment open for future use.
They are not preservation societies, however. They
look on themselves as very long-term managers,
concerned neither with "development" nor with
"preservation," but with smoothing perturbations,
keeping settlement fluid, avoiding dead ends. They
are trustees for the nonrepresented—for other species and for future human generations—whose
motives are obscure and whose chances must be preserved. They do little planning and exert little control, except to assure this. They have the power and
the narrow-mindedness of concentrated purpose.
They parcel their lands out among stable resident
groups where they can. They feel themselves as
belonging to the land, as much as the land belongs
to them.

These land trusts grant leases for the present
enjoyment of space, and at times for the exploitation of its nonrenewable resources, to individuals,
corporations, and other private and public agencies, and to resident social groups—such as families, group families, groups of families, clans, communes, and the like. There are limits to the volume
that may be leased to any one group or person. The
leases vary in length, but those made to resident
groups are the longest. The latter are renewable
and generally run for the lifetime of members, so
that a vigorous resident group, which regularly
replenishes its membership (and only such a
group), may hold a settlement space indefinitely.
When resident communities lose their members by
death or migration, break up in quarreling, or fail
economically, then their allotted lands are repos-
sessed by the trust, to be allocated anew. Communities are normally small and organized around

kinship or ethnic ties or attachment to place, but also around joint activities of production and consumption, or common life styles, and these latter bonds are often related to the nature of the place. Social ties and place ties are linked. Resident groups often maintain their own services and productive facilities. Most people belong to some resident group, although they may work or study elsewhere, be part of some other institution or corporation, and have other social ties. Nonresident land may be leased for a definite term to public agencies (roadways, schools), or to semipublic organizations, individuals, cooperatives, or private corporations.

Thus while some space is temporarily controlled by a variety of functional agencies, individuals, or corporations, most of it is in the hands of resident groups, and these holdings are more long-lived. Yet all holdings change, in response to changes in function, society, and ecology. No assignments are permanent, except for some few sacred or symbolic locations, some permanent wilderness, and the broad rights-of-way of the major transportation routes. As land holdings and uses shift, the pattern of local government and public service also shifts, while the underlying trust territories endure.

Lessees plan their own turf, while regional governments plan for the routes, the central areas, and the required infrastructure, and also control local users where necessary to prevent external harm. Interregional or international bodies may override regional decisions on crucial issues of resource allocation, transport, or social exclusion, particularly where a region has some quasi-monopoly of site, materials, energy source, or amenity. At these levels, the conflicts between regional interests must be faced and painfully resolved, although not by means of organized violence. Those peculiar warlike entities called nations no longer exist, of course. So the management of space is primarily a regional affair, rising out of the interplay between three principal kinds of actors: the land trusts, the regional governments, and the resident communities. The trusts have rather simple, long-term aims of conservation and continued openness. Governments are concerned with regional quality in the intermediate term, and with allocations of services between groups of people. They control through guidelines and performance standards, as well as by major works and services. But it is the local groups that by use and construction determine the actual form and quality of the environment.

Any person or stable small group may, in its own region, obtain a lease on a modest but adequate residential space, since the control of most land is recurrently renewed, and interregional policies control the basic ratios of men to space, so that no region is perilously overcrowded, and another empty. Anyone may have a private space, both indoor and outdoor. Children have this right as well as adults. People may camp in a wasteland for a time, or rent rooms in some urban center, but no one may multiply his permanent residential domains. He or she may not continue to hold one which is no longer used, or keep an old one after joining another resident group, or on leaving a region. However, a departing resident may ask that the lease of a relinquished domain pass on to some person who knows and loves the place and holds no other. Such a request is always carefully considered.

Migration to other regions is always possible, although interregional bodies use controls or inducements to stabilize regional rates of growth or decline. A residential space may be a piece of land; a space underground, underwater, or in the air; an unused dwelling; or a volume within a structural framework. Residents and users manage their own places and bear the consequent costs of construction and maintenance. They may design and even build, or they may call in an expert to do so, under their direction.

No rent is exacted for the few permanent assignments of land (main rights-of-way, symbolic locations, isolated wildernesses). Nor are rents imposed on the modest residential spaces allotted to individuals and small groups, including that space devoted to any minimum subsistence activity, such as local education or the production of food and clothing for local consumption. Such resident leases are not transferable; they return to the trust or government on death or abandonment of the space. The costs of maintaining essential services to such space, and of administering land allocation and planning, are borne generally, via regional taxation or lease revenues. Minimum residential space and its basic services are public utilities.

Space for larger, nonresidential activities, including space which is widely desired and in short supply and space leased to individuals and agencies in the centers and along the main routes, is leased for some definite term to the highest bidder, and the proceeds are used for trust or government purposes. These leases are transferable, are limited in size as well as in term, and are subject to restrictions to maintain future usefulness. Such lease allocations are not allowed to preempt an adequate supply of minimum residential space elsewhere, of course. Public and semipublic agencies and institutions compete in this same lease market. The consequent loss of the hidden subsidies associated with the indefinite possession of unpriced land (and the transfer of that subsidy to resident groups) has been especially difficult for large agencies, including universities and the military. All public and private institutions have found their costs inflated and must come closer to justifying them.

No one's living space is controlled by anyone else, unless by the former's choice, or because he is legally incompetent, or because his residence is temporary. Especially desirable locations are not permanently preempted. Everyone may have her own place if she wishes, or may join a resident group. Thus permanent ownership is regional, and the basic strategy of land management is set at that level, albeit by two different entities, the regional trust and the regional government. Landscape creation and maintenance, as well as the provision of local service, are decentralized and shifting. Within the framework of centers and main routes, the region is a mosaic of small, diverse territories, where inhabitant, user, manager, and temporary owner all tend to coincide.

This system of land allocation did not appear overnight, of course, and certainly not without resistance. Land began to be regionalized quite early, at first by scattered trusts set up by foundations or local governments. Initially, they took charge of open lands to be conserved. Later, public funds were put into areas ripe for development, in order to promote orderly planning. Local resident communities began to take their sites by purchase, or, like squatters, by seizure, and conveyed them to trusts to insure their title. The trusts themselves began to acquire vacant and abandoned lands as a matter of policy, as well as to regionalize development rights. Larger holdings were taken by forceful political intervention, at times softened by cash or by arranging for a terminal period during which rents could be received by former owners. Small holders were fearful of eviction and emotionally attached to their possessions. Here again, the transfer was sometimes forcible, but more often it relied on persuasion, purchase, and grants of life tenure. Although these holdings might represent a lifetime's savings, yet future residence and subsistence were assured, and rents might continue to be collected from the trust, even for a lifetime. Thus the control of land changed radically, but its use changed more slowly. Border disputes arose and still arise between the trusts, and between them and local governments, which require patient negotiations. It is not unusual to hear an individual complain about the residential space he has been allocated, or to see him seek another. Resident groups are more satisfied with their holdings, even if frictions occur at times along their edges. There are numerous enclaves not yet in trust, but by now it is clear that most lands—again excepting some permanent reservations or special cases—will eventually fall into their hands. This piecemeal local growth has meant that trust administration and control have many local variants, from region to region, even if the basic principles of land management are very general.

Each small territory may have its own style of living, its own types of buildings and landscape, even its own pattern of utilities and transport. These localized patterns are regulated by the land trusts and the regional governments to insure safety and health (both of people and of the land), and to prevent interference with neighbors. Otherwise, there is very little regulation of internal form. Thus the occupation is "patchy" and mixed with strips and pieces of wasteland, under no group's direct control (although a part of trust territory), and so open to spontaneous or deviant use. These wastes are a reservoir of species (including pests, of course). The larger wastes seem mysterious, tinged with fear and anxiety. They carry out a function once performed by the abandoned farms of declining rural areas and by the decaying "gray areas" of the inner cities.

Thus some untended land is always near at hand, while "wilderness" (in the sense of an extensive area largely untouched by people) is at least in one's mind and within one's extended reach, although the access to it may be quite difficult. Wilderness may be an island, a mountain, a great swamp, a trackless scrub, a deep sea canyon. Other lands are devoted to isolated rural retreats, or to enclaves where people may live, if they choose, in retarded or exotic modes.

In inhabited areas, there is a fine-grain mix of activity. Production, consumption, residence, education, and creation go on in each other's presence. No one need travel far to engage in any of these activities, although anyone may range widely if she wishes. The spatial and temporal integration of activity supports its functional integration. Teaching and learning is not confined to school buildings, or to childhood, or to one public agency. Any productive task has its educational and recreational aspects. Children see the world at work, and working parents watch their children learn. Rather, they work and learn together.

This new, muddled landscape contrasts with the extensive monocultures of the past, which collapsed in such a spectacular series of linked failures: the big fields of agroindustry, the great pine forests grown to be cut over, the mining regions, the empty lands, the extensive suburbs, the specialized summer resorts, the splendid hospitals and university campuses, the great office districts, the gigantic industrial estates, airfields, ports, and switching yards—all those places whose inhabitants were isolated, specialized, or temporary: migratory workers, tourists, lumberjacks, farm laborers, housewives, students, passengers, patients, secretaries. Large-scale specialization of the land is now avoided; or, where it is inescapable, it is softened by encouraging some temporary use, or by providing another home base for its temporary users.

Not that all large engineering works are gone. Dams, power stations, ports, highways, and transmission lines still exist, especially if they serve to increase the access through and between regions. There still are agencies big enough to manage them. It is the sacrifice of an extended ground to a single use that has vanished, along with the extended spatial control that that required. So, there are workshops in the fields and quiet shops among the houses. Next to them are swimming holes, picnic places, and summer cottages for people on vacation. Crops are set out in mixed plantings, garden style. The borders between different uses are thought to be the most interesting parts of a landscape. This mixing of use reduced the efficiency of production, until the measure of efficiency was recalculated.

Functional integration is matched by a degree of social integration. Small local territories are distinct in their way of life, but they are set together. No large region is closed to any people. Everyone is aware of the diversity around her. Safe on her home ground, she can maintain the norms and behavior she values. Yet she is at least in visual contact with other ways of life. And since many communities cohere around characteristics which are not permanently assigned to the person—such as a set of beliefs and interests, or a way of conducting life—it is possible for people (at substantial personal cost, of course) to shift from one group to another. Moreover, large numbers of like-minded people will at times congregate temporarily, to revel in their special kind, including camera enthusiasts, Finnish descendants, homosexuals, radical theologians, and the formerly rich. These permanent and temporary ways of distributing social groups in space could have been seen in the earlier cities, but then they were marginal compared to the overriding ethnic and class distinctions.

While the general density of occupation is now rather low, because of all this mixing of use and waste, high towers may also be seen, as well as factories and meeting halls of moderate size, and intricate, compact, group dwellings. Smaller buildings occur in tight clusters, and there are intensive public centers devoted to offices, high-density residences, specialized production, communication, distribution, and sophisticated consumption and entertainment. Footloose cosmopolites choose to live in those centers, or along the main routes, and so, for a while, do many adolescents and young adults, as well as a few older people.*

These centers of stimulus and decision are active throughout the twenty-four hours. Most of them are out-growths of earlier central places, although new centers have been established in sparsely occupied regions, so that centers may be accessible to everyone, as are the wastelands and quiet places. Central space is leased from the local government, which provides the common services. Resplendent, active, and alive, these centers unchangingly occupy historic sites in a changing way. Each has its own character, which arises out of its long history as an inhabited place. They are the symbolic points around which the loosely patterned, shifting countryside may mentally be organized, the foci of regional identity. Natural features are intensified to strengthen that symbolism. Chasms, lakes, and mountains may be manufactured where no remarkable form exists. Some people feel alienated in these changing, impersonal places, and rather enjoy it.

We have seen that parts of a region are secluded, while other lands, particularly the centers, are highly accessible. The landscape is an alternation of rest and movement, of privacy and sociability. A major grid of public transport, within a broad right-of-way, covers the entire region. It is distorted to accommodate natural features, to avoid the wild

*They are not to be called "retired" persons, however, since it is difficult to disengage from activity now, unless one is seriously ill. Sick and disturbed people are only rarely shut off from others. Lives are not segregated into eras of education, production, and rest, any more than space is segregated.

lands on the one hand and to serve the centers on
the other. Yet it is regular and continuous. This grid, like the centers, the wildernesses, and certain symbolic sites, is permanently located. Within it run the major conduits which carry people, goods, messages, wastes, and energy.

A variety of transport modes are in use. Noise and pollution have been bred out of them, or if not, their use is strictly confined. There are trains, moving walks and seats, escalators, buses, minibuses, pneumatic tunnels, trucks, group taxis, boats, horses, low-powered carts and wheelchairs, dirigibles, gliders, and light aircraft. More often than not, people walk, cycle, skate, or ski, using their own energy to get about. As we scan this list, we are dismayed to learn that this sluggish utopia has failed to invent any new modes of transport, except for fun. It has improved the old modes, makes better use of them, and is dependent on no single one.

There are regional networks, separate from the main grid, which are devoted to slow, safe movement or to the pure pleasure of motion, or which are historic pathways. Many of these special roads are maintained by volunteer "way societies," while the main grid is controlled by some regional government. Within the grid, a capillary network of roads and paths, held in many private hands, perfuses the region, and this network expands and contracts as uses change. In the centers, the transport network erupts into three dimensions. In the air, it is channeled and does not pass over certain zones. Underground, there are fantastic passage systems, but underwater one moves with less restriction. All roads are designed to make travel interesting.

Everyone is free to move. There are vehicles for the very young, the very old, and the handicapped; there are easy ways of carrying parcels or conveying small children. No curbs block a wheelchair; no obstacles endanger the blind. There are no local streets that a child cannot cross safely. Indeed, children are encouraged to roam—watching, listening, testing, wondering, learning. The right of public access, if without damage to the landscape or direct intrusion on privacy, is well established.

Seacoasts, lakes, and streams are open. Anyone can travel abroad. Although most people are locally rooted, they have spent a few years of their lives in wandering. The historical and cultural diversity of the great world is very attractive to young adults and important to their development. Travel still takes time, however, as well as personal energy. Daily or purposeful travel has decreased, since people are closer to their work, and recreation is less a running away than a renewal of self in a familiar locale. Yet people also have a greater experience of distant places than formerly.

Outside the retreats and the wilderness, simple communications devices are easy to find and free to use: local telephones, radios, TV screens, computer outlets, postal boxes, notice boards. Message sending is decentralized and two-way channels are favored. Broadcasts originate at local levels; there are wall newspapers, small printing presses, street theaters. The use of the landscape for diffuse communication has undermined the mass media. It is easy (and safe) to locate and converse with a like-minded person, in a public place, by a conference call, or through notices and the mails.

Basic transportation and communication are free public utilities, supported by public funds. Not only are the streets free to walk on, but local transit, local telephones, postcard mails, even the simpler kinds of vehicles, like wheelchairs, bicycles, and roller skates, are free to be used where found.

Most buildings use a minimum of imported material and energy. Structural technique has advanced to the use of any abundant local material— sand, earth, clay, rock, brush, grass—to the harnessing of local forces, and to building systems easy to erect and to modify. Most buildings are simple, light, and low. They are warmed and cooled by sunlight, wood, geothermal heat, evaporation, and the movement of natural currents of air, rather than by imported energy expended in sealed structures. Building skins respond to the fluctuations of weather: opening and closing, paling and darkening. Spaces are arranged to produce a variety of microclimates.

Unfortunately, many massive and uncomfortable structures remain from an earlier time. Cities cannot be transformed overnight; their inertia is very great. Much ingenuity has been expended in making these older buildings habitable—thinning them out, breaking through their walls and roofs, reducing their density of use, making internal modifications. Some still require wasteful amounts of energy. People who must live in the surviving apartments, or work in the old factories or skyscrapers, may receive some reduction of rent, or some bonus of income or prestige. Others enjoy living in these nostalgic shells. Occasionally, as we have seen, the older city areas have become a new wilderness, or are mined for their materials.

Recycled material is more often used than raw material. Wastes are converted, or their breakdown is accelerated. Structures are designed to be reused, or to be wrecked and reconstituted easily. The testing and evaluation of a design or a material includes a consideration of how it can be rebuilt or destroyed. The whole process of waste, elimination, and conversion is seen as interesting and useful, as worthy of celebration as production. Sewering, wrecking, and cleaning are trades as honorable as cooking and building.*

The low average density, the high degree of accessibility, the patchiness of development, all mean that the environment is easily changed to fit new uses and new users. Adaptations can be made with small applications of power and effort. This quality of adaptability is also prized in the design of equipment. The first question asked of a new machine is: "How can I fix this when it breaks down?" The second question may be: "Can I run it by hand?"

In many domains, we find two tiers of consumption: the one limited, standard, simple, and necessary, provided cheaply or free of charge as a common good, the other more costly, varied, and acquired by individual enterprise. Drinking water, baths and toilets, basic food and medicine, a very elementary education, basic transport and com-

*Remember the Golden Dust-
man in *News from Nowhere?*

munication, and utility clothing are the common ground of existence and the common charge. While in limited quantity and of the simplest kind, they are easily available in public places. Their production, distribution, and maintenance are a public enterprise. Despite an occasional extravaganza, the material standard of life is not elaborate, except in a symbolic sense. Levels of consumption are below resource replacement rates, or allow time for resource substitution. As regions turned toward using their local resources, there have been losses in the international carriage of goods and energy, and this has been most marked for those things that are scarce and irreplaceable at the point of origin, or which required the exploitation of human labor. Oil is now traded in small amounts as a lubricant, a shift which has brought on some very disturbing changes in the use of power (and in the balance of power) all over the world.

While the world's people now have enough food and shelter, and the material basis of a decent life, the citizens of the regions once called advanced have had to give up many luxuries. In a quantitative sense, there has been a marked leveling down of consumption. In one way, this was forced on the wealthy nations by the rising power of the developing regions. In another, it was a voluntary release—a widespread change of heart. There have been surprising changes in diet, clothing, and equipment, and a more profound change in attitudes toward material acquisition.

Since fundamental physical requirements are assured, owning a great quantity of material goods is no longer a sign of prestige, although some older people, secretly defiant, still feel it to be so. To the amusement of the young, they hoard things, measure status by property, and are disappointed when their descendants seem indifferent to an inheritance. Indeed, people still make wills, but the wills are read as an expression of feelings, as "last words" rather than as legal documents transferring property. This shift in attitudes toward the possession of material goods has proved to be one of the more difficult obstacles to communication between the generations. Theft and vandalism have lost their importance, and the family has lost its func-

tion as a device for securing and transmitting property. While physical capital is still accumulated and
maintained by groups and corporations, it is no
longer a matter of consuming importance for individuals.

In those areas of the world which still remember bitter poverty, the possession of abundant
goods is a powerful aspiration even today. But now
this attitude is shifting too, following the track of
values in the formerly dominant world. People are
by no means ascetics, however. On the contrary,
they find great pleasure in the physical world, in
creating and consuming fine things in an elegant
way. It is the exclusive control of goods, or their
sheer quantity, which has lost its savor. The joy of
things lies in making them, in using them, or even
in destroying them.

People are aware of the living process around
them and feel themselves a part of that process.
While not afraid to disturb it—as indeed they cannot avoid doing—they watch the ripples that
spread out from their gestures. They use a trail and
watch how the trailside plants respond to their
passage; abandon a building and observe the flora
and fauna which reoccupy it. Some conduct deliberate experiments, or try to communicate with
other species.

The responsibility of a group for its territory
includes the well functioning of other living things
in that place, just as much as a care for its continued
human usefulness. Residents may be brought to
account by a trust for the demise of a marsh, for
example, as well as by a regional government for
injury to a neighbor. They can be required to maintain or replenish the soil, or the water table, or a
stand of trees. People and land belong to each
other. In the early days, residents might so misuse
their land as to be dispossessed on that account, but
it is the nonresidential lands that have proved to be
the more enduring problem. Maintenance can more
easily be brought to a formal standard there, but it is
not so easy to foster an attitude of caring.

Few people keep pets, just as the converse is
rarely seen. Those pets that remain coexist with
humans on a more independent footing than

formerly. Animals which work cooperatively with man are still common, of course: horses, milk cows, sheep dogs, seeing eye dogs, rescue dolphins, rats trained to find breaks in pipes and wires. The consumption of meat has fallen, although strict vegetarians are still only a large minority. Some of these sects distinguish between the "lower" and "higher" plants, which may and may not be eaten. Other groups feed their dead to animals.

Since there are strips of waste between the developed lands, many species survive which are intolerant of man. Temporarily threatened species may be held in reservations, or introduced elsewhere, when the consequences can be foreseen. In brief, human beings are no longer an uncontrolled disease of nature, but have come to accept some responsibility for being a dominant species—stewards and not masters. That that possibility might even include a speeding, or a diversion, of evolution begins to trouble people.

Even as attention is paid to the recycling of material, so attention is given to the cycling of human settlement. Regional growth and decline may be tinkered with, but no one tries to preserve some final size or character. Change is expected; places evolve, even if explosive or irreversible change must be prevented. There are strategies for decline as well as strategies for growth. The processes of settlement, resettlement, and unsettlement are all attended to. The recent celebrated devolution of Manhattan into a cluster of small communities dependent on fishing, special recreation, and the mining of used building materials has aroused wide admiration. It is a landscape of ruins, like medieval Rome. Unlike Rome, it is also a healthy and comfortable place, and not oppressed by history. Yet it retains that magic sense of power and excitement which draws so many visitors.

World travel is encouraged, but worldly sophistication is founded on secure local attachment, just as social ease depends on a sense of personal identity. Mobility is tempered by ties of place, and by permanent symbolic locations and retreats. Of course, some groups are mobile by nature, and their stable territory is a route or sea along which they regularly pass, and a succession of places at which they regularly pause.

The great majority of people will pass their lives in one group and in one place, broken by intermittent periods of travel. Yet a certain number have experienced a permanent transfer, or their kin or neighbors have done so. Such a transfer is always a well-remembered event, carefully prepared. The move is preceded by lengthy reconnaissance and trial. Small groups will move together. There are accepted rituals for "closing" an old location, and for "opening" a new one. Moves are voluntary, but may be distant, following the incentives or persuasions of interregional authorities. Not only is the size of the world population being regulated, but its pattern is constantly being adjusted to make better use of world resources.

Environmental change has also been formalized in experimental centers. Volunteers give a trial run to some hypothesis about a modification of place and society—a new type of group family in a specially designed structure, for example, or a free-running temporal rhythm of activity in an underground habitat. The volunteers monitor their own experiment and may abandon or modify it. Should it prove workable, the experiment becomes a demonstration. Others repeat the experience for themselves—for pleasure, for confirmation, or to help them choose a way of life. Many resident groups have had their origins in some successful experiment about a placed society, although in their own evolution they may have moved some distance from the original pattern. In this way, paths to the future are being run out and their consequences examined.

All but the very youngest and oldest can remodel their own settings to some degree and are to that degree responsible for them: the young child for his corner of a room or garden, the adult for a complex landscape. Particular kinds of people may be charged with specific environmental functions. Older adolescents, since they like to play with fire, are the fire fighters, while the blind regulate noise pollution. Children manage and play with small animals, or gather trash (can we allow them to play with the trash?). Tasks are found for the retarded, the ill, and the handicapped, so that all people find meaning in a common care for place. This participation brings people to understand themselves and also binds them together. The environment is not simply the occasion for cooperative effort. It is consciously designed to reinforce cooperation, and sometimes even to require it. Since most social groups have defined spatial territories, the mental images of place and of community are usually congruent with each other. Centers and landmarks are symbols of common values. They are deliberately shaped to receive those meanings.

Elements of the landscape are also made memorable in their own right. Roads, for example, no longer have a standard cross section, or a set of details monotonously imposed. Each path has its own character. It fits into the cultural and natural landscape in its own way and reveals its own sequence of views. Buildings have personalities. Places acquire distinctive sounds and smells at special times.

Landscape design—place creation—is an admired art. Small teams are eager to take on responsibility for shaping and managing some piece of public land, for this is a route to renown. New efforts at landscape creation are widely criticized. Old settings are reworked, or, if they are considered classics, they are conserved and made the subject of critical appreciation. Some early landscapes are particularly remembered for their historic role in generating the first excitement which fueled the drive toward utopia.

Graceful land management—the way a place is used, maintained, and modified through the seasons and the peaks and valleys of activity—is as much appreciated as fine design. In fact, design and management are not distinguished. Both clarify and deepen the common image of a region and give its features a vivid presence to which meanings may attach. People learn to be aware of their surroundings, through all their senses. They perceive places actively: digging into them, moving over them, causing echoes, setting them afire. Other arts—theater, poetry, sculpture, music—sharpen this awareness and make the landscape resonant.

Tales and poems develop the meaning of a place; paintings and photography cause it to be seen in some new way. Guidebooks of a hundred kinds are written. These also are considered to be place-creating arts.

Light, motion, sound, and smell are manipulated to make places more engaging to the senses. Dim white sculpture may be placed in a dark pine grove, or wind-driven mobiles play with a water surface. A species of tree is hung with its own distinctive chimes, gives off a special, augmented odor, and has a particular way of being lit at night. A bird which is associated with that tree in some memorable poem may be deliberately attracted there. A local climate is dramatized. The spectacular, intensified melts of wet spring snow in the coastal northeast are notorious. Special celebrations are reserved to special places. There is an open hilltop used only for weddings and victories and a tiny valley saved for reminiscent picnics in spring.

Where it will not interfere with privacy, the landscape is made more transparent. Clues to its hidden functions are left on view. Economic processes are exposed. The connection between production and consumption is immediate: corn roasts are held in cornfields, people put up their own houses, fashions are modeled alongside the looms, and bicycles are chosen off the assembly line, with the advice of the assembly teams. But it remains difficult to present more remote and abstract activities in this same tangible way. How does one communicate the work of a public accountaint, or of a trader in futures?

Public activity is visible, and the symbols of resident groups are displayed. The inner workings of some functional element—a water main, perhaps, or a clock—are there to be seen if one is interested. There are guidebooks to the sewer system, with instructions on how to read the season and the time of day by watching the flow. Signs, obscure marks, the traces of activity, listening devices, diagrams, remote sensors, magnifying glasses, slow-motion films, periscopes, peepholes—any of these may be used to make some process perceptible: not immediately apparent, of course, or just presented in some canned lesson. Learning is a discovery, and no one is forced to attend to the landscape if she has other business. But the threads are there to follow, if she wants to trace them out. The environment is a great book, a drama—a rich display of information about place, function, human society, the stars, and the concert of living things. It is an education—not an illustration of the knowledge in some book, not the subject of a field trip.

Everyone is trained to read a place, just as everyone is trained to read a book. Reading a place means coming to understand what is happening there, what has happened or might happen, what it means, how one should behave there, and how it is connected to other places. Factions read their surroundings differently and press their readings on others. Two contradictory interpretations may therefore be presented simultaneously to the bemused observer. Historic traces are preserved and are modified as concepts of the past are revised. Artifacts which explain cultural traditions are considered to be landscape resources like timber, soil, and coal. They are conserved, as far as possible, within* the living, changing setting. History is marked out as it occurs. Present trends and future possibilities are displayed.* Time of day and season are dramatized, and so are the important social events and pervasive rhythms of human activity. The environment is a celebration of place and time and process.

There are "slow" places and "fast" ones; ones whose day begins at dawn and others which are alive at night. Even the periodic measures are diverse: one location may have 90-minute hours, or its weeks contain 13 days. In some locations, periods may not be sharply measured, but be elastic, to fit the work at hand, or a common mood. Of course, there remains a standard time of reference, used to maintain social coordination, just as there is a standard language among dialects and a main road system that links diverse territories. Yet people are able to match their lives to their personal rhythms.

*These will also be contradictory, of course.

The world is fitted to human feelings. There
are sacred places, mysterious and tragic ones, landscapes of aggression and of love. Through the customs and rituals associated with those places, people can experience and express their most profound emotions. One setting can be a symbol of paradise, while another expresses deep fears and anxieties. Features of the land are deliberately exploited to produce these emotive places—caves, sea coves and promontories, mountaintops, lakes and forests, gorges, waterfalls, arid mesas, jumbled badlands—as well as small places deep within the built environment—secluded courts, pinnacles, underground rooms, and tiny pools.

A network of holy places has emerged, weaving an image of the earth as a diverse and sacred unit. They are in the volcanoes, under the sea, or in the high air; they are cold, hot, wet, or dry. They expose earth time and the time of the universe. Some places look at the stars, and there are sacred satellites which regard the earth. People make pilgrimages from one such place to another, at various stages in their lives. They may visit a place briefly, to experience its special meaning, or may stay longer to contribute to its evolution. Some few remain to devote themselves to the locale, becoming, in a sense, priests of wind, fire, earth, or water. These places speak to each other by vibrations through the earth or the sea, by lights and air waves, by exchanging material substances, by messages carried by birds and fish.

Environmental rituals, special ways of acting, are as much a part of the sacred design as the place itself. In some, or at certain times, actions are rigidly controlled; speech, gesture, posture, and clothing are minutely prescribed. Other times are devoted to exuberance and disorder. Dark actions are proper to the cave and the ritual of tea to the teahouse. At home, there are similar ritual actions that every member of a community helps perform. Outdoor events celebrate the spring or the solstice, floods, the breakup of winter ice, the return of swallows and tourists, the shared mourning of a people at some place of common tragedy. The planet is a festival, a drama, and a remembrance.

People feel exposed to their surroundings. Many seek out places which challenge them, even at risk of life. Tall buildings are scaled like mountains. The polar ice is a test of survival. Men and women learn by doing. They are discovering new human abilities, new ways of perceiving, moving, and feeling, new games and resources. Or they rediscover an old, forgotten skill.

Some think themselves, like very limited gods, to be responsible for the evolution of other forms of life. Watching the changes in the animals and plants around them, they protect and encourage those changes that seem beneficial, that is, which appear to increase the viability and capability of the species itself, rather than its economic usefulness to man. A very few enthusiasts may even seek to stimulate evolutionary change, thinking of themselves as its conscious agents. Other people fear this tinkering and think that we have no such license. But all would agree that the development of oneself, of one's community, and of the living place is high art and high science, the fundamental ethical action.

These utopian notes are inadequate, because they deal with the relationship of man to place and only tangentially with those of man to man. There is nothing here about birth or death, marriage, kinship or community, power, economy, conflict or cooperation, except as these arise from a relation with place. Moreover, the narrative ignores the spatial consequences which might arise from a better social order, since they look in only one direction along the linkage between environment and society. The lack is intentional: I press a neglected theme. In this, these notes are no worse than other utopian discourses, which commit the opposite error.

But they also exhibit another critical flaw: they do not say how the millennium is to be reached, or if it really all fits together. Effective strategy requires a deep analysis of the present, the construction of an integrated future, and a grasp of the dynamics of some social and environmental change which might connect the two. This has been only a recital of wishes. Even so, wishing is a way of finding out, and a way of communicating—one method of learning how to act in the present.

So these environmental proposals have no necessary relation to some set of social proposals. Physical environment and society are not simply mirrors of each other. The former, in particular, is slow to bring forth its reflections. It retains the images of many previous historical states and emanates images of its own. So one could conceive of a number of societies which might be consonant with these environmental ideas. But not an extremely large number.

There is little similarity between these proposals and the organization of the environment in societies which have been radically restructured in recent times, such as the USSR, Cuba, or China, although Havana's Cordón is a landscape symbol of the integration of work and recreation, and the Israeli kibbutz or the Chinese agroindustrial commune may prefigure the mixed-use urban countryside, organized into local territories. The spatial settings of most of the socialist world seem to be, from this distance at least, much like those of the capitalist one, and its environmental attitudes not so very diverse. The small communes, which cling to the crevices of the western world, exhibit somewhat more advanced features, but the gap is still very wide. The indifference of classical utopian thought to the qualities of place is repeated on the plane of reality.

Ceccarelli
Frampton
Kopp
Salaff
Sawyers
Spiro
Towers

And yet the themes of this chapter are not revelations. They come from many historic and contemporary sources: from the commune, indeed, but also from the farm, the garden, the "urban village," the tribal territory, the summer house, the wilderness camp, the weedy vacant lot and the remembered landscapes of childhood, the sacred precinct, the historic city, the meadow, seashore, wood, and stream, the lively plaza, and (here I blush a little) even the despised North American suburb. Ideas come from novelists, painters, photographers, filmmakers, and poets. I hear them from students and see them in guidebooks, reminiscences, and anthropological notes.

If the picture has little resemblance to the contemporary metropolis, yet those great settlements cannot simply be wiped away, unless we are to go with them. Total rebuilding is impossible—politically, economically, and psychologically. Moreover, not all current processes and conditions are perverse. The spreading metropolis itself sets the stage for a more dispersed style of life. The technical infrastructure for the urbanized countryside is already being laid down.

Remaking the environment is a compelling idea just because it embraces so many issues: inward feelings and outward form, the integration of science, art, and ethics, the relation of the individual to his local community and yet also to the unity of mankind, the interaction and development of human and nonhuman life. The renewal of the earth and of the human settlement upon it would be the greatest human enterprise since the Neolithic.

Epilogue: A Critique

This is the end of it, and we should reconsider. The theory has a number of deficiencies. Most glaring is the lack of a complementary theory on how cities come to be and how they function. I have made assumptions of that kind, but the theory is not the comprehensive view that the cosmic or organic theories were, and that the economic and behavioral analyses are not. Until it is linked to functional assertions it remains incomplete. Functional and normative assertions are equally necessary, and neither precedes the other, whether in causation or in importance. Value and function are inseparable, and both can be considered critically. The original motive of this theory is utilitarian— how to make better cities—but it is also a legitimate intellectual inquiry into the relations between men and the things they place about themselves.

More than an accusation of incompleteness can be laid against these proposals. In comparison, say, with the organic theory, which is a coherent statement about what a city is and how it should be, based on the metaphor of a living organism, and I have presented may seem at first glance to be no more than a checklist of likeable features. Nothing within the theory explicitly tells one that all the relevant factors are listed or that they do not contradict one another.

This would be a fair criticism, if it were directed at the origin of these ideas. In the beginning, their substance was a listing of all kinds of imaginable values. As it has grown, that ragged list has been simplified and interrelated, until it appears inclusive and not self contradictory. Some traces of that process are recorded in appendix C. In the course of selection and organization, the dimensions have been linked to a more general view of the nature of cities and their fundamental value. It remains true that nothing explains why these five performance dimensions are the correct ones, and no others. Yet the structure supports and connects a rich set of speculations, if nothing more. Its internal coherence is subject to test. It seems at least a reasonable summary of a broad range of statements about valued places.

If, as we compare it with other normative theories, it seems to lack a vivid, positive affirmation about the good city, that is a result of the attempt to be general, as the older theories never were. The use of value dimensions in place of universal standards inevitably dims the force of the normative statement. The utopian sketch is perhaps more engaging, because it is a personal particular choice of position. Yet, for all its attempt to allow for diversity, it will surely be repellent to some.

Decisions about cities, if they are to be openly arrived at, require communicable reasonings. A principal motive in shaping this theory into its present form has been a political one. Points on the dimensions can be set in public processes of decision: they are negotiable. The theory is intended to be useful, not only in any cultural context, but also to nonprofessionals in open debate. Once more, this sets it off from previous normative theory.

If no ideal form is advocated, this does not mean that the theory is neutral about values. It not only deals with values, but takes a position on them. It does this in several ways. First, by the choice of the performance dimensions themselves, which already is a statement about what is valuable in a city. Second, it allows for certain universal criteria which are based on human biological regularities—standards for pollution, perception, and body capability, for example. Third, even within the dimensions, along which variations are possible, much can be said as to optimum ranges, or as to how those variations shift as culture and situation shift. The theory is value-laden, but the cargo is explicit and can explicitly be shifted according to circumstance.

Indeed, criticism can go round to the other side, just as we rush to defend one threatened wall. All normative statements, these critics will now affirm, are by their nature biased and personal. Only neutral, factual observations can be universal. While the author's cultural and personal norms are more skillfully concealed than in similar literature, they are there just the same. This is one more professional put-on in a notable series: one more attempt—perhaps now an unconscious one—to impose the values of one group upon another.

I confess to a persistent personal preference for human survival and development, but beyond that I deny the charge. It is quite true that the value dimensions originally came from personal experience, or from the personal assertions of other individuals. One can begin in no other way. Yet those assertions now seem sufficiently purged of eccentricity and bias to be universal, where they are rooted in constants of human nature, or elsewhere general because they are always dimensions of concern. Whether this is true is, like the question of internal coherence, open to test. The theory is disproven when it is shown, not that some culture puts its own peculiar value on access or control or whatever, but that it is fundamentally indifferent to them, and values some quite different aspects of settlement.

What is the use of all this, if it should be true? I discussed a number of urban issues in chapters 13–15. The theory certainly did not settle those issues; the partial conclusions reached there also rested on other considerations—primarily external costs and concepts of city form—in addition to the dimensions particular to this theory. But the application clarified the debate by indicating the more important lines of argument. Moreover, as the theory develops a richer set of propositions about the links between city form and the performance dimensions and clarifies how those links depend on context, the debate can make greater use of theory.

The dimensions can help to order an intellectual inquiry, such as a study of city history, or of the relations between persons and environment. More practically, they can be used to evaluate existing cities, to show where performance is poor and should be improved. They may help to compare alternative locations for an activity, or to judge between opposing proposals. They may play a role in exposing injustice. Mapping the accessibility of a city to diverse social groups, or their relative control of its elements, would be a radical analysis.

Programs for environmental modification can be stated in terms of the dimensions, by specifying the kinds or degrees of access, fit, etc., that are wanted. Programming is the first step in design. The most important decisions tend to be made at this point, and they are often obscure decisions. Here is a way of dealing explicitly with their influence on quality. Levels of achievement to be attained within the dimensions or subdimensions could be policy statements in a comprehensive city plan. Later, after actual achievement has been measured, the plan, or the resources devoted to it, could rationally be revised.

Detailed definition of the dimensions may suggest new possibilities. Raising the issue of city-wide access for children, for example, makes one think of new vehicles, new training programs, new roles for teenagers, new city forms. While nothing in any theory of performance leads automatically to a new means of achieving performance, nevertheless the clear statement of a problem often spurs the mind to make its creative leap. A systematic framework for discussing performance, in which performance is directly linked to form, can suggest new possibilities to a designer, and also guide her in that half-conscious game of avoidance, pursuit, and selection that is the creative process. It is true that theories can also inhibit design, by focusing the mind too sharply. Any creative person handles them a little skeptically, and preserves her ambiguities. In any case, theories serve to test alternatives, once created. Moreover, to the extent that the links between form and value are made simple and clear, they can be life rafts for those who are caught in those frantic whirlpools of decision that so often, so unfortunately, are crucial events in the long process of city development.

C. Ward 1977

It is obvious that these speculative ideas will require much more thought. As yet, the theory is no more than a group of related hypotheses. The whole idea of environmental control has hardly yet been dealt with, even if it is at the root of so many desperate conflicts, and even if it is such a well-worn topic in biology. How is environmental control exerted, and with what effect? How can conflict be mediated? How can freedom be reconciled with necessary control? How can the control system be adjusted to changing circumstances? What do we mean by just control, and how is it to be achieved? These are old themes in human affairs, but surprisingly new in city design—at least as subjects for systematic thought.

In one of its aspects, at least, sense at the city scale has been more thoroughly considered, since this is a subject dear to designers, and also of interest to those studying perception and cognition. Yet there are substantial gaps here, too, such as the perception of time in the environment, or of the means of achieving sensibility in a plural, changing society. As to vitality, for all the solid work in that area (and the less than solid application of it), we have yet to learn much about the effect of environment on the rearing of children. The ethical puzzles involved in the survival and well-being of other species are even more obscure.

Access and fit have already been well studied, if only rather narrowly in the case of the first. Careful work is now underway in regard to the latter dimension, but key issues remain to puzzle us: how to provide adaptability for the future, or how to achieve a basic fit which then allows people to adapt place and function to each other in their own creative way. So one comes on succulent questions while browsing among these dimensions.

But it will give us little nourishment, if we chew over these questions in abstract. We must look at the performance of real places for the people who live there. No theory will be mature until it shows how performance tends to vary with political and social context: the concentration of power, the homogeneity or plurality of values, the stability of a society, its political economy, its resources and technology, not to speak of the physical character of its general environment. It should indicate the positions along the dimensions that are most likely to be chosen: how a rich but threatened central power may incline to value sense, for example, in distinction to the choices of small, relatively poor, egalitarian groups. It is unlikely that theory could *predict* the positions taken. One would expect to find general tendencies to variation, due to social type and situation, yet values are also the result of the historical development of any culture. They are not predetermined by law.

The dimensions cannot be studied in isolation, either from their social context, as we have just said, or yet from each other. Which elements are mutually independent, so that their performance can be varied without affecting other types of performance? On the contrary, which must always be changed in tandem, or which are necessarily in mutual conflict? As conflicts appear, then efficiency becomes important, and the game of trade-off commences.

At the end of chapter 2, I listed a set of requirements for any useful normative theory of city form. My proposal has met many of those requirements, or at least shows promise of meeting them. On one item, however, it has made no great advance: the ability to evaluate form and process together, as they vary over a span of time. Although the problem is often referred to in the text, the theory provides no new means for evaluating a sequence. Variations in performance over time can be laid out, but they must be grasped and judged in ways that are as yet beyond rational account.

The prototype described in chapter 16 and the utopia in chapter 17 do suggest, however, how form and process can be integrated in a single model. From the standpoint of city design, research should give priority to the development and analysis of new prototypes. The design stock is depleted, and some shelves are empty. Therefore we use unthinking stereotypes, or neglect some issues entirely. Even where we possess models, we apply them in the wrong situation or are unaware of their implications. The creation of new models, linked to context and desired performance, and their testing in simulation and in reality, are crucial for city design. The design fields are not accustomed to research, and established fields are pointed toward their own research questions. Alexander's work is a beginning in this regard.

There is much to be done, which is a blessing. A useful, intellectually engaging theory of city form is quite possible.

APPENDIXES

A Brief Review of Functional Theory

This is an abbreviated catalog of the prevailing theories of city genesis and function, those theories which ask, "How did the city get to be the way it is?" and the related question, "How does it work?" These theories look at the city from quite different points of view, although a few particular viewpoints are much more fully developed. I organize the catalog by grouping the theories under metaphorical headings, that is, according to the dominant images by which they conceive of the city. These images control the elements to be abstracted and shape the model of function.

Chapin 1964
Dowall

1. *Cities are unique historical processes.* Some students of the city do not believe in the possibility of any general theory of urban genesis. They look on each city as a unique, cumulative, historical process, which has taken its present particular form through a long chain of individual events, subject to a host of accidents of history and of site, and to the broad influences of culture, climate, and economic and political structure. A city can be explained only by telling a *story*, and each city has its own tale. One cannot generalize, except about certain smaller elements which have repetitive roles, such as growth patterns which are often found just outside the city gate, or the influence of the location of the center of power, or the functions of fords, passes, and the breaks in transportation. The significance even of these common elements is culture-bound.

Abu-Lughd 1971, 1974
Hoyt
Rasmussen 1955, 1967

Bridenbaugh 1938, 1955
Briggs
Burke
Dyos
Fogelson
Mumford 1961
Reps
Warner 1972

Much of the work in urban geography was in this mode, without systematic explanatory principles. Urban historians and novelists have produced a rich literature with this point of view. Many observers of cities generalize by focusing on a technique of observing, rather than on a theory of explanation. That is, each city is unique, but at least one can learn a standard way of looking at them. These methods lay bare current function and the cumulative layers of history.

Dickinson
Vance

The power of this antitheoretical view lies in its ability to explain special character, and to admit the role of creative action. It emphasizes the unfolding

Banham
Clay

processes of history, a dynamic element too often missing in the theories I shall catalog below. The general theme is the interplay of continuity and change. Unfortunately, this stance has little general predictive power, except to point out the smoothing effect of urban inertia. In a particular case, it can predict near events, but soon the story may take a new turn.

These special historical studies are useful when one is considering local action in a particular place, when one is dealing with immediate decisions, concrete patterns, and a modification of ongoing forces. They shine when one proposes to enrich and fine-tune some special character. They convey a sense of the *quality* of the environment, as the more abstract general theories to follow cannot do. But it is difficult to extract general city values from these works, except for the value of uniqueness,* and perhaps the general sentiment that environments which have grown continuously over long periods, and still survive, are therefore good. This is the rule of "viability," the grand imperative of evolutionary development and survival.

The rule may not be very inspiring, but the literature composed in its light sets out a feast of information. It is a pleasure to read, which is true of very little of the material to follow. In two directions, this historical view shows signs of developing a more coherent and general view. One is the very recent Marxian studies of city development, which I discuss below. Another is the work of archaeologists who are attempting to explain the initial rise of the city in several regions of the world. Both of these hold promise for a more systematic historical approach. As it stands, the historical view, diffuse as it may be, remains our most interesting source of city knowledge.

2. *The city is an ecosystem of human groups.* The great bulk of our theoretical literature has taken one or the other of two views of the city. The first, the ecological view, began with the work of Robert Park and Ernest Burgess in Chicago in 1925, grew to a

*Including, one supposes, the need to conserve a unique hell?

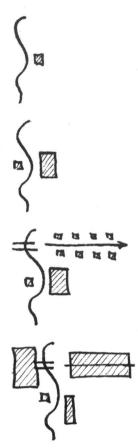

Adams
Park

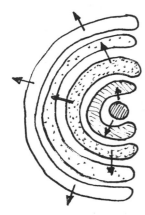

Harris

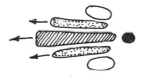

Hoyt

Berry 1977
Loudon
Morrill

dominant position, subsided temporarily, and is now being revived in a more complex form. At the beginning, it looked at cities as a map pattern of zones occupied by economic activities and by the homes of the various social classes. Taking the sociologist's view of people as a system of relatively stable groups, it tried to explain that general area pattern, including the way it changed. It employed the images of plant ecology on the one hand, and the planner's land-use patterns on the other. The contemporary Western European or North American city was its principal subject.

In this view, patterns are seen as patches on a map, people are subsumed into general groups, while the mode of analysis has become increasingly statistical. A single-centered settlement is usually assumed, spatial measurements and map patterns being referred to that center. Spatial images such as rings, waves, axes, sectors, and multiple nuclei are employed to characterize the patterns. Human groups are viewed from the outside, principally in terms of where they live and work, and how they change those locations. A simple dynamics was built up, based on successive outward growth, the "age" of an area, and principles of social attraction and repulsion. The progressive replacement of one group by another (derived from an analogy with plant succession) is an important concept. It is seen as operating within some typical general city pattern, such as a set of concentric rings, a star, or an array of sectors.* This is an empirical description, based on the development of the cities of "advanced" capitalist nations. The analysis exposes some strong generalities of pattern and provides a way of comparing the patterns of different cities. Concepts such as sectoral growth, ethnic succession, and waves of density are useful in predicting short-term future changes in modern cities, given no disturbance of the major social and economic structure.

Work in this field has recently blossomed again, in the form of "factorial ecology," which uses

*Since rings, sectors, and the like are some of the few available images for describing map forms, they are almost universally employed as a basis for analysis, even in quite diverse theories. Such is the power—and the necessity—of a mental image.

the sophisticated techniques of modern statistics to analyze the changing correlations between complex mixtures of social groups in space. The aim is to predict the detailed future distribution of work and residence by type, given some existing distribution. The work is rigorously quantitative, but still empirical, lacking a strong and coherent theoretical explanation. The massive calculations of factorial analysis and partial correlation, using computers which operate on modern census data by small localities, is a kind of intellectual fishing expedition. To date, the haul is small and rather flavorless.

These theories deal with dynamic events, but the dynamics are short-term and assume a continuation of the present set of forces. In that sense, the theory is ahistorical. Implicitly, the view is a justification of the status quo, as well as an explanation of it. The "forces" of social attraction and repulsion—ethnic cleavages, the drive to rise in income class—are right, or at least inevitable. Space is a neutral medium through which social groups communicate with one another. The city is a quantitative distribution of workplaces and living places. Other aspects of environmental quality—such as three-dimensional form, or perceptual quality, or social meaning—are more difficult to deal with. The values for cities that can be extracted, other than a buttressing of the ways things are, concern the stability and "balance" or social mix of local communities. The studies can be useful in analyses of social integration and of the equity of the distribution of spatial resources. The material, unfortunately, is tedious to read.

These criticisms are not so easily applied to some more recent ecological studies of local communities, studies which are a revival of the older Chicago tradition. The best of them are fine accounts (albeit still empirical ones) of a holistic local system of social groups, behavior, mental images, and physical form. These are a very useful background for action at the local scale. They are engaging descriptions of small human groups operating in their natural habitat.

Suttles

3. *The city is a space for the production and distribution of material goods.* The second dominant

Isard
Ratcliff
Thünen

theoretical view today is the analysis of the city as an economic engine. This has a long history and has produced the clearest and most coherent body of theory to date. Cities are looked at as patterns of activity in space which facilitate the production, distribution, and consumption of material goods. The primary idea is that space imposes an additional production cost because of the time and resources required to move things through it, and that economic activities will arrange themselves to minimize those costs. Secondarily, however, space is also a resource: it provides the room in which to produce or consume, and so activities also compete for pieces of that space, as well as for local transport locations in it. The pieces of space may have particular characteristics which influence their value for production—such as climate, steepness of surface, or fertility of soil—but this is a tertiary consideration.

These theories introduce space as a transportation cost and a room to be occupied into the optimizing machinery of classical economic theory. The basic notion is that of equilibrium: the multiple decisions of pure economic men tend to bring the spatial pattern to a balance, and that balance is the one which permits the most efficient production and distribution of goods, given the set of resources available. Thus these theories are static theories, although restorative changes occur after every shift in resources, or when obstacles to free market play are imposed or removed.

One branch of spatial economics has focused on industrial locations, particularly on resource extraction and processing, where heavy, bulky commodities must be transported across long distances. In this case, the question is: "where should a plant locate, given the dispersed locations of its various resources, markets, labor, and supporting industries?" Analysis leads to determinations of a balance point, a most efficient location, given the values of different commodities, and the various costs of transportation per unit distance. It also explains the tendencies for linked industries to agglomerate in some compromise location, and for those agglomerations, once established, to exert further locational attractions.

The economies of scale and the effect of external economies and diseconomies play an important role in these calculations. The theories not only seek to explain the past history of industrial location, but also to show where industries *should* locate, since locational equilibrium is not only what happens when the market is free, but is also an optimum. The concept has therefore been extensively used (particularly in socialist nations such as the USSR) to guide the planned distribution of new industries and the settlements linked to them. Based as it is on considerations of productive efficiency and the minimization of large transportation costs, it favors a pattern of large urban settlements founded on heavy industries.* Since the theory is most sensitive to variations in heavy transportation costs, it has been more useful in prescribing and explaining regional patterns of cities than in dealing with spatial patterns within cities, where transport costs are more obscure and complex, and a less dominant factor.

A second branch of spatial economics is central place theory. developed by Walter Christaller in 1933. This is now a clear, coherent set of ideas, well-developed in a substantial literature, and tested in numerous real situations. Like industrial location theory, it has its fullest application at the regional or national scale. In contrast, however, it is essentially mercantile, rather than industrial, its primary concern being the distribution of goods, rather than their production. Given a featureless space, uniform transportation costs, evenly distributed producers and consumers, and specified economies of scale and thresholds for different kinds of merchants who are free to move, it shows that a regular hierarchy of central places of distribution will arise. These centers will have hexagonal market areas, six of which fit within the quasi-hexagonal market area of another center next up in the hierarchical scale, and so on.

Christaller
Berry 1970

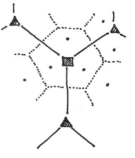

This rank ordering, hexagonal patterning, and the resulting triangular network of routes maximize the efficiency of distribution and the degree of economic communication. Given a free market and

*Behold! The ideal is what actually occurred in the urbanization of the nineteenth century!

333
Economics of location
within the city

Alonso
Hurd
Lösch
Wingo

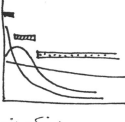

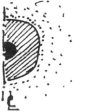

an undistorted productive space, it is inevitable and good. Arrangements of market towns which substantiate this theory are indeed to be found in regular terrains, particularly in agricultural regions. The theory has often been used to prescribe planned shopping center locations within cities, and to advocate policies which would "regularize" the hierarchy of cities at a national scale.

Both of these branches of classical spatial economics have been more successful at the regional than at the intraurban scale. Patterns of productive location within the city are more difficult to explain in theory, although they clearly show some regularities. A recent attempt at an economic explanation of intracity location, founded on concepts developed earlier by J. H. von Thünen and August Lösch, is the radial model of rent and access. This is based on free market competition for space in a city with a single center, the point of maximum access. Those engaged in different activities (owners of shops and factories, residents of various income classes) are willing to pay different prices per unit area for city ground at varying distances from that center, depending on how much they value a central location, on how willingly they bear the costs of internal transport, on the density at which they are willing to occupy space, and on their ability to pay. These variations of price can be expressed in curves which relate the rent that will be bid for a given acre to its distance from the center, for each class of activity. The highest bidder gets each location, and so the transition from one use to another, as one moves radially outward, is determined by the intersections of the rent curves. The theory is elegant and to some degree predicts the world we know: big stores and offices at the center, next the crowded poor, and so on out. But much of the complexity of the modern city escapes it; many of the most interesting features of space and society are assumed away. Like the other theories of spatial economics, it is essentially a static view, founded on an equilibrium in which space is only an empty container, affording room and imposing transportation costs. The primary value is economic efficiency, and the conclusion of the balancing process is an optimum.

This large group of theories deals with the formal economy—that part of production and distribution which is regulated by the exchange of money—and neglects the production of domestic goods, of culture, or of children. The values are the classic liberal values: increased material wealth, broad exchange, individual freedom. Justice and the distribution of resources are likely to be afterthoughts. Implicitly, these theories, quite like those of social ecology, accept the world as it is. They explain its current workings, predict the results of small changes, and prescribe enlightened tinkerings.

4. *The city is a field of force.* Some intriguing work has been done which likens cities to electromagnetic or gravitational fields of force. Cities consist of distinct particles (human individuals), distributed and moving in space, which communicate with, attract, and repel each other. More than anything else, the city is a communication network. Thus it seems plausible to import the concept of a field of force, which is such a powerful metaphor in the physicist's universe, to deal with multiple influences acting at a distance. By likening persons to point electric charges, or to bodies of equal mass, settlements and systems of settlements can be mapped as continuous fields, using the inverse square law. That is, these moving points attract or repel each other according to their relative mass or charge, divided by the square of the distance between them, since influence diminishes as it radiates out into space as the area of the spherical bubble expanding from that point increases, an area which itself is proportional to the square of its radius.*

These maps of field potential can then be used to predict future changes—including tendencies to agglomeration and the distribution of rates of growth—and also to explain the flows between different regions of the field: flows of commuters, telephone messages, freight, or whatever. The influence of barriers and initial inequalities can be accounted for, persons can be given different "mas-

Angel
Zipf

*But do urban influences operate in three-dimensional space, or on a plane, or somewhere in between?

Lobdell

Atkin

Thom

ses" according to income or other inequities, time-distances by actual routes can be used in place of straight-line distances (or the cost or capacity of routes, or even the perception of distance, can be taken into account), the exponential factor in the inverse square rule can be tinkered with to fit empirical findings, and so on. The model is elegant, simple, and testable, and it can be modified in many rational ways to fit real irregularities. So modified, it has been well fitted to many cases of real population distribution and patterns of traffic flow.

Quite naturally, this model has been the main-stay of transportation studies, being used to predict (after a local calibration) the changes in traffic flow that will be caused by some new highway, by a change in its capacity, or by a shift in the location of land uses. It also offers the possibility of a comprehensive abstract model, in which a city is a changing field of force created by the changing distribution of persons and other attractive or repellent units, and which has all the physical attributes of stress, velocity, mass, acceleration, distortions, shock waves, and so on. Concepts of hydrodynamics can be used to explain the characteristics of flows in channels. Graph theory, catastrophe theory, and other concepts of topology might be used to describe the nonmetric characteristics of spatial pattern, or the sequence of change. These theoretical openings are intriguing, and some recent efforts have been made to exploit them.

Of course there are values implied in this view. Persons are static, unthinking units which must respond in prescribed ways to the whirl of dynamic forces which surround them. The model is dynamic, but the rules are immutable. Interaction between persons is conceived as the dominant justification for a city. Implicitly, the best settlement is the one in which interaction is at its maximum. Since it is not just spatial patterns, but also technology, institutional patterns, and the human cognitive structure which impose limits on the flow of information, then one is led to propose the use of space-transcending communications, institutional reforms, and various technical intensifiers of human cognition.

Although *maximizing* communication is a dubious normative principle, it might be possible to adapt the theory to *optimizing* the rate of communication in a settlement, but this requires a definition of the optimum rate. Could that be done, it then suggests an introduction of limits, barriers, repellents and other such devices into the model, which would cause units to move to locations, and flows to seek levels, which corresponded to that defined optimum.

The model is too narrow, in its single focus on communication, and surely wrong in valuing maximum interchange. It also disregards human learning capabilities. Its strength lies in its conceptual elegance, in the intriguing possibilities of certain new mathematical models of cities, and lastly in the fact that communication is one fundamental reason for being of any human settlement.

5. *The city is a system of linked decisions.* The computer has made it possible to explore still another view of the city, one long held as an intuitive, descriptive image, but whose consequences could not previously be analyzed. This is the idea that a settlement does not grow of itself, like a biological organism, but is the cumulative product of the repeated decisions of many persons and agencies—actors who have diverse goals and resources, and who are continuously being influenced by each other's actions. This flow of decisions, and the resulting shifts in settlement form, can best be modeled as a complex *system*, that is, as a set of defined elements or quantifiable states (which in this case are things such as locational patterns, housing inventories, available sites, transport capabilities, populations, financial positions, and the like) and a set of interactions which link those elements and cause them to change. These linkages are the multifarious decisions of persons, firms, and agencies. If one can specify the classes of significant actors, with their motives and resources and how their decisions are affected by the state of the system, and if one can also define the significant elements of the system, their present state, and how each state is modified by the flow of decisions, *then* one can make an abstract machine

out of these elements and links. Once set in motion, this machine will replicate the succession of forms that a real settlement takes on.

Clearly, this is a difficult task. The significant elements and links, and their states and relationships, must be mathematically defined. The linkages typically used are the locational decisions of families seeking a residence and of firms seeking a production location. But many others can be added, including legislative moves regarding taxation, subsidy, transportation, or land control, and the various programs of public and semipublic agencies.* The sequence of decisions is usually organized in repeated stages, at regular time intervals, giving each actor his moment on the stage. The set is thereby shifted, and the play goes on. To run such a machine through its stages is too tedious for the human spirit, but not for the computer. The results of such runs are not only complex and voluminous, but often counterintuitive, just as those real happenings are that so often astonish us. If the run succeeds in replicating the development of a real place, then that development is explained, and the model is correct.

A great number of assumptions must be made to define the elements, the links, their interrelations, and their sequential timing. Different assumptions can have marked effects on the output. But at least these assumptions must be made openly, and so they are subject to criticism. Moreover, with some labor, it is possible to vary them and then to re-run the model, to see if the results are particularly sensitive to errors in that type of assumption.

When developed, such models will presumably be able to explain existing city form (in the sense of being able to replicate it), and to predict future changes. In particular, changes can be foreseen that may happen if one or another public policy is carried out, or if some uncontrollable external event occurs. These models have been extensively used to develop background predictions for

---

*These links are always limited to *human* decisions—our normal man-centeredness. Since we are the dominant species, perhaps this is not too far from the truth of cities. Let us pass on in silence.

transportation planning at the regional scale and are being constructed for more general planning use. They have been only indifferently successful in predicting short-term change up to now, but this could be no more than an ailment of youth.

One variant of this computerized decision model is the *game*, in which living persons are given defined roles, resources, and motives, and operate symbolically on various city elements (sites, developments, investments, regulations, etc.) which are linked to each other, and to the acts of the actors, in programmed ways stored in a computer. In other words, human beings, with all their unpredictable, foolish, unquantified ways, are substituted for some of the computer links. The evolution of a suburban development can be simulated, for example, with live participants, much as in real life, but in a brief time. While not so stable for prediction, these games turn out to be very useful for explaining something about the mechanism of city growth, and for giving participants a vivid feel for the process. Games have a subtle educative disadvantage, however. While exciting and revealing, they reinforce our belief that roles and rules are immutable, and that life is a competition, whose surface may be in restless motion, but whose structure is always the same.

The formal decision models themselves have other limitations. One is that, except as persons are brought in by means of gaming, the models are necessarily confined to quantifiable data and cannot accept qualities. Standardized information and values are more readily incorporated in them than are marginal or evanescent features. The high level of abstraction requires rigorous selection. Statements contained in the model must be precise, which is both an advantage and a liability, since the models cannot bear that ambiguity and fuzziness so familiar in the world we know. The metaphor used is at heart a mechanical one: the world is a vast machine, made up of distinct, independent parts and distinct, unchanging links between them. The machine works by repeated fits, like a complicated steam engine going through its cycles. It is difficult to say just what blinders this metaphor imposes, but one wonders uneasily if the city is really like a giant aeroplane.

A purely esthetic criticism can also be made. These symbolic machines and their gargantuan outputs have no seizable form. Their results not only are counterintuitive, but do not lead us to more appropriate intuitions. How can we describe how the thing works, except by repeating again the whole list of linked assumptions? Could we guess how it might come out, next time, before turning on the computer? Good theories must not only fit the external reality they purport to explain, but also our internal reality, our human cognitive structure.*

Other limitations are easier to specify. The model's advantage is that it is dynamic—it does not return to the same equilibrium point, but can construct a history. But while the elements can change, the links are assumed to interrelate those elements in an unchanging way: the game plays out, but the rules endure. When run over long periods, the models therefore either tend to damp out their fluctuations, reaching some eternal state, or, on the other hand, they blow up or collapse in a frightening manner. Radical new policies can be inserted into these models, but until the model will accept progressive changes in the linkage rules, innovations will always seem, in the long run, either to die out or to destroy us. Since they do not predict how motives and decision rules change as the situation changes—and this is our saving human capability for learning—these models are better at short-term than long-range prediction.†

The models seem to be "value-free," but they tend to accept the world as it is, predicting the effect of small changes. So they lead one to think that only such changes are possible. A further difficulty is that they are costly and time-consuming to construct, and their output is quite imposing in its quantity and precision. This encourages authoritarian decisions, since the findings are imperial, their use is restricted to those with concentrated resources, and it is costly to reprogram them, even when an assumption is questioned. Smaller, simpler, more concrete and partial models, which are open to easy reconstruction, are what we need.

*Unless we can change that, too.

†But this is true, we must admit, for all known predictive models.

Despite all these objections and the less-than-brilliant performance of these models to date, they have the virtue of forcing an explicit statement of assumptions. Moreover, the image of a city as a flow of plural decisions seems untuitively just. Through the motives of its human deciders, this view is the one which could be linked most directly to value theory.

6. *The city is an arena of conflict.* The ecological, economic, and multiple decision theories of the city all allow for competition among diverse actors. In the first two, competition is for similar resources (social position or profit), and it is considered inescapable and beneficent, leading to an optimal equilibrium. In the last, the competition is more complex, since different actors may have divergent aims, and the effects of their actions on the actions of others can be indirect and obscure. In still another view of the city, conflict is the dominant feature of city making. The city is thought of as an arena of struggle. "Who gets what?" is the important question. City form is the residue and the sign of conflict, and also something which is shaped and used to wage it.

In one way, this is a very old view. New towns have consistently been planted to dominate a subject countryside, to prevent a resource from falling into enemy hands, or to defend a border. Until modern times, a city's fortifications were its principal physical asset. They determined its shape, its density, and its particular location. The most important skill of the city designer was his knowledge of military defense. The enclosing wall was the prime symbol of the city. Internally, cities were laid out to preserve aristocratic control, or to contain some dangerous class or enclave of foreigners. Thus a substantial body of knowledge has grown up around issues of spatial defense, military communications, means of isolation, and ways of asserting dominance both symbolically and functionally. Rather than being an economic engine, the city was considered to be a spatially extended weapon.

Modern warfare has reduced, but not eliminated, the importance of these notions. Meanwhile,

Castells
Engels 1958
D. Gordon
Harvey
Lefebvre
Richardson 1977

Marxian thought, with its focus on class struggle as the engine of history, has turned to the city as an important embodiment of that struggle. Although Engels prefigured this interest in his classic description of Manchester, it is only recently that Marxists have begun to consider the role of space more systematically. The city is seen to be both an unconscious outcome of control by the capitalist class—as in the case of the "unwanted" growth of slums—and also a thing consciously shaped to further that class control—as in clearances for redevelopment, or the construction of workers' housing. It is a physical means for expropriating the social surplus. While it is also a device for increasing the efficiency of production, this is not its principal objective, since productive efficiency is not the most pressing demand on the dominant class. Moreover, there are a number of different physical forms which will permit efficient production. Rather, the key motive is the *control* of the process of production, and of the surplus it generates. In the Marxian view, this has powered the evolution of city form through the stages of mercantile, industrial, and corporate capitalism, and explains the principal features of each of these city types.*

This view of the city as the outcome of a historic conflict allows for marginal areas—local neighborhoods, for example—which are not yet completely dominated by this conflict, and acknowledges divisions within the ruling class, such as those that arise between the interests of land speculators and industrial capitalists. The theory views the city as a long-term historical sequence, just as our first group of antitheorists did, and thus admits the presence of many overlapping and contradictory features, which are either relics of the past or early manifestations of the future. This formulation clearly involves values such as equity, user control, and the desirability of struggle and social evolution in themselves.

Engels 1935
Stretton 1976

Unfortunately, the early Marxian writing focused on factory production. Housing and city

---

*The theory, however, fails to explain why cities in contemporary socialist nations are so similar to contemporary capitalist cities. Does the struggle still go on, or may new forms only now be appearing, striving to be born, against the weight of history?

services were epiphenomena, not worthy of great
attention, containing inequities which would easily be corrected, once the means of primary production was in the hands of the workers. The importance of domestic capital and domestic labor, and the issues involved in their control, were consistently neglected. While these blinders are now dropping off, they have had fateful consequences for design and investment in socialist cities, witness the low priority given to housing and local service, the rejection of low-density housing, and the acceptance of conventional roles for women and the family.

The theory is inherently dynamic, in contrast to most of the theories summarized above, which view change as a continuous, incremental reestablishment of equilibrium, operating within constant rules, and which imply a rationalization of the status quo. Marxian theory allows for the possibility of fundamental change, and, indeed, views it as inevitable. Unfortunately, it gives us little hint as to what the city will evolve into, once the socialist transformation is complete. The dynamo of history has a curious air of being about to give one last great turn, before stopping forever.* The consequence for city theory of this millennial view is that development becomes discontinuous. Even within that soon-to-be frozen image, it is unclear what the "final" city will be like.

Nevertheless, as an explanation of actual city evolution, particularly during the era of the industrial revolution, the theory is able to account for many apparent anomalies in city form, and has, like the pure historic viewpoint, the virtues of vividness and a sense of ongoing, progressive change, to which is added the virtue of a coherent generalization. As with the social physics view, however, individual motives and actions tend to be overridden by larger, more impersonal forces.

It is a peculiar fact that much of the literature on the theory of city form is outstanding for its stupefying dullness. Moreover, it is elusive in memory: it is difficult to recall the principal line of a theoretical argument. Theory is not written

*Although there are socialist voices—Mao's was among them—which call for a perpetual revolution.

for entertainment, yet when it is a successful and succinct explanation of the inner workings of a formerly confusing phenomenon, it is by its nature absorbing to read—difficult, perhaps, but unforgettable once grasped. Think only of Darwin's central ideas, or the fundamental laws of mechanics. That urban theory is so boring is more than discouraging. It must be a sign of deeper difficulties.

It is clear that urban theory is still fragmented and far from explaining the complex, shifting nature of our cities. In addition, while most of the theories pretend to be purely analytical and "value-free," they are in fact honeycombed with values. Each model includes its own criteria, as well as its own view of the world, and these concepts are related to each other. We uncover such values as viability, uniqueness, complexity, balance, stability, the status quo, efficiency, maximum interaction, equity, user control, and continuous struggle, to name a few of the more obvious ones. They make a curious list. One wonders of their adequacy as general rules, and whether they truly embrace the interrelation of human purpose and city form.

A Language of City Patterns

Martin
Passoneau

See fig. 77

In chapter 2, I said that settlement form was the spatial arrangement of persons doing things, the resulting spatial flow of persons, goods, and information, and the physical features which modify space in some way significant to those actions, including enclosures, surfaces, channels, ambiences, and objects. I then included the changes in those spatial distributions, as well as the control and perception of them. The breadth and complexity of that definition is apparent, and there are some familiar difficulties which we encounter whenever we attempt to record that form in conventional ways.

First, the accepted modes of description are two-dimensional, which may be a reasonable approximation for some purposes, but is less and less appropriate as one deals with intensive areas, or with the perception of cities. Maps have a flat quality, which is quite different from our experience of place. In geography, there are powerful ways of circumventing this difficulty, as by using contours. No similar device has yet been invented to describe the third dimension of cities. Oblique aerial photos or painstaking axonometric views can convey a strong impression of an urban area, or even a clear understanding of its solid form, especially where the area is relatively small and has a marked three-dimensional character (the towers of Manhattan, or an Italian hill town). For larger regions, or a less decisive form, these devices lose most of their power. Objects are hidden one behind another, perspective confuses the comparison of near and far, and the view from the air is nothing like the view on the ground. Vertical aerial photographs, seen in stereovision, furnish accurate and detailed three-dimensional data, but they can only be studied incrementally, and not as whole patterns. Exaggerated bird's-eye diagrams, on the other hand, can be vivid portrayals of some key feature of regional form, once that feature has been analyzed and is ready for communication by caricature.

76 As its trees and its society mature, the much ridiculed suburb acquires greater diversity and a character of its own.

77 An axonometric draw-
ing of a portion of the hill
town of Assisi in Italy.
The complicated volumes
of a small settlement are
clearly explained, but the
graphic technique is
stretched to its limit.

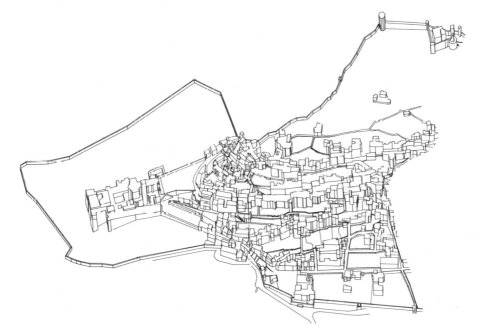

Second, the dimension of time is universally neglected (except to some degree in traffic studies). People are located where they sleep. One gets no sense of the tidal rhythms of a city, which are so important to its function and quality. Secular change is also disregarded, except in a few schematic and largely decorative historical maps. Aggregate population and economic statistics may be presented as a time series, but one gets no sense of the progressive development of spatial form. This is usually conveyed—as are so many other important qualities of cities—by verbal addenda to the maps. Further, the data on cities are so voluminous that it is very difficult to change the record frequently. City descriptions are not only static, but usually out of date.

Third, since the phenomenon under study is complex and very extended, descriptions also tend to have one or the other of two contradictory qualities. Either they show too much detail or nothing important. Many objects, such as particular buildings and minor streets, may be irrelevant by themselves at the settlement scale, although their cumulative impact is quite significant. So city maps are either a maze of lines, impossible to read, or they are empty diagrams. It is never easy to synthesize the general form of a host of objects, particularly if those objects are not easily separable, or if only some aspect of their individual configuration may be important to the whole. Population dot maps give us valuable information, despite all the things they leave out, since persons are separable, and each one is important. How does one describe a collection of varied buildings on varied streets in an equally succinct way? So we have difficulty in reading the essential information, or in making valued comparisons between different settlements.

Fourth, many of the important spatial features of cities are left out. One gains little sense of condition or management when looking at standard data, and little sense of ownership and control. While traffic flow is recorded, there is no record of the flow of communications, or of other important actions at a distance. Almost nothing can be learned about the actual experience of the place, its various qualities, or the images that its inhabitants hold of it. How could one judge the worth of a place without knowing those things?

There is still another persistent problem. While standard descriptions agree on emphasizing human activity in its relation to physical form, they are prone to confound the two in a single ambiguous description, such as "single-family house" or "church." Is it a type of building that is being denoted, or the activities of worshipping or of residing? Or, if it is the holistic idea of activity-in-place that is being recorded, why is it commonly attached to a piece of land and its buildings and presented as permanent? Churches and houses can be converted to other uses with very little physical change, and people can worship, and even reside, in all sorts of places. The failure to separate these two phenomena, so that they may later be explicitly combined, especially when their relationship is at the heart of the subject under consideration, is a source of constant confusion. Moreover, since the activity classes are conventional, they often miss the essential distinction for the purpose at hand. When one is analyzing the impact of noise, for example, it is of little help to come upon an activity classified as "public or semipublic." Does this refer to an outdoor theater, where performance may hang on a subtle sound, or to a transformer station, peopled with deaf, humming devices? That these ambiguous systems of description have survived as long as they have is due to their use in a common culture, where many things may be unexpressed but still understood, and where a supplementary verbal explanation can always be obtained from someone who knows the settlement from experience.

Much useful information is recorded in these standard exhibits, but they leave out even more. Professionals tend to use them as mnemonic devices, once they have actually experienced a place, or as stores of information which must be renewed and tediously reworked for each new and particular problem. They rely on field reconnaissance, discussions with knowledgeable local residents, and repeated resurveys. Thus it is difficult to compare the quality of two places, except for some gross features, such as size or average density. No one, however experienced, is able to look at the standard

Does:

express:

?

data for a city and evaluate that city's quality, except perhaps to note some glaring difficulties. Attempts have been made to compare cities, using only standard maps and statistics. Gross evaluations of their social or economic character can be derived from these representations. But no one thereby grasps the physical character of a place, as one might evaluate a set of architectural drawings. One must live in a city and talk to its people before one can comment. Probably this is inevitable in any comprehensive evaluation of a settlement, as compared to the evaluation of a functional object, or even of a building. Yet one wonders if there may be descriptive methods which give one a better "feel" for a place, which allow one to compare one city with another and to pick up likely problems and advantages.

While most professionals are aware of what is not conveyed, they may be less aware of how their thinking is channeled by the language they use. Zoning is a natural and obvious way of controlling changes in buildings and use, to anyone who is habituated to seeing cities represented as patches of land use, in which use and form are combined. Population statistics presented by governmental units (and originally so organized for voting purposes) obscure many important phenomena and intensify political fragmentation. Economic data which neglect productive work not done for a money return focus policy on monetary activities. Changes in ways of describing cities will not only follow on a better understanding of the city phenomenon, but could also lead to better understanding.

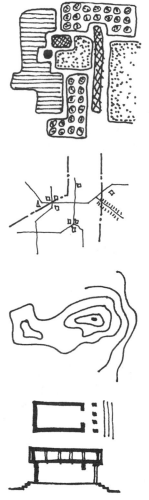

Certain types of spatial pattern languages can be cited for their economy, their accuracy, and their power to depict highly varied phenomena in an elegant way. The contour line is a fine device for explaining gradient. Precise height and slope can be read at any point, and yet the broad sweep of a piece of ground can be read at a glance. Dot maps are an economical way of conveying discrete distributions. The architectural conventions of plan and section convey the essence of a building (although not of its use) in a very small compass.

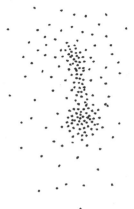

Foley
Lynch, June 1961

Brail

These conventional drawings can vary from rough sketch to precise specification, and can be used interchangeably for describing, conceiving, and controlling the erection of a structure.

The study of cities has no powerful basic language of its own. It borrows the devices of geography and architecture, but they are only partly useful. If a language particular to cities develops, it is likely that it will be a graphical one, since graphics are superior to words (but not always to mathematics) for describing complex spatial patterns.*

It once seemed reasonable to me to think that a single standard language for settlement pattern could be developed. But preparing such a description for any area proved to be very time-consuming. More important, when faced with a particular problem of analysis or design, one falls back on some other specialized language, usually a rather conventional one. Developing a standard city language may be a will-o'-the-wisp, or it may simply be premature. Just now, we are constrained to refining existing descriptions, or to inventing and testing partial, specialized modes for specialized problems.

Nevertheless, the principal features of any general description of settlement form can be laid out. Two major classes of physical things will always have to be mapped: persons acting and the physical facilities that support that action. Both of these can be subdivided once again between features that either permanently or repetitively occupy a fixed location, and those that are either moving between locations or are part of that system of movement. Thus persons can be divided between those locally active (working, playing, teaching, talking) and those in transit, while facilities have two main divisions: adapted spaces (volumes modified to facilitate localized activity, by means of enclosure, by improvement of the floor, by the provision of fixed equipment), and flow systems, or all the various pipes, wires, highways, rails, and vehicles that carry goods and people. In this way, activity and physical facility are no longer confounded: a "single-family house" will be recorded

*A question from the rear: "Why is most of this in words, *then?"* Good question. We proceed.

as an enclosed volume of a certain size and type, which at that particular time may happen to be occupied by a nuclear family residing. The combination othe two is akin to Roger Barker's "behavior setting." At other times and places, these primitive elements can be combined in other constellations to make new behavior settings.

Adapted spaces can be classified in many ways: as open or enclosed, by the character of their floor, by the scale of enclosure, by condition, by accessibility, by their ambient qualities (light, sound, climate). Flow facilities are either vehicles, channels, or terminals, and can be classified by their capacities, by the allowable speed or mode, by their local accessibility, by their "realm" or potential reach, by their liability to damage or degrade what is carried on, and so on. Neither spaces nor flow facilities need be displayed in detail, but only their intensities and typical qualities for small areas.

Persons can be classified by the familiar divisions of age, sex, and class, or by the type of activity in which they are engaged, or by the intensity or nature of the interaction between them. By recording persons in action, rather than abstract "activities," one not only escapes the confusion of behavior with facilities, but also accepts the fact that activities are carried out by human beings. Activity itself is not falsely reified; the suitability of any action is linked to the people engaged in it. "Manufacturing" is not enhanced by rearrangements of a production line. The people manufacturing may be helped, or those who derive a profit from the work. It is true, of course, that this manner of looking at a city fails to emphasize the actions of machines or of animals. Wherever there is a high degree of automation, or wherever the total ecological system is in question, then the category of people acting may have to be expanded to embrace the actions of other entities.

This two-by-two matrix of elements, classified and quantified by small regions of a settlement space, and with the key cyclical or secular changes indicated by a graphical series or by special symbols, is the essential description of the physical phenomenon that I am discussing. These categories

Barker

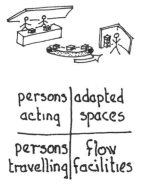

persons acting	adapted spaces
persons travelling	flow facilities

if:

• = 👤

□ = 🏠

= = 🚗

then:

equals
city.

overlap to some small degree (persons working while in transit, for example, or buildings used as sheltered walkways), but the overlaps are not critical. Otherwise, these features are independent, identifiable, measurable, capable of being localized in space, and can be indicated either in gross form or by fine subdivisions. They can be combined, to form the behavior settings which are one fundamental description of a place. It is difficult to think of a physical analysis of any settlement made for any purpose that would not require these fundamental data. In a clarified form, they correspond to the typical view of the city used by the planning profession.

Nevertheless, this basic description is not sufficient for many particular purposes. It is usually essential to know something about two other features, and they can be halved in the same manner as actions and things. One element is the information which is carried by some physical medium (books, electronic modulations, credit accounts, computer reels, speech), and which is either being transmitted, or is stored or being processed locally. The second feature is the whole set of material resources (including goods, energy, and antigoods, or wastes), which are also locally stored or undergoing processing, or which are flowing through the pipes and wires and along the roads and rail lines. Rapid communication and processing of information is the hallmark of a city—perhaps its major reason for being today—and an important gauge of its quality. Similarly, it is just beginning to occur to us that a settlement is part of the great recycling of material and energy that constitutes any natural system. As before, the localization or movement of resources and information can be quantified and classified by small regions of the space, and the classifications can be as gross or as sophisticated as desired. These distributions can now be directly related to the distributions of persons and facilities within the same spatial subdivisions, and these subdivisions can be as coarse or as fine as can be borne.

But there is more to be added, and the form of the data is not so clear, or so neatly fitted. First, one would surely be inclined to relate the description to a standard topographic map, which is a well-defined device for describing ground surface, drainage, surficial geology, and the basic ecological associations.* Second, it will be important to indicate something about the control of the space: its ownership, management, and the rights of access and use. This might be shown as a mosaic of domains of control, or by a characterization of the typical pattern of such domains by the standardized small region. Further, we have so far afforded ourselves only a very ghostly description of the sensory quality of the environment: its visual spaces, sounds, and feel. Some of this, moreover, is (like the communication of information) an action at a distance: long views, visual sequences, the way the character of a local place is modified by its context. The methods for indicating these sensory qualities, while crucial to the experience of a place, are only just now being developed for large settlements. Most difficult of all, perhaps, and quite at the heart of the city experience, is to find some objective way of recording how residents think about the place in their minds: their ways of organizing it and of feeling about it. Without some knowledge of this, one is hard put to make an evaluation, since places are not merely what they are, but what we perceive them to be.

Very likely more could be added, but already we have stirred up a thick cloud of data to record and comprehend. Little wonder that "complete" descriptions are not attempted, or that a "general" language is not yet born. All the same, this is a framework for any more specialized description.

The greater part of these data can be recorded as a spatial distribution by assignment to small subdivisions of the settlement area. For each subdivision (perhaps a grid square or a cube), we can record two things about any class of features: its modal type (or mix of types), and its intensity, or quantity per unit area or volume. So, for any subdivision of the city space, depending on our purposes, we might note such things as the quantity of enclosed floor space and the percentage in sound

*Including urban associations, of course, and not just those of the "natural" woods and meadows. Cities are phenomena of nature.

condition; the number of persons per hour in transit through the square; the number of persons by age and sex who are locally active; the weight (or monetary value) of all goods stored or in process there; the rate of information flow through it; the percentages of space controlled by different classes of persons; the typical microclimate and sound level; a set of typical views, or other characterization of the modal landscape; the relative vividness with which the general public remembers the area, as well as some measure of the value they place on it. Quantities and types can be transmuted into dot distributions, patchwork patterns, or contoured surfaces. Ratios between measures in the same square can be computed: floor space per person, or flow as a percent of capacity.

Other measurements can be made of the influence of surrounding points on any given location. One such measurement is gradient, or grain. If some characteristic is continuous (topographic elevation, or a continuously varying density of population, for example), then the measure is the steepness of gradient, that is, how quickly that characteristic changes as one moves to nearby points. If the character is discontinuous (sex or building material), then the measure is grain, or the fineness of the mix of diverse characters. A new suburb may have a very coarse grain of building or family type (or of sex, at certain times of day), while an older inner city exhibits a fine grain. One way of measuring grain is to average the distance from each point to the nearest point of diverse character. Another more qualitative description would note whether the mix was relatively blurred and indiscriminate ("gray"), or was sharply edged and clustered. The fineness of the mix of activity or class may be one of the more crucial aspects of a city. Equally crucial may be the way in which typical contrasting modules of form and activity relate to each other (how multifamily residential courtyards open off active commercial streets, for example).

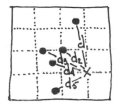

Second, it is possible to measure the potential, at any point, which is the influence at that place of all the features of a given class which occupy all the other points in the region. This measure assumes that there is a pervasive action at a distance. This is usually computed as the sum, for any one point, of

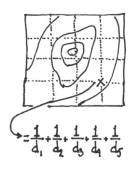

$$= \frac{1}{d_1} + \frac{1}{d_2} + \frac{1}{d_3} + \frac{1}{d_4} + \frac{1}{d_5}$$

the quantity of the chosen features at each other point, divided by the distance between those points and the original point in question. So the population potential of any block in a city can be computed, in persons per mile, by dividing the population in every other block by its distance in miles from the first and then adding up all those quotients. Blocks with the highest potential are closer to more people than any others. Any other kind of element can be used in making a similar computation. Thus we may calculate the public open space potential, the information density potential, the land value potential, the potential of nonfireproof structures (if we are worrying about the possibility of a firestorm) or even the potential of image intensity.*

Type, intensity, ratios, gradient, grain, potential, and time series are characteristics of points or small areas. They can be aggregated and analyzed in many ways. One is the familiar analysis of statistical wholes: total quantities and the relations between them, percent compositions, means and modes, measures of centrality, and changes over time. For example, one computes the modal density of population per square mile, its standard deviance, and its percent change in the last decade. While statistical in form, the raw material is nevertheless spatial data, and thus the city is still being analyzed as a spatial phenomenon.

Another manner of analysis is to look at the distribution as being itself a pattern in space—a type of analysis unfortunately less well systematized than the statistical one, but clearly crucial for our purpose. The most common mode is to prepare a map which is a patchwork of areas (a mosaic), or has an outline with a shape, or which is based on a zonal organization that approximates some familiar repetitive pattern, such as rings, checkerboards, or sectors. While striking in map form, some of these characteristics may be less important than we once believed. The gross outline of a large city is now a relative irrelevancy of this kind. But the familiar land-use map is a constant subliminal pitch, urging

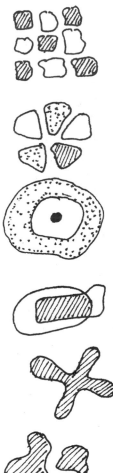

*A truly esoteric measure! When at the peak of this surface, one is closer than any- one else to more of the most vivid and valued landscapes of a settlement.

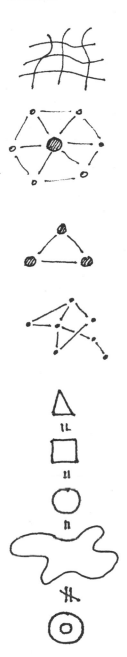

us to consider spatial patterns in this map-pattern mode.

In addition to mosaics, zone patterns, and outlines, a distribution may also be abstracted as an arrangement of focal points of special intensity or character. So a city can be single-, or many-centered; its transportation termini may be diffuse, or concentrated, or arranged in a central ring; its foci may be multipurpose or very specialized; its information flows may peak at certain points, or be broadly dispersed; and so on. A characterization by foci often allows us to make a succinct description of a complex pattern, without requiring the imposition of arbitrary boundaries. True "hard edge" features are infrequent in modern settlements, beyond the scale of buildings.

Alternatively, the pattern can be seen as a network, which itself can have a form, a degree of connectedness, a scale, or a degree of specialization. Many of these characteristics can be precisely described in the mathematical language of graph theory. A network description is clearly appropriate when describing flows and flow facilities, but it can also apply to other kinds of linkages: social, economic, or even visual ones. It is one of the prime ways, along with focal organization, in which people tend to organize their image of the city.

There can be other manners of description, such as characterizing the shape of the surface of variation of some continuous variable ("population density declines steadily from north to south, and the sharpest decline occurs as the river is crossed"). Graphic diagrams, with words appended, are still the prime ways of conveying these shapes. Mathematics is steadily becoming more important for doing so, particularly by means of topology, since many of the important spatial relations in settlements are nonmetrical. Insides and outsides, connectedness, gradients, grain, dominance, foci, enclaves, and density are form concepts likely to be more critical than such geometrical analogies as square, triangular, or round. Graph theory is useful in analyzing route networks and the networks of interaction. Numerical measures of spatial scatter and of nearest-neighbor distance are of some value. Plant ecology employs measures of this kind. The recently developed "catastrophe theory" may open up some new insights.

This review of the possible types of measurement, compounded with the review of the types of features to be measured, makes the complexity of city form all the more apparent. To describe a settlement in all of these ways on every occasion would be a fine exercise in futility. Description must fit purpose, and a good description is notable for what it chooses to ignore. Certain of these measures seem to be repeatedly important in settlement analysis, however, and have appeared more frequently than others in these pages.

Size and statistical composition may be one, but the rate of change of these could be even more important. Map patterns by patches may not be so crucial as we had imagined, while the grain or mix of spaces, persons, and behavior settings surely is, since it corresponds to the pervasive influence of access, interaction, integration, context, contrast, and choice. Intensity, whether of persons, or things, or communications, is of enduring relevance. So are the connectedness of networks, and perhaps potential, when there is in fact some influential action at a distance. Fit and misfit—the compatibility between form and activity in a behavior setting—are important. Certain nonmeasurable qualities also have to be moved up front.

These terms have recurred in this discussion. Moreover, as a theory of city form develops, we may find it more economical to describe a place directly in terms of its value, once that value can be explicitly expressed, rather than as a complex spatial form which must be linked to value. Thus we might simply map the degree of access, at any point, to the activities at other points in some settlement, and so short out a long circuit of street networks, transport nodes, social barriers, and the densities and types of local activities.

C   Some Sources of City Values

My compilation of city values is gathered from
various sources. Some of these statements are de-
ductions from city-building actions, others are implicit in the ways places are described, still others
have been more explicitly stated when prototypes
or utopias were created, or when lists of city-
building aims were constructed. I make no effort
here to organize or to justify these ideas, but only
illustrate the raw material from which the performance dimensions were shaped. The reader must
expect to be confused by the disorder of this material, irritated by its redundancy and its vagueness,
perhaps even sickened by its repetitive goodness.
Yet these motivations have often generated enormous actions.

Certain desirable things seem to have repeatedly been uppermost in the minds of those who
deliberately built cities in the course of history.
Much of this was alluded to in chapter 1. One of the
obvious motives had been security from external or
internal attack. Walls were built, entrances limited
and controlled, internal ghettoes established,
strong points fortified, wells and food supplies
protected, lookouts erected, and fields of fire
cleared. Or the city builders sought to prevent
disease, by drainage, bringing in pure water, and
avoiding unhealthy sites.

We have seen that symbolic aims were almost
always an integral part of these practical devices
and may well have preceded them. Cities were built
to secure the order of the universe and to reinforce
the dominance of one group over another. The
social space was ranked, pariahs were isolated, and
the powerful clustered together. The visible expression of power, wealth, and sophistication became important, as well as forms which induced a
sense of awe, submission, or glamor. Unpleasant
sights and sounds and unwanted people were hidden from sight. Attempts were made to recreate
familiar surroundings in some alien land.

Along with those symbolic expressions went
motives of economic control: the protection of

goods, the seizure of resources, the regulation of the productive process, and the appropriation of its output. Warehouses were built, regions dominated, route transfers and bottlenecks occupied, and the process of production brought together where it could be supervised. City builders strove to increase economic output, especially by improving the access to labor, materials, information, and credit. Transportation and communication were improved, facilities for traders and messengers established, activities brought into proximity. At times, city builders were particularly concerned with a smooth and speedy allocation of space and other resources, or with the freedom to speculate in those factors. They wanted clearly defined plots, ubiquitous access, and standardized form.

If we look at the city metaphors discussed in chapter 4, we find many of these same ideas, with additions. The earliest theory sought to maintain the cosmic order, thereby gaining a sense of oneness with the universe, achieving security from disorder, war, plague, and famine, and reinforcing the social hierarchy. Good cities convey a sense of rightness, awe, and wonder, a feeling of permanence and perfection.

The machine model thinks about efficiency, the close support of activity, good access, and easy repair or remodeling. It values the ability to exploit the material world for one's own purposes, freedom of choice, freedom to exchange or modify, freedom from imposed meanings or restraints. Ideally, this is a cool, practical world, whose parts are simple, standardized, easy to change, not in themselves significant. Equity and smooth allocation are valued. These notions may further be accompanied by a fascination with the size, intricacy, and power of the city machine itself.

The organic metaphor, on the other hand, while also concerned with security and continuity like the cosmic model, looks especially to such values as health and well-being, homeostatic balance, successful child rearing, and species survival. It is concerned with connections: the connection of the person to his environment and to the social order, the avoidance of exclusion and alienation.

Contact with nature, expression of organic order, and richness of emotion and experience are desirable things. Diversity and individuality are applauded, but only so long as individuals remain socially and biologically engaged.

A number of economists have analyzed the relative costs and benefits of various city forms. When Irving Hoch discusses city size, he deals with quanifiable (and most often negative) measures such as air pollution, noise, climate, traffic congestion, disease, crime, the money costs of infrastructure and of housing, and the monetary income realized by residents. He also quotes preference polls in order to bring in fuzzier positive measures such as excitement and stimulus, or peace and quiet. Alan Gilbert, who also analyzes city size, mulls over the same criteria, while making a few additions: job opportunity, housing adequacy, good schools, cultural and recreational facilities, and general economic growth. Perevedentsev, considering that identical issue from a quite different, socialist, perspective, uses a modified list: pollution, transport time, operating expense, and capital investment, as did the analysts above, but also: labor productivity, choice in social relationships, freedom from social control (in the USSR!), ethnic integration, the reproduction of the population, and the creation and transmission of knowledge.

We can also deduce city-building goals by considering the arguments used to advocate various form prototypes. Since the field of prototypes is so large, we flush out a swarm of motives, overlapping and conflicting with each other. Most often, the reasons cited are essentially economic ones: efficient production and efficient city construction or maintenance; the avoidance of waste, shortage, under- or over-use; the reliability and flexibility of function; the prevention of decline; adequate incomes and the abolition of poverty; the enhancement of property value, a sound tax base and a strong local finance; good profits, the freedom to use and to transfer, and a quick response to the market; adequate conservation or exploitation of resources, and the reduction of property losses. Convenient free movement, a reduction of traffic congestion and of travel time, easy communication,

Hoch 1973

Gilbert

Perevedentsev

Blumenfeld 1969

and good access to work, to recreation, to services, and to other people, are also frequently cited.

Good health, safety from fire and other disasters, a good microclimate, the conservation of land, minimizing pollution and noise, cleanliness, the extirpation of famine, the avoidance of bodily danger, are all common motives. Basic social motives are important: social stability or social mobility, the prevention or the promotion of social change, a reduction of conflict and social pathology, the reinforcement of social dominance, or perhaps the support of local community. Relations between individuals are the basis of other arguments: increased interaction, particularly between diverse ages, classes, or races; intimate or stimulating encounters; privacy and repose; liveliness, vitality, and a sense of being at the center; the ability to see and be seen; or an enhanced sense of personal identity. The freedom to act and to move about, individual choice, self-help, autonomy, equity, and diversity appear repeatedly. So do issues of behavioral control, or freedom from it, as well as participation and the democratic process. Individual development is valued by some, particularly for growing children, for example by making childhood exploration safe and interesting. In some cases, this is expanded to an evolutionary imperative: to carry on the ordained, progressive development of mankind, or the exploration of unknown worlds.

Cowan n.d.
Murtha
Wurster 1960

Other aims have more to do with direct perception and cognition: visual harmony, memorability, the expression of continuity or of grandeur, orientation and a clear image, strong sequential experience, contrast, complex coherence, human scale, a sense of the natural site, good views or the concealment of something unpleasant. Occasionally, deeper symbolic issues are cited, such as the sacredness of places, celebration and ritual, the sense of history or of the cosmos, the sense of home.

Among all the contemporary urban lamentations, some types of settled areas are cited for their desirable qualities. The dense centers of some great cities are admired for their diversity, vitality, sense of power and history, and the chance they offer for a stimulating encounter. Other boosters will point to some small historic town, remarking its beautiful form, its unique character, human scale, deep historic roots, its quiet and repose. Still others remember some old village, or some slightly (but not too markedly) decayed rural area, where one is in close touch with nature, with the fundamental processes of production, and with other people—all in a mood of ease and calm. Other respondents stress the special sensory qualities of deserts, mountains, lakes, seashores, or parklike landscapes. Most North Americans look with affection on the leafy, affluent suburb, with its perceived attributes of comfort, ease of movement, apparent lack of social conflict, prestige, security of tenure, responsive government, safety for children, good services, ample space, and pleasant planting.

Buber
Fourier
Hayden

Utopian proposals are another mine of environmental goods. Most often, their key values have to do with group identity, the strengthening of social ties, and the support for the sense of community—to which are connected such things as participation and community control, self-sufficiency, social stability, and spaces which facilitate informal social encounter. While these may be the core values, there is also frequent emphasis on equity and justice, health, cleanliness, "balance," order, the avoidance of waste, and a close relation with nature. Proposals may also touch on such additional issues as diversity and freedom, the joys of creation, the "perfectioning" of the person or the group, and even, occasionally, on comfort, efficient function, or good access.

The fantasies of high technology, on the other hand, concern themselves with esthetic coherence, rich symbolism, and the expression of power, novelty, complexity, sophistication, or dynamic change. Productive efficiency is likely to be a goal, as well as high consumption, and perhaps such cognitive issues as conveying an understanding of man's relation to his technology, or to the universe. Dreamers may declare that they are creating a superorganism, the next stage in evolution, which is to be composed of a fusion of the human community and its habitat.

The dark cacotopias—the evil dreams of hell and punishment—by contrast illuminate the same virtues. Cacotopian motives are usually clear, and clearly connected to form: excessive stimulus, sensory confusion, disorientation in space and time, ill health, isolation in the midst of intense crowding, pollution, heat, dust, cold, trash, darkness, obscuring haze or blinding light, noise, pain, meager food, barriers to movement and to use of the body, or abrupt, unpredictable change. The basic motives are external control of the individual, the breakdown of personality, the stunting of development, discomfort, and the cultivation of fear, suspicion, and hatred.

With some relief, we turn to childhood memories, which so often are suffused with nostalgia and tenderness. As people recount their time of growing, or when we read their memoirs and autobiographies, we find common explanations for the attractiveness of these childhood places. One theme has to do with the freedom to range, on the one hand, with its attendant sensations of curiosity, wonder, and excitement, and, on the other, the ability to withdraw, to dream, to be safe in one's own protected place. The opportunity to manipulate things and to test oneself is a pleasant memory, and so is the growth of an understanding of place, community, and productive function, and of the child's relation to it. Affectionate human relations, and the satisfaction of being part of a stable, small, well-knit community, are frequent explanations. Close contacts with plants and animas are valued remembrances. The grown children remember sensory delights, the pleasures of using the body, and a sense of magical meaning in the world—rich, vivid, and somewhat mysterious.

Lukashok
Hart

Novels and poetry are an important source of environmental values. Italo Calvino's *Invisible Cities* is one of the more recent and direct of these sources. He concerns himself with permanence and ephemerality, cycles and successive unfoldings, continuity, survival, and change, and the connections between the dead, the living, and the unborn. He talks of identity, ambiguity, harmony, diversity, and the satisfaction of carnal desire. He is attracted by symbolic depth in a place—how it may be encrusted with memories, signs, and reflections. The stories of Jorge Luis Borges are similarly preoccu-

Calvino

pied with the maze of time, reflections, symbols, and endless unfoldings.

Planners and social scientists have at times confected systematic lists of what they considered to be valuable in a settlement. Margaret Mead, in her brief essay entitled "What City Do We Want?," lists such things as congenial neighbors, a sense of community and of continuity, an awareness of the biosphere, and a feeling of common destiny. Ecological conservation is important. Yet she also values diversity, anonymity, mobility, choice of residence, an avoidance of social segregation, and the possibility of breaking away from social ties.

Mead

B. Ward

Barbara Ward and others presented a statement of principles to the Habitat Conference of the United Nations, concerning the essential features of a good settlement anywhere in the third world. They mention secure tenure, self-help, conservation, clean water, essential services, a viable economy, an efficient agriculture, effective social controls, participatory decisions, and a lack of social segregation. In his prescription for the "poor capitalist city," Hugh Stretton emphasizes self-help housing at low densities (via cheap land, secure tenure, good water, electricity, waste disposal, simple building materials, and moderate building standards), good access, good schools and other local services, economic development at all levels of capital, and the encouragement of incremental change.

Stretton 1978

Carp
Lamana
Michelson
Center Urban and
Regional Studies
Rapoport
Van der Ryn

F. M. Carp and others extracted a set of common environmental values from open-ended interviews with North American adults. They found frequent references to good appearance, cleanliness, careful maintenance, freedom from noise and from air pollution; a sense of openness, warmth, and tranquility, good neighbors, no feeling of alienation; safety from traffic, assault, vandalism and robbery; convenient mobility, privacy, and the presence of animals.

Cappon

Daniel Cappon and Mary Roche attempted to construct a comprehensive catalog of stress in urban life. It included pollution, resource depletion, bodily hazards and diseases, malnutrition, buildings which are too big or too tall, poor orientation, understimulus, boredom, spatial confinement, noise, social isolation, fear, an excessively homogeneous society, a lack of contact with nature, excessive travel time, inadequate outdoor recreation, too great a rate of growth, poor climate, housing in disrepair, inefficent services, poverty, and unemployment.

Planners and designers usually hold some personal point of view on cities, a characteristic cluster of values about settlement form. As we read the literature, we find one or more of the following typical, not always mutually exclusive, sets:

1. The city is to be enjoyed for its "urbanity"; its diversity, surprises, picturesqueness, and high levels of interaction.

2. The city should express and reinforce society and the nature of the world. Its critical elements are its symbolism, its cultural meanings, its historical depth, its traditional form.

3. Order, clarity, and the expression of current function are the principal criteria. One delights in the city as a fascinating, giant, intricate, technical device.

4. The proper focus of city design is simply the efficient provision and maintenance of the necessary facilities and services, that is, good engineering. The city is a neutral technical support for human life.

5. The city is essentially a managed ongoing system. Its key elements are the market, the institutional functions, the aspatial communications network, and the decision process. This is the view from above: a tight ship and a smooth voyage.

6. On the contrary, the principal values are local control, pluralism, effective advocacy, good behavior settings, and the primacy of the small social group. This is the view from below.

7. The environment is to be valued by the way in which it is individually experienced, and for such qualities as openness, legibility, meaning, educativeness, and sensory pleasure. This is the view

from inside the person.*

8. The city is a means for extracting profit or power. It is a scene of competition, appropriation, and the exploitation and division of resources. The world is a jungle, a field of opportunity, the ground of social struggle.

9. Never mind what it is, accept the environment as it is given. Learn to survive in it; take delight in its reality, its "presence," its complexity and ambiguity. Strip off its conventional meanings, and become a knowing and creative observer.

Last, it may be interesting to note that when a set of students in planning and architecture were asked, in the spring of 1977, to set forth their personal view of the good city, they responded with a rich set of value statements, which could be collected in the following compendium of city values:

Accessibility; proximity; good communication; public transport; ease of pedestrian movement; minimal individual transportation; ease of access by all modes; good access to resources, services, amenities; all parts accessible, no groups excluded; quick safe access; good information about getting about; freedom to move and to act.

Choice and opportunity; diversity of people, ethnicity, jobs, housing, activity, values, densities, recreation, shopping, life styles, and social situations; diversity of neighbors, but not neighborhoods; tolerance and appreciation of diversity.

Support of small group activity and identity; belonging, territory, turf, community scale, sense of own import, territorial clues, care and pride; individual statements, ethnic expression, places where users are in control; human scale, group identity, community proprietorship, personalization, reflection of needs and values, neighborhood organization.

Support of social interaction, a range from interaction to seclusion, privacy, meeting centers, places for large gatherings, active centers, niches.

*And is my own.

Strong social networks, coexistence, shared values, civility, no racial tension, no obstruction to development, tie of citizen to city, sense of ownership of city, encouragement of cooperation.

Safety, security, trust; freedom from accident, robbery, or vandalism.

Controllable institutions; responsive, accessible government; feedback; participation; user role in decisions; transparent planning and decision making; viable control mechanisms.

Good services, which are convenient and well-maintained; the necessary infrastructure, good schools, good housing, the comforts and benefits of contemporary technology.

Support of daily behavior, of approved behavior.

Clean, healthy, pollution-free environment; beneficial climate and ecology; environmentally responsible management.

Solid, stable, diverse economic base; macro- and microeconomic health and viability; job security; economic opportunity; low living costs; economy not under central control; no economic pockets.

Strong natural features; relation to nature; presence of wild places; form-generating natural features; good relation to landscape and climate; open spaces, sun, sky, water, trees.

Strong image, coherence, sense of place, distinctiveness, sense of the whole, a comprehensible, perceivable place, large-scale clarity and experiential complexity, articulation and integration, ordered complexity, distinct identity, strong links, dominant places and landmarks, strong centers and subcenters, defined edges, consciousness of space, elements which can be perceived on different levels, an eccentric identity, symbolism of country, uniqueness, responsiveness to specific site and culture.

Expression of time, history, tradition; sense of roots in people and land; harmony of old and new; a living museum; visible history; a continuing relation to historic roles.

Stimulus, richness; variety of experience and of scale; wealth of perceptible detail, intricacy of urban fabric, balance between overload and deprivation; a rich conflicting projection of society; surprise; a place that is fun to be in, exciting.

Opportunities for education and exchange of information, an informative setting which allows discovery; educational value; encouragement of development, imagination, creativity.

Beauty; reflects the best we have to offer.
Sense of informality.
Equality, justice.
Adaptability, flexibility.
High density; either dense city or open country.
Ability to get out of it.

The performance dimensions were shaped out of these value tangles by a process of pruning and grafting. As examples of that process, some few of the dimensions that were considered and discarded are listed below, along with brief reasons for excluding or modifying them:

1. *Social interaction, coherence, or integration; social change or stability.* All of these are frequently cited as keys to the value of any settlement. But they are features of the social system, and not of the physical, spatial one. We look for physical features that have some bearing on those social features, and must also recognize that their effect will be indirect and likely secondary.

2. *Cost.* The cost of anything is always quoted in assessing its value, as though cost were a single thing, qualitatively different than the various benefits—life being made up of (*a*) pleasure and (*b*) pain. Sometimes, the cost of something is quoted as though it were the value of it. But costs are neither unitary nor qualitatively distinct. They are simply the losses in one or more values, incurred in gaining some other value. Without that benefit to be gained, things have no value at all, whatever their cost. Thus cost, or negative value, appears in the discussion of each of our benefits, or performance dimensions. There are costs internal to the theory—losses in some performance dimension—and costs external to it—dollars, political effort, etc.

3. *Comfort, stress, nuisance, safety.* All of these rather vague, interrelated terms are well-worn criteria for good cities. I have tried to reduce them to the spatial qualities which support or avert them, and have also tried to separate those features which affect survival and good health from those which are merely matters of comfort and ease.

4. *Contact with nature.* This sometimes leads the list of wanted features in a place. But the phrase is misleading, first because of our intellectual confusion about what "nature" is, and second, because that value does not reside in things themselves, but in our perception of them, which leads us to an intuition of the web of life that entangles us. Thus "contact with nature"—like a sense of home, or of community, or of history—can be transformed and brought under the heading of the sensibility of city form.

5. *Balance.* Good environments are repeatedly characterized as "balanced." We see the world as a system of polarities—hot and cold, big and little, black and white, dense and sparse, high and low, stimulating and quiet—and expect danger at each end of the spectrum. There must then be an optimum point in between, and this incorporates the idea of equilibrium: equal and opposing forces which keep the world steady, preventing any acceleration into disaster—the yin and yang of Chinese philosophy. The metaphor is so powerful that it can be used without challenge in the sharpest of debates. Who would question that we must have a "balanced population," or a "balanced economy"? Asking what purpose is served by balancing, or, worse, advocating imbalance, is greeted with incredulity. Polarity, balance, and static equilibrium via the tension of opposites may in *some* cases be a good policy based on an insightful metaphor, but, where the polarity is only imaginary, the concept simply obscures the issue.

6. *Waste, dirt, and inefficiency.* Waste is always bad, to our way of thinking, just as balance is always good. Waste goes with decline, inefficiency, poor productivity, excessive consumption, and other puritanical evils. Dirt (except for garden soil) is unhealthy and disgusting. Our cities are wasteful and unclean. Everyone wants a clean city. No one

would run for political office on a platform of waste and inefficiency. Efficiency was discussed in chapter 12, where it was explained that the term is meaningless until basic values are defined. Efficiency was described as the trade-off criterion between different values—some of them internal to the theory and some external. The concepts of waste and dirt will require another book. Everyone decries them; but what are they, and why are they bad? Just as we are careful not to be contaminated by garbage and excrement, because of their magical, hidden dangers, so the concept of waste is best avoided until it is better understood.

7. *Order.* A well-ordered city, like a clean and efficient one, is something very generally desired. Yet it has also led to the creation of rigid and monotonous places, very orderly on paper. Recurrently, our suspicions are aroused about an excessive devotion to orderliness. As in other cases, the debate is transformed when one realizes that there is no value whatever in orderly things in themselves. Order (or rather ordering) is in the mind, and it is the ability to order things in one's mind that is valuable, since by ordering we are able to comprehend and to deal with larger and more complex wholes. Order is better understood as sensibility. Immediately, then, we are concerned with *for whom* a place is sensible, and with the *process* of ordering.

8. *Esthetics, amenity.* Many valuable considerations of city form are commonly gathered under these headings. I have already discussed the problems that emerge when esthetic values are divorced from other aspects of life. The term, moreover, bears a heavy burden of associated meanings, relics of old arguments. I prefer a term like sense, which has a more definite meaning, is more directly definable in terms of environmental form, and is free of old polemical ghosts. Unlike esthetics—and even more unlike "amenity," which can subsume so many likeable qualities—sense can be identified and tested for, and yet has clear links to human values.

9. *Diversity and choice.* The problem of defining diversity has already been discussed in chapter 10. This nonetheless important criterion has been subsumed as an aspect of access, although it

also relates to behavioral fit, in the form of the diversity of settings. The concept is not quite yet under control.

These few examples may give the reader some sense of how the performance dimensions were constructed, given the urge to generalize, to make values clear and identifiable, and to organize the welter into a structure that could be memorable and useful.

D

A Catalog of Models of Settlement Form

This is a list of the various models of city form which are in current use. The list cannot be exhaustive, and it stops short of the detailed patterns applicable at the local site planning or building scales (turnarounds, patios, boulevards, arcades, pilotis, axes of symmetry, foundation planting, tree clumps, reflecting pools, parking garages, roof terraces, podiums, and many more). The list is a survey of prototype forms at the city scale, with very brief discussions of their motives and outcomes, accompanied by one or two references to their advocacy or analysis. The organizational scheme by which they are grouped is an arbitrary one. Ideas have been separated into discrete models, although their advocates would often link them into more connected systems. Nevertheless, some overlap is inevitable. Since the list attempts to be relatively complete, at the city scale, it inevitably repeats some of the material covered in the principal chapters of this book.

Friedmann n.d.
Lang
Lynch 1961
A. E. J. Morris
Spreiregen
Wurster 1963

Some models for the general pattern of a city:

A. *The star.* According to this view, the best form for any city of moderate to large size is a radial star or "asterisk." There should be a single dominant center, of high density and mixed use, from which four to eight major transportation lines radiate outward. These lines would contain mass transit systems, as well as the main highways. Secondary centers are disposed at intervals along these lines, and the more intensive uses either cluster around these subcenters, or string out along the major lines. Less intensive uses occupy bands farther back from the main radials, and open green wedges take up the remaining space between the fingers of development. At intervals outward from the main center, there are concentric highways, which link the fingers together, but which are free of adjacent development except where they intersect the fingers themselves.

The model is a rationalization of the form which appeared spontaneously as formerly compact

central cities grew rapidly outward along newly
extended lines of public transportation. It allows for an active, dense, "urban," main center, while providing for subcenters and other uses at moderate or even low density. The mass transit system is efficient as long as most traffic is center-oriented. While most development has good access to the main center, it is also close to the open wedges between the fingers. These wedges lead directly out to the rural environs and can provide routes for pedestrians, cyclists, and horse riders. The total city can grow outward, as needed.

The most systematic exposition of this idea can be found in Hans Blumenfeld's "Theory of City Form, Past and Present." It was the basis for a plan of Washington, and also for a famous plan for Copenhagen. The general plan for Moscow is largely based on it. While some features of this form appeared in many cities in the nineteenth and early twentieth centuries, it has rarely proved possible to maintain this shape, particularly in a capitalist economy, because of the strong control required to keep the green wedges open and continuous, despite the good access to them. The concentric roads become more and more important as the radial fingers diverge farther from the center. Either the fingers become isolated from each other, or development appears along the concentrics. Thus the system, as it recedes from the center, becomes more like an open network, with major centers at the crossings. It may be difficult to relate the linear development along the fingers to the heavy traffic on them, and the dominant center may be choked by the incoming flows, if the whole becomes very large. Nevertheless, the model has many useful characteristics, particularly for cities of moderate size. The radial form is assumed in making most transportation plans, and in setting the framework for most geographic or economic studies of the city. It seems as natural to us as water to a fish.

B. *Satellite cities.* Not unrelated to the star is the concept of satellites: the idea that a central city should be surrounded, at some distance, by a set of satellite communities of limited size. The dominant center is maintained, as well as the general radial form, but growth is channeled into communities

Blumenfeld 1949

well separated from the central area, instead of spreading continuously outward along the radial arms. The limitation of settlement size is basic to the idea: cities which grow beyond a certain size are presumed to be less efficient, and also of poorer quality. The central city should be held to its present size, or even progressively reduced, while the satellites are each designed to contain some optimum population. When growth continues beyond this point, a new satellite is constructed. Satellites are separated from the mother city by broad stretches of rural land, and are themselves surrounded by greenbelts. These belted open spaces substitute for the green wedges of the star. Each satellite has its own center, services, and some productive activity. Daily commuting is intended to be local, within the satellite. The optimum size of a satellite has varied substantially, ranging from 25,000 to 250,000 persons. Historically, this assumed optimum has tended to rise.

Howard

The classic exposition of this idea was in Ebenezer Howard's *Garden Cities of Tomorrow*, in 1898. But the idea has been transmitted all over the world, and has been a basis of official policy in many nations, including the famous new towns program of Great Britain. Hugh Stretton, in *Ideas for Australian Cities*, makes a recent argument for the concept. The satellite model has by now been welded to many others, included the neighborhood concept, preferred residential forms, and ideas about the ownership of community resources. The city size debate continues today, and is still unresolved. The conviction that big is bad is fervently held, but the evidence is indecisive. While big cities contain many evils, it is not clear that those evils are due to size, rather than to poverty, class segregation, the financial structure of local government, the economic system, or other factors. While big cities are more expensive to run, they offer better services and seem to have a productive advantage. If they are badly governed, this may be due to political fragmentation. And so on. For all our fears, it is hard to catch urban bigness redhanded.

Stretton 1971

Baburov
Bull
Field
Stein 1951

Satellite cities have been built, and greenbelts successfully defended, but growth and development put constant pressures on the size ceilings, as well as the open space at the city margins. The big cities, whose overblown size they were intended to reduce, have continued to grow. It is difficult to know whether that growth might have otherwise been even greater. Nevertheless, the satellite concept has perhaps been the most influential of all the city models, and appears frequently in planning proposals in many different situations.

C. *The linear city.* The concept of a linear city has repeatedly been unfurled as a new theoretical idea, but has rarely been applied. The form is based on a continuous transport line (or perhaps a parallel series of them), along which front all the intensive uses of production, residence, commerce, and service. Less intensive, or more obnoxious, uses occupy parallel bands of space to the rear. Moving away from the line, one soon reaches rural open space. In this it is like one of the radial arms of the star, endlessly extended. Residents in the buildings along the line presumably have the best of both worlds: main line transport at their front doors, and quiet countryside at the rear. Meanwhile, such linear settlements can extend from one old city to another, over great distances, curving flexibly to adjust to the terrain. New growth is accommodated by extending the line. There are no dominant centers; everyone has equal access to services, jobs, and open land. Schools, for example, may be distributed along the line, or be placed at intervals in open country on the margins of the developed band, so that they are within walking range of all children. Mass transit works efficiently, since everyone lives right on the line.

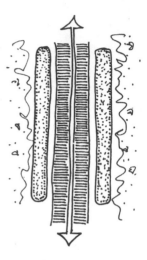

Linear roadside villages, or linear settlements along seacoasts or waterways, are old forms. But this configuration was first explicitly proposed by Arturo Soria y Mata in 1882 in Madrid, where an experimental linear suburb was actually built. Soria's ideas were later taken up by an international society, and used in different forms in many theoretical proposals, in the United States by Edgar Chambless in his *Roadtown,* by Le Corbusier in France, and the MARS group in London. Frank Lloyd Wright's *Broadacre City* is fundamentally a linear organization and so is Clarence Stein's pro-

Ash
Collins 1959

Chambless
F. L. Wright
Stein 1942

posal. N. A. Miliutin's plan for Stalingrad, and especially his ideal proposal, made in *Sotsgorod*, are thorough exemplifications of the linear idea. Current planning in Poland, for the extension of Warsaw and other cities, proposes linear forms.

The plan is rarely implemented, however, except where strong topography constrains the shape of the city, as at Stalingrad. The linear form does appear at smaller scales, such as the commercial strip. Here, ironically enough, it is almost universally condemned. It also occurs as a "megaform" in some countries—a connected string of metropolitan regions. At the city scale it has certain serious flaws. The distances between elements are much greater than in a compact city, and the choice of connection or of direction of movement much less. While everyone lives on the main line, main line transportation cannot stop at every point along that line. It necessarily stops at stations, so that while a position elsewhere on the line may be highly visible, it is no more accessible than is some more remote interior point. This is true even for the automobile on an expressway, where flows are heavy and distances long. This may explain why the linear form *does* work at smaller scales, since foot traffic, canal boats, bicycles, moving sidewalks, slow-moving streetcars, and even automobiles on low-capacity roads can all stop and start almost anywhere on the line.

Moreover, the lack of intensive centers is a handicap for the linear city. Some uses flourish in extreme propinquity, and centers are psychologically important. The supposed flexibility of the linear form is chimerical, since change without displacement can only occur at the remote ends of the line, or at right angles to it, which destroys its linearity. Thus one activity cannot grow faster than another, unless its neighbor declines with equal speed. It is, in fact, very difficult to keep development from accreting along these edges, which are so close to good access. On the other hand, it may be difficult to acquire a continuous right-of-way for extending or initiating a linear city, as Soria discovered in Madrid. It is quite likely that gradients of class or use will develop along the line, which will make for serious inequalities in access and services.

Where the linear plans, as in *Sotsgorod,* arrange use classes in parallel bands, then they are locked into a given ratio of the one use to the other. The plan fails if this ratio changes.

Yet the intermittent infatuation of theorists, as well as the spontaneous appearance of the linear form at the *local* scale, indicates that there is some substance to the idea. This form has specific utility at certain scales and for particular uses and situations. This utility is worth further thought.

D. *The rectangular grid city.* Here, on the contrary, is a proposed city form of which countless real examples exist. The essential idea is quite simple: a rectangular net of roads divides the urban terrain into identical blocks, and can be extended in any direction. Ideally, the form has no necessary boundaries and no central points. Any use can occur anywhere, since all points are equally accessible (except where they approach the margins of development), and all plots have the same shape. Change and growth can occur anywhere inside, as well as by extension outside. The standardized sites allow standardized solutions. The ground can easily be marked out, allocated, or marketed. Interestingly enough, the grid has been favored for two contradictory purposes: either to insure central control and express magical perfection, or to support an individualistic, egalitarian society.

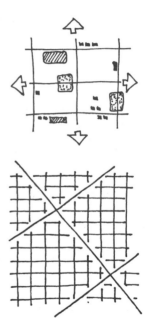

While centers hardly seem to accord with the pure, egalitarian grid, in fact they can be inserted without great distortion, unless large or intense. The grid can be arbitrarily bounded. Hierarchies of streets can be developed; minor streets can be made indirect; and the whole system can curve around irregularities in the ground—all without losing its basic properties.

The grid form has been used since antiquity—both in magical, cosmic cities, such as in China and Japan, and in more pragmatic colonial foundations, as in Greece, medieval Europe, and Spanish America. D. Stanislawski sketches some of this history, and Ferdinando Castagnoli covers the Greek and Roman experience. One hardly needs to point out the North American experience to readers from this continent, but it is well covered in John Reps's book. The discussion by the New York Commis-

Stanislawski
Castagnoli

Reps
Llewelyn-Davies

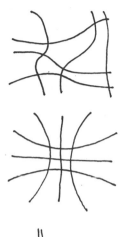

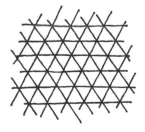

Carson
Y. Friedman

sioners in 1811 is a concise review of their motives for using a gridiron plan. The grid layout guided the planning of the latest of the English new towns: Milton Keynes.

In reality, of course, grids are not scaleless forms, any more than any other model. They cannot be extended indefinitely without changing the flows and uses in their central areas, and thus the demands on the form. Where large centers occur, they strain the undifferentiated street system. If all streets are equal, traffic may shift unpredictably, or disturb every block in an unnecessary way. If diagonals are lacking, then long trips become very indirect. If they are provided, as in Washington, D.C., they make awkward intersections with the underlying grid. Gridiron layouts are often criticized for their wastefulness when all streets are brought to the same standard, for their heedless butchery of terrain and natural features, and for their visual monotony and lack of focus.

Depending on scale and situation, many of these objections can be overcome: by developing a hierarchical grid, by using a grid as a main framework within which local streets are more indirect (as in Milton Keynes), by isolating the diagonal arterials from junctions with minor grid streets, by allowing the grid lines to curve and vary their spacing, while maintaining their topological properties, by "condensing" the grid lines as they approach major activity centers, by giving main streets varied visual characteristics and intermediate landmarks, and so on. In favorable terrain, the grid pattern is quite useful, if the designer can keep scale in mind, and knows how to vary a grid to match special character.

E. *Other grid forms.* There are many detailed variants to the rectangular grid which are worth noting. One is Christopher Alexander's "parallel roads" system, which was criticized by Daniel Carson. Non-rectangular grids are theoretically important, if of less practical value. The triangular grid has been proposed because it is a regular lattice which adds two more directions of through movement to the four afforded by the rectangular lattice. This is at times modified to give a hexagonal network. However intriguing as a geometrical concept, these nonrectangular lattices produce awkward intersections and awkward building plots. They have only rarely been applied. The layout of New Delhi is one example.

F. *The baroque axial network.* This was described, as an example, in chapter 16. The structure consists of a set of symbolically important and visually dominant nodal points, distributed over an urban area on commanding points of ground. Pairs of these are connected by arterials, which are designed as visual approaches to the nodes and to have a continuous, harmonious character of land and building facade. These arterial frontages are likely to be occupied by upper social groups, and prestigious or crowd-dependent activities. Thus an irregular triangular network of special quality covers the urban area. Within the network, buildings, streets, and uses can develop independently, as long as they do not intrude on the nodes and arterials. In that way, a visually ordered system can be created in accidented terrain or within an irregular, existing city, where a more regular form would come to grief. Moreover, it can be done with moderate investment, by focusing on the nodal points and the avenues.

First elaborated as a way of cutting sight lines in a forest, to give noble hunters quick access to game escaping from their beaters, it was then used in sixteenth-century Rome, to facilitate the movements of large numbers of religious tourists. Since then, the device has been carefully developed. The best modern accounts of this baroque approach are by Elbert Peets, and later by Christopher Tunnard.

See fig. 79

Peets
Tunnard

The device is splendid for its purpose and in its place. It was the concept, for example, that allowed L'Enfant in Washington to work so rapidly and surely. It lays the groundwork for a memorable and monumental city. It can cope with irregular ground, and even gains power from it. It achieves its ends with a minimum of control, and leaves many users free to develop at will. Indeed, it has all the advantages—and the flaws—of a "facade" solution. While it is flexible in the interstices of the net, any major shifts may undermine the necessary permanence of the symbolic nodes and avenues. Modern mechanical traffic is enraged by the resulting succession of congested multiple intersections. Nor is it appropriate to the organization of large metropolitan regions, where the grand symbolism may run thin, and the nodes become too numerous to remember. Yet for areas of moderate scale and irregular form, where symbolism is important and an effect is required rather quickly, the baroque network is a proven device.

G. *The lacework.* This name, modified from a term of Christopher Alexander's, refers to a type of low-density settlement in which the traffic ways are widely spaced, and the interstices are occupied by substantial open spaces, farmland, or "wild" land. The active urban uses front continuously along the ways, and occupy only shallow depths. This, then, is like a network of linear settlements, or a blown-up gridwork. The uses are not so intense, however, that stop-and-go entrances cannot occur all along the traffic lines. By sacrificing the density of occupation and the length of commutation, the linear ideals of flexibility and convenient access are more easily achieved. The traffic ways are not overloaded. Farms and woods are immediately at hand.

Alexander 1975

The pattern derives from our recent experience with exurbia, where new suburban uses have reoccupied the road frontages of decayed farming regions, while the backlands return to wood and brushy pasture.* But these backlands must then be defended from subsequent development, which exurbia is hardly doing today. Social contacts become more dependent on prearrangement and mechanical transport. The pattern requires lavish space, sophisticated individual transport, and some affluence. Given these, it is a very pleasant form to live in.

H. *The "inward" city.* The closed, intensely private city of the medieval Islamic world, which may still be seen in some traditional regions, is unfamiliar to us except as a romantic tourist attraction. The ruling metaphor is the container: everything is walled and gated, from the city itself, to wards, streets, and quarters of the city, to local

*It is interesting to see how many of our ideal forms are rationalizations of what are only momentary stages in evolving urban landscapes. It is difficult for us to conceive of form-in-process as a prototype model.

78 The 1971 general plan for Moscow. The open spaces are dotted, and the built ground is cross-hatched. "Green wedges" are intended to open up the historic radioconcentric form of the city, penetrating toward the center.

79 The Via del Corso and the Via di Ripetta, seen from the Piazza del Popolo in Rome. Their divergence gives one a sense of orientation and control, like that produced in the old royal hunting forests.

80 Air view of the central
area of Fez, in Morocco, a
prime example of the
medieval Islamic town.
The mosque is imbedded
at the center, and next to
it are the commercial
streets, controlled by the
separate guilds. The courtyards of the close-packed
houses are reached by a
maze of dead-end ways.

81 A sketch by Stefano
Bianca of the Madraseh al-
Attarin in Fez. The quiet
of the inner courtyard is
set off by the crowded
streets just outside.

residential clusters, to the house and its rooms. Even the major public ways are tightly confined. They lead to yet smaller local streets, which lead to extremely narrow culs-de-sac like capillaries, which lead to private doors, which lead by tight dog-leg corridors to private patios, rooms, and terraces. This arboreal system of streets is everywhere enclosed by shopfronts or the walls of houses and gardens. Even the main ways of the city can be sealed off at night at the ward boundaries, as can the various commercial streets, for secure control by the local guild corporations. Except for the great mosques or churches, and the cemeteries and wastelands outside the city gates, public open space is reduced to the streets, and to the slight enlargements at their intersections. The city is a solid built volume, in which hollows and lanes have been excavated, in contrast to our picture of a city as a collection of volumes set in an open ground. The bustle of the crowded streets contrasts sharply with the quiet calm of the interior courtyards. Nonresidential uses, although to some degree concentrated along guild streets in the city center, are strung out in narrow shops along the main ways, or occupy deep courtyards of their own which open off these ways. Each ward of the city has its mosque or church and its essential services. People of different incomes live close by each other, but ethnic and religious groups may be separated in distinctive quarters.

The essential characteristics of these cities, deeply embedded in a whole way of life, are well described in Stefano Bianca's *Architektur und Lebensform im islamischen Stadtwesen.* Perhaps they are too far from a modern style of life to be useful for us today. Yet they have an undeniable attraction, in their contrast of repose and urban stimulus, and in the quality of their spaces. They also have something to say about the techniques of living at high densities. The extreme sense of privacy, of walling-off, may be repugnant to many of us. Such cities are certainly incapable of dealing with mechanical transport. But the model can be useful for special residential quarters, and the courtyard house and the capillary street system are ideas that will reappear below.

See figs. 80, 81

Bianca 1976, 1979

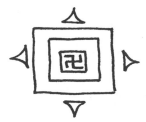

Dutt
Shukla
Smith

I. *The nested city*. The "nested-box" concept of Hindu planning theory is a highly developed theoretical model. As in the Islamic scheme, the city is a series of containers, within a city wall, but it is not irregular, nor is it laced with capillaries. The city is conceived as one ring within the other, box within box. To each box is assigned an occupational group, as well as a god of the pantheon. At the very center is the holiest place. Evil and chaos, and the lowest castes and occupations, are kept outside the city wall. The important streets are the circumferentials, not the radials, as in our tradition. The circumferentials parallel the protective walls and are the routes for the seasonal, circular, religious processions. The connecting ways are minor in scale, and often are not continuous. The dominant form and movement is round about, not in and out. The city, as in the Chinese model, is magical and protective. Ritual and form are inseparable.

While less often applied in practice than were the cosmic theories of China, the Hindu form was also the subject of a long tradition of theoretical writings. Julian Smith describes the application and present survival of that model, in one important religious center (Madurai). Even more than the Islamic model, these forms seem remote to our lives and purpose. Yet they have lessons, too, if only by contrast, and also because they reveal how links can be made between city form, world view, and ways of daily life.

J. *Current imaginings*. A number of patterns reside primarily in the imagination of contemporary designers. One professionally popular idea has been the *megaform*, in which the city is one single, vast, three-dimensional structure. Roads and utilities are integral parts of this structure, instead of being separate elements, supported directly on the earth. Houses, factories, and office clusters occupy spaces within the giant fabric, just as apartments do in an apartment building. The open spaces of the city occur on its roofs, terraces, and balconies. Storage, vehicles, automated production, utilities and waste processing are relegated to the dark, lower interiors. The idea is proposed as a way of living at very high density, both in order to accommodate future population increase, and to save rural space. The megaform takes full advantage of modern technology, and is presumably therefore efficient and comfortable. Its size and its intricacy give it a grandeur which entrances its proponents.

Plans of this kind have appeared frequently in recent times. Kenzo Tange's famous plan for the harbor of Tokyo is a linear megaform. The drawings of Paolo Soleri are another example. Perhaps the closest built example is the center of the new town of Cumbernauld, in Scotland, in which one single structure comprises highway, parking, shopping, offices, institutions, and some apartments. The result was monumental but expensive. It has proved inflexible and uncomfortable for its users. In general, these ideas are technically intriguing, but costly and complicated. If implemented, they raise many unsuspected difficulties. They require a technically advanced, centralized society for their construction and maintenance.

Buckminster Fuller and others have suggested that cities be enclosed in gigantic transparent bubbles, which let in the light, but protect the city from inclement weather. Such bubbles might be air-supported, or be light geodesic domes. The technology for making such enormous enclosures at reasonable cost is on the way; already there are greenhouses and factories covering large acreages in single spans. Once the whole is skinned over, the separate buildings of a city could be much more lightly made. The urban climate could be controlled. The distinction of inside and outside would then be overthrown, with consequences for spatial organization which no one has yet worked out. Other problems remain unsolved, such as internal condensation and pollution, storm or vandal damage to the bubble, and the political implications of creating, maintaining, and imposing a dome on all citizens. Experiments with this form are likely, however, at remote stations built in a single operation in unfavorable climates.

Other dreams have more to do with the settings of new cities than with their internal form. Floating cities have recently been suggested by Richard Meier. Paul Scheerbart proposed them earlier. Such communities might ride with the ocean currents, extracting energy from the sun, and food and raw materials from the sea. The watery wastes, which occupy the majority of the earth's surface, would become habitable, and population pressures would be relieved. Floating cities might also be useful for special purposes, such as extensions for congested coastal towns, air bases, or deep-sea mining communities. Although the engineering requirements of floating towns are currently being explored, no one has as yet developed a consistent urban form which would be consonant with that special situation. As so often happens in pioneering ventures, familiar forms, taken out of context, are applied to the new technical infrastructures. While we have a number of examples of water cities—such as Venice, Leningrad, and Bangkok—where canals substitute for streets and there is a mazy interpenetration of water and land, and while floating housing is familiar, we have no floating communities to which we can point. The prehistoric lake villages and the modern ocean oil drilling settlements are small affairs, and they are perched on stilts.

The same comment can be made about proposals for underground or undersea communities. While they may have advantages, or be necessary for certain purposes, no one has yet thought through the very special problems and opportunities—social, psychological, and political, as well as merely technical—that communities of those kinds would raise. Experiments in underwater habitats, of very small size, are just now beginning. It seems obvious that such places would of necessity have quite distinctive forms and ways of life, just as mountain settlements differ from seacoast ones.

See fig. 82

Proposals for cities in outer space have been the common fare of science fiction for generations now, and these repeated imaginary excursions have built a substantial repertoire of possible forms, as well as expectations of how to live in them. In addition, we have actually experienced the ocean liner, which is also an isolated, mobile community, encased in a single shell. So cities in space are nearer to developing a form and style of their own than are underground or floating cities. However, it is not so clear that outerspace communities would

See fig. 83

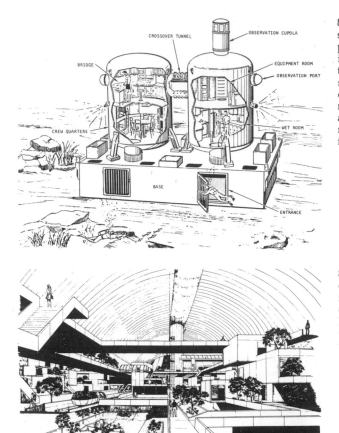

82 A small underwater station, designed for experiments in continuous, if temporary, habitation at the bottom of the sea. Note the linear sequence of the compartments and transitions, and the carry-over of nautical terms and forms from the sea's surface.

83 An artist's conception of the interior of a settlement in outer space, to be enclosed within the tubular rim of a giant rotating wheel. An earthlike (if fashionably modern) landscape is piously replicated in an alien context.

Johnson

be attractive places to live in, except as temporary adventures, or over longer spans for the few who are permanently adventurous. They raise all the social, psychological, and political problems of the megaform, but at a more intense level. In addition, they detach people from their customary earth.

The preceding models refer to the general form of a city. There are others which have to do with the organization of its central places. Central place patterns are intimately related to general patterns, of course. I separate them in order to clarify the possible combinations.

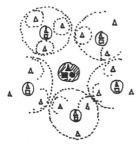

A. *Patterns of centers.* The idea of hierarchy is persistent in planning. It seems to be a natural way of ordering things, although this may be a consequence of ways in which our minds work. With regard to city centers, the hierarchical model requires that there should be one dominant center, including all the "highest," or most intense, or most specialized activities. At a distance from this center there should be a number of essentially equivalent subcenters, of lesser size, serving only a portion of the community, and containing less important, less intense, or less specialized activities, many of which will "feed into" the uses of the main center (as junior colleges feed students into a university, or community hospitals feed patients into a major teaching hospital). Each subcenter may then be surrounded by a standard array of sub-subcenters, and so on down to the degree desired. This appears to be a rational way of arranging activities which service larger and larger publics, and it provides a clear image by which people can organize complex territories in their minds. "Central place theory,"

Lösch

which came out of the work of August Lösch in south Germany, is founded on this concept, and research uncovers this form in many situations where contexts are homogeneous and linkages simple. The star city, the satellite concept, and the neighborhood idea, are all married to this hierarchic notion. But it appears in many other contexts. It permeates such disparate concepts as shopping facilities, playgrounds, political organization, and

Gruen

the provision of public services. It reinforces political or economic dominance, as well. Victor Gruen's books and plans are strong advocates of this notion.

Hierarchic centers assume that there are "lower" and "higher" functions, and that the statuses and service areas of different functions coincide, so that a person attending a junior college in a certain subcenter will also want to use its library, furniture store, and church, which are at that same level and serve the same area. Christopher Alexander has written a critique of this notion in "The City is Not a Tree." Cities which have been built on the notion (Columbia, Maryland, to take one example), find that while the system assures that local services are close to everyone, people use various centers for different purposes, and service areas overlap in complex ways. In large cities, the principal center is likely to be of great size and to have a very high density of activity. The massive, daily convergence of people to this point is marked by severe congestion, while the convergence of routes which supports that inward flow makes for poor access between points on the periphery. Once a person has battled his way to this central point, however, he may feel some exhilaration at being at the very center of such a great place, a point where the entire world seems within reach.

The contending viewpoint is that city regions are, or should be, multinucleate. That is, they should have a whole series of centers which have overlapping service areas. Many of the more important ones may service the entire region for special purposes, while also serving smaller areas for other purposes. No exclusive area can be assigned to a single center, although that center may have a general catchment range. People make choices, and go now here, now there. Of course, not all centers are of the same scale: some are larger, some smaller. But there is no sharp, steplike distribution of size and service area and no single dominant at the top. This may be a more realistic view of the proper distribution of contemporary urban centers. In contrast to hierarchy, it has advantages of choice and flexibility and may be spared heavy commuting flows. On the other hand, it requires that people seeking services have substantial mobility, and that they forego some of the pleasures of a great center where everything lies just at hand. The idea is not

Alexander 1965

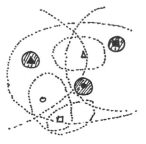

clearly developed. It provides neither a testable hypothesis of how cities work, nor a clear ideal of how they should do so. Until this is created, the hierarchic idea (just like any other partially discredited theory which lacks a challenger) continues to dominate analysis and design.

Finally—and more radically—a few theorists advocate the idea of afocal cities, that is, the abandonment of the concept of center. Now that individual transport is so rapid, and cities are so well integrated, let every function scatter at will over the city surface. There will then be no central congestion; each use will find plentiful cheap space, fitted to its own needs. Traffic will be evenly distributed, without peaks. Individual choice will be maximized, and the city will be highly flexible. Flexibility will improve even more, as communication improves. Melvin Webber puts forward this view.

Webber 1963

The form has some appeal. For some functions—such as "footloose" production or information processing—and certain sales and services whose customers come by premeditation and private car, afocality is already a reality in North American cities. On the other hand, one often finds that these "free" activities, while spread out, are not scattered at random, but are concentrated in certain areas, particularly along the major highways. Thus they tend to form linear centers, as I discuss below. Many other activities, moreover, require a close proximity to other specialized ones, or must be part of a complex in order to draw their customers. The psychological satisfaction of the notion of center, and the stimulus of being there, are persistent. Thus the murky notion of the multinucleate form, supplemented by local and linear centers, seems to be a more workable model today.

B. *Specialized and all purpose centers.* The classical notion of an urban center usually included the idea of specialization. Concentrations of distinct activities should be separated in space: a commercial center, a civic center, an office center, and so on.* The presumption behind the spatial segregation

*We are so frightened at being left out at the edge of something that it is now proper to call almost any new establishment a "center." Thus we hear of medical cen- ters, service centers, learning centers, warehouse centers, and building supply centers. If not a center, then any new thing will probably be called a "complex," since integrated

of central activities is that each use will then have its most appropriate setting, unhindered by conflicting activities. Moreover, there is an unstated assumption that some uses are "higher" than others, and suffer contamination from "lower" uses. Thus libraries, churches, and government offices are better than commercial offices and luxury shops, while these are better than second-hand stores, cheap lodging houses, and pornographic shops. This ranking of activities is in fact a social ranking of the presumed users of those activities. Where strict separation is carried out, users will be inconvenienced, if they wish to visit activities of different types (a government bureau and then a private corporation, or shopping over a range of diverse stores, or dropping in on a library or a porno shop at lunch, and so on). Moreover, separation may leave certain areas "dead" in appearance, a least at certain hours, and others overcrowded. Some of the stimulus and the spontaneous encounters possible in the great city are sacrificed.

A contrary view is that the best center is one that is thoroughly mixed in use, preferably at relatively high density, so that varied activities are cheek by jowl and the streets are full of people of all types. Such a policy, in its turn, even if achievable, may run into realistic use conflicts, and forego some of the advantages of use concentration: for example, the special character and possibilities for comparison that occur on a high fashion street, or on a street of antique stores.

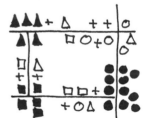

Most city centers exhibit both characteristics. The center as a whole is mixed in use, but is internally specialized, with transitions of mixed use between the specialized areas. Primarily, this is an artifact of the land market, which sorts out uses by rent-paying ability. Secondarily, it will be the effect of history, of user convenience, of complementarity between uses, or of an imposition of will by some powerful actors (as in the building of so many sterile "government centers"). In seeking a normative model, it is clear that we cannot propose either pure mix or pure segregation. Actual use linkages must

complexity also fascinates us. The third metaphor for a good place is expressed by the words garden, estate, or park. A garden center complex is very desirable.

be analyzed. The market already responds to these if users can pay. True, rather than fictitious, use conflicts (such as service congestion, street behavior, noise, etc.) must be taken into account. The more likely model is a collection of specialized nodes, linked through marginal zones of mixture, but packed closely enough together to insure easy access between them. Use clusters can be packed in three dimensions, to improve both types of connection. But such volumetric clustering may require expensive construction and impair future flexibility.

The concept of center specialization has occasionally been advocated for separate centers at the regional scale. While regional centers do have particular characters, due to history or to a preponderance of particular users (the center of a university community, or of a resort community), pure specialization at that scale is hardly to be found, and would presumably entail serious inconveniences. Regional shopping centers, however, which are established and controlled by one investor, usually exclude uses of low rent-paying ability, and most institutional occupants. While profitable, the new shopping centers thus lose many of the functions and advantages of the traditional city center.

C. *Linear centers.* Many uses, formerly found at the foci of cities and towns, are today strung out along the highways of the region, forming the so-called "commercial strip," which is such a ubiquitous feature of the North American city. Commercial, institutional, service, office, industrial, and warehouse functions all locate here, where space is cheap and there is easy access for auto-borne customers. Strips exhibit congested traffic and a shabby environment, and yet are one of the most visible features of the public city. They are universally condemned.

Yet they appear for a reason, and it is interesting that, while the linear city is popular with theoretical designers, none of them advocate linear centers, which have the same theoretical advantages at a more appropriate scale. Half-mockingly, Venturi, Scott Brown, and Izenour have lauded the strip, while the potentials and problems of the form have been analyzed by Michael Southworth. Almost all

See fig. 84

Venturi

Southworth

the remaining literature is devoted to ways of suppressing it. Is it possible that urban designers, like the confused dogs they are, are not barking up a fruitful tree? Could the very real advantages of easy individual access, low cost, and flexibility be attained in linear forms that were at the same time less irritating than present ones to passing traffic and to the eye?

D. *Neighborhood centers*. While there are differing views as to center specialization or hierarchy, there is a common acceptance of the neighborhood center prototype. This is a concentration of the commercial and service functions typically used by residents of a small community on a daily, or at least a weekly basis: the school ànd the nursery, stores for food, drugs, and the care of the person or of one's clothes; the church (if people can agree on one); the post office; the cafe, bar, or casual meeting place. The model is a replica of the local centers which persist in the inter-city fabric, however marginal or declining, and which may be seen in full vigor in more traditional settlements. It is motivated not only by considerations of convenient walking distance, but above all by a social ideal. The center is to be the focus of a small, coherent society, encouraging neighborly social interaction and a sense of community.

These local centers face serious economic competition from the shopping centers who enjoy a mass market based on automobile access. The small stores gradually close down, or specialize in serving the poor or the Sunday trade, or those unable or unwilling to patronize the big supermarkets. They become more and more marginal. The churches, now specialized by sect and serving large, scattered parishes, have already moved out to points of good highway access. For the most part, except in strong ethnic areas, they are no longer neighborhood institutions. The post offices, likewise, are being consolidated to lower their running costs. Few bars or snack bars can survive on local patronage in this country, although they are still vigorous elsewhere—the English pub is the model most often cited. Ironically, those neighborhood shops and bars that do persist are usually part of an older commercial strip, where they can draw on the auto

See fig. 85

trade as well as on the locals. The public school is still a local institution, but it is not at all clear whether there is any substantial social interaction between children and adults, or at least any relation which can be credited to the location of a school next to neighborhood stores. Moreover, the space thought necessary for a proper contemporary school makes it awkward to locate it at the center of a compact residential neighborhood.

Yet the model persists, and even becomes stronger today, as the concept of neighborhood re-emerges. The idea that convenience services should be close to houses is certainly reasonable. The hope that such centers will support or even initiate community interaction is appealing, but we need to learn the extent to which this is likely, and under what circumstances. A rethinking of the strip as a neighborhood institution may be in order. A realistic analysis of the economic viability of the neighborhood store, or whether it should be subsidized and by whom, is surely called for. The subsidies need not be governmental ones. Many local stores are possible because of the long, ill-paid hours donated by their resident proprietors. In all the sociological analysis of the neighborhood, and among all the eulogies of the neighborhood center, there is little guidance on this subject.

F. *The shopping center.* This is a familiar, well-developed model in this country: the integrated cluster of shops, all of them tenants in a single, planned structure, surrounded by parking. The shops are organized around a pedestrian mall, usually enclosed. The center is built by some major investor, and its form is carefully controlled. Traditionally, it is located in the intermediate regions of a metropolis, at some point which has excellent highway access, but where it may be totally disconnected from surrounding uses. It is a "pure" commercial center, planned from the beginning in detail. The fit between function and form in these centers has been carefully analyzed in many real cases, and the art of building and managing them is highly developed. They are a prime example of a fully tested model.

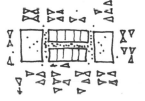

See fig. 86

The shopping center has drained much of the vitality from local shopping areas in our cities, and substantial commerce from the major downtown centers, and from those in the older suburbs. While the new centers were being constructed at a prodigious rate a decade ago, the pace has slowed remarkably, as the market has become more nearly saturated. Some of the oldest shopping centers are themselves going through the wringer of abandonment, and many others are being remodeled.

While local shopping is much decayed, the old downtown shows signs of revival, if at a more modest level than before. Meanwhile, the new shopping centers continue to be profitable. They are pleasant and lively places to be in. They have begun to attract the elderly and the teenager. To the dismay of the shop owners, these customers, bereft of credit cards, use the center primarily as a meeting place. Some centers have been built together with offices and high-density residence, in order to increase their customer base. To this extent, they are beginning to evolve from an isolated and specialized use toward a more comprehensive community center. Three difficulties persist, however. One, the center is cut off from surrounding development by its inward design and its ring of cars. It acts as a meeting place for a community on wheels, but lacks local, walk-in, casual links. Second, many uses which go to make up a full community are excluded by their inability to pay the required rentals. Third, a single hand controls the whole, which is a gain for orderliness, but a loss for freedom. Thus the model is markedly short of becoming a true community focus. Moreover, should a serious gasoline shortage occur, the access base of the shopping center will be threatened. Studies for the future rehabilitation of the modern shopping center may not now be out of place.

F. *Mobile centers.* Some problems in regard to the spatial location of central activities could be solved by moving them about, to bring them periodically within easy reach of all users, or to shift them as the load shifts. We see minor examples of this in our bookmobiles, factory canteens, traveling exhibits, and mobile clinics. It is a useful technique for meeting sudden or unpredictable requirements, or for allocating scarce services among dispersed populations. There are historic precedents in the

See fig. 87

84 The familiar commercial strip: clamorous but accessible. The example is from Los Angeles.

85 The serviceable neighborhood store, an activity now being squeezed out by the contemporary scale of development, by market competition, and by zoning prohibitions.

86 The North American shopping center, lively and protected within, barren without, and isolated from its surroundings. Teens and the elderly now choose to hang out in these private, interior streets.

87 Mobile services can
shift with demand, be
mounted with small cap-
ital, and add life to the
street. A baked potato
vendor in Kyoto, Japan,
and a barrel organ man in
Boston's North End.

circuit courts, the traveling tinkers and preachers, and the royal progress (which distributed a burden rather than a service). It seems less likely that the mobile center could be a useful model in any except unusual circumstances, because of the cost of moving complex activities and the loss of the sense of identity. Nevertheless, it has on occasion been advocated.

Next we come to a series of models which refer to the general grain or texture of a city, rather than to any particular pattern. These models range from an overall texture to the density and texture of buildings.

A. *Cells*. That a city should be an aggregate of distinct but fundamentally similar parts, as a living organism is made up of cells, has been an underlying idea of contemporary planning. Otherwise, the vast modern city seems too huge and shapeless to grasp—not just for the citizen but, more important perhaps, for the planner herself. Everyone should live and work in some small, bounded area, in which she will feel at home. The planner, meanwhile, by diagramming a city as a mosaic of these cells, can be sure of her quantities and dispositions, and be confident that every area has the local facilities it needs, since with each cell goes a proper complement of schools, shops, and other necessities.

The basic cellular notion is reinforced, in the case of residential areas, by the notion of neighborhood—a place where permanent residents are in face-to-face contact, and are on intimate terms with each other because they live next to each other. By analogy with the social structure of the villages and small towns of past generations, a sense of community will develop, and people will support each other. This will be the grass roots unit of city politics, since the neighborhood will speak for the local interests. The neighborhood idea appears in such disparate places as the massive new capital of Brasilia, the suburban new town of Columbia, Maryland, the political and economic organization of the new China, and the Model Cities program in the United States.

American Public Health Association
Dahir
Mumford 1954

Perry

The classic formulation of the idea in city planning was the neighborhood unit plan of Clarence Perry, proposed in the first regional plan of New York, who focused his units around the public elementary school. But difficulties arise when the cell is tied to any particular facility, such as to a school. The school may have an optimum size (or a standardized size) which is too large for a working social unit, or too small to support a local grocery store economically. Nor is it clear that city life does or should focus around the schoolchild, or that most social interactions begin through acquaintances gained via children. Moreover, in the particular case of the school, modern standards call for such a large amount of open space that the school is a very awkward thing to put at the center of a small community.

Isaacs

The neighborhood unit has been attacked, on broader grounds, as being a planning illusion. Urban North Americans do not live that way. They may have a casual nodding acquaintance with a handful of next-door neighbors, but their important social contacts are with old friends, workmates, and kin, who are widely scattered over the city. They shop in one community, use the school of another, go to church in a third. Their interests are no longer local. They no longer stay in one place very long. Neighborhoods have a weak voice at city hall. To plan a city as a series of neighborhoods is futile, or may support social segregation. Any good city has a *continuous* fabric, rather than a cellular one. Then it is possible for people to choose their own friends and services, and to move their residences freely, by small or large increments, as they choose.

Sims

Yet the cellular ideas persists. In planning, having been for a time widely discredited, the concept has re-emerged. The fact that people respond without hesitation when asked about their "neighborhood" indicates that the word has a popular meaning. Recent studies in Columbus, Ohio, show a surprising concordance in the way people define the local areas of the city. Social neighborhoods survive in the city, particularly in working-class and ethnic areas. But they can also be found to some degree in the suburbs. Neighborhood organizations spring up whenever outside forces threaten some damage to a locality, although they may subside again when the danger is past.

So the debate continues, and as usual it revolves about whether everybody should live in neighborhoods, or nobody. To know under what conditions the neighborhood concept is useful, for whom, and in what form, would be handier knowledge. There is no reason why everyone must be part of a local community. Some may choose to be, some not. Nor is it inevitable that the cell be the same for every purose. Social neighborhoods—meaning places where people are acquainted by reason of living nearby each other—may normally be quite small, of the order of twenty or thirty families. The service areas of most facilities will be much larger, and need not coincide, as long as those facilities are easily accessible to everyone. The physical unit, named and recognizable, to which people refer their location and their sense of place, can be different again. The latter may be a local quasi-political unit, around which people will rally when danger threatens.

The proper size of the neighborhood has been widely debated. It becomes a critical question whenever all local functions must be stuffed into the same bag. This number oscillates between 50 and 5000 persons. Most often, the neighborhood idea has also been tied to an ideal of social heterogeneity. In this view, the good neighborhood contains people of all ages, of all classes, and of varied racial and ethnic background. In this minisociety, people learn to live together. In reality, the ideal has been difficult to carry out. Most active local communities are relatively homogeneous, at least in regard to social class.

The cellular idea has almost always been applied to residential areas, and less thought has been given to its usefulness in work areas, or in other parts of the city. Naturally, planners are happy to put things on their maps in the form of standard units, since those are easier to lay down and manipulate. So industrial parks, residential neighborhoods, regional shopping centers, and standard playgrounds are comfortable planning counters. But no real thought has been given to whether there may be work communities that should be supported by city design.

or

?

Cellular theory has recently pushed beyond the neighborhood of acquaintance based on propinquity, to a more general plea for local autonomy. Local people should control their own schools, open space, police, and sanitation. They should even produce their own food and energy. This debate over autonomy was outlined in chapter 13.

B. *Sprawl and compaction.* Planning literature has generally deplored the spread-out city, because of its consumption of land, the expensive utilities and transportation it requires, and the social isolation it engenders. Most North Americans, when they could afford to, have voted the other way, and have moved out to the suburbs. They like the open space, the chance to own their own houses, better schools for their children, and the security of being with their own social kind. In return, they are willing to put more of their income into housing, to break off old local ties, and spend more time in commuting. Some will return to the inner city after a time, but most stay on, or move further out. There was a moment of return to the inner suburbs during the late lamented gasoline shortage, but it proved as volatile as that substance itself. We may see its like again, however. At present, the outwash continues, even while accompanied by some signs of inner-city renewal. Indeed, the outward tide is now flooding the old rural towns of the hinterlands, well outside the recognized metropolitan regions. The return current, which may grow to be more significant, is still small. To large degree, it is caused by the high price of the new suburban lots and houses.

There have been recent attempts to document the additional costs of suburban growth. The results are not entirely convincing, however, since in the analysis the prices of small apartments are compared to those of large houses, and crime and welfare statistics are compared across social variations. In terms of the capital cost of land, buildings, and all utilities, moderately low densities of housing are cheapest in this country, at the present.

It is clear that continued suburban growth has meant major new investments at the fringe, while housing and services are being abandoned at the center. It has also meant an increasing spatial segregation by social class, and a serious loss of the central city tax base. But these phenomena are not due directly to the change in density. Suburban densities have, however, increased our dependence on the private automobile, and thus on imported gasoline. For teenagers and the elderly, the lack of suburban public transportation can be a serious drawback in life at the fringe. Suburban densities are rising slowly, as land prices and family demands shift the market towards low density apartments. But the gradual decline of the overall density of our cities still seems irreversible.

While the broad debate has been between the dense or less dense city, either model has assumed that new development should be continuous, using the ground rationally and completely. Waste areas are surely senseless: the evil results of a lack of forethought. Only an occasional voice has argued the virtues of scattered growth, which leaves room for flexibility and fill-in, while continuous development produces monolithic, single-age areas. Arguments have been made for the social usefulness of waste ground as a place of retreat, especially for children. A larger chorus has recently sung the praises of "clustering," in which clumps of relatively high-density housing are set in open space. At a low average density, and with plenty of open space nearby, clusters achieve locally high densities, with their accompanying advantages of lower site costs and easier social interaction. Clusters are urged on communities as a way of preserving the landscape while permitting development, on developers as a way of shaving cost, and on homeowners as a new way to live. The developers are coming around, suburban communities are gradually giving way, and buyers are interested, if suspicious. The experiment looks promising. The idea of density variation within an overall limit has been the basis of numerous "planned unit development" ordinances, and has been suggested in other nonresidential contexts, as well.

Lessinger

Whyte 1964

C. *Segregation and mix.* The grain of a city, that is, how finely its physical elements, activities, or types of persons are mixed in space, is one of its fundamental characteristics. Industrial uses or Italian residents may or may not occupy extended homogeneous areas. Moreover, this granular distribution may be sharp or blurred: the industrial zone may be surrounded by a greenbelt or a high fence. Italians may never or often live next to other less gifted races, at the boundaries of their turf.

The classic planning position on this issue may be characterized as opting for a coarse grain of use and building type, but a fine grain of persons by class, race, and age. The former position is a by-product of the classified land-use map and the nature of land-use controls, both of which favor sharp distinctions. But it has also been a matter of intellectual conviction: use mixture causes conflict and nuisance, reduces property values, raises uncertainties about the future use of land, and makes rational planning for services more difficult. A fine grain of persons, however, is part and parcel of the social idealism of planning. Racial and class segregation prevent social mobility and communication, and promote inequalities of opportunity and services. The ideal community is a "balanced" one, in which all groups in the general population are present, finely mixed, and are members of one polity.

Gans 1961

In general, the North American city has heeded one piece of this advice and disregarded the other. The metropolitan region, although it contains many areas of use mix, has in general become more and more coarse-grained in regard to land use and building type. This has happened as development has been carried out at larger scales, and as zoning laws have taken stronger hold. Contrary to the planning ideal, however, the North American metropolis is also coarsening steadily in regard to the grain of persons, particularly as they are classified by socioeconomic status, but also in terms of age and family composition. Enclaves of the rich and the poor grow steadily larger, especially along the center-to-periphery gradient. The low-density suburb, or large tracts of it, is devoted to families with young children, and the elderly are concentrated more and more in special projects and communities, or at the city core. Racial and ethnic segregations continue, but it is possible that they are weakening, except as they are associated with economic status.

Not only is the ideal of social mix contradicted by real events in the North American city (and in most cities of the world with the exception of some socialist ones), but it is under a certain intellectual attack as well. Class and ethnic mixtures may be seen, not only as unrealistic, but as difficult for people to bear, leading to conflicts between ways of life, the destruction of old traditions, and a weakening of the working-class or ethnic control of a piece of urban turf. The arguments and dilemmas will be resolved only by considering the scale and conditions appropriate to each type of segregation or of mix. Small-scale segregations by class, for example, may reduce conflict and promote neighborhood interaction and solidarity. Large-scale segregation, on the other hand, will lead to gross inequalities and to a rupture of interclass communication. Thus policy might support small scale, but not extensive class segregation. Beyond these arguments, there are serious issues of implementation: how can a fine grain of class mix be enforced or induced by public power? The coarse spatial segregation by class of the modern North American metropolis is one of its outstanding features, and perhaps its most serious problem.

The traditional support of a coarse grain of use and building type has also been attacked. It produces monotony and inflexibility in the city, and, indirectly, social segregation as well. As he manipulates his clearly drawn maps and ordinances, the planner may be reducing the access to people and activities. Perhaps crops could be grown inside the city. If industrial production were carried out near the home, then those tied to the house could join in productive work, as they once did in cottage industries, or as they do in China today. From that viewpoint, zoning can be regarded as an obsolete regulatory tool. Yet it is still a powerful one in the real city, and there are strong motives at work for use segregation, including nuisance and infrastructure considerations, but also, more fundamentally, considerations of property value and social exclusion.

Once again, the question cannot be resolved at such a general level. It requires a detailed analysis which considers the scale and type of the land-use

grain. Clusterings of use with transition zones, as well as fine-grain segregations within coarser areas of mix, may be the proper answers to many of the dilemmas of access, control, fit, and flexibility. The coarse grain of development may deliberately be resisted by dividing land into small parcels, by releasing it slowly or in fragments, or even by prohibiting large-scale integrated projects. In any case, it is clear that grain, like density, is a very general and fundamental characteristic of city form, with many impacts on its quality as a human environment.

D. *Characteristic spatial texture.* There is a further way, beyond those of density, grain, or cellular organization, of describing the basic ground or texture of a city. It is immediately perceptible to us, and yet it is more difficult to define in analytical categories. This is the characteristic manner in which the spaces and masses of a settlement present themselves. There are at least three major spatial types that we are familiar with, and surely other examples might be found or invented.

In the classical European city, which is so much a part of our heritage and to which we often turn with nostalgia, the streets and squares were hollowed out of a rather compact mass of buildings of moderate height. The building facades may not have been completely continuous, but except for the occasional landmark, they appeared as a unified if articulated background for the open spaces cut into them. They faced onto those spaces, and took their identity therefrom. It was these streets and squares which were the framework of the city, named and remarkable, the vital containers of the public life. The proportions, characteristics and connections of these public hollows was the character of the city. More than anything, buildings were facades which contained and decorated those spaces. This spatial framework might be an ordered geometrical one, or more irregular and mazelike.

We have a great affection for these towns. They seem secure, legible, proportioned to the human scale, and charged with life, even if at times a little oppressive. But modern functions, particularly modern traffic, and modern styles of building and habits of living are dissolving this classic spatial

Sitte

texture, and have created a second spatial type. Buildings have become isolated objects in space. It is the objects, or clusters of them, which became the remarkable perceptual elements. The space of the streets has swollen and spilled over into the spaces between buildings. In the process, the street space has lost its form, and become a neutral background for the form of the structures.

On occasion, in a few fine, planned compositions, or more rarely by accident, these clusters of great objects in space create a splendid scene. More often, the whole disintegrates. We then depend on topographic features, or on street activities, or on symbolic connections such as signs and names, to make the city legible. We feel a certain freedom, and see some amusing scenes, but mostly we sense a loss. Repeated attempts are made, by designers at least, to recreate the bounded spaces of the first model. It is difficult to do. Whether these bounded spaces can ever be recaptured, at least as a general settlement texture, is quite uncertain. In any event, it seems that we have yet to find a way to exploit whatever potentials exist in the new spatial texture.

The third common model is the leafy suburban scene, in which streets wind with the topography, and, although not continuously enclosed, are overhung by trees, while the eye is carried forward along their planted, curving lines. Buildings appear as single objects, but always set among trees and lawns. At times buildings are completely camouflaged by the plants. Natural features are celebrated, and the ground form expressed, at least in successful examples. The *continuity* of the scene is emphasized; spaces are not blocked by walls or massive buildings, although they may dissolve in the leafy depths.

Most people do not connect the word "city" with such scenes, but in fact the great bulk of the North American city now consists of such spatial textures. The model, if somewhat bland and inexpressive of human activity, is widely admired and often passably well executed.

If these are the three principal existing types, others can be found, at least in potential. One is a three-dimensional maze of tunnels, ways, and bridges, drilled out of a neutral substance of in-

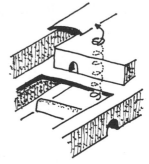

See fig. 88

definite extent. The principal image is of a complex network, full of incidents and surprises, intimate and protected in scale, intricately connected into itself: There is no outside, no facade. Everything is inside. The prototypes for this solid maze may be found in connected subways, large institutional complexes, and enclosed shopping malls. Perhaps larger settlements may soon be built in this fashion, especially in hostile environments. The model has its special delights, and also induces claustrophobia. How many tunnels are there in the world in which it is pleasant to be? The shopping arcade or the Islamic souk, perhaps?

Hybrid models are also possible. For example, a city might be spatially organized as a set of wide grand avenues, defined by trees or walls or fronting activities, and flanked or terminated by special landmarks. Having strong spatial and sequential characteristics of their own, the avenues could be clearly organized as a total structure. Just off these ways, by passing through narrow entrances, one could enter a quite separate "inside" world—private, with small interior openings and passages, nodes of activity and zones of isolated quiet. From the inside world one might get a glimpse of the busy avenue space, and from the latter a hint—through a gate or over a wall—of the inside. This would then be a bipolar organization of space: public/private, active/quiet, outside/inside, open/closed. We see spaces of this kind in some cities of the Middle East, and the model may have some application for us today, torn as we are between our desires for security and free movement.

Nevertheless, the great majority of settlements, at least among Western cities today, can be characterized by one or a combination of the three dominant spatial textures—the one historic, to which we cling, another contemporary, which makes us uneasy, and the last predominant today, basically satisfying if also a shade characterless.

E. *Housing type.* The basic texture of a city is also given by the predominant type and mix of its residential buildings, and there is a substantial literature on the subject of housing models. Most of these models can be summarized in a simple 3-by-3 matter, which pits building height against ground coverage, as follows:

Ground coverage	Building Height		
	high (over 6 stories)	moderate (3–6 stories)	low (1–2 stories)
high (over 50%)	—	dense walkups	courtyard housing
moderate (10–50%)	high slabs	ground-access walkups	attached houses
low (under 10%)	towers in the green	—	freestanding houses

1. *High slabs.* Much of the new housing being created in the world today is in the form of long, slablike, apartment buildings, twelve to twenty or even thirty stories high, with central corridors and elevators. Once one is committed to elevator apartments, this is the least expensive type to build. It is suited to prefabrication and rapid erection. Because of the density attainable, it permits compact growth, substantial local services close at hand, and good public transportation. Most urban extensions in the USSR and the socialist countries of Eastern Europe follow this model. It is also common elsewhere in Europe, and was for a time the prevailing model in Great Britain for public housing, until checked by a popular revolt. In the United States, it is found in public housing in the central city, and also in middle-class areas near the core of such giant urban regions as New York. For all of its economy in areas of high land cost, the slab elevator apartment is substantially more costly to build than the walkup apartment, or other lower-density housing types. It is a particularly difficult habitat for families with children, and is almost universally disliked. It produces a monotonous environment, beyond any human scale. The ground surfaces must be intensively used for access: parking, utilities, and organized play. Much of this surface is therefore paved,

See fig. 89

88 An interior pedestrian street in Bath, England. Interior streets need lively frontages, frequent openings to the outside, and a clear connection to the structure of the city. Most attempts at public corridors are unhappy failures.

89 Vast areas of prefabricated apartments are being built to meet a desperate need for urban housing, in a form satisfying to few. This example is at the northern edge of Leningrad in the USSR, but similar ones can be found throughout the capitalist and socialist world.

or badly worn. Vandalism and security are difficult to control. Almost everywhere in the world, this is a type of housing that is tolerated only where tenants are forced to it by politics, price, or housing shortage.

2. *Towers in the green.* High towers are a different model of high-rise housing. Widely spaced in open green areas, they preserve the natural landscape, while offering their residents broad views and all the amenities of sophisticated urban living. Roofs and balconies can be used for open space. Special common services can be provided (shops, nurseries, clinics, meeting rooms) and might be placed at mid-story within the building. The idea captured the fancy of a generation of designers. It fits the economics of urban luxury housing. In practice, except in some spectacular urban or rural locations, the outcome has been less than ideal. The towers must be pushed close together. The open ground at their feet is eaten away by parking lots. The internal services require a larger market than can be found within a single building. Despite all the people overhead, the streets are empty, even dangerous, at night. The internal corridors and lifts do not encourage neighborly interaction. Small children cannot go directly out of the house to play, under the mother's eye. Thus the crowded tower acquires most of the disadvantages of the high slab. These tall tower apartment buildings have been particularly unsuccessful as low-income housing, since they are expensive, and their elevators are difficult to patrol. But the tower, even the crowded tower, has proved acceptable for the well-to-do, for young couples, singles, or the elderly, in central city locations, where the freedom from maintenance, the ability to rise above the crowded city in a defended enclave, the glamor of modernity, and the convenient facilities within the building have proved worth the cost. In such cases it can be a preferred alternative.

3. *Dense walkups.* These were the tenements which housed the working and lower middle classes of our cities, during the nineteenth and early twentieth centuries. They are the least expensive form of housing, as long as people can be persuaded to climb four, five, or six stories without

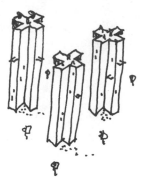

Le Corbusier

Jacobs

elevators. They establish a sufficient density to support plentiful local shops and services, perhaps as a continuous ground floor frontage, as in parts of New York or Boston, and in many European cities. The streets are full of life, and the "eyes on the street," in Jane Jacobs's phrase, tend to regulate behavior there. But there are also problems of noise, fire danger, and a lack of light and air within the apartments. These are, after all, the houses from which generations of occupants have fled, once they had the chance. While there have been some attempts to approximate their good qualities in new buildings, as with balcony access apartment slabs, or two-story row houses piled one above the other and served by skip-stop elevators, they have never been entirely successful. The Boston three-decker was a workable, low-cost variant of the model, until prohibited by fire regulations. Many existing areas of dense walkups are still serviceable, however, and even quite desirable when located in areas of special urban character. Except for the expensive tower, new building types which can sustain high urban densities and still be acceptable to most residents remain to be developed.

4. *Ground-access walkups.* At moderate coverages and building heights, it is possible to provide a mix of apartments, of which many or all have direct access to the ground, and few of whose entries are more than one flight up. An example frequently seen is the mix of two-story row houses and three-story walkup apartments, the latter so arranged that the upper apartments are duplexes, with their front doors on the second floor. More complex types can assure a private garden for each unit. The demonstration project called "Habitat" at the Montreal Exposition in 1967 was an impressive example of this type, in which roof terraces and elevated walkways within a six story structure gave every unit a private garden and an exterior private front door. It was much admired by residents and visitors, but the complicated structure proved to be very expensive. Nevertheless, since this type of housing can economically use central city land, and still provide many of the characteristics of scale and access to commonly sought by families, active design experimentation countinues. The Urban De-

velopment Corporation of New York State produced a thoroughly developed example of this housing type—one much more acceptable for family life, and also less expensive than an elevator apartment. The generic class seems a good basic model for apartment living, both in the center city and in the suburbs.

Institute for Architecture
and Urban Studies

5. *Courtyard houses.* Courtyard or patio housing is occasionally proposed as a way of achieving urban densities with single-family houses. The model goes back to the Mediterranean prototype, still in use in many traditional cities, a unit which turns inward rather than outward for light and air. A central courtyard, or a series of courtyards, provides light for every room, while the unit as a whole is packed solidly against neighboring units on two, three, or even four sides. The yard is then completely private, and the family secluded. The houses are not more than one or two stories high, so that sunlight may fill the court. The type is relatively inexpensive and workable, and particularly applicable to the warm, dry, sunny climate where it arose. Yet one of the best modern examples of its use occurs in Cumbernauld, in Scotland. North American families are still hesitant over it, but this seems to be a useful model for special urban situations. Logically, it goes with urban areas whose entire texture, somewhat alien to our culture, is one where walls predominate, privacy is a major value, and streets are narrow corridors between shop fronts or blind facades.

See fig. 12

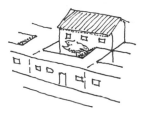

6. *Attached houses.* At moderate densities and low heights, a large array of housing types is possible: row houses, duplexes, and low "garden" apartments. One- or two-floor family units are placed side by side, or two single-floor units stack one above the other. There is a "front" side, in which each unit has its own entrance on the public street, and a "back" side, where each has its private yard, or perhaps where there is a common open space, private to a small group of units. The "quadruplex," now being used by some midwestern builders, is halfway to the denser ground-access walkup. Two units, one over the other, face forward to the street, and two, attached behind, are accessible at the side. Each has a garage, a front door, and a

tiny yard or roof space. Along with the freestanding house, these various types of low, attached houses are the work horses of the North American city. Compact and inexpensive relative to other types, they still provide the desired qualities of direct access and parking, unit identity, and private open space. Units can be owned or rented, and the duplexes offer opportunities for resident owners to secure a rental income from the attached unit. They can be built in small numbers, or repeated over large areas. Although the type has for long been considered by most North Americans as a compromised single-family house, and by designers as unimaginative, it is nevertheless the best tested of all the relatively dense forms, and is steadily gaining acceptance. In contrast to the freestanding house at these close densities, the streetscape can be modeled as a coherent whole, rather than as a repetition of small boxes. In contrast to long slab apartments, attached houses retain their intimate scale, and can be differentiated to denote the presence of each family. It is not unlikely that various modifications of this kind of housing will provide the ground texture of the future city, in our society.

7. *Freestanding houses.* These remain the ideal of most American families, and make up two-thirds of our urban housing stock. Favored by popular acceptance and federal subsidy, the postwar North American metropolis was built of single-family houses. Condemned for its reputed visual monotony, this type of housing has persisted wherever buyers could afford it. Rising construction costs and the threat of gasoline shortages are shifting demand toward the somewhat denser prototypes noted above. Lesser variations are also proposed, such as "zero-lot" houses, which have no side yard on one side, and thus sit on the lot line without being physically attached to the next unit. Since the affection for the single-family house is so strong, and it has such obvious advantages for identity and ownership, private open space, and owner maintenance and remodeling, it will be important to work out further variations on the theme, in order to lower costs and achieve higher densities. The recycling of the single-family suburbs already built will be a major design task for the future. These

See fig. 76

older suburbs, as they are modified by use, and as their landscape matures, begin to attain a special character of their own. How to enhance that sensed character, and how to "densify" these aging places by inserting attached units or scattered small walk-ups, so as to improve their access and provide a greater range of settings, is an important prototype problem.

F. *Innovations.* If those are the standard themes of housing texture, out of which almost all our cities are built, there are some additional models. If we look back at the basic list above, we see that they are all alike in at least one way: all are combinations of isolated family living units, each with its own kitchen, bathrooms, sleeping and living spaces, and its own separate entrance. This reflects, of course, the central role of the nuclear family in our society. Should the family change, then the house type will of necessity also change. The recent conversions of large single-family houses, or groups of them, into residences for communal families may indicate the sprouting of quite a new prototype. There are some previous models of this in the housing built by certain utopian communities, such as the Amana and Oneida settlements.

Another innovation has been the provision of mobile or temporary housing. The original impulse was either to provide quick housing for those temporarily homeless (as after a disaster or during a limited period of construction), or to allow people to carry their homes with them as they moved about on holiday. This simple "trailer" has grown up to become the "mobile home," compact, long, and narrow, with demountable wheels and a metal skin, packed with technical conveniences. Thus the lowly trailer became the first successful prefabricated single-family house. Some 15 percent of housing units built in the United States in any year are now of this type. Mobile homes can be moved onto sites quickly, but rarely move off again, although the illusion of potential mobility may be exhilarating. Local communities dislike them, for reasons of status and taxation, and they are relegated to marginal locations, where owners pay excessive rents for poorly laid out sites. Internally, they are well equipped, but cramped. One of the important tasks of prototype design is to show how these stepchild houses can be sited and planned to make pleasant and workable residential areas.

The mobile housing function of the old trailer has been taken up by the awkward "camper truck," which lumbers to the seashore or mountains for a weekend of "outdoor living." Still another quasi-mobile type is the houseboat, which is occasionally used as a recreational house on the rivers and lakes of the interior. In some urban situations, where buildable land is scarce, waterfronts are plentiful, and old barges are cheap, the floating house may become an important type of self-help housing, as has occurred in Amsterdam, Paris, London and other cities. It would be useful to analyze the conditions and special purposes for which floating housing could be a useful element of a city. They might provide for surges of housing demand, for example, or we might resort to them when land is scarce near a seacoast city. They have charms (and costs) of their own.

G. *Systems and self-help.* One further set of models governs our thinking about housing, and this relates to the process by which that housing is created. In our custom, the well-to-do have houses built to order, individually designed and contracted for. Everyone else occupies second-hand housing, or buys units which have been built for sale or rent by large or moderate-size developers, using stock designs and factory components incorporated into structures fabricated on the site. Or perhaps a family may purchase a prefabricated mobile home.

One planning faction believes that high-technology industrialization of housing can crack the endemic housing shortage and bring the price housing down to the relatively modest levels of food and clothing in the developed countries. Despite long advocacy in this country (including such determined governmental action as the futile Operation Breakthrough), the industrialization of housing has never taken off—except via the lowly trailer, and also, incrementally, by the progressive factory production of separate building parts: doors, windows, roof trusses, hardware, bath and kitchen assemblies, wall panels, and the like.

In Europe, however, and particularly in the socialist countries, the centralized prefabrication of housing has been developed at great length. Giant factories produce the elements of slab apartment buildings, to be assembled on the site. The result has been a rapid increase in the housing supply, even if there has been no real breakthrough on cost. The system produces vast, monotonous housing estates, often poorly finished and badly sited. The user has even less to say about the shape of his dwelling than when he rents or buys from a private housing developer.

An opposing planning faction puts its faith in self-help, rather than in systems building. Taking a cue from the history of squatter settlements in cities of the third world, it contends that the best housing is made by, or under the direct supervision of, the ultimate user, and that the labor and ingenuity of the dweller is a vast, unused resource for housing construction. Public policy, therefore, should be directed toward supporting that local enterprise: encouraging small contractors, and providing cheap land, cheap small-scale building materials, teachers of construction skills, and basic services such as water and electric power. The urban texture will consist of individual buildings of simple but varied form, at the moderate densities which can be achieved by low buildings at relatively high coverage. Rather than by imposing a repeated building model, a coherent city form results from the pattern and character of the street and utility system, from the nature of the building materials and simple building elements that are supplied to owner-builders, and perhaps because of some quite elementary building regulations.

Turner

See figs. 90, 91

Abrams
Beinart
Habraken

Pure self-help, where residents build everything with their own hands, may in practice be restricted to traditional societies building by traditional means, or, on the contrary, to very affluent societies where people do it themselves because they have the time and the desire to do so. Nevertheless, houses can be built by professionals, partially and incrementally, while under close user control, and subsequently modified and finished by residents. More advanced theories of this kind have proposed the construction of uniform supporting structures, in addition to the public streets, within which families could erect their shelters in any form they prefer. It seems unlikely, however, that such an elaborate support system would be feasible.

While we can talk at length about residential models, it is interesting that there is relatively little said in the literature about nonresidential building types other than the shopping center. Houses make up the bulk of any city, but why is so little consideration given to the workplace, for example, in which such a large percentage of our waking hours are passed? In reality, standard models for workplaces exist, and are repeated: the downtown office tower, the suburban office block, the industrial estate with single-floor machine rooms fronted by offices and lawns, the vast factory shed set in yards and parking lots, the warehouse and truck terminal, the houses converted to small offices, and so on. These are "unconscious" models, used by firms as the natural way to build their premises, and never examined for their impact on the people who work within them, or on the city as a whole.

See fig. 92

See fig. 67

Another series of city models refers to patterns of internal circulation:

A. *Modal choice.* There are many ways of carrying people about, and much of the discussion about city form revolves about the choices that should be made between them. Running through all the bewildering array of devices—trolley cars, cable cars, buses, railroads, subways, elevateds, "elephant trains," wagons, bicycles, boats, horses, feet, litters, wheelchairs, automobiles, taxis, group taxis, dial-a-bus, moving sidewalks, "people movers," hovercraft, rickshaws, roller skates, minibusses, ice boats, airplanes, helicopters, dirigibles, mopeds, motorcycles, elevators, and escalators—there are two fundamental dimensions which serve to distinguish their qualities:

(1) The technical continuum, from the simple and muscle-powered to the complex and automated (with such familiar mechanical devices as autos and buses somewhere in the middle); and

(2) The control continuum, from largely free individual movement to scheduled and spatially

90 Will the housing shortage be solved by using
high technology, or will
people do it by using their
own labor?

91 A typical squatter settlement in a disused quarry in Fez, Morocco. People are housing themselves with scant resources and regulating their own environment. Government-built middle-income housing can be seen in the distance.

92 The clean, empty facade of the modern industrial estate. Who uses it? Who looks at it? What lies behind it?

fixed mass transit (with group taxis in between).

To some degree, these two dimensions are not independent, but tend to parallel each other. There are, however, high-technology modes which allow a fair amount of individual freedom (such as moving sidewalks and "people movers"). There are also low-technology modes which are mass transit devices, such as horsecars and packet boats. But the complex and the controlled, and the simple and the free, tend to associate with each other.

Concentrated, mass modes are more frequently advocated in the professional literature on city design, since they require less space than individual modes (both in the channel and also when storing the vehicle), they are more energy efficient (if the alternatives are not muscle-powered), and presumably are more cost efficient. Since they are provided by social rather than personal capital, and are guided by specialists, they are available to a larger range of the population: the poor, the disabled, the young, and the elderly. On the other hand, they provide less flexible routes and stops, and they require large initial capital investments and a more concentrated set of origins and destinations to operate efficiently. In this country, and in many others, people have opted for individual transportation whenever they could afford it, since it means privacy, door-to-door access, the ability to go and come at will, and the opportunity of living and working at low densities. This choice, in its turn, has brought with it massive air pollution, accidents, dependence on oil, road congestion, a demand for extensive parking space, and a worsening of access for all those who do not drive a car. While there has been some dismay at the price, and some improvement of transit service in central cities, the individual vehicle has not yet lost ground. A severe gasoline shortage may change this picture, but the resistance will be tenacious and ingenious.

Blumenfeld 1977

True mass transit requires high concentrations of users, and may thus be appropriate only in the central areas of large cities. Its cost superiority is not clear, and recent fixed rail transit lines in this country have proved expensive and inequitable. Public vehicles which use the familiar internal combustion engine—bus, minibus, and group taxi—are at present better devices for moving large numbers of people, since they are reliable, flexible, and relatively cheap. But they also pollute the air, and cannot offer the convenience of the personal car. Nor is it easy to service far-flung suburbs at reasonable prices and schedules. One proposed resolution of this modal dilemma is the construction of a mixed-mode system—one in which individual vehicles running on local, low-density roads can be linked together on belts or guideways or into trains, when they are on the main routes and near the high-density centers, so that large numbers of people can move without conflict at high speeds. But this not only requires a very expensive technical device for carriage and control on the main routes, but also that individual vehicles be made compatible with that device. The idea attracts us as a splendid technical fix, but the price is a highly complex, inflexible, and all-embracing system.

The key issue is not the car versus mass transit, or how to develop a super mode, but rather how to develop two devices: (1) an individual vehicle which is less polluting, less murderous, less expensive, less space-demanding, and less of an energy sink than our beloved automobile (a safe, weatherproof, and motor-assisted bicycle with a capacity to carry packages?), and (2) a means of group transit which is flexible in its routes and schedules and can serve low-density areas efficiently. The freedom to move over a wide area at will is a pleasure that is not easily given up, once achieved. Solutions should not entail a denial of this freedom, but a mitigation of its costs, of which unequal access to the transport system and the burden of accidents and air pollution are undoubtedly the most serious.

Much the same may be said of the low-technology–high-technology dimension. Walking (or running) is the healthiest way to move about, for those able to do so. But most urban trips now require other means. It is less than likely, however, that the answer lies in sophisticated devices such as "people movers" or hovercraft. It is the small, familiar, personally guided vehicle that will be most useful, from bicycles to small buses or group taxis. The proper modal mix depends on the political economy and spatial form of the city in question. Management and control of the transport system can well be more critical than its technology. The qualities needed are simplicity, flexibility, lack of pollution, and openness to all users, rather than speed or technical splendor.

B. *Circulation pattern.* The spatial pattern of the circulation system is often a matter of debate. Once more, the concept of hierarchy is rarely challenged. A good circulation system is one in which minor lanes feed into local streets, which feed into arterials, which feed into expressways. The hierarchy may be composed of three levels instead of four, or any other reasonable number. Thus the capacity of a channel may be sized to its expected flow, and uses which prefer much traffic or little traffic can locate where they are confident of finding the bustle or the quietness they prefer.

Such hierarchies develop with time in many unplanned cities.* Public intervention may sharpen this "natural" hierarchy, and new cities are usually laid out to that model. In this case, the model seems unquestionable, but small doubts do arise. One doubt has to do with how many levels are proper, although the minor street/collector/arterial/expressway ladder is widely accepted. Another doubt has to do with the ability to predict future flows, and thus to know where and how often a higher-ranking channel should occur. Still another has to do with the flexibility of movement at any given time, that is, whether a strict hierarchy may hinder local movements by forcing one to clamber up and down the branching system, in order to reach some point nearby. Therefore, strict hierarchy is often compromised by interconnecting the lower-level channels as well, so that bypass movements are possible. Nevertheless, the general concept of circulation hierarchy is widely used.

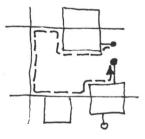

Beyond this general idea, there are several alternatives for the pattern itself, and these are closely linked to other features of urban form. The two principal models of pattern—the grid and the radioconcentric—have already been described. The

---

*Of course, no city is a natural growth, and therefore none is unplanned. This rather misleading term refers to an absence of centralized, comprehensive planning.

Okamoto

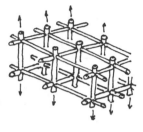

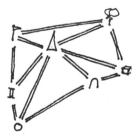

grid is usually a rectangular one, in most North American cities, and indeed throughout the world. With its advantages of simple layout, regular building plots, flexible traffic flow, and logical orientation, come familiar problems: visual monotony, a disregard of topography, difficulties for travel on the diagonal, and the threat of fast traffic on any street. Many of these difficulties can be overcome, however, as has been noted above.

The rectangular grid may also be expanded in the third dimension, so that there is a coordinated set of vertical ascents and of horizontal paths at superimposed levels. This has often been proposed for very dense areas, in order to exploit a total volume of space. Joining the horizontal and vertical flows is not easy, since a change of mode is necessary there. But in some of our downtown areas, as in Minneapolis, we are beginning to build an extended three-dimensional grid of second-floor walkways and escalators. Other cities, such as Toronto, are building underground networks. Subsurface shopping centers are common enough. While they protect pedestrians from the weather, these passages tend to be oppressive and disorienting, and may drain off the vitality of surface streets.

The radioconcentric form has been the chief competitor of the regular grid. It appears frequently in historic cities, often without any regular concentric components. It is well suited to flows in a city with a dominant single center, but to the degree that flows are not central, the fit is poor. If the concentric routes are missing, as may often occur in an older city, then travel across the city is awkward, and central congestion may be intense. At the regional scale, many freeway systems still follow this radial model. See, for example, the continued dominance of the model in the Boston expressway system, or even that of Los Angeles. It may be that a rectangular grid, distorted to fit local circumstances, is a much better model for large freeway systems serving extensive urbanized regions.

The axial network, described above under the baroque form, approximates a rough triangular grid. Although this form has substantial advantages in other ways, it is difficult for general traffic, since the multiple at-grade intersections are vicious. For slow foot or carriage traffic, it may be quite workable, however. For ceremonial processions, the axial network is a splendid device. It is interesting that, at a national scale, the interstate highway system in the more developed areas of the United States follows the triangular grid form rather closely.

While grid and radial are the two principal pattern models, other concepts refer to the general texture of channels, rather than to their total pattern. The capillary system, described above, for example, is often seen in old, dense, pedestrian cities, particularly where the competition for living space presses on access space to the limit. This is a hierarchy in pure form, where each minor access street is a dead end, and is connected to the whole only through a succession of merging branches. The overall pattern is a maze, which pervades the total space. Privacy is maintained and through traffic excluded, at the cost of enforced detours. Today, a pattern of this type is suited only to small enclaves used only by local people and occasional visitors.

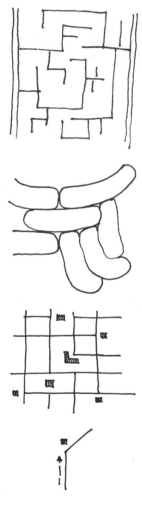

At this smaller scale, many other patterns are possible, including the familiar "kidney" shape, which is the result of fitting long superblocks to rolling ground by means of curving streets. Local streets within a grid can also be interrupted by T-intersections and swastika patterns, to discourage through traffic without creating dead ends. The T-joints have the further advantage of providing definite visual closure to the street and good positions for important buildings. Similar visual results can be obtained by bending the street sharply at special places.

C. *Modal separations*. Every city uses more than one transport mode: at very least, foot and pack animal, or foot and boat. Modern cities use a vast range of modes, most of which travel together in the street channel. To some extent, these modes are separated by use of the sidewalk or bicycle lane, but conflicts persist. Much thought has been devoted to ways of separating foot movements from autos and trucks, with cycles and transit vehicles falling now with one, now with the other of these two groups.

Buchanan 1963

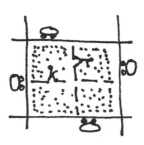

One idea has been to set up bounded areas within which motor vehicles would not be allowed to penetrate. Such pedestrian precincts are frequently created in historic center cities. The superblock interior is another example, the wilderness zone a third. The privacy, quiet, and safety of such zones is much valued. Certain standard problems always arise in conjunction with these schemes: the carriage of goods, the entrance of emergency vehicles, the relation to transit, and the relation of the parked vehicle to its owner. These have limited the size of the areas to which exclusion can be applied, but have not dimmed the popularity of the idea. A compromise concept is to allow autos to intrude at very low speeds, while giving the pedestrian an unrestricted right-of-way in the entire street space. Drivers must proceed cautiously, like waiters in a crowded restaurant, since they are made legally liable for any accident. It takes ingenuity to achieve local safety and quiet without serious loss of individual mobility, but it has been done.

The other form of modal separation is linear. A path is restricted to one form of movement: the freeway, the parkway, the bus lane, the railroad line, the bikeway, the bridal path, the footpath. Once specialized, a channel can be efficiently designed to fit its mode, and many conflicts can be avoided. Finding a new right-of-way for a separate mode can be difficult, and the intersections between modes are troublesome, unless they are grade-separated at major expense. The idea of the bikeway, the reserved transit lane, or the inner block, underground, or elevated pedway, are all part of the intellectual baggage of the planner. A multiplication of these separations, however—especially in crowded central areas—may not only be difficult to accomplish, but, once accomplished, force activities to provide multiple entrances, and cause an existing multifunctional street to lose its importance and vitality. Therefore, modal specialization requires a careful study of site and a good prediction of types of future flow. It is not a universal cure.

D. *Managing travel distance.* Reducing transportation time is the ideal, since it is considered to be unproductive and unsatisfying idleness. A close

See fig. 93

93 Pedestrians are protected in the broad center strip of Las Ramblas, a famous boulevard in Barcelona.

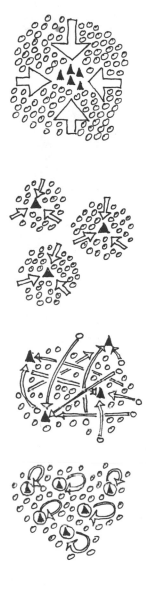

proximity of work and home is recommended, to keep travel time to a minimum. Such proximity is rare today, except in company towns, with all *their* disadvantages. A few people will locate their residence close to their work by preference, or will work at home. More will accept a relatively long commutation in order to live in a better neighborhood. If one is limited to work which is near home, one's occupational opportunities are sharply curtailed. The shortening of the average home-to-work trip may be an unattainable goal. It may even be doubtful that it would increase production, if it were achieved. It may be more important to arrange the city so that more people can live close to their work if they choose to do so, and then arrange for the travel experience itself to be a pleasure. Perhaps travel could even be a social or a productive event?

We have also hoped that the new electronic communications would shorten or abolish the trips from home to work, school, shop, or friends. People can now work in their living rooms and be in touch with the central office. They can shop by telephone, learn via programmed video instruction, and be within easy call of distant kin. It is not clear, however, that these new devices are actually reducing urban traffic flows, or will do so. The introduction of the telephone at an earlier date seems to have had the effect of expanding the communications of the ordinary family, without reducing their moving about. Moreover, the prospect of families spending their lives secluded in their houses, in rapt dialogue with their videophones, is slightly chilling. It is just possible that transport may not be the utter waste that we all consider it to be.

E. *Channel prototypes.* There are a number of models for the design of the channels themselves, streets in particular. Now we verge on the site planning scale, but the models are worth listing, if only because they have been the frequent subject of city designs, are typically under public control, and have so much to do with the quality of a settlement.

Perhaps the most influential model has been the boulevard: the broad, arterial street, with one or more rows of trees on either side, wide sidewalks, and possibly parallel service drives. Important buildings front along its flanks. It can carry heavy traffic, and yet provide many amenities. Wherever uses are sufficiently intense, the model works well, even if it requires a broad right-of-way. Empty of people, or barren of its trees, it is a discouraging sight. The boulevard has also been used in the form of the residential avenue, along which imposing houses sit behind deep lawns. The nuisances of traffic have killed this variant, and its remaining examples are now mostly converted to institutional use. The boulevard has a fine application along a waterfront or a large park, where both the passing traffic and the important uses on one side of the street can enjoy the land- or waterscape before them, while the city gains a memorable facade.

The modern concept of a major street is the familiar freeway, with its divided lanes of traffic, landscaped central island and shoulders, and access only at grade-separated intersections. Traffic flows easily and enjoys a bland natural setting. Passing through a city, the road is often depressed, removing the traffic from view and allowing city streets to pass overhead. One district is divided from another as if by an ancient moat, and the driver is denied any view of what he is passing through. If not depressed, the road is elevated above the city streets, which improves the drivers' view, but imposes even more of his noise on the abutters. The division of the city is more severe, and there are dark, unusable spaces under the roadway. While the freeway in the country is often a beautiful accomplishment of modern engineering, its insertion into the urban fabric has never been properly solved. Proposals have been made for the joint development of roadway and flanking use in one single, designed structure, but these have never been implemented. Tunnels remove the traffic nuisance. They are expensive, and for the driver are dreary in the extreme.*

The parkway, or motor road designed for pleasure movement, on the other hand, has been done well in many instances. Here we have a model that responds to terrain and can take particular advan-

See fig. 94

See fig. 95

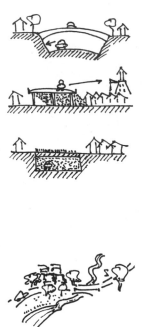

See fig. 96

*No one has ever designed a fine tunnel, whether for cars, subway trains, or people on foot. This is an important gap in our store of prototypes.

See fig. 97

See fig. 98

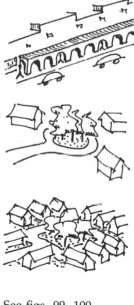

See figs. 99, 100

See fig. 101

tage of a linear natural feature, such as a stream. It is unfortunate that its opportunities for sequential visual and aural experience have not been exploited, as well. But the greater difficulty is that most of these pleasureways have been taken over by heavy general traffic, except in some of the national parks.

The pedestrian promenade, designed with the same motive as the parkway, but for a different mode, is today rarely seen, although it may be re-emerging (in confined form) in the central malls of our shopping centers. With our reawakened interest in walking and jogging, might it be possible to build promenades once again? The pedestrian shopping street, on the other hand, is very much alive, and not only in the shopping centers. Furnishing, lighting, and intensifying such pedestrian ways has recently been a prime effort of urban design. We still have things to learn, however, about achieving the humanization of the city sidewalk. The continuous arcade is one historic device still useful for important streets, since it provides weather protection, traffic protection, and a means of unifying uncoordinated street facades. Arcades may be built into the abutting structures, or may allow them to project over the public walk. With some problems of jointing, they can be added to the fronts of existing buildings. In their shelter, the walk can be used for many social purposes.

Strict control of the design of the facades of diverse buildings along a street, which gives many historic cities their special character, is rarely attempted today except along special avenues of power. The old device of building the facades together with the street itself, and then allowing private builders to construct the remainder of the structure behind those facades, is no longer used.

We also have several familiar and workable models for minor streets: the curving suburban street, the cul-de-sac with its planted turnaround, the close, and the fenced and planted English square around which the residential street divides. But we are bereft of ideas at the scales in between these major and minor extremes: the chaotic commercial strip, the barren arterial, with all its empty turning lanes and half-used frontages, or the arid

94 A waterfront boulevard makes a handsome face for a city, and permits bathers, strollers, drivers, and apartment dwellers to enjoy the water simultaneously. Here we look north from the Oak Street beach along the "Gold Coast" of Chicago, fronting on Lake Michigan. The older mansions of the wealthy have largely been replaced by a line of luxury apartments, yet the lakefront is open to all the ordinary citizens who live behind that facade.

95 The view from the road is not very inspiring when an urban expressway is set below street level.

96 It is difficult to create good sense in underground places. The central subway station in Boston has been rebuilt since this dispiriting picture was taken, and yet even today the station is oppressive and confusing.

97 The George Washington Parkway in Virginia. A split-lane expressway can be well fitted to the ground and convey a fine sense of motion.

98 The street arcade is an old device for protecting the pedestrian while maintaining the life of the street.

99 The innovative use of the cul-de-sac in Radburn, New Jersey, created the car-free "superblock." and allowed the separation of motor and foot entrances to the house.

100 Louisburg Square, on Beacon Hill in Boston, in the nineteenth century. It remains a prime American example of the English residential square, fenced and gated, surrounded by the fine town houses of its proprietors.

101 A typical arterial street in an industrial zone: ill-defined, ill-cared-for, open to rapid change of use—a low-value, single-function space.

industrial route, almost lost among its goods yards and chain-link fences.

Pages could be devoted to terminals, the other essential element of the circulation system. I will do no more than lament the faded grandeur of the city railroad station, the crowded shabbiness of the contemporary bus station, the worldwide confusion and inhumanity of the modern airport, the barren discomfort of the parking lot, and the desolation, disorientation, and terror of any parking garage. Alas, we cannot even find a comfortable place to wait for the bus!

A final set of spatial patterns clusters around questions of public open space:

A. *The distribution of open space.* There are two contrasting points of view about this distribution. In the one, open spaces should be concentrated and continuous, in order to "give form" to the remainder of the city. Thus they will be linked together, and by their size they will afford a true relief to crowded city conditions. In the other view, open spaces should be small and widely dispersed throughout the city fabric, to make them as accessible as possible. In large part, the divergence of these views is due to different conceptions of the function of open space: whether it is a normal and integral place of daily life, like a front stoop or a playground, or whether it is an experience in contrast to city life, which sets it off in thought, and, on particular occasions, in experience. One faction sees open spaces as places in which to carry out certain normal activities, such as conversing or playing ball, while the other thinks of them as places of special quality, which offer an important experience in which one should be totally immersed, acting and perceiving in a different way than during one's usual routine. The latter proponents also believe that a good environment is one in which the parts of a settlement have distinguishing characteristics, such as dense city versus open country. This distinction makes them memorable, and allows one to choose one's habitat. Large open spaces are useful for creating that contrast. By defining the built-up edge, they give a recognizable form to the city as a whole. The opposing view is

436
Open space
continuous or
dispersed

See figs. 102, 103,
104, 105

that such contrast is not important, and that most people do not think of a city as a map shape, defined at its edges.

Indeed, continuous open space may be an ineffective definition of city form, unless that space is itself a powerful landscape: an ocean, a mountain range, or a great river. Moreover, linking open spaces directly together can be unnecessary, if adequate walks and bikeways have been provided elsewhere, since few people make continuous journeys from one open space to another. But open space has many functions, among which are immersion, contrast, and the rural experience, and also immediate daily use for normal activity. A good settlement will include the total range. These two views are therefore complementary, rather than alternative, concepts. In a concrete case, with limited resources, the issue may be real enough, however. For example, it may be necessary to decide whether to enlarge a suburban regional park or to create a series of center-city playgrounds.

B. *Map shapes.* Among the models for distributing large open spaces in a settlement the greenbelt, the wedge, and the network stand out. Being large-scale patterns, they are allied to the large city form patterns with which we began. The first conceives of open space as an enclosure, which surrounds a settlement and prevents its further growth. It is allied to the satellite form and the concepts of optimum city size. While often discussed in the garden city theory, it has been less often applied. When applied, it has been difficult to maintain, since the immediate periphery of any growing city is always the most favorable place to locate new activities. London's greenbelt has required a major administrative effort to secure, and in doing so has imposed additional costs on the development forced to jump beyond the barrier. Undoubtedly it provides a special amenity for the suburbanites nearby. It would be interesting to know how many city residents make use of it, or are aware of its presence. Havana's Cordón was achieved by complete nationalization of the land. The greenbelt of Greenbelt, Maryland, ironically enough, was first invaded by war housing, and later sold off when the government disposed of the town.

Lynch 1972

M. Williams

See fig. 106

102 The old city railroad station gave a certain dignity to waiting and traveling.

103 But the city bus terminal is crowded and shabby.

104 And the airport is clean, empty, and cold, an alien place in which to sit or to run for the plane.

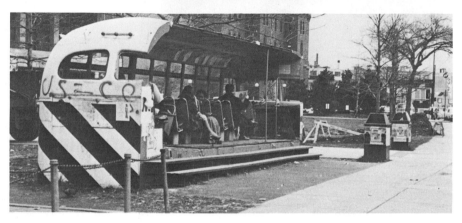

105 Waiting for the bus is no pleasure—wondering when it will come and how to get one's packages on board—although the ride may be interesting enough if one gets a seat. Bus shelters are a help, but the problem has not been solved.

106 Picnicking in Epping Forest, a part of the great greenbelt that surrounds London—a belt preserved at substantial cost, but used with pleasure by its adjacent population.

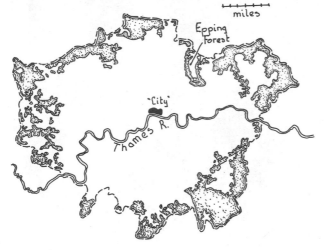

miles

Epping Forest

"City"

Thames R.

See fig. 78

The "green wedge" idea is almost the reverse of the greenbelt concept. In this view, open space should penetrate into the heart of a settlement and radiate outward to the periphery. Thus all developed land will have open space nearby, although there will be less of it toward the center, as the rays converge. Open spaces are linked together, and connect to the rural environs of a city, however distant. Yet growth at the periphery, along the major access routes, is never blocked. Clearly, the wedge idea is linked to the star form discussed above, but it may also be applied in the linear city. The idea has not often been carried out in practice, although it occurs when natural radial features, such as rivers, penetrate the city and offer the opportunity. The general plan for Moscow provides for wedges of this kind, penetrating the entire metropolitan region. Where circumferentials occur, the green wedge may be as difficult to keep inviolate as the greenbelt. Moreover, the way in which the relationship to open space changes, as one moves from center to periphery, must be accounted for. But in a large settlement, the wedge form brings open space closer to everyone.

The open network concept, naturally allied with the grid form city, is less clearly developed, and nowhere applied to my knowledge. This model abandons the idea of giving form to the whole by any pattern of green edges, and focuses on an equitable distribution of open space throughout the fabric, coupled with a general interconnection of the open space system. The open space grid is the complement of the street grid, set off half a phase, so that it runs through the centers of street blocks, and crosses between intersections. Thus one can easily reach the open system from any part of the city, and move anywhere along it. As the complement of the street grid, the open grid could be used for recreational travel: foot, horse, skis, bicycles, or the like. Connections can be pinched down to narrow ways near the major roads, so that little prime development land is usurped, while the open space expands in the interstices of the street grid. As in the "green wedge," activity spaces for daily use can be placed along the edges of the open network, while larger and more "rural" areas might be found deeper inside. Since the model is an interconnected system, and yet intimately meshed with the entire urbanized area, it presupposes comprehensive control, and may require grade separations where it crosses the major streets.

C. *Open space classes.* There is a set of open space classifications, which are commonly accepted as models for design:

1. *The regional park.* This is a large rural area, at the periphery of a metropolitan region, which is meant for use by people making full or half day trips on weekends or holidays. It must be large and varied enough to absorb mass access, transit, and parking, and to provide for a variety of activities for all ages, plus natural landscapes for hiking and perhaps camping. Water sports, picknicking, and field games are some of the explicit activities most commonly provided for. Traditionally, about 600 acres is thought to be a minimum size, and the area should have some special natural character of its own, preferably including a stream or lake. Users should be within a half hour to an hour of such a park, whether by car, bus, foot, or cycle.

2. *The urban park.* This is a much smaller park landscape, well within the urban area and visually a part of it, which is intended for daily local use of a rather leisurely and informal kind: walking, running, sitting out, picknicking, and informal games. The landscape of the English "park" is the prototype: clumps of trees set in meadows, with winding walks, ponds, and occasional shrubberies or flower beds. This landscape is carefully designed and highly managed. These parks, so familiar to us, are found in the center city and in some older residential neighborhoods. They have typical problems of maintenance and overuse, conflicts between users, and safety at night. Nevertheless, they are a much loved urban feature. In places, they become the central image and meeting place of a city (the Boston Common; New York's Central Park; the London parks). At other times, they are the important focus of some local area, as in the "neighborhood commons" concept.

3. *The square or plaza.* This is a different model for an urban open space, one taken primarily from the historic European cities. Books on city design

are full of its possibilities, at times it has almost appeared that urban design might simply be a matter of plaza design. The plaza is intended as an activity focus, at the heart of some intensive urban area. Typically, it will be paved, enclosed by high-density structures, and surrounded by streets, or in contact with them. It contains features meant to attract groups of people and to facilitate meetings: fountains, benches, shelters, and the like. Planting may or may not be prominent. The Italian piazza is the most common prototype. In some North American cities, where the density of people on the street has been high enough, this form has succeeded handsomely. Elsewhere, these borrowed plazas can be rather melancholy and empty.

4. *Linear parks.* Other open spaces are designed primarily for movement, whether on foot, on horseback, in carriages, or in cars. Linear in form, they lead from one destination to the next. A river or stream provides a very natural setting for such a park, and so we frequently find river parks in cities, with the stream as the central feature, paths along its banks, and trees and shrubs masking the urban development along the edge. River parks may be large enough to contain a major road, as Rock Creek Park in Washington, or be as narrow and intimate as the famous Paseo del Rio in San Antonio. Similar linear open spaces can be disposed along an old canal or a waterfront.

Elsewhere, the dominant motive is one of pleasurable motion, and of seeing and being seen, rather than the experience of nature. The nineteenth century saw the creation of many promenades, intended for fashionable carriages, of which the Viale dei Colle in Florence is a splendid example. Planted promenades for strollers are an older legacy. The idea was carried forward to the parkway, intended for automobiles driven for pleasure. But under the pressure of traffic, these fine parkways have degenerated into general-purpose highways.

The design model for linear parks has either been the winding stream valley, flanked by woods and curving with the stream or around landscape incidents, or the avenue, lined with regular rows of trees and leading straight to some visible destination. Whether to exclude the flanking urban development from sight, or, if not, how to integrate it into the park scenery, has been one question. Many linear parks fail to accomplish either. While they are designed for movement, it is very rare to find a linear park that exploits the sequence of visual events, except by accident. The craft of designing for the moving experience in the city is not yet mature, although the Japanese long ago created compact "stroll gardens" in a limited space. The cycleways and pedestrian ways, so often shown in green on contemporary designs, are only lines of segregated movement, and are rarely conceived as linear open spaces or an unfolding succession of views.

5. *Playgrounds and playfields.* This is a class of open spaces which are intended primarily for use in the games of children, teenagers, and active adults. Sizes, features, and locations are based on the organized games thought to be appropriate to the various age groups. There is a large literature on these standards. At least two subclasses are distinguished: the *playground* for children up to early adolescence, which is to be attached to the elementary school and should be within easy walking distance of all houses, and the *playfield* for the more extensive and organized games of older children and adults. The playfield must be larger, and can be more distant. In theory, it is attached to a high school. To these two is sometimes added the *play lot*, intended for the informal play of preschool children, and meant to be very close to the house, for easy parental supervision.

The design of these features is tied to the active games which are presumed to occupy a child's leisure, and so they are rather rigidly laid out, furnished with standard play equipment, and favor flat, open land. They can be noisy and rather barren in appearance. The direct link to the school, and the substantial flat area demanded, often pose problems for school location.

These spaces are used, and it is clearly important to provide for standard, organized games. Yet playgrounds may not be as central to the lives of our children as we formerly supposed. The model can be criticized for a neglect of the role of manage-

See fig. 107

ment, for its narrow view of the scope of the child's activity, and for the way its equipment and layout impose (or try to impose) adult conceptions of play. Originally, the playground idea grew out of the active, supervised use of large city parks, which was intended to promote the health and broad education of both children and adults. In focusing on games, segegated ages, and physical equipment, the model has gained clarity, but may have lost some of its original importance.

6. *Wastelands and adventure playgrounds.* An alternative model of children's play has recently evolved out of studies of how children actually use the city, and its waste corners in particular—those areas where adult control is weaker and children are freer to act in their own ways. From this has arisen the model of the "adventure" (or "junk" or "action") playground, where a flat space and a large collection of discarded material are furnished, and children are left free to construct what they will: clubhouses, play equipment, imaginary environments, or whatever. A supervisor prevents the building of any dangerous structures, mediates conflicts, and provides technical construction advice, if asked. There must also be some mechanism for occasional clearance, so that new groups can build for themselves. The resulting landscapes are imaginative and intricate. The children are deeply engaged. Neighboring adults are likely to consider the place dangerous, and an eyesore, and so it must be screened off. The children are learning by doing, which was part of the original motives of the playground movement. Much depends on the quality of the supervision. If it is sensitive enough, a relatively small space can provide for a great range of activity, including nature study and secluded niches for dreaming.

While the adventure playground focuses on the intensive, supervised use of defined plots of ground, the concept has spread to thinking about how children use the city as a whole: streets, alleys, rooftops, yards, shops, and so on. Models are developing for the multifunctional use of the sidewalk, for example, or of the role of waste and abandoned lands in child development. None of these are direct substitutes for the activities of the

107 Given the means, children make their own worlds.

organized playground. They are extensions of our thinking about the child in the city. They conflict with typical adult concept of safety, control, visual tidiness, and the place of children.

Certain models for city design refer to the temporal organization of a city, rather than to its spatial pattern. These are strategies, or successions of actions:

A. *The management of growth.* Concepts of ideal city size have already been referred to. This is only one aspect of a larger set of concepts: how settlement growth should be managed. In one view, assuming that there are optimum city sizes, growth should occur in one settlement after another. Let each fill to its optimum size, and then divert growth to a new one. The result is a series of cities of best size, in which very few, at any one time, are racked with the agonies of expansion. But it turns out to be difficult to turn growth on and off in so decisive a fashion, not to speak of the problems of determining optimum size.

The opposite view is that there is no reliable evidence about good size, and nothing wrong with growth if it is well organized. In fact, growth is the sign of health and prosperity, while its cessation is stagnation. The proper strategy, then, is to encourage growth, while periodically removing obsolete tissue, and making sure by preplanning that new areas will be of good quality and well integrated to the old.

Still another view is that, while it is true that there is no such thing as optimum size, nevertheless too rapid a growth can cause severe disruption, and should be avoided. It is the *rate* of growth that is crucial, and not the resulting size at any one time. Therefore, the proper strategy is to determine an optimum rate, and to endeavor to keep growth near that optimum for all settlements. The concept is intuitively attractive as a way of managing a dynamic situation. To date, however, little work has been done on determining optimum rates of growth for different situations. That there are such optima seems reasonable, but they may in the end prove as elusive as optima for size. Nevertheless, many suburban communities are today taking steps

Thompson

to limit their rates of growth, well in advance (as usual) of theory.

A variation of this stand is to say that difficulties do not arise simply when growth is too rapid or too slow, but when successive thresholds are reached—points at which major new infrastructure is required, when new areas for expansion must be opened up, or where new services are suddenly needed. Costs do not rise evenly along with size increase, but tend to jump at critical points. Breaking through such a threshold inflicts a special burden, with little concomitant gain. Thresholds will vary for different cities. Once a threshold is determined, the proper strategy is to restrain growth below it as long as possible, and then move rapidly beyond it, in order to reap the benefits of the added cost as quickly as possible. Thus a small town whose houses use septic tanks may have to install an entire new central sewer system when it reaches a certain size. Knowing this, the town fathers should strive to keep the town small enough to make a sewage plant unnecessary. If goaded beyond that point, they should encourage a surge in growth, to acquire enough residents to pay for the new plant. Proper growth, then, is a series of leaps and ambles. The model is sensible, but it turns out to apply best to small settlements, where single public investments loom large, or to cases of extraordinary expenditure. In larger, more complex settlements, there are many thresholds of growth, and these are generally so uncoordinated that no one point is truly critical. The threshold model is not incompatible with the growth rate model. They can be used together.

It is notable that all these models deal with the problems of growth, and none with decline. Decline is as familiar to us as growth, and usually poses more severe problems. We dislike to confront it. Most solutions to problems of decline are attempts to turn it into growth. We have no conceptual models about managing decline in any optimum way. This is one of the troublesome difficulties of the "zero-growth" idea. Since absolute stasis is a balance too fine to be maintained, a lapse into decline is as likely to happen as a fall into growth, when one tries to keep close to the zero point.

Without convincing models for good decline, the possibility of incurring it induces panic.

B. *Strategies of development and renewal.* Certain models of city design deal with patterns for successive actions, when changing a place by renewal or by new development. One of them takes its cue from an observation of how cities have experienced "waves" of change, waves that seem to ripple outward from the center, crests of population density, of ethnic locations, and use successions. An effective strategy, therefore, is to begin at some point (usually the most accessible one, or where it is easiest to start), and then to advance changes outward continuously, until the entire area is covered. Each successive area of change is supported by the adjacent area last renewed. Current opportunity lies at the margin. This seems so obvious to us as not to be worth mentioning. Being beneath notice, the model has a pervasive effect. Much real estate development and pricing is based on it. If the outward spread is radial, however, more and more ground must be renewed, to maintain a constant outward rate of change.

An accompanying idea is that of the wave barrier. If change propagates like a wave, then when one wants to limit it one makes a barrier to check the wave, or to divert it in some other direction. The barrier may be a heavily trafficked street or railroad line, a cutting off of access,* a natural movement barrier, a large open space, or a rise in elevation. Such barriers frequently occur by accident, but they are also deliberately created and vigorously defended. Once breached, they are quickly abandoned. The wave of change seems to wash over them, quite in accordance with the hydraulic model. This is the spatial analogy of the temporal idea of threshold.

Another model is the focal point, or "infective," strategy. According to this image, change is best effected by building a number of new foci throughout an area. If these points are strategically placed, and strong enough to survive for a time on their own, then they will "infect" the areas around

*As was done by the land developers who separated the "good" south side of Boston's Beacon Hill from its infamous north slope.

them, and cause the whole to change. This was the
baroque strategy, which relied on the creation of
new focal points to renew a city. L'Enfant did the
same in his plan of Washington, deliberately separating the White House and the Capitol from
Georgetown, so that each would be an incentive to
the growth of a larger territory. The same idea
appears, at the regional scale, in "growth pole
theory." The model can also apply to unwanted
change: the presence of some undesirable use (a
porno shop) or a condition (a building in disrepair)
is thought likely to infect and degrade its entire
setting.

The model is doubtful, since cities are not
organisms. Whether a new focal point will cause its
environs to change, or will itself succumb, or will
survive as a local anomaly, depends on detailed
relations of use and perception.

Still another strategy, perhaps, is the network.
First, provide an area with a network of essential
infrastructure, such as highways, boulevards, sewers, electric power, schools, and the like. Private
development, which depends on these coordinated
services, will then fill in the remainder without
further public intervention. Clearly, this is akin to
the "supports" model of John Habraken and other
enthusiasts of self-help housing. It is also reflected   Habraken
in David Crane's idea of the "capital web."   Crane
Whether it will work depends on the degree to
which the chosen infrastructure is in fact a key. In
the case of new suburban growth in the United
States, for example, the locations of highways and
sewer lines do indeed seem to govern the location
of new housing. But the effect will not be so powerful in built-up areas, which are already well provided with a utility net.

C. *Permanence.* According to the prevailing
idea, that which lasts is good. Permanence means a
saving of material resources, a minimizing of disorder, and strong links with the past. It means that
the original thing was well-fitted to its function.
Stone, and other "eternal" materials, settled
populations, and the maintenance of form and custom are all commendable. Discarded things and
behaviors are losses. New objects and new ways of
living, being untested, expose us to dangerous

risks. This is probably a majority view today, in regard to the cities we live in. If a firm or a family or a building or a district or a custom has endured, then it must be a good one.

The opposing view (which used to be considered the North American outlook) is that value lies in change. The failure to change not only makes it impossible to respond to the inevitable flux of events, but it is also a failure to improve. Old buildings are generally obsolete buildings: old habits are constrictive. The initial costs and recurring maintenance costs of permanent things far outweigh the resources needed to replace them periodically with new materials. Cities should be built of light, temporary structures, so that people can easily change them as their lives change. Historical associations can be maintained symbolically, rather than by acres of cumbersome buildings. Young people, in particular, need the opportunity to explore new possibilities. Early in the century, at least, this was the dominant mood of the avant-garde intellectual. Not today.

Both models are applied indiscriminately. Once more, each concept is apt in certain situations, inapt in others. This will vary not only with the external situation—that is, with the value of relict buildings, or with the relative discounted costs of temporary versus permanent structures, or with the rate at which function is actually changing—but also with internal feelings about change and stability. Given the heterogeneity of large-city populations, it is evident that our cities must contain both stable and temporary environments. Thus it may be proper to zone different areas, not simply for their use or physical form, but also for their rates of change.

Nevertheless, the idea of physical conservation is taking hold more and more. It has progressed from the preservation of singular historic landmarks to that of notable historic districts, and is moving thence to the preservation of older areas of good character, but without a "special" history or outstanding architectural quality. To this is being joined a separate image of preserving the "natural" ecology of any region, that is, that presumably stable and beneficient interrelation of living organ-

isms which approximates the balance which most
recently existed, prior to any major urban development. As ecologists turn their attention to the city,
and the historians turn to "everyday" areas, their
agendas begin to merge. To this can be added a
concern about the uprooting of social communities.
If these concerns can be fused successfully, they
will be a potent conservative force.

Preservation is itself shifting toward conservation, that is, toward an attempt to manage change so
as to maintain links with the past and to conserve
resources which still have present value: rehabilitation rather than historic reconstruction, the recycling of structures and of waste materials, rather than
preservation or abhorrence. There is some interest
in "soft" forms, that is, in ways of building which
will be responsive to future piecemeal change. To
the degree that these concepts reveal a desire to
accept and manage change, they transcend the
earlier arguments about temporariness and
permanence.

D. *The timing of use.* A final set of temporal
models deals with the timing of activity. The idea of
scheduling the time of an action is itself an important concept. Activities may be prohibited at certain
times to prevent conflict or profanation, as by "blue
laws." They may be separated in time to alleviate
congestion, or be brought together in time to allow
connections and a sufficient density of use, as by
the establishment of market days. Schedules are
established to permit the coordination and predict-
ability of service. Activity timing is as essential a
part of city design as activity spacing, but it is less
often consciously manipulated.

We have tended toward a greater precision of
activity timing, and greater time specialization:
weekends, office hours, peak travel, and the like.
Many spaces are used intensively for certain
periods, and then stand empty for longer times.
The crush and emptiness of a city's financial district
is a cliché of urban journalism. Similar phenomena
occur in transport systems, entertainment districts,
parks, and many other places.

Some will argue that this spasmodic use is
quite wasteful. If we planned the timing of use as
well as its spacing, we could carry on our lives with

Browne

a great saving of resources. Moreover, it is psychologically depressing and even dangerous if an area of the city, particularly a central one, lies unused much of the time. Thus the central district, at least, should be designed so that it will be "lighted"—be in active use throughout the 24 hours, or at least for a good portion of them. One part of the city would not be "dead" at night, and people would be free to be active at any hour of their choice. Of course, they could enjoy a similar freedom simply if *some* area of the settlement were active at every hour, even if all were closed most of the time. But in order to enjoy this particular freedom, one would require flexible transport and a good knowledge of the prevailing timing.

Time specialization and time integration each have their place. Resources may be saved or wasted by either one, but it is true that we do not pay sufficient attention to the role of time in city design. As to the "deadness" of certain city zones: buildings are not psychologically depressed by being closed down. "Lifelessness" is only hard for people to bear, when they enter these closed zones. "Lighted" areas and sharply time-specialized ones can both be pleasant. It is the ambiguously timed areas, feebly active at times, but never completely shut down, which are the problem.

This catalog is not an encyclopedia. Its cutoff is arbitrary. As one goes down to the site planning scale, for example, the listing could unfold marvelously, as we paraded models of streets, building types, site plans, and small open spaces.

It is apparent, however, how rich the catalog is in certain areas—such as housing and open space design—and how lean in others, such as workplaces, streetscapes, and terminals, as well as the form of process, temporal organization, and models for decline. Even where the models are numerous, there are many uncertainties about their impacts, or about the situations they are best adapted to. Developing and analyzing prototypes would be a useful field of urban design research.

Second, it may be apparent that many of these models are held as articles of faith. They are set in opposition to other models on extremely general grounds, as though there were only one correct way to build a city. In truth, models are no more than alternatives. Some are useful in special circumstances. At other times, diverse ones can be used simultaneously. A good designer has them all in mind, with all their different strengths and weaknesses, knows the context in which they are apt, and employs them flexibly and willfully. This presentation has been defective, moreover, because the models were too often stripped of the institutions of management that make them viable, and were described as if independent of the culture and political economy in which they must be applied. But since the presentation has been mechanical, it can at least be summarized mechanically—as a simple outline:

1. General patterns
A. The star or asterisk
B. Satellite cities
C. The linear city
D. The rectangular grid city
E. Other grid forms
F. The baroque axial network
G. The lacework
H. The "inward" city
I. The nested city
J. Current imaginings

2. Central place patterns
A. Patterns of centers
B. Specialized and all-purpose centers
C. Linear centers
D. Neighborhood centers
E. The shopping center
F. Mobile centers

3. Textures
A. Cells
B. Sprawl and compaction
C. Segregation and mix
D. Perceived spatial textures
E. Housing types
    1. High slabs
    2. Towers in the green
    3. Dense walkups

"If there was a Paradise it
included the whole world,
which must be completely
made over if we are to find
and enjoy it once more."
Fernando Ortiz

Bibliography

Charles Abrams, *Man's Struggle for Shelter in an Urbanizing World*. Cambridge, Mass.: The MIT Press, 1964.

Jānīt Abū-Lughd, *Cairo: 1001 Years of the City Victorious*. Princeton, N.J.: Princeton University Press, 1971.

Jānīt Abū-Lughd, "The Legitimacy of Comparisons in Comparative Urban Studies." Mimeo. School of Architecture and Urban Planning, University of California, Los Angeles, 1974.

Robert M. Adams, "The Natural History of Urbanism," in *The Fitness of Man's Environment*. Washington, D.C.: Smithsonian Institution, 1968.

Christopher Alexander, "The City Is Not a Tree," *Architectural Forum*, Vol. 122, Nos. 1 and 2, April/May 1965.

Christopher Alexander, *Notes on the Synthesis of Form*. Cambridge, Mass.: Harvard University Press, 1964.

Christopher Alexander, Sara Ishikawa, and Murray Silverstein, *A Pattern Language: Towns, Buildings, Construction*. New York: Oxford University Press, 1975.

William Alonso, *Location and Land Use*. Cambridge, Mass.: Harvard University Press, 1964.

Alan Altshuler, "The Goals of Comprehensive Planning," *Journal of the American Institute of Planners*, Vol. 31, No. 3, August 1965.

American Public Health Association, *Planning the Neighborhood*. Chicago: Public Administration Service, 1960.

G. F. Andrews, *Maya Cities: Placemaking and Urbanization*. Norman, Okla.: University of Oklahoma Press, 1975.

S. Angel and G. M. Hyman, "Urban Spatial Interac-
tion." London, Center for Environmental Studies, Working Paper #69, July 1971.

R. P. Appelbaum, "City Size and Urban Life: A Preliminary Inquiry into Some Consequences of Growth in American Cities," *Urban Affairs Quarterly*, Vol. 12, No. 2, December 1976.

Donald Appleyard, *Planning a Pluralist City: Conflicting Realities in Ciudad Guayana*. Cambridge, Mass.: MIT Press, 1976.

Maurice Ash, "The Linear City Fad," *Town and Country Planning*, Vol. 34, No. 3, March 1966.

William Ashworth, *The Genesis of Modern British Town Planning*. London: Routledge & Kegan Paul, 1968 (orig. 1954).

R. H. Atkin, "Urban Structure Research Reports II and III," Department of Mathematics, University of Essex (England), August 1973.

A. Baburov, *The Ideal Socialist City*, trans. R. N. Watkins. New York: Braziller, 1971.

G. Bachelard, *The Poetics of Space*, trans. Maria Jolas. Boston: Beacon Press, 1969 (orig. 1958).

William Baer and T. Banerjee, "Environmental Research, Environmental Design and the 'Applicability Gap,' " in Peter Suedfeld et al. (eds.), *The Behavioral Basis for Design, Book 2: Session Summaries and Papers*. Stroudsburg, Penna.: Dowden, Hutchinson & Ross, 1977.

Mark Baldassare, *Residential Crowding in Urban America*. Berkeley, Calif.: University of California Press, 1979.

Reyner Banham, *Los Angeles: The Architecture of Four Ecologies*. London: Allen Lane, 1971.

Roger Barker. *Ecological Psychology: Concepts and Methods for Studying the Environment of Human Behavior*. Stanford, Calif.: Stanford University Press, 1968.

Julian Beinart, "Government-Built Cities and People-Made Places," *Architectural Yearbook*, Vol. 13, 1971, pp. 185–207.

Leonardo Benevolo, *The Origins of Modern Town Planning*. London: Routledge & Kegan Paul, 1967; Cambridge, Mass.: The MIT Press, 1971.

B. J. L. Berry, *Land Use, Urban Form, and Environmental Quality*. Chicago: Department of Geography, University of Chicago, 1974.

B. J. L. Berry and F. E. Horton, *Geographical Perspectives on Urban Systems*. Englewood Cliffs, N. J.: Prentice-Hall, 1970.

B. J. L. Berry and J. D. Kasarda, *Contemporary Urban Ecology*. New York: Macmillan, 1977.

Stefano Bianca, *Architektur und Lebensform im islamischen Stadtwesen*, 2d ed. Zurich: Verlag für Architektur Artemis, 1979.

Stefano Bianca, "The Structural Unity of the Islamic Town: A Study in Urban Patterns," revised paper, Colloquium on the Islamic City, World of Islam Festival, London and Cambridge, England, 1976.

R. H. Bletter, "Paul Scheerbart's Architectural Fantasies," *Journal of the Society of Architectural Historians*, Vol. 34, May 1975.

Hans Blumenfeld, "Theory of City Form: Past and Present," *Journal of the Society of Architectural Historians*, Vol. 8, July 1949.

Hans Blumenfeld, *The Modern Metropolis: Its Origins, Growth, Characteristics, and Planning, Selected Papers of Hans Blumenfeld*, ed. Paul D. Spreiregen. Cambridge, Mass.: The MIT Press, 1967.

Hans Blumenfeld, "Criteria for Judging the Quality of the Urban Environment," in H. J. Schmandt and W. Bloomberg (eds.), *The Quality of Urban Life: An Urban Affairs Annual Review*, Vol. 3. Beverly Hills, Calif.: Sage, 1969.

Hans Blumenfeld, "Beyond the Metropolis," Department of Urban and Regional Planning, University of Toronto, 1977.

Murray Bookchin, *The Limits of the City*. New York: Harper & Row, 1974.

Philippe Boudon, *Lived-In Architecture: Le Corbusier's Pessac Revisited*, trans. Gerald Onn. Cambridge, Mass.: The MIT Press, 1972.

Serge Boutourline, "The Concept of Environmental Management," *Dot Zero IV*, September 1967.

A. C. H. Boyd, *Chinese Architecture and Town Planning*. Chicago: University of Chicago Press, 1962.

R. K. Brail and F. S. Chapin, Jr., "Activity Patterns of Urban Residents," *Environment and Behavior*, Vol. 5, No. 2, June 1973.

David Braybrooke and Charles E. Lindblom, *A Strategy of Decision*. New York: Free Press of Glencoe, 1963.

Carl Bridenbaugh, *Cities in the Wilderness*. New York: The Ronald Press, 1938.

Carl Bridenbaugh, *Cities in Revolt: Urban Life in North America, 1743–1776*. New York: Knopf, 1955.

Asa Briggs, *Victorian Cities*. New York: Harper & Row, 1965.

Enrique Browne, *El Uso de las Ciudades y de las Viviendas*. Buenos Aires: Ediciones SIAP, 1978.

Martin Buber, *Paths in Utopia*. Boston: Beacon Press, 1958.

Colin Buchanan & Partners, *Traffic in Towns*. London: HMSO, 1963.

D. A. Bull, "New Town and Town Expansion Schemes," Parts I and II, *Town Planning Review*, Vol. 38, No. 2, July 1967 and Vol. 38, No. 3, October 1967 (see under Field for Part III).

Gerald Burke, *The Making of Dutch Towns*. London: Cleaver-Hume Press, 1956.

Ian Burton, Robert Kates, and Gilbert White, *The Environment as Hazard*. New York: Oxford University Press, 1978.

D. Calabi and M. Folin (eds.), *Eugène Hénard*. Padova: Marsilio, 1972.

Daniel Callahan, "What Obligations Do We Have to Future Generations?," *American Ecclesiastical Review*, Vol. 164, No. 4, April 1971.

Italo Calvino, *Invisible Cities*, trans. William Weaver. New York: Harcourt Brace, 1974.

Cambridge Institute, "Prospects for New City Project." Mimeo. Cambridge, Mass., September 1970.

D. Cappon and M. Roche, "A Catalogue of Stress and Strains in Urban Life," *Habitat*, Vol. 19, Nos. 5/6, 1976.

F. M. Carp, R. Zawadski, and H. Shokrkon, "Dimensions of Urban Environmental Quality," *Environment and Behavior*, Vol. 8, No. 2, June 1976.

Daniel Carson, "Comments on 'The Pattern of Streets' by C. Alexander," *Journal of the American Institute of Planners*, Vol. 33, November 1967.

Ferdinando Castagnoli, *Orthogonal Town Planning in Antiquity*, trans. Victor Caliandro. Cambridge, Mass.: MIT Press, 1971.

Manuel Castells, *The Urban Question: A Marxist Approach*, trans. Alan Sheridan. Cambridge, Mass.: MIT Press, 1977 (orig. *La Question Urbaine*, 1972).

Paolo Ceccarelli (ed.), *La Costruzione della Città Sovietica, 1929–1931*. Padova: Marsilio, 1970.

Center for Urban and Regional Studies, University of North Carolina, "Evaluation of New Communities: Selected Preliminary Findings." Chapel Hill, N.C., 1974.

Edgar Chambless, *Roadtown*. New York: Roadtown Press, 1910.

F. S. Chapin, Jr., and Shirley F. Weiss, *Factors Influencing Land Development*. Chapel Hill: Institute for Research in Social Science, University of North Carolina, 1962.

F. S. Chapin, Jr., "Selected Theories of Urban Growth and Structure," *Journal of the American Institute of Planners*, Vol. 30, No. 1, February 1964.

F. S. Chapin, Jr., and E. J. Kaiser, *Urban Land Use Planning*, 3d ed. Urbana: University of Illinois Press, 1979.

Françoise Choay, *L'urbanisme: Utopies et Réalités*. Paris: Éditions du Seuil, 1965.

Walter Christaller, *Central Places in Southern Germany*, trans. C. W. Baskin. Englewood Cliffs, N.J.: Prentice-Hall, 1966 (orig. 1933).

Grady Clay, *Close-Up: How to Read the American City*. New York: Praeger, 1973.

William Cobbett, *Rural Rides in the Counties . . . 1821–1832*, ed. E. F. Daglish. New York: E. P. Dutton, 1932 (orig. 1830).

George Collins, "The Cuidad Lineal of Madrid," *Journal of the Society of Architectural Historians*, Vol. 18, May 1959.

George Collins, "Linear Planning throughout the World," *Journal of the Society of Architectural Historians*, Vol. 18, October 1959.

George Collins, *Visionary Drawings of Architecture and Planning*. Cambridge, Mass.: MIT Press, 1979.

George Collins and Carlos Flores, *Arturo Soria y la Ciudad Lineal*. Madrid: Revista de Occidente, 1968.

Ulrich Conrads and Hans G. Sperlich, *The Architecture of Fantasy*, trans. G. Collins and C. Collins, New York: Praeger, 1962.

Peter Cook (ed.), *Archigram*. New York: Praeger, 1973.

Peter Cowan, *Studies in the Growth, Change and Aging of Buildings*, trans. Bartlett Society, University College, London, 1963.

Peter Cowan, "On Irreversibility," *Architectural Design*, Vol. 39, September 1969.

Peter Cowan, "What Makes a Good City?" Mimeo, no date.

David Crane, "The City Symbolic," *Journal of the American Institute of Planners*. Vol. 26, November 1960.

Gordon Cullen, *The Concise Townscape*. New York: Van Nostrand, 1971.

James Dahir, *The Neighborhood Unit Plan: Its Spread and Acceptance*. New York: Russell Sage Foundation, 1947.

Robert E. Dickinson, *The West European City*, 2d ed. London: Routledge & Kegan Paul, 1962.

David Dowall, "Theories of Urban Form and Land Use: A Review," Working Paper #295, Institute for Urban and Regional Development, University of California, Berkeley, Calif., September 1978.

Anthony Downs, "Alternative Futures for the American Ghetto," *Daedalus*, Fall 1968.

C. A. Doxiadis and René Dubos, *Anthropopolis: City for Human Development*. New York: Norton, 1975.

Patricia Draper, "Crowding among Hunter-Gatherers: The !Kung Bushmen," *Science*, Vol. 182, 19 October 1973.

Peter Droege, "Floating Shelter," M.Arch.A.S./ M.C.P. Thesis, School of Architecture and Planning, Massachusetts Institute of Technology, 1978.

R. Dubos, *Man Adapting*. New Haven, Conn.: Yale University Press, 1965.

Edgar S. Dunn, Jr., *The Development of the U.S. Urban System, Vol. 1: Concepts, Structures, Regional Shifts*. Baltimore: The Johns Hopkins University Press, 1980.

B. B. Dutt, *Town Planning in Ancient India*. Calcutta: Thacker, Spink, 1925.

John Dyckman, "Planning and Decision Theory," *Journal of the American Institute of Planners*, Vol. 27, No. 4, November 1961.

H. G. Dyos and M. Wolff (eds.), *The Victorian City.* London: Routledge & Kegan Paul, 1973.

Duane Elgin et al. "City Size and the Quality of Life," Stanford, Calif.: Stanford Research Institute for the National Science Foundation (RANN), November 1974.

Friedrich Engels, *The Housing Question.* New York: International Publishers, 1935 (orig. 1872 and 1887).

Friedrich Engels, *The Condition of the Working Class in England.* Stanford, Calif.: Stanford University Press, 1958 (orig. 1844).

A. H. Esser and R. Deutsch, "Environment and Mental Health: An Annotated Bibliography," *Man-Environment Systems*, Vol. 5, No. 6, November 1975.

Norma Evenson, *Paris: A Century of Change, 1878–1978.* New Haven, Conn.: Yale University Press, 1979.

Nan Fairbrother, *New Lives, New Landscapes.* New York: Knopf, 1974.

Andreas Faludi, *Planning Theory.* Oxford: Pergamon Press, 1973.

D. Field, "New Towns and Town Expansion Schemes," Part III, *Town Planning Review*, Vol. 39, No. 3, October 1968 (see under Bull for Parts I and II).

Walter Firey, *Land Use in Central Boston.* New York: Greenwood Press, 1947.

Robert Fogelson, *The Fragmented Metropolis: Los Angeles, 1850–1930.* Cambridge, Mass.: Harvard University Press, 1967.

D. L. Foley, "An Approach to Metropolitan Spatial Structure," in M. Webber (ed.), *Explorations into Urban Structure.* Philadelphia: University of Pennsylvania Press, 1964.

Jay Forrester, *Urban Dynamics.* Cambridge, Mass.: MIT Press, 1969.

Charles Fourier, *Design for Utopia*, ed. Charles Gide,

trans. Julia Franklin. New York: Schocken, 1971 (orig. *Selections from the Writings of Fourier*, 1901).

Kenneth Frampton, "Notes on Soviet Urbanism, 1917–1932," in D. N. Lewis (ed.), *Urban Structures*. New York: Wiley Interscience, 1968.

Marc Fried and P. Gleicher, "Some Sources of Residential Satisfaction in an Urban Slum," *Journal of the American Institute of Planners*, Vol. 27, No. 4, November 1961.

Yona Friedman, *Toward A Scientific Architecture*. Cambridge, Mass.: The MIT Press, 1975.

John Friedmann, "Normative Planning: Outline of Methodology," class notes. Mimeo, July 1960.

John Friedmann, "Metropolitan Form and Social Choice: A Review." Mimeo, no date.

Ralph Gakenheimer, "Determinants of Physical Structure in the Peruvian Town of the Sixteenth Century," doctoral dissertation, University of Pennsylvania, 1964.

Herbert Gans, "The Balanced Community: Homogeneity or Heterogeneity in Residential Areas," *Journal of the American Institute of Planners*, Vol. 27 No. 3, August 1961.

Herbert Gans, *People and Plans*. New York: Basic Books, 1968.

Patrick Geddes, *Cities in Evolution*. New York: Howard Fertig, 1968 (orig. 1915).

Alan Gilbert, "The Arguments for Very Large Cities Reconsidered," *Urban Studies*, Vol. 13, No. 1, February 1976.

Mark Girouard, *Life in the English Country House: A Social and Architectural History*. New Haven, Conn.: Yale University Press, 1978.

Artur Glikson, *The Ecological Basis of Planning*. The Hague: M. Nijhoff, 1971.

J. R. Goldsmith and Erland Jonsson, "Effects of Noise on Health in the Residential and Urban Environment," Report to the Bureau of Community Environmental Management, 1970, unpublished.

Brian R. Goodey, *Interpreting the Built Environment*. Elmsford, N.Y.: Pergamon, 1979.

Paul Goodman and Percival Goodman, *Communitas*. Chicago: The University of Chicago Press, 1947.

Robert Goodman, *After the Planners*. New York: Simon and Schuster, 1971.

David Gordon, "Capitalism and the Roots of Urban Crisis," in R. Alcaly and David Mermelstein (eds.), *The Fiscal Crisis of American Cities*. New York: Vintage, 1977.

Lincoln Gordon, "Limits to the Growth Debate," *Resources for the Future*, No. 52, Summer 1976.

J. Gottman, *Megalopolis*. New York: The Twentieth Century Fund, 1961.

Etienne Grandjean, *Ergonomics of the Home*, Harold Oldroyd trans., Davis ed.. New York: Halsted Press, 1973.

Etienne Grandjean and A. Gilgen, *Environmental Factors in Urban Planning: Air Pollution, Noise, Urban Open Spaces, Sunlight, and Natural Lighting Indoors*, trans. Harold Oldroyd. London: Taylor and Francis, 1976.

Cathy Greenblat, *Gaming-Simulation: Rationale, Design, and Application*. New York: Sage Publications, 1975.

Victor Gruen, *The Heart of Our Cities*. New York: Thames and Hudson, 1965.

Robert Guttman, "Site Planning and Social Behavior," *Journal of Social Issues, October 1966*.

John Habraken, *Supports: An Alternative to Mass Housing*. New York: Praeger, 1972.

Gary Hack, "Environmental Programming: Creating Responsive Settings." Ph.D. Thesis, Department of Urban Studies and Planning, Massachusetts Institute of Technology, 1976.

Jorge Hardoy, *Urban Planning in Pre-Columbian America*. New York: Braziller, 1968.

C. D. Harris and Edward L. Ullman, "The Nature of Cities," *Annals of the American Academy of Political and Social Sciences*, Vol. 242, November 1945.

Roger Hart, *Children's Experience of Place*. New York: Irvington, 1979.

David Harvey, *Social Justice and the City*. London: E. Arnold, 1973.

Dolores Hayden, *Seven American Utopias: The Architecture of Communitarian Socialism, 1790–1975*. Cambridge, Mass.: The MIT Press, 1976.

Heikki von Hertzen and P. Spreiregen, *Building a New Town: Finland's New Garden City, Tapiola*. Cambridge, Mass.: The MIT Press, 1971.

Morris Hill, "A Goals-Achievement Matrix for Evaluating Alternative Plans," *Journal of the American Institute of Planners*, Vol. 34, No. 1, January 1968, and discussion, Vol. 35, No. 2, March 1969.

L. E. Hinkle and William C. Loring, *The Effect of the Man-Made Environment on Health and Behavior*, Publication #CDC 77–8318, Public Health Service, U.S. Department of H.E.W. Washington, D.C.: USGPO, 1977.

Irving Hoch, "Urban Scale and Environmental Quality," *Resources for the Future*, Reprint #110, August 1973.

Irving Hoch, "City Size Effects, Trends, and Policies," *Science*, Vol. 193, 3 September 1976.

F. Hosking, "Psychological Aspects of Extreme Environmental Stress," *Diseases of the Nervous System*, Vol. 31, No. 8, August 1970.

Ebenezer Howard, *Garden Cities of To-Morrow*, introduction by F. J. Osborn. London: Faber & Faber, 1945 (orig. 1898).

Homer Hoyt, *One Hundred Years of Land Values in Chicago*. Chicago: University of Chicago Press, 1933.

Homer Hoyt, *The Structure and Growth of Residential Neighborhoods in American Cities*, Washington, D.C.: USGPO, 1939 (for the Federal Housing Administration).

Richard Hurd, *Principles of City Land Values*. New York: The Record and Guide, 1903.

Phyllis W. Ingersoll, *Ideal Forms for Cities: An Historical Bibliography*. Council for Planning Librarians, Exchange Bibliography #10. Oakland, Calif., 1959.

Institute for Architecture and Urban Studies, "Another Chance for Housing: Low-Rise Alternatives," an exhibition at the Museum of Modern Art, for the New York State Urban Development Corporation, New York, 1973.

Reginald Isaacs, "The Neighborhood Theory: An Analysis of its Adequacy," *Journal of the American Institute of Planners*, Vol. 14, No. 2, Spring 1948.

Walter Isard, *Location and Space Economy*. Cambridge, Mass.: The MIT Press, 1956.

Walter Isard and R. Coughlin, "Municipal Costs and Revenues Resulting from Community Growth," Parts I and II, *Journal of the American Institute of Planners*, Vol. 22, Nos. 3 and 4, Summer 1956 and Fall, 1956.

J. B. Jackson, *Landscapes: Selected Writings of J. B. Jackson*, E. H. Zube (ed.). Amherst Mass.: University of Massachusetts Press, 1970.

Jane Jacobs, *The Death and Life of Great American Cities*. New York: Random House, 1961.

R. D. K. Johnson and C. Holbrow, eds.. *Space Settlements: A Design Study*. National Aeronautics and Space Administration, SP 413. Washington, D.C.: USGPO, 1977.

John Kain, "Urban Form and the Costs of Urban Services," Joint Center for Urban Studies, Cambridge, Mass.: Harvard University, May 1967.

G. N. Kates, *The Years That Were Fat: The Last of Old China*. Cambridge, Mass.: MIT Press, 1967 (orig. 1952).

A. D. King, *Colonial Urban Development: Culture, Social Power and the Environment*. London: Routledge & Kegan Paul, 1976.

R. E. Klosterman, "Foundations for Normative Planning," *Journal of the American Institute of Planners*, Vol. 44, January 1978.

Ralph Knowles, "Solar Access and Urban Form," *Journal of the American Institute of Architects*, Vol. 69, No 2, February 1980.

Anatol Kopp, *Town and Revolution*. New York: Braziller, 1970 (orig. 1967).

J. B. Kracht, "Municipal Efficiency and Its Relation to the Problem of Optimum City Size," *Bulletin of the Illinois Geographical Society*, Vol. 12, No. 2, June 1970.

Peter Kropotkin, *Fields, Factories and Workshops*. New York: Harper & Row, 1974.

Arthur Kutcher, *The New Jerusalem: Planning and Politics*. Cambridge, Mass.: The MIT Press, 1975.

R. Lamana, "Value Consensus among Urban Residents," *Journal of the American Institute of Planners*, Vol. 30, No. 4, November 1964.

S. Lang, "The Ideal City from Plato to Howard," *Architectural Review*, Vol. 112, No. 668, August 1952.

Ira Lapidus, *Muslim Cities in the Later Middle Ages*. Cambridge, Mass.: Harvard University Press, 1967.

Le Corbusier (C. E. Jeanneret-Gris), *The City of Tomorrow*, trans. Frederick Etchells. Cambridge, Mass.: The MIT Press, 1971 (orig. *Urbanisme*, 1924).

Henri Lefebvre, *La Droit à la Ville*. Paris: Editions Anthropos, 1968.

M. Leff, J. F. Roatch, and W. E. Bunney, "Environmental Factors Preceding the Onset of Severe Depressions," *Psychiatry*, Vol. 33, No. 3, August 1970.

Llewelyn-Davies, Weeks, Forestier-Walker & Bor, *The Plan for Milton Keynes*, Volumes I and II, Wavendon, near Bletchley, Milton Keynes Development Corp., March 1970.

Lars Lerup, "Environmental and Behavioral Congruence as a Measure of Goodness in Public Space: Two Case Studies in Stockholm," *Ekistics*, Vol. 34, No. 204, November 1972.

Lars Lerup, *Building the Unfinished: Architecture and Human Action*. Beverly Hills, Calif.: Sage, 1977.

J. Lessinger, "The Case for Scatteration," *Journal of the American Institute for Planners*, Vol. 28, No. 3, August 1962.

P. H. Levin, "The Design Process in Planning," *Town Planning Review*, Vol. 37, No. 1, April 1966.

Norman Lobdell, "Models of Urban Transportation." Columbus, Ohio: Battelle Memorial Institute, monograph #9, 1967.

N. Lichfield, "Economics in Town Planning." *Town Planning Review*, Vol. 39, No. 1, April 1968.

August Lösch, *The Economics of Location*, 2d rev. ed., trans. W. Woglom and W. Stolper. New Haven, Conn.: Yale University Press, 1954 (orig. 1939).

B. Loudon and W. G. Flanagan, "Comparative Urban Ecology: A Summary of the Field," in J. Walton and L. Masotti (eds.), *The City in Comparative Perspective*. Beverly Hills, Calif.: Sage, 1976.

Ira S. Lowry, "Comments on Harris, 'The City of the Future: The Problems of Optimal Design'." Mimeo, Regional Science Association, November 1966.

W. H. Ludlow, "Urban Densities and Their Costs," in C. Woodbury (ed.), *Urban Redevelopment: Problems and Practices*. Chicago: University of Chicago Press, 1953.

Alvin Lukashok and Kevin Lynch, "Some Childhood Memories of the City," *Journal of the American Institute of Planners*, Vol. 22, No. 3, Summer 1956.

Kevin Lynch, "Environmental Adaptability," *Journal of the American Institute of Planners*, Vol. 24, No. 1, 1958.

Kevin Lynch, "A Classification System for the Analysis of the Urban Pattern," typescript, paper presented to the Seminar on Urban Spatial Structure of the Joint Center for Urban Studies of Massachusetts Institute of Technology and Harvard University, June 1961.

Kevin Lynch, "The Pattern of the Metropolis," *Daedalus*, Winter 1961.

Kevin Lynch, "The Visible Shape of the Shapeless Metropolis." Mimeo, 1965.

Kevin Lynch, *Site Planning*. 2d ed. Cambridge, Mass.: The MIT Press, 1971.

Kevin Lynch, *What Time Is This Place?* Cambridge, Mass.: The MIT Press, 1972.

Kevin Lynch, "The Openness of Open Space," in G. Kepes (ed.), *Arts of the Environment*. New York: Braziller, 1972 (orig. 1964).

Kevin Lynch, *Managing the Sense of a Region*. Cambridge, Mass.: The MIT Press, 1976.

Kevin Lynch, "City Design: What It Is and How It Might Be Taught," *Urban Design International*, Vol. 1, No. 2, 1980.

Sandra Major, "A Review of Futurist Literature," University College, London, Joint Unit for Planning Research, 2d Series Seminar Paper #8. Mimeo, no date.

Fumihiko Maki, "Investigations in Collective Form," special publication #2, School of Architecture, Washington University, St. Louis, June 1964.

B. Malisz, "Implications of the Threshold Theory for Urban and National Planning," *Journal of the Town Planning Institute*, Vol. 55, No. 3, March 1969. (Then see: W. Lean, "Urban Threshold Theory: An Economist's Note," *Journal of the Town Planning Institute*, Vol. 55, No. 7, August 1969.)

L. Martin and L. March (eds.), *Urban Space and Structures*. Cambridge, England: Cambridge University Press, 1972.

Margaret Mead, "The Kind of City We Want," *Ekistics*, Vol. 35, No. 209, April 1973.

Richard L. Meier, *A Communications Theory of Urban Growth*. Cambridge, Mass.: MIT Press, 1962.

Richard L. Meier, "A Stable Urban Ecosystem," *Science*, Vol. 192, 4 June 1976.

Jeffrey Meyer, *Peking as a Sacred City*, Vol. 81 of the Asian Folklore and Social Life Monographs. Taipei: Chinese Association for Folklore, 1976.

William Michelson, "An Empirical Analysis of Urban Environmental Preferences," *Journal of the American Institute of Planners*, Vol. 32, No. 6, November 1966.

N. A. Miliutin, *Sotsgorod: The Problem of Building Socialist Cities*, ed. G. R. Collins and W. Alex, trans. A. Sprague. Cambridge, Mass.: The MIT Press, 1974 (orig. 1930).

René Millon (ed.), *Urbanization at Teotihuacán, Mexico*. Austin: University of Texas Press, 1973.

Rafael Moneo, "Aldo Rossi: The Idea of Architecture and the Modena Cemetery," *Oppositions*, Summer 1976.

Roger Montgomery, "The Urban Design Product," mimeo, presented at University of California at Berkeley, AIA Urban Design Short Course, May 1966.

R. Moos and R. Brownstein, *Environment and Utopia: A Synthesis*, New York: Plenum, 1977.

R. L. Morrill, *The Spatial Organization of Society*. North Scituate, Mass.: The Duxbury Press, 1974.

A. E. J. Morris, *History of Urban Form: Prehistory to the Renaissance*. London: George Godwin Ltd., 1972.

William Morris, *News from Nowhere*, James Redmond (ed.). London: Routledge & Kegan Paul, 1970.

Lewis Mumford, *The Culture of Cities*. New York: Harcourt Brace & Co., 1938.

Lewis Mumford, "The Neighborhood and the Neighborhood Unit," *Town Planning Review*, Vol. 24, No. 4, January 1954.

Lewis Mumford, *The City in History*, New York: Harcourt Brace & World, 1961.

D. M. Murtha, "Dimensions of User Benefit: Overview of User-Oriented Environmental Design Criteria." Washington, D.C.: American Institute of Architects, 1976.

Raymond Neutra and Ross McFarland, "Accidents and the Residential Environment," report to the Bureau of Community Environmental Management and the American Public Health Association, unpublished, 1970.

Oscar Newman, *Defensible Space: Crime Prevention Through Urban Design*. New York: Macmillan, 1972.

Joan Oates, *Babylon*. London: Thames and Hudson, 1979.

E. P. Odum, *Ecology*. New York: Holt, Rinehart, and Winston, 1963.

Rai Okamoto and F. E. Williams, *Urban Design Manhattan*, prepared for the Regional Plan Association. New York: Viking, 1969.

Fernando Ortiz, *Cuban Counterpoint: Tobacco and Sugar*, trans. Harriet de Onis. New York: Vintage, 1970 (orig. 1960).

R. E. Pahl, "Spatial Structure and Social Structure," Chapter 11 in R. E. Pahl, *Whose City?* Harlow, England: Longman, 1970.

R. J. Paquette, N. Ashford, and P. H. Wright, *Transportation Engineering: Planning and Design*. New York: Ronald Press, 1972.

Robert Park, "Human Ecology," *American Journal of Sociology*, Vol. 42, July 1936.

Joseph Passoneau and R. S. Wurman, *An Urban Atlas of 20 American Cities*. Cambridge, Mass.: The MIT Press, 1966.

Elbert Peets, *On the Art of Designing Cities*, ed. P. Spreiregen. Cambridge, Mass.: The MIT Press, 1968.

V. Perevedentsev, *The Concentration of Urban Popula-* 476
tion and the Criterion of Optimality of a City, translated Bibliography
from Akademia Nauk SSR, Institut mezhdunarodo-
nogo rabochego dvizhenia, *Urbanizatsia i rabochii*
klass v ysloviiakh naucho-tekhnicheskoi revolutsii, Moscow, 1970.

Constance Perin, *With Man in Mind.* Cambridge,
Mass.: The MIT Press, 1970.

Constance Perin, *Everything in Its Place.* Princeton,
N.J.: Princeton University Press, 1977.

J. Perraton, "Urban Systems: Collection and Management of Data for a Complex Model," Working
Paper #46, Centre for Land Use and Built Form
Studies, Cambridge University, Cambridge, England, September 1970.

Clarence Perry, "The Neighborhood Unit," in *The*
Regional Plan of New York and Its Environs. Vol. 7.
New York: Regional Plan Association, 1929.

P. Pinchemel, A. Vakili, and J. Gozzi, *Niveaux Op-*
tima des Villes. Lille, France: Comité d'etudes ré-
gionales économiques et sociales (CERES), 1959.

R. A. B. Ponsonby-Fane, *Kyoto: The Old Capital of*
Japan, 794–1864, rev. ed. Kyoto: Ponsonby Memorial Society, 1956.

Donald Preziosi, *The Semiotics of the Built Environ-*
ment: An Introduction to Architectonic Analysis.
Bloomington, Ind.: Indiana University Press, 1978.

L. Rainwater, "Fear and the House as Haven in the
Lower Class," *Journal of the American Institute of*
Planners, Vol. 32, No. 1, January 1966.

A. Rapoport, *Human Aspects of Urban Form.* New
York: Pergamon, 1977.

Steen Eiler Rasmussen, "Commentary on Clark's
'Ideal Cities: Past and Present, ' " in R. M. Fisher
(ed.), *The Metropolis and Modern Life.* New York:
Russell & Russell, 1955.

Steen Eiler Rasmussen, *London: The Unique City.*
Cambridge, Mass.: The MIT Press, 1967.

R. U. Ratcliff, "Efficiency and the Location of Urban Activities," in R. M. Fisher (ed.), *The Metropolis and Modern Life*. New York: Russell & Russell, 1955.

John Rawls, *A Theory of Justice*. Cambridge, Mass.: Harvard University Press, 1971.

Real Estate Research Corporation, *The Costs of Sprawl*, for the Council on Environmental Quality, U.S. Department of H.U.D. Washington, D.C.: USGPO, 1974.

T. F. Reddaway, *The Rebuilding of London after the Great Fire*. London: Edwin Arnold, 1951 (orig. 1940).

Jesse Reichek, "On the Design of Cities," *Journal of the American Institute of Planners*, Vol. 27, May 1961.

Thomas Reiner, *The Place of the Ideal Community in Urban Planning*. Philadelphia: University of Pennsylvania Press, 1963.

E. C. Relph, *Place and Placelessness*. London: Pion, 1976.

John Reps, *The Making of Urban America: A History of City Planning in the United States*. Princeton, N.J.: Princeton University Press, 1965.

H. W. Richardson, *The Economics of Urban Size*. Lexington, Mass.: Lexington Books, 1973.

H. W. Richardson, *The New Urban Economics, and Alternatives*. London: Pion, 1977.

David Riesman, "Some Observations on Community Plans and Utopia," *Yale Law Journal*, Vol. 57, December 1947.

Lloyd Rodwin, *Nations and Cities*. Boston: Houghton Mifflin, 1970.

Colin Rowe and F. Koetter, *Collage City*. Cambridge, Mass.: The MIT Press, 1978.

Edgar Rust, *No Growth: Impacts on Urban Areas*. Lexington, Mass.: D. C. Heath, 1975.

Howard Saalman, *Haussmann: Paris Transformed*. New York: Braziller, 1971.

Eliel Saarinen, *The City: Its Growth, Its Decay, Its Future*. New York: Reinhold, 1943.

Janet Salaff, "Urban Communities after the Cultural Revolution," in J. W. Lewis (ed.), *The City in Communist China*. Stanford, Calif.: Stanford University Press, 1971.

F. Savigeau, "A Quantitative Measure of Accessibility," *Town Planning Review*, Vol. 38, No. 1, April 1967.

Larry Sawyers, "Urban Planning in the Soviet Union and China," *Monthly Review*, Vol. 28, March 1977.

P. Scheerbart, *Glass Architecture*, trans. S. Palmer. New York: Praeger, 1972 (orig. 1914; bound with Bruno Taut, *Alpine Architecture*).

K. Schlager, "A Land Use Plan Design Model," *Journal of the American Institute of Planners*, Vol. 31, May 1965.

R. C. Schmitt, "Density, Health and Social Disorganization," *Journal of the American Institute of Planners*, Vol. 32, No. 1, January 1966.

A. L. Schorr, *Slums and Social Insecurity*, Washington, D.C.: USGPO, 1963 (for the U.S. Department of H.E.W.).

Roger Scruton, *The Aesthetics of Architecture*. Princeton, New Jersey: Princeton University Press, 1979.

Irving Shapiro, "Urban Land Use Classification," *Land Economics*, Vol. 35, No. 2, May 1959.

D. N. Shukla, *Vastu-Śāstra: The Hindu Science of Architecture*, Volume 1. Poona: Poona Book House, 1960.

William R. Sims, *Neighborhoods: Columbus Neighborhood Definition Study*. Columbus, Ohio: n. pub., 1973.

Camillo Sitte, *City Planning According to Artistic Principles*, trans. G. Collins and C. Collins. New York: Random House, 1965 (orig. 1889).

Julian Smith, "Madurai, India: The Architecture of a City," M.Arch. Thesis, Department of Architecture, Massachusetts Institute of Technology, Cambridge, Mass., 1976.

Paolo Soleri, *Arcology: The City in the Image of Man.* Cambridge, Mass.: The MIT Press, 1969.

Michael Southworth and Kevin Lynch, "Designing and Managing the Strip," Joint Center for Urban Studies, Cambridge, Mass., October 1974.

M. E. Spiro, *Kibbutz: Venture in Utopia.* New York: Schocken, 1963.

Paul Spreiregen, "Roots of Our Modern Concepts," in M. Branch (ed.), *Urban Planning Theory*, Stroudsburg, Penna.: Dowden, Hutchinson & Ross, 1975.

Dan Stanislawski, "The Origin and Spread of the Grid Pattern Town," *Geographical Review*, Vol. 36, No. 1, January 1946.

Clarence Stein, "City Patterns, Past and Future," *Pencil Points*, June 1942.

Clarence Stein, *Toward New Towns for America.* Chicago: Public Administration Service, 1951.

P. A. Stone, *The Structure, Size and Costs of Urban Settlements,* Cambridge, England: Cambridge University Press, 1973.

A. L. Strauss, *The American City: A Sourcebook of Urban Imagery.* Chicago: Aldine, 1968.

Hugh Stretton, *Ideas for Australian Cities.* Melbourne: Georgian House, 1971.

Hugh Stretton, *Capitalism, Socialism and the Environment.* New York: Cambridge University Press, 1976.

Hugh Stretton, *Urban Planning in Rich and Poor Countries.* New York: Oxford University Press, 1978.

Louis Henry Sullivan, *A System of Architectural Ornament According with a Philosophy of Man's Powers.* New York: Eakins Press, 1967 (orig. 1924).

Superstudio, "Twelve Cautionary Tales for Christmas," *Architectural Design*, Vol. 62, December 1971.

Anthony Sutcliffe, *The Autumn of Central Paris*. London: E. Arnold, 1970.

Gerald Suttles, *The Social Order of the Slum*. Chicago: University of Chicago Press, 1968.

Bruno Taut, *Alpine Architecture*, trans. S. Palmer. New York: Praeger, 1972 (orig. 1919; bound with P. Scheerbart, *Glass Architecture*).

René Thom, *Structural Stability and Morphogenesis*. Reading, Mass.: W. A. Benjamin, 1975.

Wilbur Thompson, "Planning as Urban Growth Management: Still More Questions Than Answers," *American Institute of Planners Newsletter*, December 1974.

John M. Thomson, *Great Cities and Their Traffic*. London: Gollancz, 1977.

J. H. von Thünen, *Isolated State*, trans. C. Wartenburg. London: Pergamon, 1966 (orig. 1826).

Graham Towers, "City Planning in China," *Journal of the Royal Town Planning Institute*, Vol. 59, No. 3, March 1973.

Yi-Fu Tuan, *Topophilia: A Study of Environmental Perceptions, Attitudes and Values*. Englewood Cliffs, N.J.: Prentice-Hall, 1974.

Christopher Tunnard, *The City of Man*. New York: Scribner, 1953.

John F. C. Turner and R. Fichter (eds.), *Freedom to Build: Dweller Control of the Housing Process*. New York: Macmillan, 1972.

U.S. Department of Housing and Urban Development, Division of International Affairs, *Urban Growth Policies in Six European Countries*. Washington, D.C.: USGPO, November 1972.

J. E. Vance, *This Scene of Man: The Role and Structure of the City in the Geography of Westrn Civilization*. New York: Harper College Press, 1977.

Sim Van Der Ryn, "San Francisco Community Renewal Program: Amenity Attributes of Residential Locations," Technical Paper #3, Arthur D. Little, San Francisco, May 1965.

Robert Venturi, Denise Scott Brown, and Steven Izenour, *Learning from Las Vegas*. Cambridge, Mass.: The MIT Press, 1972.

R. K. Wagoner, "Urban Structuring Techniques," *Journal of Environmental Systems*, Vol. 1, No. 3, September 1971.

Barbara Ward (Jackson), "Human Settlements: Crisis and Opportunity," report of meeting, 1973, in preparation for U.N. Conference on Human Settlements. Ottawa: Minister of State for Urban Affairs, rev. ed., 1975.

Colin Ward, *Housing: An Anarchist Approach*. London: Freedom Press, 1976.

Colin Ward, *The Child in the City*. London: The Architectural Press, 1977.

David Ward, "The Industrial Revolution and the Emergence of Boston's Central Business District," *Economic Geography*, Vol. 42, 1966, pp. 152–171.

Sam Bass Warner, *Streetcar Suburbs*. New York: Antheneum, 1969.

Sam Bass Warner, *The Urban Wilderness: A History of the American City*. New York: Harper & Row, 1972.

Melvin Webber, "Order in Diversity," in L. Wingo (ed.), *Cities and Space*. Baltimore: Johns Hopkins Press, 1963.

Melvin Webber, "The Urban Place and the Nonplace Urban Realm," in M. Webber et al., *Explorations into Urban Structure*. Philadelphia: University of Pennsylvania Press, 1967.

Melvin Webber, "Planning in an Environment of Change," Parts I and II, *Town Planning Review*, Vol. 39, No. 3, October 1968 and Vol. 39, No. 4, January 1969.

David Weinberg, "The Social Relations of Living: London 1830–1880, The Dialectics of Urban Living and City Form," M.Arch.A.S./M.C.P. Thesis, School of Architecture and Planning, Massachusetts Institute of Technology, 1974.

P. Wheatley, *The Pivot of the Four Quarters*. Chicago: Aldine, 1971.

A. G. White, "Urban Futures: Science Fiction and the City," Monticello, Ill.: Council of Planning Librarians Exchange Bibliography #418, 1973.

Walter Muir Whitehill, *A Topographical History of Boston*. Cambridge, Mass.: Harvard University Press, 1959.

Dora Wiebenson, *Tony Garnier: The Cité Industrielle*. New York: Braziller, 1969.

Michael Williams, "The Parkland Towns of Australia and New Zealand," *Geographical Review*, Vol. 56, January 1966.

Raymond Williams, *The Country and the City*. New York: Oxford University Press, 1973.

R. L. Wilson, "Livability of the City, Attitudes and Urban Development," in F. S. Chapin and S. Weiss (eds.), *Urban Growth Dynamics*. New York: Wiley, 1962.

Morton and Lucia White, *The Intellectual versus the City, from Thomas Jefferson to Frank Lloyd Wright*. New York: New American Library, 1964.

William H. Whyte, *Cluster Development*. New York: American Conservation Association, 1964.

William H. Whyte, *The Social Life of Small Urban Spaces*. Washington, D.C.: The Conservation Foundation, 1980.

A. G. Wilson, P. H. Rees, and C. M. Leigh, *Models of Cities and Regions: Theoretical and Empirical Developments*. New York: Wiley, 1977.

Lowden Wingo, *Transportation and Land Use*. Washington, D.C.: Resources for the Future, 1961.

Arthur Wright, "The Cosmology of the Chinese City," in G. W. Skinner (ed.), *The City in Late Imperial China*. Stanford, Calif.: Stanford University Press, 1977.

Frank Lloyd Wright, *The Living City: When Democracy Builds*. New York: New American Library, 1958.

Catherine Wurster, "Framework for an Urban Society," in President's Commission on National Goals, *Goals for Americans*. Englewood Cliffs, N.J.: Prentice-Hall, 1960.

Catherine Wurster, "The Form and Structure of the Future Urban Complex," in L. Wingo (ed.), *Cities and Space*. Baltimore: Johns Hopkins Press, 1963.

R. E. Wycherley, *How the Greeks Built Cities*. London: Macmillan, 1949.

Tadeusz Zalski, "Polish Plans for Linear Cities," *The Architect*, Vol. 1, No. 3, April 1971.

George K. Zipf, *Human Behavior and the Principle of Least Effort: An Introduction to Human Ecology*. New York: Hafner Publishing Co., 1965 (facsimile of 1949 edition).

Addenda

J. S. Adams (ed.), *Comparative Metropolitan Analysis Project*, Vol. 1, *Contemporary Metropolitan America: Twenty Geographical Vignettes*, and Vol. II, *Urban Policymaking and Metropolitan Dynamics: A Comparative Geographical Analysis*. Cambridge, Mass.: Ballinger, 1976. Vol. III, *A Comparative Atlas of America's Great Cities: Twenty Metropolitan Regions*. Minneapolis, Minn.: University of Minnesota Press, 1976.

Donald Appleyard, *Livable Streets*, Berkeley, Calif.: University of California Press, 1981.

Canon S. A. Barnett, "The Ideal City," in H. E. Meller (ed.), *The Ideal City*. Old Woking, Surrey: Leicester University Press, 1979.

Jonathan Barnett, *An Introduction to Urban Design*, New York: Harper and Row, 1982.

G. H. Pirie, "Measuring Access: A Review and Proposal," *Environment and Planning A,* Vol. 11, No. 3, March 1979.

Aldo Rossi, *The Architecture of the City*, Cambridge, Mass.: The M.I.T. Press, 1982.

J. Rykwert, *The Idea of a Town*, Princeton, N.J.: Princeton University Press, 1976.

C. Schorske, *Fin de Siecle Vienna*, New York: Vintage, 1981.

William Whyte, *The Social Life of Small Urban Spaces*, Washington, D.C.: The Conservation Foundation, 1980.

Sources and Credits

Material is quoted from Italo Calvino, *Invisible Cities*, trans. William Weaver (New York: Harcourt Brace Jovanovich, 1974) with the permission of Harcourt Brace Jovanovich.

Figs. 42, 60, 61 (bottom), 63, 65, 67, 69, 71 (bottom), 76, 85, 86, 87 (top), 92, 95, 101, 103, and 104 are by Julie Messervy.

Figs. 41, 46, 51, 52, 53, 54 (top), 55, 56, 57, 58, 71 (top), 72, 79, 88, 89, 91, 93, 98, and 106 (bottom) are provided by the author.

Other illustrations:

Frontispiece
Reproduced with the permission of the American Institute of Architects. Further reproduction, in part or in whole, is not authorized.

2
From Sir Leonard Woolley, *Excavations at Ur* (London: Ernest Benn Publishers, 1954).

3
From J. Oates, *Babylon* (London: Thames and Hudson, Ltd., 1979).

5, 6
From René Millon (ed.), *Urbanization at Teotihuacán, Mexico*, vol. 1, part 1, © René Millon.

7
Reprinted from G. William Skinner (ed.), *The City in Late Imperial China*, with permission of Stanford University Press. © 1977 by the Board of Trustees of the Leland Stanford Junior University.

8
From The American Geographical Society Collection of the University of Wisconsin–Milwaukee.

9
From Nelson Wu, *Chinese and Indian Architecture* (New York: Braziller, 1963). Courtesy of the author.

10
From *The Geographical Review*, vol. 62, 1972, with the permission of The American Geographical Society.

11
From Ferdinando Castagnoli, *Orthogonal Town Planning in Antiquity*, © 1971, The MIT Press. Courtesy of the author and of the British School at Rome.

12
From Richard E. Wycherley, *How the Greeks Built Cities*, 1949, with the permission of Macmillan Co., London and Basingstoke.

13
Reprinted with permission of The Amon Carter Museum of Western Art, Fort Worth, Texas.

14
From Instituto de Estudios de Administraccion Local, *Planos de Ciudades Iberoamericanas y Filipinas Existences en el Archivo de Indias*, vol. 1, Seminario de Urbanismo, Madrid, 1951.

15
From Jaqueline Tyrwhitt (ed.), *Patrick Geddes in India*, 1947, with the permission of Lund Humphries, London.

16
Courtesy of Julian Beinart.

17, 18
Courtesy of the Society for the Preservation of New England Antiquities.

20
Courtesy of The Bostonian Society.

21
Courtesy of the Boston Public Library, Print Department.

22
From Sam Bass Warner, *Streetcar Suburbs* (Cambridge, Mass.: Harvard University Press, 1962).

23
Courtesy of The Bostonian Society.

24
Courtesy of the Society for the Preservation of New England Antiquities.

26
Ebenezer Howard, *Garden Cities of To-Morrow* (Cambridge, Mass.: The MIT Press, 1965).

27
From *Taliesin*, vol. 1, no. 1, Taliesin Fellowship, Spring Green, Wisconsin, October 1940, with the permission of the Frank Lloyd Wright Memorial Foundation, Scottsdale, Arizona.

28
From Le Corbusier, *The City of Tomorrow* (Cambridge, Mass.: The MIT Press, 1971, orig. 1929).

29
From N. A. Miliutin, *Sotsgorod* (Cambridge, Mass.: The MIT Press, 1974, orig. 1930).

30
From Umbro Apollonio, *Antonio Sant'Elia* (Milan: I1 Balcone, 1958).

31
From P. A. Alexandrov and S. O. Khan-Mahom medov, *Ivan Leonidov* (Moscow: Izdatelstuo Literaturi po Stroitelstru, 1971).

32
From Bruno Taut, *Alpine Architecture* (New York: Praeger, 1972, orig. 1919).

33
From Paolo Soleri, *Arcology: The City in the Image of Man* (Cambridge, Mass.: The MIT Press, 1969).

34
Reproduced by permission of *The Magazine Antiques*.

36
"A completed section of Poston," in Alexander Leighton, *The Governing of Men*, © 1945, 1973 by

Princeton University Press. Reprinted by permission of Princeton University Press.

37

From R. A. B. Ponsonby-Fane, *Kyoto: The Old Capital of Japan, 794–1869*, rev. ed. (Kyoto: Ponsonby Memorial Society, 1956).

38

From Andreas Volwahsen, *Living Architecture: Indian* (London: MacDonald and Co., 1969).

39

Courtesy of Julian Smith.

40

View of an Ideal City, Central Italian School, 1490–1495. Courtesy of The Walters Art Gallery, Baltimore.

43

From Eliel Saarinen, *The City* (New York: Reinhold, 1943).

44

From Albert Ballu, *Guide Illustré de Timgad* (Paris: Levy-Neurdin, 1910.

45

"Vertical Aerial View of Santa Fé, Spain, 1958," in John W. Reps, *The Making of Urban America: A History of City Planning in the United States*, © 1965 by Princeton University Press. Reprinted by permission of Princeton University Press.

47

From G. R. Collins and Carlos Flores (eds.), *Arturo Soria y la ciudad lineal*, 1968, by permission of Alianza Editorial, S.A.

48

Courtesy of Martha Beck, The Drawing Center, New York.

49

Courtesy of Map Division, New York Public Library, Astor, Lenox and Tilden Foundations.

50

From Clarence Stein, *Toward New Towns for Amer-*

ica, © 1957 by Litton Educational Publishing, Inc. Reprinted by permission of Van Nostrand Reinhold Company.

54 (bottom)
From E. S. Popko, *Transitions*, © 1978, Dowden, Hutchinson & Ross, Inc., Stroudsburg, Pa.

59
Courtesy of Nishan Bichajian.

61
Courtesy of Robin Moore.

62
From A. W. Burin, *Geschichte des russischen Städtebaus bis zum 19. Jahrhundert* (Berlin: Henschelverlag, 1961).

66
From G. A. Jellicoe, *Motopia: A Study in The Evolution of Urban Landscape* (New York: Praeger, 1961).

68
Courtesy of Mr. Yoshio Watanabe, Tokyo.

70
From a drawing by F. Cresson Schell, *Leslie's Magazine*, July 25, 1895.

73
Courtesy of Mayer Spivack.

74
Courtesy of Nishan Bichajian.

75
From Paul Spreiregen (ed.), *On the Art of Designing Cities* (Cambridge, Mass.: The MIT Press, 1968).

77
Courtesy of Julian Beinart.

78
A. V. Ikonnikov, *Kamennaya Letopis Moskvi: Puteveditel* (Moscow: Moskovski Rabochi, 1978).

80, 81
From Stefano Bianca, *Architektur und Lebensform*,

reproduced by permission of Artemis Verlag und Verlag für Architektur, Zurich.

82
From *Man-Environment Systems,* vol. 5, no. 5 (1975).

83
From T. A. Heppenheimer, *Colonies in Space* (Harrisburg, Pa.: Stackpole Books, 1977).

84
From Reyner Banham, *Los Angeles: The Architecture of Four Ecologies* (London: Penguin Press, 1971). Courtesy of the author.

87 (bottom)
Courtesy of Nishan Bichajian.

90
From E. S. Popko, *Transitions,* © 1978, Dowden, Hutchinson & Ross, Inc., Stroudsburg, Pa.

94
The Bettmann Archive.

96
Courtesy of Nishan Bichajian.

97
From Lawrence Halprin, *Freeways,* © Litton Educational Publishing, Inc. Reprinted by permission of Van Nostrand Reinhold Co.

99
From Clarence Stein, *Toward New Towns for America,* © 1957 by Litton Educational Publishing, Inc. Reprinted by permission of Van Nostrand Reinhold Co.

102
By permission of the Historic American Buildings Survey, Heritage Conservation and Recreation Service, U.S. Department of the Interior. Photo by Arthur Ziegler, 1901.

106 (top)
From Nan Fairbrother, *New Lives, New Landscapes* (New York: Alfred A. Knopf, Inc., 1970).

107
Courtesy of Yanni Pyriotis.

Acknowledgments

Lloyd Rodwin and I began this inquiry in an experimental seminar, twenty-five years ago. He will find some of his ideas here, no doubt distorted. I take ideas where I find them, and forget my sources. Most of them come from talking with students: Robert Kramer and Robert Manoff are two whose insights I will not forget. Julian Beinart taught a seminar on city form with me, during the last several years, and this book comes directly out of that collaboration. My partner, Stephen Carr, read an early draft, and helped me to sharpen my ideas. Julie Messervy collected many of the illustrations, and Anne Simunovic kept me organized. When I think of the longer, underlying influences, I think of my high-school teachers in Chicago, of Frank Lloyd Wright, and of Hans Blumenfeld, who is still today the wisest head in the planning profession.

Index